JOURNAL FOR THE STUDY OF THE NEW TESTAMENT SUPPLEMENT SERIES
193

Executive Editor
Stanley E. Porter

Editorial Board
Elizabeth A. Castelli, David Catchpole, Kathleen E. Corley,
R. Alan Culpepper, James D.G. Dunn, Craig A. Evans, Stephen
Fowl, Robert Fowler, George H. Guthrie, Robert Jewett,
Robert W. Wall

STUDIES IN NEW TESTAMENT GREEK
6

Sheffield Academic Press

Diglossia and Other Topics in New Testament Linguistics

edited by
Stanley E. Porter

Journal for the Study of the New Testament
Supplement Series 193

Studies in New Testament Greek 6

Copyright © 2000 Sheffield Academic Press

Published by
Sheffield Academic Press Ltd
Mansion House
19 Kingfield Road
Sheffield S11 9AS
England

Typeset by Sheffield Academic Press
and
Printed on acid-free paper in Great Britain
by Bookcraft (Bath) Ltd, Midsomer Norton

British Library Cataloguing in Publication Data

A catalogue record for this book is available
from the British Library

ISBN 1-84127-091-1

CONTENTS

Part I
DIGLOSSIA IN THE FIRST CENTURY

Part II
OTHER TOPICS IN NEW TESTAMENT LINGUISTICS

PREFACE

This volume is the fourth that draws upon papers that have grown out of the Biblical Greek Language and Linguistics Section of the Society of Biblical Literature. The first three volumes in their order of appearance are as follows: S.E. Porter and D.A. Carson (eds.), *Biblical Greek Language and Linguistics: Open Questions in Current Research* (JSNTSup, 80; SNTG, 1; Sheffield: JSOT Press, 1993); S.E. Porter and D.A. Carson (eds.), *Discourse Analysis and Other Topics in Biblical Greek* (JSNTSup, 113; SNTG, 2; Sheffield: JSOT Press, 1995); and S.E. Porter and D.A. Carson (eds.), *Linguistics and the New Testament: Critical Junctures* (JSNTSup, 168; SNTG, 5; Sheffield: Sheffield Academic Press, 1999). Like previous volumes, this one is divided into two parts. The first part contains the papers that were delivered at the session dedicated to a particular topic at one of the annual meetings of SBL. Part I of this volume contains papers delivered in 1998 in Orlando, Florida, in the session dedicted to the topic of Diglossia. The second part brings together papers on a range of subjects of concern to the Section. I wish to thank the many contributors for making their papers available for this volume, and being responsive to suggestions for changes and improvements, so that we could produce as cohesive a volume as possible. Sheffield Academic Press is, as usual, to be thanked for its willingness to publish a volume such as this in the JSNT Supplement Series and Studies in New Testament Greek sub-series. Speaking for numerous scholars, I am grateful for the Press's efficiency and desire to promote academic research. I wish also to thank the Centre for Advanced Theological Research, and University of Surrey Roehampton, for the facilities that it provides for my and others' work. I can only imagine how much poorer my work would be without my colleagues in the Centre, and the stimulating environment that it provides. Finally, I wish once again to thank my wife, Wendy, for her support. This volume was finished in the midst of a temporary move to another country, and she helped to ensure that this project, as well as so many others, came to completion. Thank you.

ABBREVIATIONS

AB	Anchor Bible
AnOr	Analecta orientalia
ATR	*Anglican Theological Review*
BARev	*Biblical Archaeology Review*
BDF	Friedrich Blass, A. Debrunner and Robert W. Funk, *A Greek Grammar of the New Testament and Other Early Christian Literature* (Chicago: University of Chicago, 1961)
BHS	*Biblia hebraica stuttgartensia*
Bib	*Biblica*
BLG	Biblical Languages: Greek
BN	*Biblische Notizen*
BNTC	Black's New Testament Commentaries
BO	*Bibliotheca orientalis*
BTB	*Biblical Theology Bulletin*
BWANT	Beiträge zur Wissenschaft vom Alten und Neuen Testament
CBQ	*Catholic Biblical Quarterly*
ConBNT	Coniectanea biblica, New Testament
CRINT	Compendia rerum iudaicarum ad Novum Testamentum
CTL	Cambridge Textbooks in Linguistics
DJD	Discoveries in the Judaean Desert
EncJud	*Encyclopaedia Judaica*
ExpTim	*Expository Times*
FFNT	Foundations and Facets: New Testament
FN	*Filología neotestamentaria*
GAG	*Grundriß der akkadischen Grammatik* (AnOr, 33; supplementary edition, AnOr, 47; Rome: Pontifical Biblical Institute).
GBS	Guides to Biblical Scholarship
GKC	*Gesenius' Hebrew Grammar* (ed. E. Kautzsch, revised and trans. A.E. Cowley; Oxford: Clarendon Press, 1910)
HSS	Harvard Semitic Studies
ICC	International Critical Commentary
IDB	George Arthur Buttrick (ed.), *The Interpreter's Dictionary of the Bible* (4 vols.; Nashville: Abingdon Press, 1962)
Int	*Interpretation*

JBL	*Journal of Biblical Literature*
JETS	*Journal of the Evangelical Theological Society*
JJS	*Journal of Jewish Studies*
JNES	*Journal of Near Eastern Studies*
JNSL	*Journal of Northwest Semitic Languages*
JQR	*Jewish Quarterly Review*
JSNT	*Journal for the Study of the New Testament*
JSNTSup	*Journal for the Study of the New Testament*, Supplement Series
JSOT	*Journal for the Study of the Old Testament*
JSOTSup	*Journal for the Study of the Old Testament*, Supplement Series
JSPSup	*Journal for the Study of the Pseudepigrapha*, Supplement Series
JSS	*Journal of Semitic Studies*
JTS	*Journal of Theological Studies*
LCL	Loeb Classical Library
LLL	Longman Linguistics Library
LSJ	H.G. Liddell, Robert Scott and H. Stuart Jones, *Greek–English Lexicon* (Oxford: Clarendon Press, 9th edn, 1968)
NICNT	New International Commentary on the New Testament
NIGTC	The New International Greek Testament Commentary
NovT	*Novum Testamentum*
NovTSup	*Novum Testamentum*, Supplements
NTCS	New Testament Commentary Series
NTOA	Novum Testamentum et orbis antiquus
NTS	*New Testament Studies*
NTTS	New Testament Tools and Studies
RB	*Revue biblique*
RevExp	*Review and Expositor*
RILP	Roehampton Institute London Papers
SBG	Studies in Biblical Greek
SBLDS	SBL Dissertation Series
SBLRBS	SBL Resources for Biblical Study
SBLSBS	SBL Sources for Biblical Study
SBLSCS	SBL Septuagint and Cognate Studies
SBLSP	SBL Seminar Papers
SD	Studies and Documents
SNTG	Studies in New Testament Greek
SNTSMS	Society for New Testament Studies Monograph Series
SNTW	Studies of the New Testament and its World
SWJL	*Southwest Journal of Linguistics*
TDNT	Gerhard Kittel and Gerhard Friedrich (eds.), *Theological Dictionary of the New Testament* (trans. Geoffrey W. Bromiley; 10 vols.; Grand Rapids: Eerdmans, 1964–)

TynBul	*Tyndale Bulletin*
WBC	Word Biblical Commentary
WUNT	Wissenschaftliche Untersuchungen zum Neuen Testament
ZAW	*Zeitschrift für die alttestamentliche Wissenschaft*
ZNW	*Zeitschrift für die neutestamentliche Wissenschaft*

LIST OF CONTRIBUTORS

Edward Adams, King's College London, University of London

Dirk Büchner, University of Durban-Westville, South Africa

Matthew Brook O'Donnell, University of Surrey Roehampton, UK

Christina Bratt Paulston, University of Pittsburgh, Pennsylvania

Stanley E. Porter, University of Surrey Roehampton, UK

Jeffrey T. Reed, University of Surrey Roehampton, UK

Scobie P. Smith, Harvard University, Cambridge, Massachusetts

Jonathan M. Watt, Geneva College and the Reformed Presbyterian Theological Seminary, Pittsburgh, Pennsylvania

INTRODUCTION:
DIGLOSSIA AND OTHER TOPICS IN NEW TESTAMENT LINGUISTICS

Stanley E. Porter

The technical dimensions of the topic of diglossia will not be familiar to many New Testament scholars, although they are probably more familiar to some scholars of the Hebrew Bible. With this knowledge in mind, the first part of this volume is dedicated to this topic of recent linguistic discussion, and attempts to redress this lack of familiarity by presenting several contributions to the debate over what diglossia is and how it, and related concepts such as code-switching, are of relevance to scholars interested in first-century Palestine. The recent debate over the concept of diglossia dates very specifically from the inciting article by Charles Ferguson on 'Diglossia', which appeared in 1959.[1] In the four decades that have passed since this article was first published, there has been a veritable groundswell of work in the area, with linguists using the category in a number of different, and yet potentially useful, ways. As Jonathan Watt notes in his paper, there have been over 3,000 items published in the last four decades on this subject. In the area of New Testament studies, however, the concept has been far less important. Nevertheless, as virtually all scholars who are concerned with the study of Palestine in the first century soon come to realize, issues regarding language, especially the interplay between Aramaic and Greek, should be very much at the forefront of their concerns. That they are not always so is to be lamented, and is one of the reasons for the papers that follow here.

In discussing this vital subject, we have gone beyond the confines of simply bringing together a number of New Testament or Hebrew Bible scholars to discuss this topic. Instead, we have enlisted a group that has background and demonstrable expertise in the area of linguistics. This includes inviting Dr Christina Paulston to respond to the papers here.

---

1. C. Ferguson, 'Diglossia', *Word* 15 (1959), pp. 325-40.

Dr Paulston is Professor of Linguistics in the Department of Linguistics at the University of Pittsburgh, and works regularly in the emerging area of historical sociolinguistics. Dr Paulston is not the only one on the panel to work in this area, however, and the papers, I think, reflect the expertise of those involved. Jonathan Watt opens the section by offering an overview of the topic. Noting the two major definitions of diglossia currently being utilized in research, he offers an analysis of these definitions, and then adapts them to how he sees the linguistic situation of first-century Palestine. Since many studies on diglossia are applied only to modern linguistic contexts, Watt provides a valuable service in refining the terminology for discussion of ancient languages. The second essay, by Scobie Smith, examines the Semitic linguistic situation of the Second Temple period, focusing upon Hebrew. Taking a cautious approach, Smith notes changes between biblical and mishnaic Hebrew, and treats several case studies to illustrate what he sees as the dialectal situation of the first century. Stanley Porter examines the Greek of the New Testament. After recognizing some of the difficulties with how diglossia has been defined, he takes a functional approach to the topic. Using Halliday's concept of register, Porter examines four of Paul's letters in an attempt to quantify various registers of Greek usage. This part concludes with Christina Paulston's assessment of the work that has been presented. Paulston uses a historical sociolinguistic approach to offer a useful critique of not only the papers presented, but other issues raised in such a discussion. These include useful questions regarding evidence, quantification, and even definitions of what Palestine was. She draws on helpful analogies from modern diglossic situations (while questioning the concept as well), brings us back to the major proponents of the concept, and suggests useful ways forward in the discussion.

The second part of this volume contains a variety of papers. Nevertheless, there is a surprising amount of continuity with the first part of this volume to be found in their apparent diversity. The section opens with Dirk Büchner's paper on the translation technique in Septuagint Leviticus. Though not specifically treating the Greek of the New Testament, his discussion has application to this area, besides addressing issues in Septuagint studies. Drawing upon principles developed for the New English Translation of the Septuagint (NETS), he analyses a translational continuum, with particular concern for what are called stereotypes and calques. Not only is insight gained into the particular translational difficulties of Leviticus, but Büchner offers methodological insights as well.

Jonathan Watt presents a paper on dialects. The Synoptic Gospels present an episode in which Peter is apparently identified by the way he speaks, and Watt, noting how little research has been undertaken on the linguistic significance of this episode, attempts to shed light on it. He concludes that there were both recognizable dialectal features of Peter's speech, and sociolinguistic stigmatization that went along with this way of speaking. In this essay, Watt makes us aware that there is often much to be learned about the linguistic situation in first-century Palestine from the biblical documents themselves.

Jeffrey Reed's paper on linguistic change in Paul's writings is in several ways an extension and development of some of the ideas introduced in Watt's paper. Reed, noting the changes that Paul makes in the Hellenistic letter form, in particular in the opening and thanksgiving, draws conclusions regarding Paul's linguistic varieties. In the discussion of whether Paul follows a Hellenistic or a Jewish letter-writing style, Reed concludes that Paul is charting his own course, by selecting and refining various linguistic features from each of the strands. Reed challenges future Pauline scholars to take more seriously not only the formal characteristics of the Pauline letter form, but the linguistic implications of the use and development of this form as reflecting the Pauline perspective.

In a study that resonates with Reed's work on the Pauline letter form, Stanley Porter and Matthew O'Donnell take up the topic of semantics and argumentation in the book of Romans. Beginning from a historical survey of work in semantics over the last 40 years, they suggest and present several recent developments as ways forward in semantic analysis. These ways forward are seen as providing the backdrop for a more complete analysis of the argumentative structure of the book of Romans. A Hallidayan functional model provides the means of presenting the semantic information of Romans in terms of its letter form.

In one of the few essays in New Testament studies devoted to critical linguistics, Edward Adams first defines the concept and then applies it to Galatians 1–2. This sociolinguistic method attempts to come to grips with the social issues involved in Paul's writings, especially the power relations indicated in the letter. Temporal and spatial language, point of view, and psychological and ideological issues are all examined, within a Hallidayan functionalist standpoint.

The final essay, by Matthew O'Donnell, builds on previous work regarding corpus linguistics. O'Donnell examines recent efforts to provide computer-searchable databases, making an important distinction between an archive and a corpus. He concludes by applying his findings to building a corpus for New Testament study.

Several concluding comments are warranted in the light of these essays. One is the recognition of the importance of the subject of linguistic analysis for thorough exegesis of the biblical text, in particular that of the New Testament. Virtually all of these essays include not only methodological and theoretical comments—as foundational and important as these are—but also analysis of specific texts, often on a verse-by-verse basis. This should provide encouragement for other exegetes to draw upon the best of this kind of linguistic work in their own efforts to understand the texts that they are studying. This is not to say that there are not some technical terms or concepts that need to be mastered in order fully to utilize such work. Any academic discipline has its own ways of referring to methods and data. Nevertheless, the results presented here should encourage others at least to attempt to assimilate some of these results into their own study.

A second conclusion is that much of this work is tentative in its conclusions. Some of this tentativeness is caused by the initial application of methods designed for the study of modern living languages, with native speakers, to the study of ancient languages, where there are only written texts for examination. There is no denying the fact that the study of ancient languages from an informed linguistic perspective has appreciable differences from the study of modern languages. These differences should not, however, hinder us from pushing forward with development of appropriate methods, which will then be employed and refined in the process of definition and development. There is much front-line scholarship represented in several of these essays. This should encourage others to join in the discussion, as well as to appropriate the results in their own study. Although no one can predict the direction in which biblical linguistics will move in the years ahead, this collection of essays alone has certainly more than enough provocative analysis and tempting suggestions to show that linguistic approaches to the biblical documents have established themselves not as an area merely appropriating the models of others, but as one that is developing and refining its own models as a foundation for much future research.

Part I

DIGLOSSIA IN THE FIRST CENTURY

THE CURRENT LANDSCAPE OF DIGLOSSIA STUDIES: THE DIGLOSSIC CONTINUUM IN FIRST-CENTURY PALESTINE

Jonathan M. Watt

1. *Introduction*

Of approximately 3000 articles and books on diglossia that have appeared in print during the past four decades, only a handful have applied the concept to the language situation of Palestine during the late Second Temple period. Yet despite the small number of these applications, no fewer than seven variations of the paradigm have appeared already in the literature. The variations seem to arise less from philosophical differences between the conflicting traditions of Charles Ferguson (1959, 1991) and Joshua Fishman (1967, 1971)—something that has animated much of the broader literature on diglossia—than from the imprecise application of both of these authors' works to the linguistic repertoire of the first-century Jewish Palestinian community.

This article addresses the promises and the problems of invoking the concept of diglossia in relation to the Levantine speech community that cradled the New Testament writings. It will survey the discussions that have appeared in print so far, and consider their strengths and shortcomings. I will suggest that Ferguson's self-modified (1991) version of his landmark 1959 article contains the necessary definitions and constraints needed for a productive application of the term, and that it comprehends the undeniable fact that tertiary languages and spoken variants of high forms are present in the speech repertoire of many communities, including the first-century Palestinian situation.

2. *Toward a Definition of Diglossia*

Although the term 'diglossia' long predated Ferguson, his groundbreaking article by the same name (1959) became its defining moment. Using four modern language situations as the legs for his table (Swiss German, Arabic, Haitian Creole, Modern Greek), Ferguson described a particular form of bilingual community in which a special relationship existed between its primary languages, which he labeled simply the *high* and *low* 'codes'. He suggested that diglossia represents a diachronically stable variant of bilingualism, due in part to the highly specified functional distribution of the codes.

According to Ferguson, a 'high' (H) form of a language is used for public, formal and official speech situations, while a low (L) variety of the same language, which in some speech communities may be spoken only or at least is not normally in written form, is used for informal and especially private speech situations involving intra-community conversation. The high form is generally associated with religion and traditional texts, and is the basis for the Received Pronunciation (RP) of the language, while the low form is considered the language of the collective soul, so to speak. The terms 'variety', 'code' and 'form' are typically preferred over 'language' and 'dialect' so as to allow maximum flexibility in the accommodation of the paradigm to different linguistic communities.

For example, in Haiti, French is the official language of government and public events, while Haitian Creole serves in the informal encounters of everyday life. Among the Amish of North America, Modern High German is the language of worship services and the Bible, while Pennsylvania Dutch is its daily interactional counterpart. In the Pitcairn Island community comprised of descendants of the famous H.M.S. Bounty mutiny of 1789, something approximating modern English is still used for worship services and periodic interaction with outsiders, while a Tahitian-influenced vernacular is routine for personal dialogue between local residents. Such is the stuff that is consistent with, if not original to, Ferguson's four-decade-old model.

However, Ferguson's paradigm was to undergo extensive surgery when Fishman, prompted by certain inadequacies that were being discovered in the then-prevailing model—something Ferguson himself would acknowledge in 1991—chose to re-construe the concept significantly. He proposed that multilingual communities tend toward two of four possible combinations: either diglossia with bilingualism or diglossia without bilingualism. (The other two combinations he described as 'transitional', as when bilingualism is present without diglossia, or 'moribund', that is, neither diglossia nor bilingualism, which 'tends to be self-liquidating'.)

What Fishman effectively demonstrated was the need for increased flexibility in Ferguson's paradigm; what he appears to have lost in the process was definition, for the application of 'diglossia' to multilingual situations would soon become so broad, one might wonder what multilingual situation in the world today is *not* diglossic. The trend in publications on the subject indeed indicated the appeal of Fishman's broader version: according to Fernandez (1993), 156 diglossia articles appeared during the 1960s—a number that increases fivefold in the 1970s and tenfold throughout the 1980s! If Ferguson opened a window to the rain, Fishman channeled the gutters right into the living room.

The differences between the Fergusonian and Fishmanian paradigms have become legendary—future linguistic mythologies may indeed portray two Herculean linguists with disciples in tow, each out to cut the Gordian knot of multilingualism in his own unique way. But are the differences seminal, or merely token? Surely they are substantive, and already cries are being heard for a return to a 'canonical' concept of diglossia, a 'classic diglossia' as some have labeled it (should Fishman's be identified as *neo*-diglossia?!). These genuine philosophical differences, compounded with misapplication or free-wheeling definitions, as I will demonstrate below, threaten to stretch even the relatively small circle of ancient Palestinian studies into a misshapen ovoid. These articles on diglossia, we hope, will be timely and productive in the study of the ancient speech community in Palestine.

3. *Classic Versus Neo-Diglossia*

In his 1991 revisitation, Ferguson emphasized that his work originally aimed at understanding the function of language at the *community* level, and that his choice of the terms 'code' and 'variety' had been intentionally ambiguous in order to be inclusive. He identified nine factors in what might otherwise have been labeled 'bilingual' communities that became essential to a diagnosis of diglossia:

(a)   the two codes had highly specialized *functions*;
(b)   the more widely established code was more *prestigious*;
(c)   the prestige code had a strong *literary heritage*;
(d)   the non-prestige code became the *first acquired* language (L1/NL);
(e)   the prestige code was supported by formal study and *standardization*;
(f)   the use and function of these codes was diachronically *stable*;

(g) the prestige code had a more highly developed *grammatical* structure;

(h) both codes shared most of the *lexicon*, but the prestige code was broader;

(i) the *phonology* of the prestige code was a subsystem of the derived code.

Ferguson's decision to organize along these lines was intentional, if subtle. He wanted to understand the function and development of the codes in question *as they related to the speech community as a whole*. Despite the necessary linguistic components of his work, his attention was geared toward their function within the *speech community*, as his subsequent observations indicated. For example, Ferguson stated that by virtue of the specific *social* functions of the H and L varieties, a diglossic speech community—in contrast with generically bilingual communities—evidenced considerable diachronic stability in its repertoire. This was made possible, in part, because the H-form in his original formulation had no native speakers; the high tradition existed 'on paper', as it were, while the low form was living and active in the oral realm.

Ferguson observed that the H-proponents living in a diglossic community constituted a literary elite that often pushed for its acceptance because 'it connects the community with its glorious past', while L-proponents would typically claim that their code was 'closer to the real thinking and feeling of the people'. Both parties, Ferguson observed, 'seem to show the conviction…that a standard language can simply be legislated into place' (1959: 337). There were no native speakers of the high form in his diglossic situations. Throughout, Ferguson was attempting prediction and inviting others to see if what typified his four test cases was indeed a pattern in other speech communities of the world. His arrangement at that point, however, applied only to variant forms of the same language, or genetically closely related languages.

Having used those four modern language legs on which to construct his first table, Ferguson wondered whether researchers elsewhere were seeing like patterns, stating at the conclusion (1959: 340):

> This paper concludes with an appeal for further study of this phenomenon… Perhaps the collection of data and more profound study will drastically modify the impressionistic remarks of this paper, but if this is so the paper will have had the virtue of stimulating investigation and thought.

Ferguson's RSVP triggered a landslide of responses which often left the 'yes/no' boxes unchecked while adding a third option, namely, 'interested, and willing to experiment with your original taxonomy'. Typically, researchers extracted from his piece the following points, which, when re-construed as I am about to do, led to inevitable shifts of direction. Numerous diglossic situations were being identified on the grounds extracted from Ferguson, but then one or more of these factors were brought out that did not match. Naturally, Ferguson held no copyright to the word 'diglossia'. How could he? It had been in use for decades prior to his birth. He was its definer, systematizer and popularizer, but never sole owner.

Thus entered Fishman. He was not the only theoretician who set out 'to extend, to narrow, or to differentiate Ferguson's original definition' (Hudson 1991: 7), but he certainly cast the longest shadow, and so the antithesis (antipathy?) was born. Fishman's four-part paradigm (1967: 30) really centered upon just two options, what he called 'diglossia with/without bilingualism'. A number of differences emerged between him and Ferguson, but three important ones have been the most obvious:

(a)   whereas the L-form is a daughter dialect of the H-form in Ferguson's original work, the two codes need not be genetically related in Fishman's (1980: 4) and many subsequent constructions;

(b)   whereas politico-geographic boundaries do not figure in Ferguson's work, social compartmentalization by a diglossic community may take place either by social consensus *or* by virtue of territorial or political boundaries, according to Fishman;

(c)   while Fishman's paradigm allows for native speakers of the H-variety, Ferguson's emphasis had been upon a more abstract classical form which, strictly speaking, had no native speakers—'no segment of the speech community in diglossia regularly uses H as a medium of ordinary conversation, and any attempt to do so is felt to be...pedantic and artificial...[by the community]' (Ferguson 1959: 327).

If the differences between Ferguson and Fishman were mere matters of definition and taxonomy, then a 'separate but equal' statute might suffice and some clever scholar could coin a new word and publish it. Hudson (1991) himself avoids taking sides, yet the anthology he introduces, leaning as it does toward Ferguson's 'uniform' and 'consistent' definition, is said (1991: 17) to contribute to the study of diglossia in the '*classical* sense of the term'—a rather unsettling adjective to those of us who are about the same age as Ferguson's seminal article.

By the admission of its own author, Ferguson's original work contained inadequacies; due to various pressures, 'multiple ambiguity... crept into the term diglossia as a result of its use with reference to quite disparate sociolinguistic situations', says Hudson (1991: 16), adding (1991: 16; and quoting Hymes), that 'a return to a consistent definition of whatever kind is therefore essential if the study of diglossia is to contribute in a significant way to understanding "the organization and change of verbal repertoires in relation to the main processes of societal evolution"'. And similarly, Spolsky (1991: 91) maintains that: 'Pure Fergusonian diglossia is an abstract conception, existing often as one element in a much more complex sociolinguistic pattern'. Even sympathizers want to subject Ferguson to the rack, at least momentarily.

Further proof of the need for improved definition is seen in Fernandez's bibliography, which includes an index of references arranged by language; no fewer than 173 different 'diglossic' language situations had been identified at the time of its publication in 1993, many of which do not conform to Ferguson's original construct. Though Ferguson had then expressed the hope (1959: 38) that what he was seeing in his four 'defining' language situations *might* appear with *some* frequency elsewhere, one might now be tempted to ask whether there is *any* language situation that will not, someday, be slipped under the diglossic umbrella. This is not to attribute total lack of definition or restraint to Fishman any more than it is to attribute perfection to Ferguson, who has acknowledged (1991: 214) the 'weaknesses in his own original conceptualization'. But if a concept becomes too inclusive, then what is its heuristic advantage? Lack of *ex*clusion will likely correspond to diminished predictability. As Hudson implies, neither 'organization' nor 'change' in a community's repertoire will be comprehensible when the doors are opened too widely.

4. *Form or Function? Repertoire in a Diglossic Community*

Diglossia is concerned with *function* as much as *description*. Ferguson came to regret (1991: 220) his failure to make this clear from the outset, noting that he had been 'describing speech communities rather than languages'; 'This is a central issue', he said. To clarify and underline this fact, he went on to offer (1991: 221) a more specific definition of a *speech community* as 'a social group sharing features of language structure, use, and attitudes that functions as a sociolinguistic unit for the operation of linguistic variation and/or change; it may be monolingual or multilingual'.

Ferguson's eye toward the 'larger picture' is a vital feature of this present study. He came to acknowledge explicitly (1991: 224-25) the presence of other languages in the community's repertoire beside the diglossic pair, hence the terminological variants others were starting to employ, such as 'polyglossia' (Platt 1977), 'triglossia' (Rabin 1976), tetraglossia, quadriglossia, schizoglossia, and more (for an extended list of these terms see Fernandez 1993: ix). Ferguson himself stated (1991: 231) that he had come to realize that the H-variety, which he had connected solely with the written tradition, could also be spoken, though he said 'it would be useful to know the extent to which the H variety is used for formal spoken purposes' (1991: 231) in other communities.

The matter of repertoire is emerging as a necessary key to the refinement of diglossia studies. Platt (1977) carefully distinguishes between what he calls the *speech repertoire* ('the set of functional codes utilized by a particular speech community to which the speaker, as a member of the community, has access') and the individual speaker's own *verbal repertoire*, which of course might equal, or be narrower than, the community's range. I would add, however, that within the latter of these lists exists a sub-repertoire that would include *styles* (or possibly even *registers*) which could be employed or created for metaphoric effect.

Platt's (1977) work in Malaysia and Singapore led him to propose 'a range with possibly more than one H-variety, one or more M(edium) varieties, not to mention one or more L-varieties', which he would label (in order of preference) *H1, H2, M, L1, L2*, and so forth (1977). As I will demonstrate shortly, I concur in part, though would prefer to speak not of 'polyglossia' but instead of a diglossic continuum (however, see Errington 1991 on the pros and cons of this).

Diglossia in any manifestation must attend simultaneously to three areas in order to be productive. It must concern itself with: (1) genetic relationship on some level (otherwise, it would be no different than generic bilingualism); (2) concern for accuracy in the area of repertoire (otherwise, classic diglossia would have sufficed all along); and (3) the functional distribution of the language varieties (in order to present an accurate prediction and explanation of a speech community's behavior).

The Palestinian language situation in the late Second Temple period indeed may offer a suitable vehicle for refinement of this concept.

5. *The Language Repertoire of First-Century Palestine*

Diglossia pertains to verbal repertoire, thus any application of the term to the Palestinian situation of the late Second Temple period must reckon first with the territory. Four languages, in one form or another, enter into the picture. The literature on this topic is extensive and this paper must presume, rather than try to defend, the currently most widely accepted scenario.

First, Aramaic is now generally regarded as the first language, that is, the native language, of Jews in Palestine during the first century. Secondly, Hellenistic Greek is clearly in use in Palestine at this time as well. That the Septuagint was more than two centuries established by Jesus' day attests to the strength of Hellenistic Greek at this time (Mussies 1976). Thirdly, though classical Hebrew has been widely regarded as a dead language that was revivified in the latter half of the twentieth century, it should probably be conceded that pockets of scholarship kept it 'alive' over the past two millennia. Strictly speaking, a dead language has no living *native* speakers; consequently, its use by select scholars who *acquired* it for scholarly forum would not thereby render it 'living'. In any case, Hebrew may well have been the language of the temple, and, in some cases, even of some synagogues as well, and should be considered part of the community's repertoire even if it did not fit into the repertoire of every speaker in that community. Fitzmyer (1979: 38-39) comments:

> If asked what was the language commonly spoken in Palestine in the time of Jesus of Nazareth, most people with some acquaintance of that era and area would almost spontaneously answer Aramaic. To my way of thinking, this is still the correct answer for the *most commonly* used language, but the defense of this thesis must reckon with the growing mass of evidence that both Greek and Hebrew were being used as well [emphasis his].

Fourthly, a note must be made with regard to Latin. Fitzmyer (1979) places it first in his language catalogue even though he identifies it as 'the latest language to appear on the scene'. Latin appears in public Roman inscriptions and on tombstones, with its best-known New Testament usage being one of the three languages of the inscription placed on the cross above Jesus. It comes as no surprise that Fitzmyer should identify 'an official use of Latin in Palestine by Romans...[as] expected' (1979: 31) while qualifying its usage even after a century of occupation (i.e. since Pompey's invasion of 63 BCE) because 'Greek was still a common means of communication not only between Romans in the provinces, but also between the capital and the provinces. Greek was still more or less the *lingua franca* in the Near East' in Jesus' day (1979: 32).

It could hardly be argued, therefore, that Latin would occupy anything more than a peripheral place in the verbal repertoire of the early Jewish Palestinian community. That local residents would willingly acquire the language code of the occupation administration seems too unlikely; that certain words or phrases may have been comprehensible to them, and even borrowed into their native codes, is quite reasonable. However, Latin should not be considered as enjoying competency in the early Jewish Palestinian community.

In summary, then, the consensus has been that Aramaic and (some variety of) Hellenistic Greek saw oral and written usage in the Jewish communities of the Levant. (For recent comments on the kinds of Greek used in the New Testament, see Porter 1997: 99-130.) These codes can be given first- and second-language positions, respectively, in the speech repertoire of Jewish Palestine at this time. But this is not to claim that every resident of Palestine was bilingual; rather, that in the speech repertoire of the community *as a whole*, Aramaic–Greek bilingualism was likely to have been widespread.

6. *Experimental Paradigms for Palestinian Diglossia*

Variations on the diglossic paradigm now invoke the Fergusonian or Fishmanian concepts of diglossia for the purpose of describing the first-century Palestinian situation. Some of these arise because of difficulties in matching theoretical concept with reality; others because of theoretical differences at the foundational level, while still others seem to have arisen from simple misconceptions about linguistic terminology.

1. Rendsburg (1990, 1991, 1996) argued for an identifiable distinction between written biblical Hebrew, which he classifies as the H-form, and mishnaic or spoken Hebrew, which he says is the L-form. Rendsburg was intentionally striving for consistency with Ferguson's 1959 vision

of the concept, yet in highlighting the written (biblical Hebrew) *versus* oral (mishnaic Hebrew) codes, his paper evidenced a functional short-coming: neither the high nor the low forms in his arrangement matched up to the informal, daily language usage that Ferguson had been envisioning for the L-form. Rendsburg's form was consistent, but the function he assigned to the low code stressed the Fergusonian paradigm.

2. Rabin (1976) coined the neologism 'triglossia' in order to bring the three primary language codes of first-century Palestine into simultaneous consideration—written biblical Hebrew, spoken Hebrew and Aramaic. Though keeping within the same language family (Northwestern Semitic) in order to bring the paradigm to bear upon the language community, he brought two distinct, albeit closely related, languages into paradigmatic relationship. Rabin reflected Fishman's subsequent broadening of the concept, yet changed the term in order to adapt the linguistic concept to the language community under consideration.

Spolsky (1991: 85) commented that Rabin's triglossia 'shares...features both with Ferguson's (1959) definition of diglossia in that it includes two varieties of Hebrew, and with Fishman's wider use of the term, by adding the more distantly related Aramaic'. But he notes as well that Rabin's 'innovation', though useful, omits practical reference to Greek and Latin, the former at least deserving a place in the community's repertoire. Furthermore, Rabin's arrangement distracts from the atypical 'functional allocation' of the H and L varieties of Hebrew. In fact, any diglossic situation involving spoken H-forms must necessarily stretch the paradigm, since a simple picture can remain so only as long as the language is absolutely dead. It is axiomatic that living languages, and therefore the repertoires in which they live, will change.

3. Spolsky himself (1983) also used the term 'triglossia', but incorporated three different languages under this terminological variant. Whereas Rabin had included biblica Hebrew, mishniac Hebrew and Aramaic, Spolsky proposed the inclusion of Hebrew (in general), Aramaic and Greek. Spolsky evidences Fishman's influence, describing diglossia *with* bilingualism.

4. My own invocation of the diglossia term (Watt 1989, 1997) involved retention of the term but a relaxation of the standards, steering a course close to Ferguson's 1959 rendition while allowing for genetic distance

between the H- and L-forms. It stopped short of the broadening accomplished in Fishman's 1967 piece, which to my thinking makes it possible to label nearly any multi-code situation 'diglossic'. My adjustments seem to me to be consistent with Ferguson's subsequent acknowledgment in 1991 of the need to allow for variation of the spoken forms
of the high code. I listed Hebrew (generally) as the high form and
Aramaic as the low, with Greek treated as a tertiary language that does
not, strictly speaking, impinge upon the diglossic aspect of the repertoire. This shows consistency with Ferguson's interest in the language
of daily interaction, the L-variety; however, it gave a nod to Fishman's
hybrid concept of diglossia *with* bilingualism. The liberties I took by
virtue of placing two languages in contradistinction (Hebrew and Aramaic) were counterbalanced by attempting an adequate functionality—
namely, Aramaic, not mishnaic Hebrew, was the low code of daily interaction. In other words, Rendsburg's strength was my weakness, and
vice versa.

5. Zerhusen (1995) applied the term 'diglossia' somewhat idiosyn-
cratically. The abstract that opened his article defined diglossia as 'a
situation in which a multilingual community uses different languages,
each with a distinct set of social functions'. Zerhusen helpfully elimi-
nated a number of unclear comments about Acts 2 that had been made
by other writers, noting that numerous ethnic groups, and not necessarily language communities, were represented on the day of Pentecost.

Yet his article used the term with the indefinite article, I believe being
unique in that respect. For example, he labeled as diglossic certain language situations that are nothing more than generically bilingual, such
as the traditional Christian European use of Latin as the supposedly
high code, with German, French or whatever as the low codes, claiming
(1995: 125) that 'William Tyndale was killed for violating the ecclesiastical *diglossia* present in England'—another idiosyncratic feature of
his article. Zerhusen identified Hebrew (generally) as the high form,
and *both* Aramaic and Greek as low forms, in the ancient Palestinian
situation. Functionally, Zerhusen falls in line with Ferguson; paradigmatically, he is consistent with Fishman; grammatically, he stands in
his own category.

6. Eric Meyers (1985), in a discussion of Galilean regionalism that
involves interaction with Sean Freyne, defined the term 'diglossia' (on

behalf of Freyne as well, he claims) as a situation in which 'two languages are used by one people...[as] in all of Galilee' (119). Specifically, he applies the term to Greek plus Hebrew or Aramaic, but then adds that diglossia exists

> as a result of the relationship between Hebrew and Aramaic: Hebrew could be the language of cult and worship, Aramaic the language of everyday life... Greek was on the ascendancy... A theory of diglossia thus presupposes a population in Galilee that is at least bilingual if not tri-lingual.

His passing comment on p. 122, though confusing, is tantalizing: he asks why Aramaic, 'at one time a *lingua franca*, [cannot] serve as a surrogate holy language' for special Jewish ceremonies such as synagogue dedications and tombstone inscriptions. I would add: with Aramaic being identified in some New Testament passages as *Hebraisti*, 'in Hebrew', one wonders whether in the early mindset, the two sister languages were not virtually regarded as being one, albeit with variations, because they shared the same orthography. After all, if the infamous folk-etymologies of the ancient Hebrew corpus are allowed to stand on the grounds that they were psychologically 'real' to their creators even though they do not adhere strictly to a formal philology, then why not permit a community's perception of language identity to stand over and above a strict genetic differentiation?

7. Fredericks (1998), in the most recent study I am aware of, loosely relates the 'cumbersome and grammatically inappropriate and irritating [language of the] opening chapter of Ezekiel' to the concept of diglossia. Noting 'the weakening of gender consistency' and various examples of abnormal affixation, he asks whether 'the aberrations of Ezekiel 1 could be attributed confidently to a well-known dialectal source' (i.e. what is conventionally called a regional dialect).

Fredericks concludes (1998: 198) that the unusual grammar may have been triggered by 'the emotional effect of Ezekiel's experience', or that it was 'a garbled attempt to form grammatically correct sentences [as would have been done] by a foreigner'; possibly, it was 'an intentional, artificial corruption of the language designed to contrast with an acceptable literary language—a rough form of grammar', or perhaps is merely 'the looser grammatical conventions of the daily language, a vernacular dialect', this last option being his preference. His use of the term 'diglossia', which he correctly says 'will not explain all of the abnormalities in Ezekiel 1', remains largely undefined and only vaguely invoked, at least in that article.

The foregoing applications of the concept of diglossia to the ancient Palestinian language situation, and the seeming chaos they imply, surely evidence the value *and* the limitations of the term. Can order be imposed on this primeval chaos by the authoritative word of an omnipotent linguist? An accounting of the languages in question would be a good place to start. The speech repertoire (to use Platt's term) of the first-century Jewish Palestinian community consisted of numerous codes, which we can cautiously suggest were as follows:

- (a) written biblical Hebrew
- (b) mishnaic Hebrew (presumably, written and spoken)
- (c) perhaps two regional dialects of Aramaic, Judaean and Galilean (which may have been written identically but were orally distinguishable)
- (d) Koine Greek in fairly standard and perhaps Semiticized varieties (written and spoken)
- (e) Latin (written or spoken)—presumably used rarely, if at all

Ferguson's 1959 narrow gate obviously cannot accommodate such a repertoire; however, in my opinion, Fishman's broad gate leads to linguistic perdition, and many are those who find it. Hence, the following preferable option.

7. *Synthesis of Palestinian Models*

For the most part, the seven variations on the concept of diglossia which I have outlined above evidence tensions that are *structural* and *conceptual*. If the Ferguson–Fishman differences were removed, and moderns could somehow ascertain with precision the functional distribution of the languages in question, the problems would remain, for the following reasons.

First, it has become clear after four decades of research since Ferguson's landmark article that many living language situations are simply too variegated to comply with an essentially bipolar model (i.e. H- vs. L-forms). Though it may be sufficient for some language communities (e.g. that of Norfolk Island), too many others comprise round pegs that cannot be pounded into this square hole. The dividing line between *language* and *dialect* is fuzzy, and the compounding problematics posed by register and/or style and community/individual repertoire contribute even further to the tension. Some allowance *must* be made for variants and tertiary codes!

Secondly, even those who agree upon an optimum school of diglossia show tensions arising between *form* and *function*. This can most easily be seen in the variants proposed by Rendsburg and myself: where one lacks the other gains. Rendsburg is *structurally* consistent with Ferguson by identifying the two forms of Hebrew (biblical vs. mishnaic) as the high and low codes, respectively, but cannot match the functional distribution necessitated by everyday spoken Aramaic. My own work was *functionally* consistent with Ferguson's criteria for the low code, namely, the daily interactional use of Aramaic, yet it failed to account for the different forms of Hebrew. Ferguson's multivalent definition of diglossia prompted conflicting match-ups even as it had attempted (see his 1991 comments on his earlier aims) to address largely functional issues. All discussion has also neglected to allow for register variations—for example, the language of the New Testament, though certainly Koine Greek, shows at many points some entrance of Semitic features which likely were unconscious in certain writers (such as Markan parataxis) while conscious in others (such as Luke's probably artificial use of the periphrastic imperfect).

Thirdly, Errington's (1991: 189) desire to return to 'something like a canonic or fundamentalist sense of the term' is vital, though it may be impossible, for this reason: Fishman's broader usage has had as its inevitable fruit that virtually any multilingual situation that evidences functional differentiation (and, I wonder, which one does not?) can be called diglossic. A taxonomy that fails to characterize certain data *and* exclude others is unhelpful, unproductive and unpredictive.

Fourthly, until it is established with certainty that Aramaic, not Greek, was the native language of the majority of Palestinian Jews—a likelihood that yet remains unproven—then allowance will have to be made for flexibility in NL/L2 assignments. It may be that the situation of Hippos in the Decapolis (Greek as NL?) differed from that of the hamlet of Nazareth in Galilee (Aramaic as NL?) or that of certain aristocratic Jerusalemites (Aramaic and Hebrew as simultaneous NLs?). Community diglossia may not extend to every individual, even within the same community. Scholarly humility is usually a good policy, and tentativeness is not usually a fatal disease.

8. *Toward a Solution: Diglossic Continuum*

In order to reach beyond paradigmatic congestion, I suggest that either form or function must be chosen as priority. Perhaps Emerson's comment in his 'Essay on Self-Reliance' is appropriate: 'A foolish consistency is the hobgoblin of little minds, adored by little statesmen and philosophers and divines'. Thankfully, he mentioned nothing about linguists. Ferguson said he wanted all along to understand the function and development of language codes *as they related to the speech community as a whole*. Non-conforming particulars must not become the tail that wags the dog. Concluding his observations (1991: 101) on the ancient Palestinian situation, Spolsky aptly observed:

> The sociolinguistic pattern of Jewish Palestine in the late Second Temple period provides a rich example for the study of Ferguson's concept of diglossia and for seeing the strengths and limitations of the concept. It tests the Fergusonian model by providing a striking case both of two varieties of a language in clearly distinguished functional roles and the added complexity caused by the existence of other significant languages in the pattern. It calls in other words for more social contextualization than the originally linguistic conception provided for; the added light that a sociologist like Fishman cast on the issue is clearly revealing. But the beauty and fitness of the original notion is clearly brought out.

The use of a T (tertiary) category is vital for isolating the specifically diglossic relationship of the genetically related (sister) languages, Hebrew and Aramaic. For if Greek is directly entered into the diglossic feature (as the low form), not only would the situation be nothing more than generic bilingualism, but it would fail to allow for the multiple roles of Greek that do not parallel those of the Semitic languages. Strictly speaking, diglossia can apply only to the Semitic languages (or, theoretically, to the Greek alone), but not to Hebrew (or Aramaic) *and* Greek simultaneously. If diglossia is applied to the ancient Palestinian situation, Greek does not belong within the diglossic portion of the community repertoire. Although the repertoire may include diglossic features within it, the whole is not to be crammed into a diglossic packet.

Furthermore, we might observe that given the apparent perception of ancient Palestinian Jews that Hebrew and Aramaic were essentially the same language—such that Aramaic is referred to as *Hebraisti*, 'Hebrew', in Jn 19.20, for example—then the treatment of Aramaic and

Hebrew together under the same umbrella seems warranted on community, even if not purely on genetic, grounds. For it is the ability of speakers to treat the high and low forms as in some way complementary in their substance and application—whether or not they are, truly, variants of the same language—that renders diglossia distinctly useful. The tightly-knit functional distribution made possible by the affinity of the high and low varieties appears to be the key ingredient for the diachronic stability of diglossia, and hence its functional particularities.

Consequently, I suggest that while the term 'diglossia' might be applied generally to a community as a whole, it still should be understood as pertaining specifically to parts of the repertoire. By designating certain languages as tertiary in the paradigm—if indeed, genetically or functionally, they are—then the concept can be kept alive and productive. Furthermore, it can be presumed that an international and/or traditional literary standard (Hebrew, Greek, Aramaic, Latin) may have spoken variants (Ferguson 1991); it can remain, simply, the H-form if structurally and functionally it remains that way. A simple sub-listing method is possible, for example H1, H2, L1, L2 and so forth. In such an arrangement, variations in dialect, style or register can still be incorporated without distorting the holistic concept.

I recommend against the creation of certain neologisms ('triglossia', 'tetraglossia', 'multiglossia', 'polyglossia', etc.) because they mask the functional issues and problems even as they sacrifice formal precision; in the long run, they lead to confusion, and, in fact, are unnecessary. For example, even if it were discovered that Palestinian Jews at the time of the New Testament spoke numerous other languages in addition to those already acknowledged, or that there was a multiplicity of regional Aramaic varieties, the issue of the relationship between the ancient speakers' use of Hebrew and Aramaic is the key issue. Even the Greek, a vital second language in the Palestinian repertoire, can reflect but should not distract from the Semitic language issues. The term 'diglossia' must be related strictly to the Semitic languages; any other usage would constitute an essential redefinition or maladaptation of the concept, such that it could degenerate to the point of impotent generalization.

My suggestion, therefore, for a flexible yet 'canonical' application of the term 'diglossia' to the Palestinian situation, which borrows partly from Platt (1977), is to assign language positions as follows:

High 1 = biblical Hebrew (written)
High 2 = mishnaic Hebrew (spoken, written)
Low 1 = Judaean Aramaic (spoken, written)
Low 2 = Galilean Aramaic (distinguishable in speech only)
T1   = Koine Greek (spoken and written)
T2   = Latin (spoken? written?)

Without such differentiation, diglossia cannot serve as a viable model for understanding the first-century Palestinian language community. The essential components of such a paradigm continue to be the same, or sister, codes (a nod to Fishman), while the fundamental community functions are exemplified (per Ferguson).

BIBLIOGRAPHY

Bangura, Abdul Karim
    1991   *Multilingualism and Diglossia in Sierra Leone* (Lawrenceville, VA: Brunswick).
Black, Matthew
    1967   *An Aramaic Approach to the Gospels and Acts* (Oxford: Clarendon Press, 3rd edn).
Blom, J.-P., and J. Gumperz
    1972   'Social Meaning in Linguistic Structure: Code-Switching in Norway', in J. Gumperz and D. Hymes (eds.), *Directions in Sociolinguistics* (New York: Holt, Rinehart & Winston): 407-34.
Britto, Francis
    1986   *Diglossia: A Study of the Theory with Application to Tamil* (Washington, DC: Georgetown University Press).
    1991   'Tamil Diglossia: An Interpretation', *SWJL* 10: 60-84.
Caton, Steven
    1991   'Diglossia in North Yemen: A Case of Competing Linguistic Communities', *SWJL* 10: 143-59.
Comrie, Bernard
    1991   'Diglossia in the Old Russian Period', *SWJL* 10: 160-72.
Errington, Joseph J.
    1991   'A Muddle for the Model: Diglossia and the Case of Javanese', *SWJL* 10: 189-213.
Fasold, Ralph
    1984   *The Sociolinguistics of Society* (Oxford: Basil Blackwell).
Ferguson, Charles
    1959   'Diglossia', *Word* 15: 325-40.
    1963   'Problems of Teaching Languages with Diglossia', in *Report of the 21st Annual Round Table Meeting* (Georgetown University Monograph Series on Languages and Linguistics; Washington, DC: Georgetown University Press): 355-68.

1991   'Diglossia Revisited', *SWJL* 10: 214-32.

Ferguson, Charles (ed.)
1960   *Contributions to Arabic Linguistics* (Cambridge, MA: Harvard University Press).

Fernandez, Mauro
1993   *Diglossia: A Comprehensive Bibliography 1960–1990* (Amsterdam: John Benjamins).

Fishman, Joshua A.
1967   'Bilingualism With and Without Diglossia; Diglossia With and Without Bilingualism', *Journal of Social Issues* 23: 29-38.
1971   *Advances in the Sociology of Language* (The Hague: Mouton).
1980   'Bilingualism and Biculturism as Individual and as Societal Phenomena', *Journal of Multilingual and Multicultural Development* 1: 3-15.

Fitzmyer, Joseph
1979   *A Wandering Aramean* (Atlanta, GA: Scholars Press).
1992   'Did Jesus Speak Greek?', *BARev* 18.5: 58-63, 76-77.

Flint, E.H.
1979   'Stable Diglossia in Norfolk Island', in W.F. Mackey and Jacob Ornstein (eds.), *Sociolinguistic Studies in Language Contact* (The Hague: Mouton): 295-333.

Fredericks, Daniel C.
1998   'Diglossia, Revelation, and Ezekiel's Inaugural Rite', *JETS* 41: 189-99.

Hudson, Alan
1991   'Toward the Systematic Study of Diglossia', *SWJL* 10: 5-15.

Hudson, R.A.
1980   *Sociolinguistics* (Cambridge: Cambridge University Press).

Hudson-Edwards, Alan
1984   'Rediscovering Diglossia', *SWJL* 7: 5-15.

Meeus, Baudewijn
1979   'A Diglossic Situation: Standard vs. Dialect', in W.F. Mackey and Jacob Ornstein (eds.), *Sociolinguistic Studies in Language Contact* (The Hague: Mouton): 335-44.

Meyers, Eric
1985   'Galilean Regionalism: A Reappraisal', in William Scott Green (ed.), *Approaches to Ancient Judaism*, V (Atlanta, GA: Scholars Press): 115-31.

Mussies, G.
1976   'Greek in Palestine and the Diaspora', in Safrai and Stern (eds.): 1040-64.

Niehoff-Panagiotidis, Johannes
1994   *Koine und Diglossie* (Wiesbaden: Harrassowitz).

Peyraube, Alain
1991   'Some Diachronic Aspects of Diglossia/Triglossia in Chinese', *SWJL* 10: 105-24.

Platt, J.T.
1977   'Aspects of Polyglossia and Multilingualism in Malaysia and Singapore' (paper presented to the 12th International Congress of Linguistics, Vienna) (Also in *Language and Society* 6: 361-78).

Porter, Stanley E.
    1997   'The Greek Language of the New Testament', in *idem* (ed.), *Handbook to Exegesis of the New Testament* (Leiden: E.J. Brill): 99-130.
Rabin, Chaim
    1976   'Hebrew and Aramaic in the First Century', in Safrai and Stern (eds.): 1007-39.
Rendsburg, Gary
    1990   *Diglossia in Ancient Hebrew* (New Haven, CT: American Oriental Society).
    1991   'The Strata of Biblical Hebrew', *JNSL* 17: 81-99.
    1996   'Linguistic Variation and the "Foreign" Factor in the Hebrew Bible', in Shlomo Isre'el and Rina Drory (eds.), *Israel Oriental Studies*, XV (Leiden: E.J. Brill): 177-90.
Safrai, S., and M. Stern (eds.)
    1976   *The Jewish People in the First Century*, II (2 vols.; Philadelphia: Fortress Press).
Sankoff, G.
    1982   'Language Use in Multilingual Societies: Some Alternative Approaches', in J.B. Pride and Janet Holmes (eds.), *Sociolinguistics* (Harmondsworth: Penguin Books): 33-51.
Schiffman, Harold F.
    1991   'Swiss-German Diglossia', *SWJL* 10: 173-88.
Smith, Scobie
    1996   'Can We Find Diglossia in Biblical Hebrew?' (Unpublished revision of a graduate class paper given at Harvard University).
Spolsky, Bernard
    1983   'Triglossia and Literacy in Jewish Palestine of the First Century', *International Journal of the Sociology of Language* 42: 95-109.
    1991   'Diglossia in the Late Second Temple period', *SWJL* 10: 85-104
Watt, Jonathan M.
    1989   'L1 Interference in Written L2: A Comparison between the Koine Greek and Pennsylvania German Situations', in Werner Enninger *et al.* (eds.), *Studies on the Languages and the Verbal Behavior of the Pennsylvania Germans*, II (Stuttgart: Franz Zteiner): 103-15.
    1997   *Code-Switching in Luke and Acts* (New York: Peter Lang).
Zerhusen, Bob
    1995   'An Overlooked Judean Diglossia in Acts 2?', *BTB* 25: 118-30.

THE QUESTION OF DIGLOSSIA IN ANCIENT HEBREW

Scobie P. Smith

Ancient Hebrew provides a challenging case study for understanding the concept of diglossia and its complexities. Several problematic issues arise, such as the following: (1) the linguistic data are available only in certain extant writings, many of which are literary; (2) the sociological background motivating code-switching is usually not well documented or corroborated; (3) several different dialects and languages are involved, making for a complex multilingual scenario; and (4) genetic relationships between earlier and later dialects of Hebrew have not been definitively established. These problems raise fundamental linguistic questions as to the definition of diglossia and the valid methods of demonstrating its existence. Hence, an ancillary purpose of this paper is to illustrate both the need for clarity in our linguistic concepts and the importance of traditional historical-linguistic methodology (i.e., comparative and internal reconstruction).

There are two roughly-defined periods that concern us here regarding ancient Hebrew diglossia: (1) the late Second Temple period, including Qumran Hebrew (QH)[1] and the dialect corresponding to the Mishnah (MH), and (2) the biblical age, including both standard and late biblical Hebrew (BH). This study looks at both, because a relationship between them has been claimed. In particular, diglossia in BH has been argued on the basis of later diglossia involving MH (Rendsburg 1990). There are therefore important implications for the linguistic landscape (and hence, criticism)[2] of the biblical literature.

---

1. Abbreviations used in this paper: BH = biblical Hebrew, LBH = late biblical Hebrew, MH = mishnaic Hebrew, QH = Qumran Hebrew, H = high, L = low, 1cp = first person common plural, 1cs = first person common singular.

2. For example, Rendsburg (1990: 173-74) applies the concept of diglossia to the question of text criticism.

Late Second Temple Period

Diglossia in this period has most recently been discussed by Spolsky (1991), as well as by Rendsburg (1990). A summary of the case for diglossia during this period runs along these lines (following Spolsky).

1. It is granted that there were several languages in use in different quarters and for different purposes: Greek, Aramaic, Hebrew, Latin. Although this makes for a more complex overall picture of socio-multilingualism, a two-way relationship between high and low Hebrew can also be discerned.

2. Contrary to old notions of MH as an artificially sustained language of scholarship (e.g. Geiger 1845), MH was in fact a living language of ordinary speech (Segal 1907–1908; 1910–12; 1927). That is to say, the mishnaic dialect is a written record of that spoken language. Various evidences combine to support this. (a) A literary dialect was already in use at the same period, namely QH, and this dialect differed from MH (more on this below). (b) The Mishnah was orally composed and passed down, making the language of its later written record more likely to be the spoken variety. (c) Grammatical similarities between MH and the Bar Kokhba letters corroborate the use of this dialect for non-literary, or low, functions (Spolsky 1991: 87-91).

3. In addition, BH (i.e., a descendant literary dialect) continued in use for formal, religious, or specialized functions. The differences between BH and MH are significant (dialectal and not merely stylistic), involving such grammatical constructions as verbal tense/aspect, possessive modifiers, etc. The Qumran dialect (QH) provides evidence of this literary dialect in use for formal and religious writing. Talmudic references to a vernacular dialect in contrast to the biblical dialect also indicate a linguistic consciousness of an existing distinction. The distinctive function of this high dialect was literacy for reading or writing sacred texts, both among scribes and other educated persons (Spolsky 1991: 90, 97).

There is therefore evidence for some sort of Hebrew diglossia during this period. There are, to be sure, other languages involved in the overall picture, and including Aramaic the situation has been called triglossia (Spolsky 1991: 85; Rabin 1976). The precise functional distribution of the several languages is another issue, beyond the scope of this paper. Nevertheless, two varieties of Hebrew co-existed, one regarded as vernacular and one as literary/sacred.

Gary Rendsburg is in agreement with this case, in particular the vernacular status of MH and the literary status of QH (Rendsburg 1990). That MH was the spoken language of ordinary discourse is supported both internally, by the oral nature of the topics and genres expressed (Rendsburg 1990: 10, following Segal 1927: 6, §7), and externally, by the Bar Kokhba letters. On the latter, indeed, Rendsburg can affirm: 'The Bar Kokhba letters have so clinched the argument that today every Hebraist recognizes the colloquial nature of MH' (1990: 11). The Talmudic evidence is also cited in corroboration (Rendsburg 1990: 11 n. 33).

Moreover, QH is properly viewed as an authentic descendant of classical literary Hebrew—not as an archaizing imitation. Support is again found internally and externally. Internally, the stylistic quality and similarity to post-exilic BH indicate a natural development of the language. Externally, the continuity of literary Hebrew from LBH through the Second Temple period (e.g. Ben Sira, second century BCE) presents difficulties for our determining the end of the literary dialect and the beginning of archaizing. Thus, as Rendsburg says, 'Without such a break, the Hebrew of the DSS cannot be considered archaistic or imitative of a dead literary tradition; rather it is the direct continuation of BH, specifically LBH' (1990: 14).

MH and QH thus stand as two roughly contemporary dialects in a diglossic relationship (Rendsburg 1990: 14-15). The problem of the time gap between Qumran and mishnaic evidence is answered by Rendsburg in two ways (internally and externally): (1) the Mishnah quotes sources as old as c. 200 BCE and appears older in origin than our source from about 400 years later. (2) Other, earlier texts indicate earlier use of this dialect, namely the Copper Scroll (written in the dialect, pre 70 CE) and the Isaiah Scroll (1QIsa[a], showing MH influence; following Kutscher 1974).

Overall, then, there is a case for late Second Temple diglossia. Certainly, there is evidence of the literary character of QH and the vernacular status of MH. A significant weakness, one might argue, lies in relating the two as a contemporaneous diglossic pair with clearly defined sociolinguistic motivations. Nevertheless, even here the Talmudic evidence is suggestive of an awareness of two dialects for high and low functions.

Biblical Period

Diglossia in the late Second Temple period has gained added significance by virtue of its application and extrapolation to the biblical period. Rendsburg has developed the thesis that MH may be 'retrojected' to biblical times, forming together with the literary BH idiom a situation of diglossia (1990: 15-33). That is, we may project the existence and vernacular status of MH back to the biblical period. This means that anomalous grammatical features found in BH that are distinctive of MH (vs. QH) may be regarded as biblical colloquialisms.

There are two overall arguments used to support this claim. First, given that MH is the spoken dialect of late Second Temple diglossia, distinctively mishnaic linguistic features found in BH may be regarded as colloquial intrusions (Rendsburg 1990: 14-15, 22-23). Secondly, vernacular dialects among cognate languages may be searched for comparative evidence of the colloquial status of a BH form. The idea here is that when a grammatical feature occurs in the colloquial idiom of a cognate language and not in the literary idiom, and a similar feature is instanced in the biblical text, the Hebrew occurrences of this feature are likely to be colloquialisms just as they are in the cognate (Rendsburg 1990: 4-6, 24-25). Rendsburg's study then proceeds to investigate certain linguistic phenomena in order to show that they fit these criteria and so are colloquial.

As attractive as the hypothesis might be, however, there are three flaws in the above approach. First, the selection of grammatical features is at times *ad hoc* and isolated. A wider look at paradigmatically related forms and words reveals that the 'discovered' colloquialism is based on a gratuitous choice. This is an error in the synchronic perspective. Secondly, the appeal to cognate colloquialisms is faulty historical linguistics. The comparative method establishes cognate relationships and reconstructs proto-languages, but it cannot infer a transference of linguistic status (vernacular, literary, etc.) from one language to another. This is an error in the diachronic perspective. Thirdly, the method of retrojecting MH neglects early Hebrew epigraphic materials that one would classify as 'non-literary' and thus potentially indicative of colloquial usage. This is of great importance, since otherwise we have no proximate check on ancient Hebrew 'as it was spoken' at all. This is a synchronic error in corpus selection.

To illustrate these issues, I have selected for closer examination three linguistic features used by Rendsburg: the relative pronoun, the 1cp independent pronoun, and the waw-consecutive imperfect. The approach here will be to apply sounder linguistic methods and relevant epigraphic data to cast doubt on the colloquial status of these features, especially as the low variety of a diglossic pair. The epigraphic data are the letters from Arad, Lachish, and Yavneh Yam, whose non-literary status is here assumed.[3]

The three phenomena have been selected in particular to illustrate the methodological issues. The case of the relative pronoun illustrates the application of the contemporary epigraphic corpus. The 1cp independent pronoun illustrates especially the use of complete synchronic systems, but also introduces the relevance of internal reconstruction. Finally, the waw-consecutive illustrates the proper application of the comparative method.

The Relative Pronoun

The distribution of the relative pronouns אֲשֶׁר and ־שֶׁ in the Hebrew Bible has been difficult to explain. One possibility is that אֲשֶׁר existed in southern Hebrew, and ־שֶׁ in northern (Dahood 1952: 44-45). Another view, to which Rendsburg subscribes, espouses a combination of diglossia with this geographical consideration, an idea proposed already by Segal (1927: 42-43, §78) and Rabin (1979). In this view, ־שֶׁ was colloquial northern Hebrew and progressively invaded southern colloquial, while אֲשֶׁר continued in the literary idiom. This view is intended, then, to explain both the mixed distribution of אֲשֶׁר and ־שֶׁ in books of northern origin (intrusion of the colloquial), and the intermittent presence of ־שֶׁ in southern books (dialectal borrowing) (Rendsburg 1990: 115-18).

Since this putative spread of spoken ־שֶׁ southward must have occurred well before the exile in order for it to appear later in the literary medium,[4] we would expect ־שֶׁ to appear at least some time in the low

---

3. This assumption obviously warrants qualification: formulaic features and social norms in the epistolary genre might well not reflect ordinary speech. The assumption is held, then, for the sake of argument, since letters have already been accepted as evidence of the colloquial in the case of the Bar Kokhba letters (e.g. Rendsburg 1990: 10-11).

4. Rendsburg 1990: 116-17: 'During the period of the monarchy, 1000–586 BCE, a standard literary Hebrew was utilized in which אֲשֶׁר was the sole relative

register as evidenced by our letters dating from just prior to the exile. This, however, is not the case. ־ש never occurs in the Arad or Lachish letters, while אשר is found twelve times. A few examples follow:[5]

Arad 18.6-8[6]

ולדובר אֲשֶׁר צוותני שלם

As regards the matter concerning which you gave me orders: it is fine (now).

Arad 40.4, 5

ועת הטה [ע]בדך [ל]בה ׀ אל אֲשֶׁר אמ[ר]ת

And now, your servant has applied himself to what you ordered.

Lachish 9.4-9

השב ׀ [ל]עבדך דובר בויד שלמיהו אֲשֶׁר נעשה מוחר

Return word to your servant by way of Shelemyahu as to what we are to do tomorrow.

Lachish 4.2-4

ועת ככל אֲשֶׁר שלח אדני ׀ כן עשה עבדך כתבתי על הדלת ככל אֲשֶׁר שלח[תה א]לי

And now, according to everything which my lord has sent thus has your servant done. I have made a record according to everything which you sent to me.

pronoun. The colloquial form, which existed side-by-side with the classical form, was ש, which in a very few instances infiltrated literary composition. The upheaval of 586 BCE, with the resultant exile and restoration, effected changes in the Hebrew language, and one of these was the further penetration of ש into written records.' Cf. also Rabin (1979: 73), from whom Rendsburg draws this idea.

5.   This is the complete list of occurrences in these letters (Pardee *et al.* 1982: 216): Arad 5.[4], 10; 8.9; 18.7; 21.[7], 40.5, [6], [15]; Lachish 2.6; 3.5, 11; 4.2, 4; 9.7-8; 18.1; and P. Mur. 17.2 (dated to the seventh century; Pardee *et al.* 1982: 119). Also Yavneh Yam 6.8 has כאשר. (Brackets signify that textual reconstruction of the word is involved.) There are two other instances at Arad (the only other relatives there), both in fragmentary texts (and not letters): Arad 29.7; 71.2, this latter being interesting in that it reads]טאשרל[, which may involve the possessive construction אשר ל־ (cf. Rendsburg 1990: chapter 8).

6.   The ׀ character is used to show line divisions in the original text.

Lachish 4.10-12

כי אל משאת לכש נחנו שמרם ככל האתת אשר נתן ן אדני

...we are watching the Lachish (fire-)signals according to the code which
my lord gave (us)...

The fact that אשר is always used in the letters at our disposal suggests
that this was the relative pronoun of ordinary speech. Since, however,
all our early letters are of southern origin, we are unable to address the
geographical question whether אשר is distinctly southern and ־ש distinctly northern. Unfortunately, extra-biblical evidence of northern Hebrew is sparse by comparison. The little that is available in the Samaritan ostraca, for example, provides no instances of a relative pronoun.
Nevertheless, diglossia seems unlikely in light of the uniformity of the
above evidence. If the Bar Kokhba letters, which uniformly use ־ש,[7]
argue for ־ש as colloquial, so should these earlier letters.

The 1cp Independent Nominative Pronoun

The 1cp independent pronoun אנו is also cited by Rendsburg as colloquial when contrasted with putatively literary אנחנו (1990: 139-41, §89).
Retrojection of MH should also lead us to this conclusion. Several considerations, however, invalidate this approach in this case. The selection
of the suitable grammatical element is *ad hoc*. If instead we had chosen
the first singular pronouns, אני and אנכי, the exclusive use of אני in MH
(Segal 1927: §67) would again produce a new 'colloquialism'. This
perception could then be buttressed by *a priori* impressions of the sort
that find longer forms more suited for literary use and shorter forms for
colloquial.[8] Attempts to find 'comparative' support would also produce
several cases in which cognates of אני are regularly used in other Semitic languages.[9]

7. See Pardee *et al.* 1982: 230 for a list of the 29 occurrences.
8. Segal unfortunately borders on this mentality: 'In earlier Hebrew alone are
the two forms found existing side by side, but אני, being the shorter of the two,
gradually came to be employed more frequently, especially in colloquial speech,
until the longer form disappeared entirely from common use' (§67). Yet Segal, as
we can see here, still explains the development in diachronic terms.
9. Many of these, though, Rendsburg would probably not count, since he
would regard them as literary. For example, Aramaic אנה, Ugaritic *an* (and *ank*),
Ge'ez *'ana*, Arabic *'anā*, Old South Arabian *'n* (Beeston 1984: §22:1), and Akkadian *ana* (a literary OB alternate to *anāku*, *GAG* Erg. §41-42). אני is also the only

This view of the singular pronouns would obviously be incorrect. The abundant use of אני in the Hebrew Bible voids any idea of 'creeping colloquialism' here. More specifically, if we recognize an increasing frequency of אני in later books (e.g. in 1 and 2 Chronicles, 15 occurrences of אני but only one of אנכי), then a diachronic change accounts for the distribution without any involvement of diglossia. Regarding the 1cp pronoun, however, the sole instance of אנו in Jer. 42.6 (*Kethib*) unfortunately precludes any significant distributional analysis, as could be done with אני, and this fact rescues Rendsburg's proposal of diglossia from immediate contradiction. The argument, however, should not rest on silence of this sort.

What is more, we can reconstruct an alternative history of אנו that is at least as plausible as diglossia. Here again, the 1cs pronouns prove relevant. Whereas אני, אנכי,[10] and (א)נחנו should all be considered proto-Semitic in origin (their cognates are found in East and West Semitic), אנו appears to be an internal Hebrew development. By internal reconstruction, I offer the explanation that אנו came about by analogy with the singular form:[11] אנכי:אנחנו::אני: *X*, where *X* = אנו. The implication follows that an alternative history of the *use* of אנו may be posited over against diglossia. It is at least as likely that the increased use of אנו and ultimate replacement of אנחנו followed a diachronic path similar to that of אני in its displacement of אנכי. That is, אנו was perhaps no more colloquial than אני, on which its form was in part based. The larger lesson in this example is that grammatical features should be studied in the *systems* to which they belong and not in isolation.

To the above remarks may be added this datum from the early letters: נחנו in Lachish 4.10-11:

Lachish 4.10-11

כי אל משאת לכש נחנו שמרם ככל האתת אשר נתן ן אדני

> ...that we are watching the Lachish (fire-)signals according to the code which my lord gave (us)...

form attested in epigraphic Hebrew (Garr 1985: 79), though Garr cites only two occurrences in the early epigraphic material.

10. The 1cs -*k* element (cf. Akkadian stative suffix -*āku*, Ethiopic perfect suffix -*ku*) appears to have been added to a base ***'ana*, so אנכי would then not be quite as old in its origins as proto-Semitic.

11. This appears also to be the view of Bauer and Leander (1922: §28o): 'Durch Anlehnung an die 1. Sg. entstanden אנו אנחנו (oben h)'.

This form of the 1cp pronoun also occurs six times in the Hebrew Bible, five of which could be classified as direct discourse.[12] Taken together with the Lachish example, this distribution might then lend some support (if direct discourse has any bearing) to an alternative hypothesis, namely that נחנו is colloquial.[13] The scanty evidence and the ambiguous origin[14] respecting נחנו bestows only some plausibility on this hypothesis, yet this once again presents a viable alternative to the diglossia interpretation of these pronouns.

The Waw-Consecutive Imperfect

In Rendsburg's view, the waw-consecutive form is literary and not spoken, notwithstanding its usage in direct discourse (Rendsburg 1990: 19-20, n. 61). The basis for this view, as well as Rendsburg's hypothesis for the origin of the waw-consecutive, can be found in an earlier article, in which Rendsburg compares the Hebrew waw-consecutive with classical Egyptian *'iw* plus perfective verb. Indeed, Hebrew *wa-* is 'to be identified with' Egyptian *'iw* (= 'is, are'), leading Rendsburg to label *wa-* an 'existential particle (or copula)', and thus making the waw-consecutive a 'compound verb' (Rendsburg 1981: 668-71). This comparison is pursued even to the level of syntactic style,[15] leading to the conclusion that waw-consecutive verbs are 'reserved for literary style' (Rendsburg 1981: 670). My study takes issue with this Egyptian comparison in its totality, explaining the waw-consecutive by way of the proto-Semitic *yaqtul* preterite, along more traditional lines.[16]

12. Gen. 42.11; Exod. 16.7, 8; Num. 32.32; 2 Sam. 17.12 ('direct discourse'); Lam. 3.42 (poetry: acrostic section using initial *nun*).

13. If נחנו is derived from אנחנו by aphaeresis, it is possible that this irregular reduction occurred via a 'fast speech' process (Hock 1991: 49-50).

14. Proto-Semitic (cf. Akkadian *nīnu*, Ge'ez *neḥna*, Arabic *naḥnu*) or secondary aphaeresis of *aleph* (Garr 1985: 51)?

15. 'The Egyptian is used most often at the beginning of narrative sentences and moreover "gives a certain smoothness and elegance to recitals of past events" (Gardiner). The same holds true for the Hebrew form. Phonetically, morphologically, syntactically, and stylistically, they are to be identified with the Egyptian compound verbs...' (Rendsburg 1981: 670).

16. See the following works for linguistically more plausible accounts of the origin of the waw-consecutive in the proto-Semitic *yaqtul* preterite (with Semitic conjunction *wa-*): Bauer and Leander 1922: §36e; Lambdin and Huehnergard 1985: 72-73; Smith 1991: 3-5.

Rendsburg's argument, to be sure, does not hinge entirely on this Egyptian comparison. Appeal is also made to the diglossia of the late Second Temple period. The case is made explicit in the following paragraph:

> To back up my suggestion that the Hebrew consecutive tenses were used solely for the written dialect, we may again turn to the diglossia of Greco-Roman times. In the spoken dialect of the time as represented by MH, these forms are completely absent (Segal). In the written dialect of the time as represented by the Hebrew of the DSS and of certain liturgical pieces, these forms are used (Segal, Kutscher). The same must have been true during the Biblical period. The written dialect used the consecutive tenses, viz., their regular appearance in BH. The spoken dialect doubtless did not (Rendsburg 1981: 671).[17]

There is an analogical leap in this argument that in fact begs the question of diglossia in BH. Linguistic change over the centuries, including external influence from Aramaic, internal dialectal effects, and stylistic factors such as archaism, invalidate straight extrapolation from MH to BH. In fact, epistolary evidence, as we will see, suggests that waw-consecutive forms were not reserved for literary purposes.

Thus, Rendsburg's case is based on a comparative argument (Egyptian) and retrojection of MH. My purpose is to argue instead that retrojection ignores the real nature of language change and is contradicted on comparative and diachronic grounds. Moreover, epistolary evidence supports usage of waw-consecutive forms in hypothetically low idiom. That is to say, they were not reserved solely for literary purposes and so cannot serve as a reliable indicator of diglossia during the biblical period.

To begin, it must be remembered that the waw-consecutive tenses were at one time innovations, since the tense cannot be reconstructed for Proto-Semitic from comparative evidence. Innovations, such as this tense form, arise in 'ordinary' speech. Linguistic change is to be expected in spoken language, not an archaizing or conservative high idiom. Furthermore, the later loss of the waw-consecutive was also an

---

17. Rendsburg is drawing on an idea expressed earlier by Segal in 1927: 73 (§ 157): 'It may even be doubted whether the consecutive construction ever attained in popular speech that dominating position which it occupies in the literary dialect. It may be plausibly assumed that the more convenient construction with the simple tenses had survived in the every-day speech side by side with the more difficult construction by means of the consecutive tenses.'

innovation, which also must be sought in spoken language. Hence, methodologically, we cannot transfer grammatical features from one period back to an earlier time in neglect of the diachronic developments in the language. As for the waw-consecutive, we may merely have a diachronic change along the following lines. First, the waw-consecutive arose as an innovation within the developing Hebrew language (and perhaps more broadly in Canaanite).[18] This grammatical feature became distinct as a result of changes from the old northwest Semitic verbal system, in which the *yaqtul* preterite was productive. Secondly, the memory of the old preterite waned and the waw-consecutive became increasingly marginalized as an operative verbal tense during the period of LBH (Kutscher 1982: 45, §67). Thirdly, a further restructuring in the verbal system occurred, producing the changes seen in MH, including complete loss of waw-consecutives and the rise of a productive periphrastic present/future using היה plus participle (Kutscher 1971: 1600-1601; Segal 1927: 150, 156-57). This picture is simplistic, to be sure, but it underlines the point that it is precisely the *spoken* language that *changes*.

Comparative methodology supports the view that the waw-consecutive imperfect developed from the old *yaqtul* preterite. East Semitic (Akkadian) maintains its *iprus* preterite, and there is evidence of prefix-conjugation forms in use in restricted contexts as preterites in a number of West Semitic languages. Specifically, in certain contexts the Arabic jussive *yaqtul* (e.g. after *lam*), Ge'ez subjunctive *yeqtel* (after *'em-qedma* and *za'enbala*), Sabaean *yaqtul* (after *lm*), Ugaritic preterite *yaqtul* (e.g. sometimes after *'idk*, *hl*), and Hebrew imperfect *yiqtōl* (e.g., after *bəterem*) represent vestiges of an earlier *yaqtul* preterite (cf. Smith 1991: 1-15). To this we may add the internal evidence that the *yaqtul* preterite without prefixed waw occurs in Hebrew poetry[19] and appears to be historically antecedent to the waw-consecutive (GKC §107b; Waltke and O'Connor 1990: §31.1.1; Rainey 1986: 15-16).

Important evidence for the West Semitic *yaqtul* preterite is also found in the western peripheral Akkadian of the Amarna letters (Moran 1950: 49-52; 1961: 63-64; Rainey 1986: 4-5; 1990: 407-13; 1996: II, 221-27). The Canaanizing Amarna letters contain a mixture of an Akkadian dialect (or dialects), used for diplomacy, with the local dialect, leading

---

18. Cf. the 'waw-consecutive' in the Moabite stone (Jackson 1989: 104); also Punic (Harris 1936: 39), but note Friedrich and Röllig (1970: § 266).

19. And sometimes in prose; e.g. Judg. 2.1.

us to infer that the local dialect visible in the letters is the native, spoken language. The implication, therefore, is that preterite forms in the Amarna corpus are non-literary and colloquial.

Our most direct evidence for the non-literary usage of BH waw-consecutives comes from the ancient letters. Although these letters lack the quantity of the narrative content necessary to require frequent use of waw-consecutive imperfects, inclusion of the Yavneh Yam letter produces unambiguous evidence. The only occurrences of waw-consecutive imperfect are found in the following two passages:

Lachish 4.6-7

וסמכיהו לקחה שמעיהו <u>ויעלהו</u> העירה

As for Semakyahu, Shemayahu has seized him and taken him up to the city.

Yavneh Yam 4-9

<u>ויקצר</u> עבדך...
<u>ויכל</u> ואסם כימם לפני שב
ת כאשר כל [ע]בדך את קצר וא
סם כימם <u>ויבא</u> הושיהו בן שב
י <u>ויקח</u> את בגד עבדך כאשר כלת
את קצרי זה ימם לקח את בגד עבדך

Your servant did his reaping,
finished, and stored (the grain) a few days ago before stopping.
When your servant had finished his reaping and
had stored it a few days ago, Hoshayahu ben Shabay came
and took your servant's garment. When I had finished
my reaping, at that time, a few days ago, he took your servant's garment.

This passage demonstrates a consistent sequence of waw-consecutives for past consecution: ויקצר, ויכל, ויבא, and ויקח. The waw-less perfect in l. 9, לקח, is a case of altered word-order, in which the temporal adverbial (זה ימם) precedes the verb.

Semantic consecution in past narrative is uncommon in a typical letter, so waw-consecutive imperfects are not often called for. Frequently, other particles intervene before the verb, such as ועת and כי, or word order may not be verb-first, with an object or subject before the verb. For example, Lachish 3 illustrates both of these situations:

Lachish 3.13-18

ולעבדך הגד...
לאמר ירד שר הצבא
כניהו בן אלנתן לבא

מצרימה ועת
הודוייהו בן אחיהו ו
אנשו שלח לקחת מזה

Now your servant has received
the following information: General
Konyahu son of Elnatan has moved south in order to enter
Egypt. He has sent (messengers) to take
Hodavyahu son of Ahiyahu and
his men from here.

Line 13 begins with altered word-order (ולעבדך), introducing direct discourse, which therefore does not begin with a consecutive tense. The past-tense direct-discourse, however, is continued using ועת followed ultimately by a perfect שלח.

A sequence of waw-less perfects need not indicate diminishing use of waw-consecutive imperfects if there is no consecution implied, as in the following example.

Lachish 4.2-4

...ועת ככל אשר שלח אדני
כן עשה עבדך כתבתי על הדלת ככל
...אשר שלח[תה א]לי...

And now, your servant has done
everything my lord sent (word to do). I have written down everything
you sent me (word to do)...

The writer states in a list-like fashion that he has fulfilled instructions. No consecution is involved.

Thus, the waw-consecutive imperfect finds its typical biblical usage in the non-literary correspondences from Lachish and Yavneh Yam.

Conclusion

Diglossia cannot be simply extrapolated backwards from MH to the biblical period. We are lacking the kinds of evidence available for late Second Temple diglossia, such as sociolinguistic awareness of dialectal distinction and corroboration from non-literary sources. Consideration of synchronic systems, diachronic processes, and contemporary texts argues rather that we should at best suspend judgment on the question for BH. The present case for BH diglossia becomes, in fact, a counter-example of sound historical linguistic methodology. The case for Hebrew diglossia in the late Second Temple period, on the other hand, finds support in the roughly contemporaneous existence of two distinct dialects that are also recognized within the speech community as filling different sociolinguistic roles. Within the larger multilingual setting of this period, a form of diglossia within Hebrew appears to have existed.

BIBLIOGRAPHY

Bauer, H., and P. Leander
1922   *Historische Grammatik der hebräischen Sprache* (Halle: Max Niemeyer; reprint: Hildesheim: Georg Olms, 1991).
Beeston, A.F.L.
1984   *Sabaic Grammar* (JSS Monograph, 6; Manchester: University of Manchester Press).
Dahood, Mitchell J.
1952   'Canaanite-Phoenician Influence in Qoheleth', *Bib* 33: 30-52, 191-221.
Driver, G.R.
1958   'A Lost Colloquialism in the Old Testament', *JTS* 8: 272-73.
1970   'Colloquialisms in the Old Testament', in D. Cohen (ed.), *Mélanges Marcel Cohen* (The Hague: Mouton): 232-39.
Fellman, Jack
1977   'The Linguistic Status of Mishnaic Hebrew', *JNSL* 5: 21-22.
Ferguson, Charles A.
1959   'Diglossia', *Word* 15: 325-40.
Friedrich, Johannes, and Wolfgang Röllig
1970   *Phönizisch-Punische Grammatik* (Rome: Pontifical Biblical Institute).
Garr, W. Randall
1985   *Dialect Geography of Syria-Palestine, 1000–586 B.C.E.* (Philadelphia: University of Pennsylvania Press).
Geiger, Abraham
1845   *Lehr- und Lesebuch zur Sprache der Mischnah* (Breslau: F.E.C. Lenckart).
Harris, Zellig S.
1936   *A Grammar of the Phoenician Language* (New Haven: American Oriental Society).
Hock, Hans H.
1991   *Principles of Historical Linguistics* (Berlin: Mouton de Gruyter, 2nd edn).
Jackson, Kent
1989   'The Language of the Mesha Inscription', in Andrew Dearman (ed.), *Studies in the Mesha Inscription and Moab* (Atlanta: Scholars Press).
Kutscher, Eduard Y.
1971   'Hebrew Language: Mishnaic', *EncJud* 16: 1590-1607.
1974   *The Language and Linguistic Background of the Isaiah Scroll (1QIsaᵃ)* (Leiden: E.J. Brill).
1982   *A History of the Hebrew Language* (ed. Raphael Kutscher; Jerusalem: Magnes Press).
Lambdin, Thomas O.
1971   *Introduction to Biblical Hebrew* (New York: Charles Scribner's Sons).

1978 *Introduction to Classical Ethiopic* (HSS, 24, Atlanta: Scholars Press).
Lambdin, Thomas O., and John Huehnergard
1985 'Historical Grammar of Biblical Hebrew: Outline' (Cambridge, MA: Department of Near Eastern Languages and Civilizations, Harvard University).
MacDonald, J.
1975 'Some Distinctive Characteristics of Israelite Spoken Hebrew', *BO* 32: 162-75.
Moran, William L.
1950 'A Syntactical Study of the Dialect of Byblos' (PhD dissertation, Johns Hopkins University).
1961 'The Hebrew Language in its Northwest Semitic Background', in G. Ernest Wright (ed.), *The Bible and the Ancient Near East* (New York: The Biblical Colloquium; reprint Winona Lake, IN: Eisenbrauns, 1979): 54-72.
Pardee, Dennis, S. David Sperling, J. David Whitehead, and Paul E. Dion
1982 *Handbook of Ancient Hebrew Letters* (SBLSBS, 15; Atlanta: Scholars Press).
Rabin, Chaim
1976 'Hebrew and Aramaic in the First Century', in S. Safrai and M. Stern (eds.), *The Jewish People in the First Century: Historical Geography, Political History, Social, Cultural and Religious Life and Institutions* (CRINT, 1.2; Assen: Van Gorcum): 1007-39.
1979 'The Emergence of Classical Hebrew', in A. Malamat (ed.), *The Age of the Monarchies: Culture and Society*, Part 2 (Jerusalem: Massada): 71-78, 293-95.
Rainey, Anson F.
1986 'The Ancient Hebrew Prefix Conjugation in the Light of Amarnah Canaanite', *HS* 27: 4-19.
1990 'The Prefix Conjugation Patterns of Early Northwest Semitic', in T. Abusch (ed.), *Lingering over Words* (Atlanta: Scholars Press): 407-20.
1996 *Canaanite in the Amarna Tablets* (3 vols.; Leiden: E.J. Brill).
Rendsburg, Gary
1981 'Diglossia in Ancient Hebrew as Revealed through Compound Verbs', in Y.L. Arbeitman and A.R. Bomhards (eds.), *Bono Homini Donum: Essays in Historical Linguistics in Memory of J. Alexander Kerns* (Amsterdam: John Benjamins): 665-77.
1990 *Diglossia in Ancient Hebrew* (New Haven: American Oriental Society).
Segal, M.H.
1907–1908 'Mišnaic Hebrew and its Relation to Biblical Hebrew and to Aramaic', *JQR* 20: 647-737.
1910–12 'Hebrew in the Period of the Second Temple', *International Journal of the Apocrypha*: 79-82.
1927 *A Grammar of Mishnaic Hebrew* (Oxford: Oxford University Press).
Smith, Mark
1991 *The Origins and Development of the* waw-*Consecutive* (HSS, 39; Atlanta: Scholars Press).

Spolsky, Bernard
    1991   'Diglossia in Hebrew in the Late Second Temple Period', *SWJL* 10.1: 85-
                104.
Waltke, Bruce K., and M. O'Connor
    1990   *An Introduction to Biblical Hebrew Syntax* (Winona Lake, IN: Eisen-
                brauns).

THE FUNCTIONAL DISTRIBUTION OF
KOINE GREEK IN FIRST-CENTURY PALESTINE

Stanley E. Porter

Diglossia (if this is the correct term to use—see below) in first-century Palestine is a complex issue, which must inevitably face two major theoretical questions. These are the definition of diglossia, and the problems faced in the reconstruction of the linguistic milieu of the first century. Rather than treat these in detail here, I wish simply to review these questions briefly, before turning to the title of my paper, the functional distribution of Koine Greek. In this section, having defined diglossia in its narrower sense, I wish to place it in what I consider its proper context, that is, as a small part of the larger question of Greek register analysis.

1. *Diglossia and Bilingualism*

Studies of diglossia have traditionally revolved around two major definitions of the concept, although there has also been a large amount of revisionist thinking regarding the term (see Errington 1991; Britto 1986; Platt 1977). Ferguson (1959; 1991), following the work of Weinreich (1953), argued for a particular kind of linguistic situation in which there were two distinct varieties of a language used by the same speech community, what he labeled the 'high' or 'superposed' variety that was not used in ordinary conversation but rather learned through formal education (taught) and in which literary texts were produced, and what he labeled the 'low' variety or dialect that was learned by children in the home and used in everyday communicative contexts. Each of these varieties has definable functions, with the high variety the prestige language and hence tending towards a standardized language, often having more complex grammatical features not present in the low variety (e.g. case and verb structure) and a more formal vocabulary. Although Ferguson differentiated this kind of linguistic situation from other instances of bilingualism, a differentiation some question (see below), even these categories are not as clearly defined as they might be. Part of the problem was that Ferguson's initial analysis was of the varieties, of which he selected four, rather than speech communities (1991: 220). Further, a given linguistic context might result in a speaker having a repertoire that consists of three or more strata, with one variety being the superordinate for another, but itself the subordinate of a third. An instance might be users of Arabic (in Baghdad), where in some linguistic contexts there may be at least three varieties, including classical written Arabic as the highest form, with Muslim spoken Arabic and Christian Arabic below that (see Watt 1997a: 47-48). This suggests that one may well need to differentiate numbers of high and low varieties (H1, H2, L1, L2) (see Platt 1977; cf. Watt 1997b). A further difficulty is with regard to syntax, with the theory being that the high form has a more subordinated or hypotactic syntax due to its formal nature, and the low form being more non-subordinated or paratactic due to its casual nature. However, recent studies of the differences between writing and speaking indicate that many of these kinds of differentiations are not as clear-cut as once was thought (Biber 1988; cf. Hudson 1994). Despite these difficulties (and others to be noted below), Ferguson's model has persisted, and is to be found in a number of sociolinguistics books that discuss diglossia (e.g. Wardhaugh 1992: 90-96), since it seems to avoid several of the terminological difficulties of the alternative position (noted below), by giving diglossia a specific application.

The other development in diglossic studies follows the work of Fishman (1967; 1980), who explicitly puts diglossia within the context of bilingualism. These coordinates allow for a speaker to be diglossic and bilingual, diglossic and not bilingual, bilingual and not diglossic, or neither diglossic nor bilingual, depending upon whether analysis is of the individual speaker or the nature of the functions of language within a social context, and how these interact. Some of these varieties might be defined as forms of the same language (hence, Ferguson's definition), and the speaker is considered diglossic, while others might be varieties of different languages, in which case the speaker may be bilingual, but, depending upon other factors, diglossic or not (there are only a few transitionary instances of neither diglossia nor bilingualism). Fishman's scheme also suffers from problems of definition and differentiation, with very little being offered in terms of how one might go about establishing both his categories and how individual speakers and language communities relate to them (Dittmar 1976: 176-78). The result is, in fact, that virtually any society can be seen to be diglossic, rendering the differentiations less than useful for distinguishing features of complex linguistic situations (Hudson 1980: 53-55). Many recent treatments of diglossia, however, utilize variations of Fishman's categories, undoubtedly due to the wider definitional scope of his terms, and their applicability to contexts that go beyond the constraints of the specific linguistic situation defined by Ferguson (Baetens Beardsmore 1986; Hamers and Blanc 1989).

This is a brief summary of the discussion of diglossia, pointing out some of its more obvious limitations. Despite these limitations, the category of diglossia has continued to be used in discussion of multilingualism, either in its more restricted or in an expanded sense.

2. *Diglossia or Bilingualism in First-Century Palestine*

The broad conceptual problems with discussing diglossia or bilingualism in first-century Palestine are notoriously difficult, and cannot be explored in detail here. I merely chronicle some of these difficulties as a prelude to discussion of several particular difficulties. Besides the obvious drawback of having no native informants (of course, a problem for dealing with the linguistic or sociological situation of any time before the advent of the recording era), for diglossia there is the inherent limitation of any evidence that exists only in written form. This is especially the case with regard to Ferguson's categories, in which the high variety is often a written language, whereas the low variety is often spoken. The relationship between written and spoken forms of ancient languages is also a highly complex one. The limitation of the evidence to what is found in written documents runs contrary to the instincts of many modern linguists, whose methods have often been developed for analysis of spoken language, or at least for situations in which both spoken and written language forms are available for comparison. Not only is it difficult to determine and analyse the relation between spoken and written forms of epigraphic languages, but the possibilities of both the conservatizing tendency of written forms and interference of written and spoken forms with each other must also be taken into account (Horrocks 1997: 5-6). A further difficulty is that there is a restricted range of evidence, both in terms of the entire sociolinguistic situation of first-century Palestine, and in terms of the linguistic repertoire of any given speaker, and that speaker's representative function within a speech community. We also know little of the context in which a given discourse was produced. The history of textual transmission also makes it difficult to differentiate the idiolect of the original user, when a manuscript such as the New Testament has undergone a regularizing influence in the hands of Atticistic copyists, who tended to conform syntax and even spelling to their idealized classical norms.

Despite these difficulties, there have been numerous studies of the languages of Palestine in the first century (see Porter 1994 for a recent survey). Very few of these studies, however, are concerned to analyse the languages in use in terms of sociolinguistic categories (but see Silva 1980). Instead, they are content to suggest whether a language may or may not have been used, without scrutinizing its functional relationships within a diglossic or multilingual environment. Several exceptions are worth noting, however. The first two are by Niehoff-Panagiotidis (1994; cf. Blomqvist 1995) and Horrocks (1997). Writing without any apparent knowledge of each other's investigations, they provide insightful analyses of the development of the Greek language. Niehoff-Panagiotidis argues against the concept of a 'Middle Greek' and sees the Koine as an adequate description of the form of Greek that first developed during the late classical period as a form of spoken language, followed by development of a written form. This developmental pattern continued until the early Byzantine period, laying the foundation for modern Greek developments (which proved instructive for Ferguson). The Koine was not simply based upon the Attic-Ionic dialect, but had a number of features of the various dialects of the dialect period, not because of drawing specifically upon these dialects, but because many of the features cannot be localized in one dialect and because the dialects persisted longer than many have thought. Horrocks argues similarly to Niehoff-Panagiotidis, with the major distinction being that he sees the Koine language developing from the Attic-Ionic dialect, with the written form developing somewhat independently of the spoken form, and reflecting a persistent 'fossilized' character, which, with the spoken form, laid the foundation for the development of modern Greek.

As insightful as these studies are, however, they do not address the situation of how Greek 'fit' within a multilingual context of first-century Palestine. Two recent studies attempt to look at this linguistic situation in terms of diglossia (see Horsley 1989 for bibliography). Spolsky (1991: esp. 95; cf. 1983) claims to have shown that Jews in the Diaspora in Egypt, Rome and Asia Minor used Greek, but in Babylon used Ara-

maic and Hebrew. Non-Jews in Palestine, if they were government officials, used Greek and some Latin; if they lived in coastal cities (Greek
colonies), used Greek; and elsewhere used Aramaic. For Jews in Palestine, however, in the Judean villages they used Hebrew and Aramaic, in
Galilee they used Aramaic, Hebrew and Greek, in the coastal cities they
used Greek, Aramaic and Hebrew, and in Jerusalem, if they were upper
class they used Greek, Aramaic and Hebrew, and if they were lower
class they used Aramaic, Hebrew and Greek. There is much of merit in
Spolsky's study. This includes his useful differentiation between Jews
inside and outside of Palestine, in the sense that he does not make the
Jews of Palestine representative of all Jews of the Mediterranean world.
Also, he differentiates between Jews and non-Jews in Palestine. Further, his list of the languages cited above orders the languages according to their probable frequency of use and the level of proficiency.

Unfortunately, there are some severe limitations to his study. One of
these is the failure to be able to provide any kind of quantifiable comparative data for these estimations, even though they may well be correct in many instances. Thus, there is no real way of determining why
Hebrew would have been the language of the Judean villages, but Aramaic that of Galilee. Further, there is a useful appreciation of the evidence for the use of Hebrew, but not one that convincingly links the
abstract data with actual contexts of usage, probably resulting in a
higher valuation of the language than is appropriate, especially in the
light of the development of the targums during this period even in
Palestine (and Aramaic may have then become the 'surrogate holy
language'; see Meyers 1985: 121). It is highly improbable, to my mind,
that Hebrew was a language of widespread use by any except perhaps
the highly educated Jewish scribe in Palestine (and certainly not by
Judean villagers, most Galileans, or the lower class of Jerusalem). There
is the further difficulty of there being much evidence that Spolsky
leaves uncited or unappreciated, including the Greek Judean desert
documents for assessing the widespread use of Greek by Jews in the
eastern regions of Palestine, and the role of Greek in Galilee due to its
location in the midst of the Decapolis. Thus, despite Spolsky's use of
the term 'diglossia' in his title, he is concerned to define the multiliter-
ate and multilingual environment of Palestine (Spolsky 1991: 97). What
he shows is that, although Ferguson's categories may appear elegant, he
must use something closer to Fishman's model to appreciate the range
of languages in use in Palestine.

In contrast to Spolsky's study, Watt (1997b) has proposed a clearer form of Ferguson's theory, treating Hebrew and Aramaic as forms of the same language because of their genetic relationship. As a result, he proposes that biblical Hebrew (written) was a 'high 1' variety and mishnaic Hebrew (written and spoken) was a 'high 2' variety, while Judean Aramaic (written and spoken) was a 'low 1' variety and Galilean Aramaic (written and spoken) a 'low 2' variety. Watt uses this configuration to retain specific diglossic features of the relationship between Hebrew and Aramaic, while recognizing also that if Greek (as well as Latin) is included in the linguistic equation, its variety of uses would necessitate that the situation be regarded as one of bilingualism. As he admits, strictly speaking, the category of diglossia can only be applied to either Hebrew and Aramaic or to Greek, but not to both. Hence he treats Greek and Latin as what he calls tertiary languages. The strengths of Watt's analysis are that he tries to isolate diglossic features of the relation between Hebrew and Aramaic and their varieties. The weakness of this analysis is inherent in the use of Ferguson's model. Rather than Greek being seen as a form of low variety, or bracketed out of discussion, the evidence, I believe, points in another direction (see Porter 1989; 1994). Recent discussion of Hebrew has provided convincing evidence for its use in a number of circles (perhaps the 'language miracle' of Acts 2; see Zerhusen 1995), but there still does not appear to be much vernacular usage, as there was of Aramaic. The Greek evidence, including the composition of religious texts in Greek in Palestine (1 Esdras, 2 Maccabees, as well as the importance of the LXX), points away from Hebrew's preservation as a prestige religious language—except in perhaps certain restricted religious linguistic contexts. Greek was, I believe the evidence shows, the prestige language of Palestine in the first century. Although it was perhaps not the first language for many Palestinian Jews, the evidence for its widespread vernacular use is also undeniable.

The recently published documents from the Judean desert have a number of interesting texts that shed further light on the multilingualism of the region at about the time we are considering. Two examples must suffice. One is the well-known correspondence between Bar Kokhba and his followers (see Porter 1997). A cache of letters discovered in the Cave of Letters of Nahal Hever/Wadi Habra has a number of Aramaic (around eight or more, depending on whether some are actually in Hebrew) and a few Hebrew letters (three to five), but also two

Greek letters. There has been much made of these Hebrew letters, since they are often used to confirm that Hebrew continued to be used as a language in certain Jewish circles during the first century, including the Qumran sectarians and the later Bar Kokhba rebels. The Aramaic letters, most think, were to be expected, due to this being a Jewish rebellious movement. However, one of the Greek letters is the most instructive (*P.Yadin* *52 = 5/6Hev 52 = SB VIII 9843), since it says that the letter was written by Soumaios to Jonathe and Masabala in Greek, because (here the text is subject to reconstruction, and hence a variety of interpretations; see Porter 1997: 315-16) the desire or opportunity was not to be found to write in Hebrew/Aramaic. Either no one wanted to work that hard, or no one was capable of writing in Hebrew/Aramaic, so it was written in Greek. The papyrus implies that the context was such that both a writer and a reader at the other end could be expected to be able to communicate through this linguistic medium. The letter conforms in all regards to the model of how letters were written based upon the numerous documentary papyri found in Egypt, including its syntax and lexis. However, it also tends to indicate that the use of the Semitic language, whether it was Aramaic or Hebrew, was restricted (while Greek was not). It seems most likely that Greek was a major component of the rebels' linguistic repertoire, even though, because of various political and religious beliefs at the time, they tried to use Hebrew or Aramaic to create a sense of corporate identification and nationalism (much like the role of the modern revivals of Welsh or Gaelic).

A second, and even more pertinent, example, is found in the several archives of documentary papyri from the Cave of Letters, one of Babatha and the other of Salome Komaïse, as well as some other manuscripts. Several of these documents have multilingual elements to them. For example, the body of the text is written in Greek, but the names or signatures are written in another language, such as Aramaic or Nabataean. There are other words in Semitic languages as well. It is disputed what this evidence indicates. Some have taken these documents as evidence for a particularly Hellenized group of Jews, who had perhaps been associated because of their material holdings with the Bar Kokhba rebels. A more convincing explanation, however, is that we have a group of Jews, living on the easternmost frontiers of the Roman Empire, who were probably bilingual. Even though some signatories to the letters may not have been literate, there were scribes or other writers who had facility in Greek and the other languages. More to the point for establishing the cultural environment that led to these documents, the people participate fully in the Roman legal system, reflecting Roman law and business practice of the time (a conclusion suggested by Cotton and Yardeni 1997: 154). Rather than indicating Hellenization, this evidence probably indicates that these Jews, like so many other religio-cultural groups within the Roman Empire, were fully integrated within the Greco-Roman world of their times, of which multilingualism was a part.

One document in particular to note is XHev/Se 64, a deed of gift, also now thought to come from Nahal Hever/Wadi Habra (Cotton and Yardeni 1997: 203-21). Recently published, this document is a Greek text noted for its ungrammatical and non-idiomatic features, including a disregard for case endings and grammatical gender. The editor argues that the document was probably a rendering of an Aramaic original text, although we no longer have that specific original, only a number of other similar texts. The editor further notes that this text is unparalleled by any other Greek papyrus from the Judean documents.

This is not the only explanation of this document, however. It is noteworthy that this is the only one written in this way from the Judean documents, as is the fact that the items of linguistic note are the matters of case endings and gender. These two features—fewer cases and a simplified gender system—are typically noted as characterizing the lower variety in a diglossic context. Further, this is a double document, well known in the ancient world, especially in Egypt of a slightly earlier period, for having what amounts to the same text on both the inside and the outside of a (sealed) document. The inner document was sealed as a means of guaranteeing that the legal statement was not tampered with or in any way altered. What is noteworthy with XHev/Se 64, however, is that the supposed grammatical irregularities are far from irregular. Virtually every instance of alteration of case or gender is found in both the outer and the inner texts (e.g. lines 5 and 24, 6 and 25, 7 and 26, 10 and 31, 11 and 32-33, 13 and 34; there are also instances of changed number: 9 and 28). The cases used reveal that the author consistently changes the dative case to the genitive or accusative, and the genitive to the accusative case. This is the general tendency of the Greek language with regard to cases, with the dative case being assimilated with the genitive, and then the genitive being assimilated with the accusative (see Horrocks 1997: *passim*). Far from being unmindful of case endings and grammatical gender, the author is entirely consistent, both in terms of his own idiolect and in terms of the tendencies of Greek language development.

Studies of the multilingualism of Palestine, especially in terms of diglossia, have been few, and have also probably neglected the most important of the languages of the region. The recent publication of a number of documents illustrates that Greek must be given its due in discussion of the multilingualism of first-century Palestine.

3. *Diglossia as an Instance of Register Variation*

One of the major issues that has often been overlooked in discussion of diglossia is that of *context*. Much of the emphasis of the discussion has been on determining the two (or more) languages, describing their differences, and then comparing the results. Ferguson (1991: 220) noted that his comments in 1959 had been interpreted as comments about *languages*, when he had been meaning to speak about *speech communities*. Although often mentioned, the context in which the varieties are used is not often developed. This is an area that has been developed in more recent studies of register and diglossia. Often when register has been mentioned in studies of diglossia, however, it is equated with the concept of style. There is some merit in this equation, since one is attempting to describe a number of distinguishing features of a particular variety of language. The focus is upon the features of the language being used. However, register studies that have paid greater attention to varieties and their context of situation, to use Hallidayan terms (see Halliday and Hasan 1985), rather than those of stylistics, seem to me to have greater promise of advancing discussion of diglossia, since there is an attempt to link description and analysis of features of language with contexts of usage. Hallidayan register studies address the major components of the context of situation—the field and its ideational semantic component, the tenor and its interpersonal semantics, and mode and the textual component—within a context of their functional employment (i.e. varieties), whether this is in terms of written or spoken texts. Rather than requiring full knowledge of the context of situation before being able to appreciate the linguistic issues at play, as is the case in many studies of diglossia, Hallidayan register encourages, on the basis of analysis of the semantic components, the reconstruction in linguistic terms of the major features of the context of situation (see Porter 2000).

As designated above, diglossia, especially when narrowly defined, becomes a special instance of register variation (Hudson 1994). The matter of the informal and formal, or casual and non-casual language use (to use Hudson's terminology) that diglossia emphasizes becomes a part of the range of varieties, or even languages, discussed by register, with register studies extending the language repertoire beyond simply two distinct varieties of the same language (cf. Ferguson 1991: 222, 229). The advantage of register studies over diglossia (at least for an epigraphic language such as the Greek of the New Testament), as a part of the discussion of bilingualism, is that the criteria for discussion shift from anthropologically-based studies of language contact to socio-linguistically-based and formally-based studies (cf. Hudson-Edwards 1984). As a result, discourse-pragmatic criteria come to the fore, as the entire communicative context, including the context of culture, and the particular context of situation, enters into the analysis. The kinds of rigid distinctions between high and low varieties in diglossic studies give way to quantification of multivariate analysis of individual registers as they are used in various communicative situations. Along with this re-assessment of the categories comes a necessary re-examination of such terms as 'high variety' and 'low variety'. These terms carry with them connotations that may not be the most helpful to assessment of language use. The term 'prestige language' is more accurate in expressing what social realities might have existed with regard to language use, without labeling such a language either 'high' or 'low'— automatically elevating or denigrating a particular form of usage (see Williams 1992: 95-122; cf. Ferguson 1991: 227-29). There is the further departure from the potentially diachronic view of diglossia, in which the development of particular varieties of language (e.g. those that become standardized) are seen to have triumphed over lesser varieties, to a synchronic one, in which varieties of usage (i.e. registers) reflect choice within a given context, and say little to nothing about the history of their usage. In this sense, it is perhaps possible to speak of differentiated strata of linguistic usage according to the repertoire of a given speaker (see Platt 1977; Watt 1997a).

In the light of Hallidayan register studies, of which diglossia becomes a part, there are two ways to pursue discussion further. I wish to spend some time with each, but emphasize the second. The first means of assessing the functional distribution of Koine Greek is to note the range of types of text to be found in Palestine in the first century. The non-casual or formal register levels would include inscriptions of various types in Greek (the situation with Aramaic and Hebrew inscriptions is complicated by a number of factors that cannot be addressed here). The formalized language of the inscriptions is designed to stand as a permanent record for others to read, regardless of their relation to the actual context that elicited the erection of the inscription. As a result, the field of discourse is often (though certainly not always) of an official nature, such as laws, edicts, announcements of significant political and military victories, and the like. The tenor is usually in the third person, conveying a resolution by an authoritative person or body. The mode is often a highly stylized and formulaic inscriptional language, with set phrases, such as honorifics to the erector of the inscription, and inscriptional syntax such as the use of the infinitive as the main verb of clauses.

Throughout Palestine, the number of inscriptions in Greek is largest. Even in Jerusalem, there is roughly an even number of Greek and Semitic-language inscriptions, with Jewish tombs at Beth She'arim being predominantly in Greek (see van der Horst 1991). An interesting example is the inscription at the Temple in Jerusalem forbidding Gentiles to pass a certain point in the Temple precinct (Boffo 1994: 283-90). The inscription was reportedly written in Greek and Latin (so Josephus says [*War* 5.193-94; 6.124-25; *Ant.* 15.417], although he may be kowtowing to his Roman audience), but only the Greek version has survived. The circumstances of its erection are unknown, but its message is very clear. It has several features of inscriptions, including the commanding use of the infinitive in lines 1-2, and a third-class conditional structure for the punishment of violators, addressed to 'whoever' might commit such an act. It is clear, nevertheless, that the inscription was erected to warn off any foreigners (non-Jews) who might be tempted to enter forbidden territory. The question of who could actually read it aside, the inscription seems to assume at the least that non-Jews would have been able to understand the inscription in Greek, since the Greek warning suffices for all, including foreigners (apart possibly from Latin-speaking Roman officials and soldiers). This might well also imply that the inscription was written to Jews as well in Greek. There is no report of any other inscription clarifying access to the Temple for Jews to read.

At the opposite end of the continuum must be the documentary papyri. Several of these from Palestine have already been mentioned above. Although from Egypt, one of the most interestingly and instructive papyri giving insight into the kind of private language often used within constricted contexts is that of a husband to his wife (*P.Oxy.* 744;

see Davis 1933: 1-7). There is so much of interest in this 1 BCE papyrus, yet there is so much that remains private to the corresponding couple. For example, the author, Hilarion, addresses the letter to his 'sister' Alis, almost assuredly his wife and probably also his natural sister, although this is not certain, since he also addresses Berous, 'my lady', possibly though not certainly his mother. Hilarion lets them know that 'we' are still in Alexandria, probably because he is working (he later refers to wages), but without any further explanation of who 'we' refers to, although he says that 'all of them', but not apparently himself, might return to Oxyrhynchus. He says that if Alis gives birth *pollapollōn*, a term that remains obscure, and if it is not male, she is to leave it, but if it is female to cast it out. Is this a case of commanding the wife to expose a female child? It may well be, although it may have something to do with animals. The meaning is elusive. There are also a number of non-standard grammatical features, such as aphaeresis (deleting an initial letter), the present subjunctive in a prohibition, and the use of the adverbial form for the adjective form, several instances of use of the accusative case for the dative (see above), and unusual morphology. The author probably wrote the papyrus himself, or had it written by one of those with him, for his family back home, giving them assurances that he was all right, and that he was thinking of them. The field of discourse concerns almost entirely personal matters, with a high degree of interpersonal elements (e.g. use of the first and second persons), conveyed on a small piece of papyrus. I am sure that Hilarion would be amused to know that we are still reading his private mail 2000 years later.

Within these two extremes, we might well note a number of different broad, literary registers (note that in Porter 1989: 153, a scale of registers is given, with what Ferguson might have called the 'high' forms on the bottom; however, I would wish to change the chart in other ways). For example (again drawing on authors from outside Palestine), more formalized registers might include those by the Atticistic writers such as Dionysius of Halicarnassus, Plutarch or Lucian. These authors were reacting to their immediate context of linguistic usage and, by invoking archaic forms and vocabulary, intending to place their texts within an identifiable literary/linguistic tradition. Less archaically formal but still non-casual would be various literary writers, including Philo, Josephus, Polybius, Arrian and Appian. Perhaps more casual, and hence more identifiably linked to their immediate contexts of situation, would be non-literary authors, many of them perhaps purporting to be (though to varying degrees actually) reflecting spoken language. These would include official papyri, scientific texts (the so-called *Zwischenschichtsprosa*; see Rydbeck 1967), and popular philosophers such as Epictetus, geographers and travel writers such as Strabo and Pausanias, and others such as Apollodorus.

The question that emerges from this discussion of register is where to place the various books of the New Testament (I realize that few, if any, were actually written in Palestine, but believe that this is the natural extension of this discussion). This is a highly contentious issue, since the discussion of these texts has a lengthy history that involves so many other discussions that are now brought to bear upon the linguistic discussion. It is often difficult to sort through this wealth of data to determine which pieces of information regarding, for example, cultural context or context of situation have actual bearing upon determination of register. Recent studies have attempted to analyse the register of various New Testament books, including the gospel of Mark and the book of Philippians, from a Hallidayan perspective (Porter 2000; Reed 1997).

The second approach that I mentioned above regarding diglossia within the context of register would require that we analyse several texts by the same author, where we might have a chance of describing and analyzing their differences in context of situation. The major author to emerge from such a consideration is, of course, Paul. His writings have been bedeviled ever since the days of F.C. Baur by often useless discussions of authorship, shrinking his corpus down to four letters, and then gradually expanding it again to seven to ten books in the eyes of most scholars. Nevertheless, the Pauline corpus, and hence the available data for analysis within that corpus, is thirteen letters. Before I am willing to eliminate any of them from the corpus, I will need to see far more convincing linguistic evidence that, for example, the Pastoral Epistles, or Ephesians, Colossians or 2 Thessalonians, do not belong. By 'convincing linguistic evidence', I do not mean inconclusive studies of authorship based upon supposed analysis of word statistics, which are based upon too small a sample size utilizing methods that require much larger sample sizes (see O'Donnell 1999).

As a result, I wish to analyse some of the quantifiable features of register in a number of the Pauline letters, to see if we can begin to find a functional distribution of uses of Koine Greek among Paul's letters. The letters I have chosen to analyse are Romans, 1 Corinthians, Philippians and the Pastoral Epistles. I have chosen these letters for a number of reasons (see McDonald and Porter forthcoming: ch. 10). The first is their respective historical contexts, so far as these can be known. Romans was addressed by Paul to a church that he had never visited, about a situation that he was anticipating, that is, support for his visit to Rome (Rom. 1.10, 15). It would seem that there should be a number of features of non-casual language within Romans that would place it in a more formal and less personal register, due to the personal distance between the author and addressees, and the subject-matter discussed. 1 Corinthians, on the other hand, is a response to communication in both oral and written forms from the Corinthian church to Paul, a church that Paul had founded on a previous missionary trip, and for which he had personal regard and interest (Acts 18.1-18). There were issues of apparent unrest between various factions, especially in their relation to Paul (1 Cor. 5.1; 7.1), and he is responding to these immediate needs. Pauline authorship is not in doubt for either Romans or 1 Corinthians. Philippians is a letter that, although its authenticity was once doubted, is now firmly entrenched within the Pauline canon, even if some take it to be a composite of a number of smaller Pauline letters. It too is addressed to a church that Paul had founded and for which he had much personal regard (Acts 16.12-40), but in which there does not appear to have been the personal strain in relations that is brewing in the Corinthian context. Nevertheless, like Romans and 1 Corinthians, Philippians is a letter written to a church context, and shares that feature in common with the others.

The Pastoral Epistles, however, are the most difficult letters to deal with from a higher-critical perspective. Their authorship is doubted by all but the most recalcitrant (of which I account myself one), but there are also other features that distinguish them. Unlike virtually all other Pauline letters, except possibly Philemon (and Philemon has some questionable features in this regard), the Pastoral Epistles purport to be personal letters, that is, letters not addressed to churches, whether Pauline or otherwise, but to single individuals (Reed 1993). These individuals are not simply people whom Paul knows, but two of his closest colleagues and fellow workers, according to what we can piece together from the rest of the New Testament, two who were probably instrumental in ultimately resolving the crisis at Corinth. There are undoubted difficulties regarding where the Pastoral Epistles fit within the Pauline compositional chronology, but nevertheless the two figures to whom they are addressed are plausible people to receive personal Pauline letters. It is on that basis that these letters are examined. The findings may well be instructive on several accounts, including what we can learn about a level of Pauline writing that in some ways would be the most context-specific of any of his writings. If the results prove promising for this relatively small body of data, a next important step would be to extend analysis to a much larger corpus, in order to validate these findings.

In order to facilitate this register analysis, in this paper I draw on the empirical register study of Biber, who identified a number of textual dimensions, indicated by sets of linguistic features that co-occur in texts (Biber 1988: esp. 101-69). The most significant dimension was whether a text had more informational or involved features (see Table 1 and Dimension 1 below). Since his sets of features (called dimensions) are based on English, they needed to be reconfigured for analysis of Greek. Here is not the place to justify this method fully, except to note that Biber's findings regarding spoken and written English have helped to establish an empirical approach to register analysis. I assume that it is also possible to identify similar determinative features for the study of register in an ancient language, such as Greek. For example, on the basis of knowledge of the person system, and its semantic features regarding the relation between speaker and addressee, first and second person were placed within the dimension of interaction, and third person in the dimension of narrative. Similar estimations were made regarding other linguistic features, creating six testable textual dimensions. These six dimensions form the basis of a multifactor analysis of each of the Pauline letters, as a means of testing hypotheses regarding these letters determined through other, more conventional critical means. (The tables below [1-6] record instances per thousand words of text of each of the linguistic features for each book. These features are individually rated on a scale of 1-4, and then summed for each dimension. The rankings are based on simple calculations, and the lower the number indicates the larger number of features.)

Dimension 1 (see Table 1 below), the most important and powerful of the set of features, is designed to determine personal interaction versus informational production. This dimension directly addresses the tenor and field components of Halliday's register analysis. Factors that indicate interaction are such things as private verbs (e.g. thinking, feeling), use of first and second person pronouns and verb endings (implying involvement by speaker or hearer in interactive discourse), and a number of individual features, such as imperfective aspect (with more of a heightened sense of immediacy than perfective aspect), analytic negation (a negating word, such as *ou* or *mē*), demonstrative pronouns/ adjectives, the use of *eimi* ('be') as a main verb, the use of verbs (as conveyors of processes), and several other features. These features are characteristic of interactive discourse, with pronouns indicating reduced surface forms to heighten the verbal elements. Informational production is characterized by more linguistic substance and hence semantic density, and is determined by the use of nouns (significant for the ideational component), the noun–verb ratio, word length (especially important in a synthetic and transparent language such as Greek), type–token ratio regarding lexis (with the idea that a larger ratio indicates more information-conveying words), and several other features.

On the basis of these features, 1 Corinthians has the highest interaction indicated. If one selects only the most important indicators of interaction (private verbs, imperfective aspect, first and second person, analytic negation and demonstrative pronouns and adjectives), the same result is found, indicating that the lesser features do not skew the results. Philippians is the next most interactive discourse of the four, perhaps reflecting the writer's personal involvement with a church that he had founded and that strongly supported him in his ministry. Romans is very similar to Philippians in its interactive level. Even though in Romans it is Paul alone who addresses his readers (this is also true of the Pastoral Epistles), his use of the first person is not as high as in 1 Corinthians and Philippians, and just above that of the Pastoral Epistles. It comes as somewhat of a surprise to find the Pastoral Epistles as the least interactive by these criteria, until one examines the informational factor. Here the Pastoral Epistles are clearly the highest in information production, with the largest number of nouns, the second largest noun–verb ratio, the longest word length, the largest type–token ratio, and the largest number of attributive adjectives, all seen as information-conveying features. Nouns and type–token ratio not only indicate that there is information conveyed, but, when combined with the number of attributive adjectives, indicate a precise selection of information to be transmitted. Whereas 1 Corinthians has the largest number of verbs, it has the smallest number of nouns, and the smallest noun–verb ratio, contributing to its position as the least informational of the letters. Again, Romans is in the middle, closest to the Pastoral Epistles, tending toward being informational, but not predominantly so. As noted above, one might have expected Romans to be more informational and less interactive, especially compared to 1 Corinthians and the Pastoral Epistles. Its middle ground is perhaps commensurate with a position that suggests a certain amount of interaction with the audience, due to Paul's desire to ingratiate himself with the Romans as a means of advancing his ministry, but less full of information than he would be in a letter that gives explicit guidance and directions to a trusted co-worker such as Timothy or Titus. 1 Corinthians, being highly interactive, is directly commensurate with Paul's concern for a church that he had founded but that is obviously enquiring about important ecclesial matters. He is less concerned to give information than he is to be responsive to the matters that concern them. The Pastoral Epistles have less concern for interaction, and more for information. This reflects a more informative and direct style of writing, a feature of these letters that perhaps mirrors the immediacy of their being written near the end of Paul's life.[1]

Dimension 2 (see Table 2 below) indicates whether a discourse is narrative or non-narrative in its concerns, and analyses questions of mode in register analysis. Non-narrative includes, but is not limited to, descriptive and expositional discourse. Those features that establish narrativity are the use of the perfective aspect (to be expected in narrative), third person singular and plural verbs, as well as stative aspect (since this aspectual form is often used in a series of items to heighten emphasis) and synthetic negation (phrasal rather than individual word negation). Those features that indicate non-narrative features are the imperfective aspect (to be expected in discursive discourse), attributive adjectives and word length. Several of these features are similar to those tested in Dimension 1, although here they are used differently. A surprising, if not logically impossible, result of the findings is that the Pastoral Epistles score the highest for both narrative and non-narrative. It may also seem inappropriate to use a test of narrativity on epistolary material; however, the test of narrativity is not a test of historicality, but of a discourse style. Although one is tempted to posit that this dimension determines that both types of discourse are found in the Pastoral Epistles, this test instead indicates that elements of both types of discourse, hence narrative and non-narrative features, are prominent. In any

---

1. I wish to thank my colleague, Brook W.R. Pearson, for his insights regarding the Pastoral Epistles.

case, the Pastoral Epistles emerge clearly as the leaders in both features. Romans and Philippians both score lowly for both narrativity *and* non-narrativity, while 1 Corinthians, by contrast, is in the middle. Again, this does not indicate that 1 Corinthians is neither narrative nor non-narrative; rather, it suggests that it does not have distinguishing tendencies in either direction, but some features of each.

Dimension 3 (see Table 3 below) concerns explicit versus non-explicit reference, and hence whether that reference is situation-independent (such as by means of relative pronouns, coordination of phrases, nominalizations and proper nouns) or is situation-dependent (such as by means of various deictic indicators such as adverbs). The Pastoral Epistles are clearly the most explicit of the discourses: they have the largest numbers of all features except proper nouns, which have the second highest frequency of occurrence. This evidence is commensurate with the concentration in the letters upon Timothy and Titus and their specific situations being addressed, but not with those features that are context-dependent (such as the general concepts of church leadership, rather than a specific problem with a particular person in the church), as is perhaps found in Philippians. Philippians scores highest in non-explicit or situation-dependent factors, with the largest number of adverbs. This situation-dependent orientation of the letter perhaps accounts for the difficulty on the part of interpreters in determining the nature of references to 'dogs' in Phil. 3.1, etc. This is not because of the use of adverbs in this particular episode, but because these adverbs are linguistic indicators of the general situation-dependent character of the text. Romans and 1 Corinthians avoid high levels of both explicit and non-explicit reference. This indicates that there is a relative avoidance of reference to situation-dependent material.

Dimension 4 (see Table 4 below) consists only of features that indicate overt expressions of persuasion, features of the tenor component (Porter 2000). These include infinitives, suasive verbs (e.g. commanding, demanding), conditionals (to indicate the conditions under which something might occur), and imperatives (used to direct behaviour). Both suasive verbs and imperatives are designed to indicate intentions or to direct actions. In the light of the analysis above, it is not surprising to find that 1 Corinthians, the most interactive discourse, is also the most overtly persuasive by some measure, with suasive verbs and conditional subordinate clauses the most heavily used. None of the other letters is relatively highly persuasive, with Philippians being the least so. This can perhaps be accounted for by the personal relations involved, in which Paul charts a firm but gentle course with the Romans, but is on friendly terms with the Philippians and recipients of the Pastoral Epistles

Dimension 5 (see Table 5 below) is concerned with abstract versus non-abstract information. The use of discourse conjunctions often goes along with discourse that requires guidance through abstract information, the kind of indirect information that is often transmitted by passive forms of verbs, whether the passive agent is expressed or not. Non-abstract language is indicated by a high type–token ratio, indicating a high degree of lexical variety and an attempt by the writer to disambiguate information. 1 Corinthians, according to this set of features, is the most abstract of all of the discourses, followed by Romans and then Philippians and the Pastoral Epistles. The opposite is found regarding non-abstract information, with the Pastoral Epistles having the highest type–token ratio, followed by Romans and Philippians, and 1 Corinthians. There may be a correlation between the level of overt persuasion and the abstract nature of the language of 1 Corinthians, indicating that the highly persuasive language is more explicitly interactive than it is specific. On the other hand, the language of the Pastoral Epistles is non-abstract and highly informational, perhaps in keeping with the explicit referencing of the text.

Dimension 6 (see Table 6 below) stipulates the features that designate that there is elaboration within a discourse taking place. The primary features of elaboration include demonstrative pronouns and adverbs, causative subordination, and relative pronouns. By contrast, phrasal coordination is the primary feature of non-elaborative discourse. In both instances, Philippians has the largest frequency of features. This feature is designed to quantify the kind of elaboration that takes place, with the first resulting in the possibility of adding clauses on to previous ones, rather than coordinating such addition.

Once these six dimensions have been studied, it is possible to create a multifactor analysis of each of the letters, and to compare the results. This multifactor analysis could be performed in a number of ways. For example, one could list the components in which each book had the highest number. This would result in a description of the register of each book in terms of its most evident or strongest dimensions, but at the expense of neglecting lesser dimensions. Another method would be to find a way of assigning ratings to each dimension, so that all of the dimensions of each book are described. On the basis of these lists, specific similarities and differences could be more closely analysed.

4. *Conclusion*

Although 'diglossia' is one of the most frequently used terms in soci-olinguistics, and although it has obviously been of use in describing the linguistic repertoires of a number of language users, when it comes to defining the senses in which the word is used, problems begin. These are compounded by the fact that the most consistent definition, that of Ferguson, seems to run counter to the complex linguistic milieu of first-century Palestine. Ferguson's definition of diglossia in terms of a single language with several varieties only has potential explanatory power for a limited range of the evidence of linguistic usage in the first-century world. Fishman's expanded definition, with its significant overlap with the concept of bilingualism, does not redeem the use of the term. Instead, I have proposed that the study of register, a concept already introduced in rudimentary form into diglossic studies, has much more potential benefit to the study of the language-world of the New Testa-ment. Register studies are able to describe the strata of usage across a number of languages. Biber's attempt to quantify through empirical study a number of these results adds a further dimension. I have started with the study of a few of the Pauline letters, concentrating upon Greek usage (cf. Biber 1995, for application to other modern languages). The results do not entirely coincide with usual higher-critical findings, but present a challenge for further study.

BIBLIOGRAPHY

Baetens Beardsmore, H.
    1986   *Bilingualism: Basic Principles* (Clevedon: Multilingual Matters, 2nd edn).
Biber, D.
    1988   *Variation across Speech and Writing* (Cambridge: Cambridge University Press).
    1995   *Dimensions of Register Variation: A Cross-Linguistic Comparison* (Cam-bridge: Cambridge University Press).
Blomqvist, J.
    1995   'Diglossifenomen i den hellenistiska grekiskan', in T. Engberg-Pedersen, P. Bilde, L. Hannestad and J. Zahle (eds.), *Sproget i Hellenismen* (Hellen-ismestudier, 10; Aarhus: Aarhus Universitetsforlag): 25-38.

Boffo, L.
    1994   *Iscrizioni Greche e Latine per lo studio della Bibbia* (Brescia: Paideia).
Britto, F.
    1986   *Diglossia: A Study of the Theory with Application to Tamil* (Washington, DC: Georgetown University Press).
Cotton, H., and A. Yardeni
    1997   *Aramaic, Hebrew and Greek Documentary Texts from Nahal Hever and Other Sites* (DJD, 27; Oxford: Clarendon Press).
Davis, W.H.
    1933   *Greek Papyri of the First Century* (repr. Chicago: Ares).
Dittmar, N.
    1976   *Sociolinguistics: A Critical Survey of Theory and Application* (London: Edward Arnold).
Errington, J.J.
    1991   'A Muddle for the Model: Diglossia and the Case of Javanese', *SWJL* 10.1: 189-213.
Ferguson, C.A.
    1959   'Diglossia', *Word* 15: 325-40; repr. in P.P. Giglioli (ed.), *Language and Social Context: Selected Readings* (Harmondsworth: Penguin Books, 1972): 232-51.
    1991   'Diglossia Revisited', *SWJL* 10.1: 214-34.
Finegan, E., and D. Biber
    1994   'Register and Social Dialect Variation: An Integrated Approach', in D. Biber and E. Finegan (eds.), *Sociolinguistic Perspectives on Register* (New York: Oxford University Press): 315-47.
Fishman, J.A.
    1967   'Bilingualism with and without Diglossia; Diglossia with and without Bilingualism', *Journal of Social Issues* 23.2: 29-38.
    1980   'Bilingualism and Biculturism: As Individual and as Societal Phenomena', *Journal of Multilingual and Multicultural Development* 1: 1-15.
Flint, E.H.
    1979   'Stable Societal Diglossia in Norfolk Island', in W.F. Mackey and J. Ornstein (eds.), *Sociolinguistic Studies in Language Contact: Methods and Cases* (The Hague: Mouton): 295-333.
Halliday, M.A.K., and R. Hasan
    1985   *Language, Context, and Text: Aspects of Language in a Social-Semiotic Perspective* (Geelong, Victoria, Australia: Deakin University Press).
Hamers, J.F., and M.H.A. Blanc
    1989   *Bilinguality and Bilingualism* (Cambridge: Cambridge University Press).
Horrocks, G.
    1997   *Greek: A History of the Language and its Speakers* (London: Longman).
Horsley, G.H.R.
    1989   *New Documents Illustrating Early Christianity*. V. *Linguistic Essays* (New South Wales: Macquarie University).
Horst, P.W. van der
    1991   *Ancient Jewish Epitaphs* (Kampen: Kok).
Hudson, A.
    1991   'Toward the Systematic Study of Diglossia', *SWJL* 10.1: 1-22.

1994   'Diglossia as a Special Case of Register Variation', in D. Biber and E. Finegan (eds.), *Sociolinguistic Perspectives on Register* (New York: Oxford University Press): 294-313.

Hudson-Edwards, A.
1984   'Rediscovering Diglossia', *SWJL* 7: 5-15.

Hudson, R.A.
1980   *Sociolinguistics* (Cambridge: Cambridge University Press).

McDonald, L.M., and S.E. Porter
forthcoming   *Early Christianity and its Sacred Literature* (Peabody, MA: Hendrickson).

Meyers, E.M.
1985   'Galilean Regionalism: A Reappraisal', in W.D. Green (ed.), *Approaches to Ancient Judaism. V. Studies in Judaism and its Greco-Roman Context* (Atlanta: Scholars Press): 115-31.

Niehoff-Panagiotidis, J.
1994   *Koine und Diglossie* (Mediterranean Language and Culture Monograph Series, 10; Wiesbaden: Otto Harrassowitz).

O'Donnell, M.B.
1999   'Linguistic Fingerprints or Style by Numbers? The Use of Statistics in the Discussion of Authorship of New Testament Documents', in S.E. Porter and D.A. Carson (eds.), *Linguistics and the New Testament: Critical Junctures* (JSNTSup, 168; SNTG, 5; Sheffield: Sheffield Academic Press): 206-62.

Platt, J.T.
1977   'Aspects of Polyglossia and Multilingualism in Malaysia and Singapore', Paper presented at XIIth International Congress of Linguistics, Vienna, Austria, August 1977.

Porter, S.E.
1989   *Verbal Aspect in the Greek of the New Testament, with Reference to Tense and Mood* (SBG, 1; New York: Peter Lang).

1994   'Jesus and the Use of Greek in Galilee', in B. Chilton and C.A. Evans (eds.), *Studying the Historical Jesus: Evaluations of the State of Current Research* (NTTS, 19; Leiden: E.J. Brill): 123-54.

1997   'The Greek Papyri of the Judaean Desert and the World of the Roman East', in S.E. Porter and C.A. Evans (eds.), *The Scrolls and the Scriptures: Qumran Fifty Years After* (RILP, 3; JSPSup, 26; Sheffield: Sheffield Academic Press): 293-316.

2000   'Dialect and Register in the Greek of the New Testament: Theory' and 'Register in the Greek of the New Testament: Application with Reference to Mark's Gospel', in M.D. Carroll R. (ed.), *Rethinking Contexts, Rereading Texts: Contributions from the Social Sciences to Biblical Interpretation* (JSOTSup, 299; Sheffield: Sheffield Academic Press): 190-208, 209-29.

Porter, S.E. (ed.)
1991   *The Language of the New Testament: Classic Essays* (JSNTSup, 60; Sheffield: JSOT Press).

Reed, J.T.
    1993   'To Timothy or Not? A Discourse Analysis of 1 Timothy', in S.E. Porter and D.A. Carson (eds.), *Biblical Greek Language and Linguistics: Open Questions in Current Research* (JSNTSup, 80; Sheffield: Sheffield Academic Press): 90-118.
    1997   *A Discourse Analysis of Philippians: Method and Rhetoric in the Debate over Literary Integrity* (JSNTSup, 136; Sheffield: Sheffield Academic Press).

Rydbeck, L.
    1967   *Fachprosa, vermeintliche Volkssprache und Neues Testament: Zur Beurteilung der sprachlichen Niveauunterschiede im nachklassischen Griechisch* (Uppsala: n.p.).

Silva, M.
    1980   'Bilingualism and the Character of Palestinian Greek', *Bib* 61: 198-219; repr. in Porter (ed.) 1991: 205-26.

Spolsky, B.
    1983   'Triglossia and Literacy in Jewish Palestine of the First Century', *International Journal of the Sociology of Language* 42: 95-109.
    1991   'Diglossia in Hebrew in the Late Second Temple Period', *SWJL* 10.1: 85-104.

Wardhaugh, R.
    1992   *An Introduction to Sociolinguistics* (Oxford: Basil Blackwell, 2nd edn).

Watt, J.M.
    1997a   *Code-Switching in Luke and Acts* (Berkeley Insights in Linguistics and Semiotics, 31; New York: Peter Lang).
    1997b   'Beyond Diglossia: The Diglossic Continuum in First Century Palestine' (unpublished paper, Biblical Greek Language and Linguistics Section, Society of Biblical Literature).

Weinreich, U.
    1953   *Languages in Contact: Findings and Problems* (New York: Linguistic Circle of New York).

Williams, G.
    1992   *Sociolinguistics: A Sociological Critique* (London: Routledge).

Zerhusen, B.
    1995   'An Overlooked Judean *Diglossia* in Acts 2?', *BTB* 25: 118-30.

Tables 1-6: Register Analysis of Pauline Textual Dimensions[2]

Table 1. *Dimension 1: Interactive vs. Informational Production*

(+) [Interaction]	Rom.	1 Cor.	Phil.	Past.
Private Verbs	25.03	23.28	33.76	22.65
Imperfective Aspect	88.17	119.78	92.69	106.36
2nd Person Reference	44.29	51.99	68.75	44.15
Analytic Negation	28.97	37.78	12.28	19.50
Demonst. Pro. & Adj.	7.73	10.54	9.21	11.75
1st Person Singular	30.94	43.69	84.10	29.25
1st Person Plural	22.22	19.48	7.98	16.91
'Be' as Main Verb	10.69	18.01	4.91	10.32
Causative Subordination	7.88	8.79	12.89	5.73
Indefinite Pronouns	2.11	7.91	6.14	6.31
Wh-questions	6.05	4.69	1.23	0.86
Adverbs	33.89	38.07	52.18	32.97
Conditional Subordin.	9.00	16.25	7.98	6.88
Verbs	168.75	195.78	166.97	184.35
Summed Ranks	37	**23**	36	44

(-) [Informational]	Rom.	1 Cor.	Phil.	Past.
Nouns	235.83	200.91	224.06	249.14
Noun–Verb Ratio	1.40	1.03	1.34	1.35
Word Length	4.66	4.63	4.74	5.24
Type–Token Ratio	0.28	0.24	0.28	0.34
Attributive Adj.	2.53	4.25	2.46	8.31
Place Adverbs	0.00	0.59	0.61	0.29
Agentless Passives	15.05	17.43	8.59	12.90
Summed Ranks	17	21	20	**12**

2.   I wish to thank my colleague, Matthew Brook O'Donnell, for his work on creating the computer searches that enabled the production of these charts.

Table 2. *Dimension 2: Narrative vs. Non-Narrative Concerns*

(+) [Narrative]	Rom.	1 Cor.	Phil.	Past.
Perfective Aspect	52.59	46.13	42.36	52.47
3rd Singular Verb	53.44	71.46	23.33	44.44
3rd Plural Verb	13.22	14.06	4.30	20.07
Stative Aspect	11.11	14.06	12.28	15.19
Synthetic Negation	0.98	3.66	3.68	4.59
Summed Ranks	14	11	17	**8**

(-) [Non-Narrative]	Rom.	1 Cor.	Phil.	Past.
Imperfective Aspect	88.17	119.78	92.69	106.36
Attributive Adj.	2.53	4.25	2.46	8.31
Word Length	4.66	4.63	4.74	5.24
Summed Ranks	10	7	9	**4**

Table 3. *Dimension 3: Explicit vs. Non-Explicit Reference*

(+) [Explicit]	Rom.	1 Cor.	Phil.	Past.
Relative Pronouns	12.94	9.08	9.21	14.62
Phrasal Coordination	8.86	7.61	22.10	24.37
Nominalizations	1.69	1.17	1.23	2.29
Proper Nouns	30.80	22.70	47.88	38.70
Summed Ranks	10	16	9	**5**

(-) [Non-Explicit]	Rom.	1 Cor.	Phil.	Past.
Time Adverbs	1.41	1.76	3.68	4.30
Place Adverbs	0.00	0.59	0.61	0.29
Adverbs	33.89	38.07	52.18	32.97
Summed Ranks	11	7	**4**	8

Table 4. *Dimension 4: Overt Expression of Persuasion*

(+) [Overt Persuasion]	Rom.	1 Cor.	Phil.	Past.
Infinitives	14.20	14.64	23.94	22.65
Suasive Verbs	17.16	23.87	12.89	16.92
Conditional Subordin.	9.00	16.25	7.98	6.88
2nd Per. Sing. Imperative	2.95	0.73	0.61	21.79
2nd Per. Plur. Imperative	5.20	7.32	14.12	0.00
3rd Per. Sing. Imperative	1.27	6.00	1.23	2.29
3rd Per. Plur. Imperative	0.28	1.03	0.00	2.58
Summed Ranks	19	**13**	21	17

Table 5. *Dimension 5: Abstract vs. Non-Abstract Information*

(+) [Abstract]	*Rom.*	*1 Cor.*	*Phil.*	*Past.*
Discourse Conjuncts	39.23	31.63	23.33	20.36
Agentless Passives	15.05	17.43	8.59	12.90
BY-passives	0.56	1.32	1.23	0.29
Summed Ranks	6	**4**	9	11

(-) [Non-Abstract]	*Rom.*	*1 Cor.*	*Phil.*	*Past.*
Type–Token Ratio	0.28	0.24	0.28	0.34
Rank	2	3	2	**1**

Table 6. *Dimension 6: On-Line Informational Elaboration*

(+) On-Line Elab.	*Rom.*	*1 Cor.*	*Phil.*	*Past.*
Demonst. Pro. & Adj.	7.73	10.54	9.21	11.75
Causative Subordination	7.88	8.79	12.89	5.73
Relative Pronouns	12.94	9.08	9.21	14.62
Summed Ranks	9	8	7	**6**

(-) Not On-Line Elab.	*Rom.*	*1 Cor.*	*Phil.*	*Past.*
Phrasal Coordination	8.86	7.61	22.10	24.37
Rank	3	4	2	**1**

LANGUAGE REPERTOIRE AND DIGLOSSIA IN FIRST-CENTURY PALESTINE: SOME COMMENTS

Christina Bratt Paulston

Palestine, the crossroads of mighty empires in Mesopotamia and Egypt, has long been of interest to scholars in history and religion and, in recent times, namely the last century, to linguists. The traffic of these crossroads, of this multitude of ethnic groups in contact for purposes of administration, trade, conquest, and worship, resulted in a veritable profusion of multilingualism.

Palestine was also the birthplace of two of the world's great religions. Exegesis of the Torah and exegesis of the New Testament have the same purpose in their linguistic analysis—a better understanding of the word of God. But the Old Testament and the New Testament are also studied for their historical significance—they are among our very few literary sources from this time. My own interest lies in accounting for the language shift of the Jewish people from Hebrew to Aramaic, referred to in Porter's chapter. To this date, there is no satisfactory explanation why God's chosen people shifted from their sacred Hebrew to the common lingua franca of the Fertile Crescent for centuries, Aramaic. Whatever our questions, a better understanding of the perplexing situation of the languages in contact and their use in first-century Palestine will clearly give us a better insight into the lives of the people who used those languages, what their values and priorities were, and where their loyalties lay.

Palestine of the first century was a site of many languages but also of various language shifts between the ethnic groups, a condition which enormously confuses the situation. Not that language shift was a new phenomenon in Palestine; the Philistines, who gave their name to Palestine (the land of the Philistines, from Hebrew, via Greek), left no record of their language and shifted—probably—to Canaanite, then to Aramaic and later to Koine Greek. The Jews can be said to have begun their shift to Aramaic with the Babylonian exile in 537 BCE and the Egyptian diaspora.[1] The Idumeans shifted from Arabic to Hebrew/ Aramaic; Herod was by lineage all Arab although raised as a Jew. The final shift of the region came later, with Islam and the shift to Arabic.

The real difficulty in attempting to account for the language repertoire in first-century Palestine lies in the paucity of data. *Working with No Data*[2] necessitates very robust concepts, models, and theories, and, in a sense, that is what these four chapters are all about. One can of course simply work, as does Rendsburg,[3] 'in analogy with other situations', but that is a risky business because without data one cannot tell whether other situations are actually analogous, and Scobie Smith duly and convincingly takes him to task. One can also use the few data there are, preferably from text in the original language, with models which allow for a quantitative approach (maybe with statistical analysis for significance). Quantification is not proof, nor do correlations imply casuality, but they do give us a powerful summary of dispersed and sparse data as even a cursory glance at Porter's charts will make clear. Porter uses Hallidayan register features for his theoretical framework, but his chapter holds as much, if not more, significance as a model for possible alternative analytical procedures as it does in terms of the actual findings of his register analysis.[4]

---

1. There is no agreement in the scholarly literature on when the Jews shifted to Aramaic. The existence of Aramaic as a lingua franca from Egypt to Babylon is generally acknowledged as well as an Aramaic-speaking Jewry; the disagreement rather concerns the duration of Hebrew–Aramaic bilingualism and the demise of Hebrew as a common, spoken language. Porter, in this volume, argues for a shift, complete by the first century; for another view see Bernard Spolsky, 'Diglossia in Hebrew in the Late Second Temple Period', *SWJL* 10.1 (1991), pp. 85-104, esp. p. 215. I expect both are partially right; in all likelihood, different groups of Jews shifted at various rates, depending on region and social class. As long as biblical Hebrew and mishnaic Hebrew were prestige languages, the upper strata were slower to shift than the lower; Judaea slower than Galilee. Once Greek had become the prestige language, the upper classes became bilingual in Greek and Aramaic or shifted completely to Greek at a quicker rate than the lower strata.

2. The title of a Festschrift for Professor Lambdin of Harvard University: David M. Golumb (ed.), *'Working with No Data': Semitic and Egyptian Studies Presented to Thomas O. Lambdin* (Winona Lake, IN: Eisenbrauns, 1987).

3. Gary Rendsburg, *Diglossia in Ancient Hebrew* (New Haven, CT: American Oriental Society, 1990).

4. See also Jonathan M. Watt, *Code-Switching in Luke and Acts* (Berlin: Peter Lang, 1997).

Another promising approach is that of historical sociolinguistics. Bernard Spolsky points out that the Jewish languages provide an excellent field for the study of historical sociolinguistics, which he defines as 'the application of sociolinguistic principles and models to questions of language use at earlier times'.[5] He goes on to demonstrate the contribution of theory to the solution of a problem of historical language use, examining the way the notion of diglossia and Jackendoff's preference linguistics[6] cast 'light on the available contemporary evidence and reveal the pattern of language use among Jews of Palestine in the first century of the Common Era'.[7]

Historical sociolinguistics then becomes a search for the most appropriate models and key concepts to use in the explanation and even basic description of historical situations. With present-day scholarly work in sociolinguistics, we seek to reach an adequate explanation so that we can predict the coming situation. As an example, in 1982 the Swedish National Board of Education asked me to do a review and analysis of Swedish research on bilingual education as the Board was responsible for the language instruction of immigrants: 'Sweden is an immigration country. Within a few decades, Swedish society has been transformed from ethnic homogeneity and virtual monolingualism to heterogeneity and a plurality of languages.'[8] Given certain social factors among which the most important were the immigrants' shift to Swedish (much like the United States a hundred years ago) and the children's desire to assimilate, the prediction that mother-tongue instruction was laudable, but only indispensable for linguistic minority groups with a record of back-migration, was fairly obvious (if controversial). Time has proved that report accurate.

But with historical sociolinguistics, we begin with the consequence or results; we already know what happened, and instead we are looking

5.   Bernard Spolsky, 'Jewish Multilingualism in the First Century: An Essay in Historical Sociolinguistics', in J.A. Fishman (ed.), *Readings in the Sociology of Jewish Languages* (Leiden: E.J. Brill, 1985), pp. 35-50 (35).

6.   Ray Jackendoff, *Semantics in Cognition* (Cambridge, MA: MIT Press, 1983).

7.   Spolsky, 'Jewish Multilingualism', p. 35.

8.   From Inger Marklund, Head of Research Division, National Swedish Board of Education, Introduction to Christina Bratt Paulston, *Swedish Research and Debate about Bilingualism* (Stockholm: National Swedish Board of Education, 1982), p. 3.

for description and explanation. We know that Jesus spoke Aramaic and we know that 500 years earlier the Jews spoke Hebrew, so, says Spolsky, 'we must assume a situation in which the status attached to being a Hebrew speaker was less than that attached to speaking the other language'.[9] One difficulty in selecting assumptions and speculations based on our present-day theories and models is that those theories are almost all based on present-day situations, such as the modern nation-state. (Sociolinguistics itself is less than a half-century old.[10]

The notion of Palestine itself is easily misleading. It was neither a country nor an empire but a geographic area, consisting of petty kingdoms and city-states, variously independent, colonized, or occupied with in-between stages like client-kingdoms; with steadily shifting borders due to conquests and re-conquests, much like eastern Europe. Most of our models for multilingualism refer to ethnic groups within a modern nation-state.[11] We do not really know to what degree such generalizations will hold for an area like Palestine, and we need to specify whether we are talking about multilingualism in Judaea, Galilee, Caesarea, Scythopolis or Elephantine as the situations all differed with regard to languages and language use. Comparing the Palestinian situation to historical empires for which we do have adequate data about language use, such as the Hapsburg, the Romanov or the Ottoman Empires, and against which we can test the strengths of modern-day generalizations, might be a fruitful approach. We know, for instance, that language shifts in multilingual nations take place only if there are opportunities and incentives to learn the national language. Such opportunities of access would include participation in social institutions like universal schooling, exogamy, military service and religious institutions; access to mass media such as television; demographic factors such as urbanization, and so on. The delayed urbanization and industrialization in eastern Europe[12] contributed to ethnic group and language

9. Spolsky, 'Jewish Multilingualism', p. 48.

10. Christina Bratt Paulston and G. Richard Tucker (eds.), *The Early Days of Sociolinguistics: Memories and Reflections* (Dallas: Summer Institute of Linguistics, 1998).

11. See Christina Bratt Paulston, *Linguistic Minorities in Multilingual Settings* (Amsterdam: Benjamins, 1994) and its references.

12. Christina Bratt Paulston, 'Introduction', in *idem* and D. Peckham (eds.), *Linguistic Minorities in Central and Eastern Europe* (Clevedon: Multilingual Matters, 1998).

maintenance there, and the reverse also holds true for the Palestine area: urbanization, as in Caesarea, resulted in the spread of Greek, whether in bilingualism or in shift.

We know that negative sanctions for language use (such as forbidding or urging against the use of a particular language) do not seem to be very effective. Such sanctions did not work in the Hapsburg Empire and they did not work in Judaea where the rabbis' strictures against Greek were not effective. Many modern conditions, like mass media or universal schooling, do not apply to the Judaean situation, but some of the same principles can be extracted, inherent in those situations: Jesus' knowledge of Hebrew is probably tied up with reading (and learning to read) the Torah in the Temple (Lk. 4.16). The Greek city-states may not have had television but they provided public entertainment in Greek and so provided access to willing listeners.

Many of the other social factors were as effective then as they are today. Exogamy was most certainly a major factor in the Jewish shift to Aramaic as were forced population movements (cf. Stalin's deportation of the Tartars). That Hebrew is the national language of modern-day Israel is directly due to its role as a sacred language and its function in religious worship. My point here is that this kind of comparison with similar historical situations for which we do have data will allow us to test the robustness of our theoretical models and so allow us to speculate with more assurance about language situations for which there is a paucity of data.

These then are some background thoughts that bring us to the topic of the language repertoire and diglossia in first-century Palestine. What can we hope to achieve by using the notion of diglossia? Watt, in his very useful overview of relevant studies of diglossia as they relate to our topic, spells out three objectives. First, 'The Palestinian language situation...indeed may offer a suitable vehicle for refinement of this concept' (p. 25 in this volume), in other words, we can use Palestine as a case study to clarify the concept. As I hope the previous pages have made clear, I would object to this aim for partially the same reasons Scobie Smith objects to Rendsburg: we have virtually no data for the unwritten form. Equally, it would lead to circularity of argument to use shaky (non-existent) data to refine the concept of diglossia which we then turn around to employ to clarify our data. Watt goes on to identify another objective in the literature, namely using the concept of diglossia 'for the purpose of describing the first-century Palestinian situation'

(p. 24 in this volume), and continues some pages later with the (rhetorical) question whether some order can be imposed on the 'chaos' of the biblical literature about these language issues. While in principle—as I have discussed above—using the theoretical model of diglossia to describe a historical situation may be well worth the effort, I have my doubts about imposing order on chaos. One of the side effects of working with little or no data is that it becomes very difficult to refute scholars whom one disagrees with: the strength of the argument lies within the argument, not with the facts. The more important then the clarity of the theoretical concepts.

Charles Ferguson himself was very clear about his intentions with his diglossia model (I shall not repeat his definitions here; see the preceding three papers):

> I wanted to characterize a particular kind of language situation, taking a clear case that was relatively easy and uncontroversial to characterize. However, the idea of doing that was to make the clear case just one slot in a taxonomy of some sort... Ultimately the taxonomy would be replaced by some set of principles or frame of reference in terms of which this kind of thinking about language and this kind of research should be done. My goals, in ascending order were: clear case, taxonomy, principle, theory.[13]

Ferguson clearly had theory building in mind, and he was interested in language situations 'which seemed to have implications for the writing of grammars and for theories of language and language change'.[14] Ferguson expressed the hope that other people would write articles about other cases, and so they have. The writing of grammars took another turn with the Chomskyan revolution in linguistics, while historical linguistics have turned to Fergusonian thoughts and sociolinguistics for elucidation in accounting for language change.[15]

---

13. Charles Ferguson, 'Diglossia Revisited', *SWJL* 10.1 (1991), pp. 214-34 (215).

14. Ferguson, 'Diglossia Revisited', pp. 216-17.

15. Unfortunately, this socio-historical linguistics is often misnamed historical sociolinguistics, which it is not, as in, for example, T.W. Machan and Charles T. Scott (eds.), *English in its Social Contexts: Essays in Historical Sociolinguistics* (Oxford: Oxford University Press, 1982) or James Milroy, *Linguistic Variation and Change: On the Historical Sociolinguistics of English* (Oxford: Basil Blackwell, 1992). Suzanne Romaine discusses under the heading of 'Historical Sociolinguistics: Problems and Methodology' (in Ulrich Ammon *et al.* [eds.], *Sociolinguistics: An International Handbook of the Science of Language and Society* [Berlin: Walter

Ferguson continues to discuss Switzerland as an example of 'four different language situations in a nation',[16] and it is perfectly clear that he recognized bi/multilingualism as co-existing with diglossia as well as dialectic diversity at the same time. If we apply this description to the various (semi-)autonomous units in Palestine, it is obvious that Galilee's language situation was not the same as Judaea's, nor like those of Caesarea and the Decapolis, and that Jerusalem (much like Brussels) was an exception to all. There is obviously no need to extend Ferguson's clear case of Arabic diglossia to all these language situations (nor to the Jewish diaspora); the result is conceptual confusion.

Watt comments several times that one cannot 'copyright' a theoretical concept like diglossia (Ferguson himself had after all borrowed the term);[17] one more comment here from Ferguson: 'diglossia when it is used by a French linguist nowadays always implies the oppression of some lower classes by upper classes and I never even thought of that when I was writing about diglossia'.[18] Oppression of an ethnic minority rather than of a social class may be more accurate because most French writers have used Fishman's definition and have applied diglossia to bi/multilingualism.

> One has thus the impression that the success of the concept of diglossia can be explained by the historical moment in which it was introduced. At the time of the African independencies, numerous countries were confronted with a complex linguistic situation: on one hand, multilingualism and on the other, the official predominance of the colonial language. Providing a theoretical framework for this situation, diglossia tended to present this situation as normal, stable and to erase the linguistic conflict

de Gruyter, 1988]) the goals, methods and data of what she quite accurately refers to as socio-historical linguistics, accounting for language change. See her *Socio-Historical Linguistics* (Cambridge: Cambridge University Press, 1992).

16. Ferguson, 'Diglossia Revisited', p. 215.

17. D. Sotiropoulos mentions in 'Diglossia and the National Language Question in Modern Greece', *Linguistics* 19 (1977), pp. 5-31, that the term 'diglossia' was first used by Karl Krumbacher in 1902 in his book *Das Problem der Neugriechischen Schriftsprache* (Munich: Verlag der Akademie, 1902). Other references are to the coinage of the term by the French linguist W. Marcais in 'La diglossie arabe', *L'enseignement public* 97 (1930).

18. Charles Ferguson, 'History of Sociolinguistics', in Paulston and Tucker (eds.), *Early Days of Sociolinguistics*, pp. 77-86 (83).

to which it bore witness, to justify in some way that nothing changed (which was after all the case in most of the decolonized countries)'.[19]

Slight wonder that Ferguson had not thought of this application of diglossia because he was trying to describe the language situation of one ethnic group, be it Arabic, Greek or Swiss German. He certainly did not have in mind the 'tendency to obfuscate the conflicts which characterize situations of diglossia and to represent as normal a situation of domination',[20] as Calvet quite inaccurately put it, but his statement illustrates two important points: (1) extending diglossia to include bilingualism merely contributes to confusion and dilutes the concept, and more importantly (2) different scholars will interpret differently what they see as the most salient feature of diglossia. For the French, it was the conflict inherent in the contact situation between ethnic minorities and the dominant group in ex-colonial settings, and this conflict situation was later extended to any kind of group conflict involving languages.

Joshua Fishman saw functional complementary distribution of the language varieties as the most salient feature of diglossia and extended it to bilingual situations. This is not a new insight in multilingual settings.

Charles V is reputed to have claimed that he spoke German to the horses, Italian with the ladies, French with the men, but Spanish to God; in other words, he chose his language according to the addressee. Maybe more to the point here is the frequently cited saying from the Jerusalem Talmud: 'Rabbi Jonathan of Bet Gubrin said, "Four languages are of value: Greek for song, Latin for war, Aramaic for dirges, and Hebrew for speaking"'.[21] The choice here is according to genre or purpose. Ferguson divided his language varieties according to what he called 'situations'; these are reminiscent of Rabbi Jonathan's genre division, such as sermon in church, speech in parliament, conversation with family, and so on, but he also includes addressee, as in instruction to servants and workmen (who do not know the H form). The major difference between Rabbi Jonathan and Ferguson is that the former writes about different languages echoing ancient Greece's distribution

19. Louis-Jean Calvet, *La sociolinguistique* (Paris: Presses Universitaires de France, 1993), p. 45, my translation.

20. Calvet, *La sociolinguistique*, p. 120.

21. This version of the translation is taken from Bernard Spolsky and Robert L. Cooper, *The Languages of Jerusalem* (Oxford: Clarendon Press, 1991), p. 24.

of dialects such as Ionic for history, Doric for choral and lyric works, and Attic for tragedy,[22] while Ferguson's break with tradition in writings on diglossia lay in that he was attempting a description of the speech community, not linguistic descriptions as had earlier writers.

It is quite clear that the notion of functional complementary distribution can include separate languages (and language families) as well as varieties of the same language. It is also quite clear that not all bi/multilingual situations necessarily involve functional distribution. Where languages are legally protected by territorial linguistic rights, as in Switzerland and Belgium, those languages co-exist with no functional distribution. When languages co-exist within a nation-state without the protection of language rights and without functional distribution in a super–subordinate relationship, the norm is shift to the dominant language, although the rate of that shift may vary, as with Gaelic in Scotland over hundreds of years compared to Swedish in Minnesota over a three-generation shift. But shift is normal, given the absence of internally or externally imposed boundary maintenance.[23] The Jewish dietary and marital regulations with insistence on endogamy reinforced the group's religious boundary maintenance, but for the Jews language did not seem to have been an absolute for group membership; the translation of the Torah into Greek for the Alexandrian Jews is evidence of that.

What we need at this point is a very clear set of guidelines for selecting robust theoretical models and frameworks for use in historical sociolinguistics, and obviously we have not yet arrived at that point. Let me here very briefly outline some thoughts in considering whether diglossia is a useful construct in describing 'the language repertoire in first-century Palestine'. As I hope to have made clear, 'Palestine' is a misleading notion to begin with and should be reconsidered in this context.

We do know that the region we call Palestine was bi/multilingual so we need to consider what sub-concepts are implied or entailed in using a concept like diglossia in contrast to bilingualism.

In diglossia the Low (L) form is not standardized and often not written while in bilingualism the L form (or subordinate language) can be standardized and written just as well as the High (H) form, as, for example, Spanish and English in the US Southwest. In a putative Hebrew–

22. Einar Haugen, 'Dialect, Language, Nation', in J. Pride and J. Holmes (eds.), *Sociolinguistics* (Harmondsworth: Penguin Books, 1972), pp. 97-111.

23. Paulston, *Linguistic Minorities*, pp. 20-21.

Aramaic diglossia, Aramaic had been written for centuries and presumably owed its spread and what prestige it had to its written nature. We do not need diglossia to explain this feature, but it is useful for the shift to Aramaic. Diglossia is characterized by a stable language situation with an increasingly wide split between the written and spoken word, and we find this situation in the biblical Hebrew and Aramaic. When we do get shift in a diglossic situation, the shift is to the L form, here Aramaic, while in bilingualism the shift typically is to the H form, the dominant language (as Spolsky suggests with the Jewish shift to Greek).

In diglossia, there are no native speakers of the H form, but there are in bilingualism. Having no native speakers of the H form entails great pressure on book learning and education, especially in the form of economic resources and leisure time for study, a situation which very much favors the elite classes and ultimately serves to legitimate their status.[24] Jewish rabbinical studies neatly fit this characterization but, interestingly enough, it also extends to the study of Greek within the Jewish community.

Ferguson's notion of diglossia specified dialects of the same language or very closely related varieties,[25] which in turn entailed that both the H and the L form were spoken by members of the same ethnic group, and for present-day conditions with frequent strife and competition between groups along ethnic lines, this is of crucial importance in diglossic versus bilingual situations. But ethnicity as we think of it did not really exist in first-century Judaea and Galilee. Israel was a theocracy as much as an ethnic nation (nationalism in the modern sense did not exist either; political scientists typically date the birth of nationalism to the time of the French Revolution), and there were monolingual Greek-speaking Jews. King Herod, in fact, was ethnically Arab, but this was of no concern because religiously he was Jewish. So this highly salient feature in contrasting diglossia with bilingualism explains very little in our first-century situation. Finally, as implied above, one does not need the concept of diglossia to deal with complementary distribution, which also occurs with bilingualism.

In other words, I find very little explanatory power in the concept of

24. Richard A. Horsley, *Galilee* (Valley Forge, PA: Trinity Press International, 1995).

25. Language and dialect are notoriously difficult to define linguistically; see David Crystal, *The Cambridge Encyclopedia of Language* (Cambridge: Cambridge University Press, 1987).

diglossia when applied to first-century Palestine and considerable—and unnecessary—conceptual confusion, or in Watt's terms the 'chaos', which follows from these implications. On the other hand, I find Watt's suggestion of a diglossic continuum quite intriguing, although at this time I would avoid the term 'diglossic' and simply call it a language continuum, calqued on the notion of a Creole continuum. In a Creole continuum, the opposing poles of the continuum are simply (H) acrolect and (L) basilect and there is no reason I can see why this notion could not be extended to plural acrolects (Greek, Latin, biblical Hebrew) and basilects (Aramaic, Arabic, unwritten languages) with mesolects sketched in (perhaps mishnaic Hebrew, 'educated' Aramaic, etc.). Here the conceptual weight of the continuum is placed on the individual speaker's repertoire, similarly but not identically to a Creole continuum where the proficiency includes a continuum of the same language variety but here would include different language varieties. The locus, however, remains the individual speaker's proficiency.

I am here obviously only playing with ideas of how best to characterize and explain the various language situations in first-century Palestine, but I do think that this is the direction that Watt and fellow biblical scholars should take in future studies: the development of solid theoretical models and concepts for use in a historical sociolinguistics which will allow us to speculate with more accuracy and in so doing perhaps discover data we had not thought of as significant before. Porter's sugggestive use of quantificational analysis of text within a theoretical framework shows us the way to test such new speculations and generalizations, always heeding Scobie Smith's admonition not to ignore the context of those generalizations, be they linguistic or social. I would only add the hope that such a direction of biblical studies would give impetus to a more general development of historical sociolinguistics as a recognized field of study with its own methodology.

Part II

OTHER TOPICS IN NEW TESTAMENT LINGUISTICS

TRANSLATION TECHNIQUE IN THE SEPTUAGINT LEVITICUS

Dirk Büchner

This paper is an illustration of some translational and linguistic matters that have arisen in the course of my translation of the Septuagint Leviticus for the New English Translation of the Septuagint (hereafter NETS). Some aspects of Septuagintal semantics will be raised and then several things will be said about the particular methodology that this series is following. This methodology will then be illustrated by a number of examples from Leviticus. Lastly, I shall point out the usefulness of comparing the Septuagint with the Midrash *Sifra* to Leviticus.

1. *Methodological Aspects*

a. *Septuagintal Semantics: General Remarks*

Essential to any enterprise of rendering into English a work of translation such as LXX Leviticus is a correct view of the semantics of Septuagintal Greek or what has been described as the extremely difficult business of deciding the meaning of a word in the LXX.[1] Those who entered Septuagintal studies via Semitic studies, as I did, know that the Septuagint is replete with Jewish rather than Hellenistic ideas,[2] and that the translators were in the first place Jews, who sought to convey the intention of the original into Greek. This knowledge makes it all the more inviting to assume that the Greek terms the translators used bear the semantic content of the Hebrew words they translate.[3] Whether or

---

1. S.P. Brock and J.A.L. Lee, 'Memorandum on the Proposed LXX Lexicon Project', in R.A. Kraft (ed.), *Septuagintal Lexicography* (SBLSCS, 1; Missoula, MT: Scholars Press, 1975), pp. 20-24, esp. p. 20.

2. Literature on this topic is extensive. See my 'Jewish Commentaries and the Septuagint', *JJS* 48 (1997), pp. 250-61, esp. p. 250 nn. 3 and 4; and J. Cook, *The Septuagint of Proverbs—Jewish and/or Hellenistic Proverbs? Concerning the Hellenistic Colouring of Proverbs* (Leiden: E.J. Brill, 1998).

3. An assumption underlying most of the entries labelled 'LXX' in LSJ.

not words in the Septuagint are to be given Hebrew meanings is what this paper is all about. Moisés Silva's chapter on 'Semantic Change and the Role of the Septuagint'[4] contains an excellent review of the history of this debate. In it, he evaluates the contributions of, among others, Hatch,[5] Deissmann,[6] Ottley[7] and Hill,[8] and sums up by cautioning that the Hebrew may be an important guide to the meaning of the Greek. Nevertheless, it may not be assumed that, if the meaning of the Hebrew word corresponding to the Greek has been identified, the meaning of the Greek is automatically established. Addressing the same point, Chamberlain stresses that LXX words should be taken to mean exactly what they mean in Classical Greek, unless this is impossible, or until 'the Greek context forces an expansion of their semantic range'.[9] Brock and Lee indicated at the inception of the LXX lexicon project that it is incorrect lexical procedure to equate the meaning of a Greek word with that of the Hebrew word it represents, thereby giving too much weight to the Semitic original. Also, they underlined the importance of investigating non-biblical Greek.[10] Finally, Tov suggests that the only way to determine the real meaning of words in the LXX is to grasp the intention of the translators by way of analysing their translation techniques.[11]

b. *The NETS Approach to Semantics*
The NETS approach to the Septuagint is based largely on the above principles. This approach is outlined in the *General Introduction to*

4. M. Silva, *Biblical Words and their Meaning: An Introduction to Lexical Semantics* (Grand Rapids, MI: Zondervan, 2nd edn, 1994), p. 72.
5. E. Hatch (*Essays in Biblical Greek* [Oxford: Clarendon Press, 1889], p. 20) wrote: 'A word which is used uniformly...as the translation of the same Hebrew word, must be held to have in Biblical Greek the same meaning as that Hebrew word'.
6. A. Deissmann, *The Philology of the Greek Bible: Its Present and Future* (London: Hodder & Stoughton, 1908).
7. R.R. Ottley, *A Handbook to the Septuagint* (London: Methuen, 1920).
8. D. Hill, *Greek Words and Hebrew Meanings: Studies in the Semantics of Soteriological Terms* (SNTSMS, 5; Cambridge: Cambridge University Press, 1967).
9. G.A. Chamberlain, 'Method in Septuagint Lexicography', in L.M. Hopfe (ed.), *Uncovering Ancient Stones: Essays in Memory of H. Neil Richardson* (Winona Lake, IN: Eisenbrauns, 1994), pp. 177-92, esp. p. 191.
10. Brock and Lee, 'Memorandum', p. 20.
11. E. Tov, 'Three Dimensions of LXX Words', *RB* 83 (1976), pp. 529-44, esp. p. 532.

NETS.[12] One unique aspect of the NETS translation method is the principle that the *translationese* dimension of the Septuagint's Greek be allowed to shine through in the English rendition. In the words of Al Pietersma, in correspondence via e-mail with a member of the translation team,

> In NETS terms there is a fundamental difference in translating an original and translating a translation. When one translates an original, one makes two basic assumptions: (a) that the original text was written in idiomatic language and (b) whatever conundra are in the text are the products of transmission history. In the light of (a) one has full justification for translating idiomatic language with idiomatic language. In the light of (b) one has justification for correcting mistakes. On the other hand, when one translates Septuagintal translationese, (a) one does not have idiomatic Greek (a fact one admittedly first has to establish) and (b) many conundra are original to the translation. Hence in the light of (a) one lacks justification for translating into fully idiomatic English. In the light of (b) one lacks justification for correcting original mistakes. Thus the warts are passed on in NETS.

Take for example again this comment made by Pietersma in correspondence with me over the meaning of ἁμαρτία, one of whose meanings is given by Muraoka in his lexicon as 'slaughtered animal to atone sins':[13]

> Muraoka unfortunately does lexicography of the LXX by standard lexicographical rules. That is to say, a word means whatever the context makes it mean. That procedure is strongly circumscribed when it comes to translationese, where the primary consideration is to represent the parent text at a word-for-word level, and contextual meaning plays second fiddle at best. In other words, the integrity of translationese, (or for that matter any Greek text) demands that one reads Greek as Greek until proven otherwise. And such proof can only come from non-translational use.[14]

c. *Difficulties in LXX Leviticus*

Having determined that the LXX translationese should at the outset be read as standard Hellenistic Greek, one begins to pick one's way

12. A. Pietersma and B. Wright, 'To the Reader of NETS', currently found on the NETS home page http://ccat.sas.upenn.edu/nets.

13. T. Muraoka, *A Greek–English Lexicon of the Septuagint: Twelve Prophets* (Leuven: Peeters, 1993), p. 11.

14. Cf. Brock and Lee, 'Memorandum', p. 22 and Tov, 'Three Dimensions', p. 536.

through the Greek Leviticus, and soon finds that this cannot uniformly be maintained. That is, it seems as if the translator viewed certain Greek words, as Tov puts it, merely as symbols for the Hebrew.[15] And so it becomes a question whether some of the terminology would have made sense to Greek readers were the semantic content of the Hebrew words not assumed.[16] That this was indeed the case is not easy to prove, since it is very difficult to find attestations of all the Levitical cultic terms in non-biblical literature, and particularly in non-translational Hellenistic Greek. Some, as we shall see, do appear in 2 Maccabees and Josephus. This difficulty is partly due to the incompleteness of the lexica and partly because translators simply do not have the time to allot the same energy to each problem word in a biblical book that a lexicographer would have in scanning the meaning of, let us say, only the words for cultic action in all the available literature.[17] This brings us to the next step which is to determine when one has no alternative but to let the meaning of the Hebrew serve as an indicator of the Greek meaning.[18]

d. *Determining the Semantic Range of Septuagintal Greek*
In the translation manual,[19] Al Pietersma constructs the following diagram:

Contextual------------------Stereotypes | Calques------------------Isolates
     (Greek meanings)   (Hebrew meanings)

He continues: 'Lexemes ranging from contextual to stereotypes[20] are dealt with in accord with normal Greek meanings; those ranging from

---

15. 'Three Dimensions', p. 536.

16. This does not imply that a supposed Jewish-Greek dialect was spoken by Alexandrian Jews, nor that they already knew Hebrew. See Chamberlain, 'Method', p. 182.

17. See for example the guidelines given to prospective lexicographers in Brock and Lee, 'Memorandum', p. 23.

18. One such case, mentioned by Tov, is when Greek words are polysemous ('Three Dimensions', p. 531).

19. A. Pietersma, *Translation Manual for 'A New English Translation of the Septuagint' (NETS)* (Michigan: Uncial Books, 1996), p. 13.

20. Tov ('Three Dimensions', p. 533) introduces the term *stereotyped or automatic representation of Hebrew words* in discussing lexical Hebraisms. To the best of his knowledge, he says, the terminology derives from M. Flashar, 'Exegetische Studien zum Septuagintpsalter', *ZAW* 32 (1912), pp. 81-116, esp. p. 105.

calques[21] to isolates[22] are effectively assigned the meaning of their Hebrew counterparts (= so-called Hebraisms)'.[23] Practically, this means that translators need to determine where Greek words fit on the continuum in order to render the Greek accurately. Lexical items on the isolate end of the continuum are likely to cause the English translator most grief. This is partly true for Leviticus, which, though a fairly literal translation, is nevertheless full of unusual terminology, most of which is Hebrew cultic language, strange to Greek ears. From some of the e-mail traffic between members of the translation team regarding this semantic scale, I have filtered out the following comments particularly about stereotypes and calques:

1. *Stereotypes*

- A stereotype carries the meaning of the target language, but the needs of the target language have not always been taken into account.
- The choice of the Greek lexeme is based on perceived Hebrew–Greek verbal equivalency.
- For many translators, the word in the target language becomes merely a symbol representing the word in the source language. Thus that meaning cannot be included as such in the lexica.[24]
- If a stereotype becomes fully contextualized through continued use within the Greek-reading/-speaking community, it turns into a calque, that is, a Greek word with a Hebrew meaning.

21. Defined by Silva (*Biblical Words*, p. 218) as 'a French word meaning "imitation" and used by linguists to describe various forms of borrowing'. See further, below.

22. A good example of an isolate is the Greek ἱκανός found in Ruth and *kaige*-Theodotion, 'he who is sufficient' for the Hebrew שׁדי, where the translator read די + שׁ. Hence the meaning for ἱκανός in Ruth must be given as what the translator thought the Hebrew to mean, rather than what the Hebrew actually means (Tov, 'Three Dimensions', p. 540).

23. Pietersma, *Manual*, p. 14. Tov ('Three Dimensions', p. 533) defines a Hebraism as follows: 'a Greek word, phrase or syntagma which transfers certain characteristic Hebrew elements into Greek in an un-Greek fashion'.

24. Tov cites the example of how εἰρήνη as stereotypical rendering for שׁלום had led several LXX translators to use εἰρήνη contrary to ordinary Greek usage. Moreover, LSJ incorrectly created an entry ἐρωτῆσαί τινα εἰς εἰρήνη 'to greet a person, inquire after their health' on the basis of the LXX alone ('Three Dimensions', p. 536).

Thus, if ἐρωτῆσαί τινα εἰς εἰρήνην, mentioned in the previous note, were to be found outside the LXX, then it would be fine to let it assume the same meaning as לשאול אתו לשלום.

2. *Calques*[25]

- A calque is a Greek word with a Hebrew meaning. It has become normal Greek and part of the living language.
- Only the main sense is taken from the source language.
- The meanings of calques are attested in non-translational Greek, for example, in books like Maccabees and Wisdom of Solomon. A good example of a calque is διαθήκη for the Hebrew ברית.[26]
- The translator decides that his default rendering does not fit at all and so he either generates a calque or uses an already generated calque.
- One can attribute Hebrew meaning to a Greek lexeme when the lexeme is seen to convey that Hebrew meaning in a productive sense, that is, in the generation of novel utterances,[27]

---

25. I am indebted to Moisés Silva for directing me to the relevant literature. For further references, see his *Biblical Words*, pp. 88-90. T.E. Hope, *Lexical Borrowing in the Romance Languages* (Oxford: Basil Blackwell, 1971), pp. 637ff. treats calque under the rubric of Semantic Loans, and mentions that the subject of semantic borrowing, where a word acquires new meanings under the influence of related words in a foreign language, is a controversial one. He defines what he calls *semantic calque* as a case where 'translation of form occurs between source and borrowing languages during transfer of meaning', such as the German *Ente* meaning 'lying newspaper report' under the influence of French *canard* (p. 639). On p. 643 he stresses the need to distinguish between semantic calque (where translation of the formal element rather than unaltered adoption or simple adaptation has taken place) and ordinary, straightforward semantic loans so that the formal shift peculiar to calque would be taken into account. If no such distinction were made, some of the semantic loans would have to be classed as loan-homonyms which implies lack of semantic affinity.

26. Tov also gives the example of ἐξομολογέομαι which is used in an un-Greek way in the LXX as 'to thank' as equivalent for הודה. But when that special meaning was quoted from the LXX and used outside the framework of that translation in a Greek source, it became part and parcel of the Greek language ('Three Dimensions', p. 543).

27. In this regard Hope comments that 'semantic calque presupposes a high degree of intention, an effect of deliberate adaptation and therefore a strongly

or, in other words, in non-translationese. Calques are not peculiar to translationese.

- If an item is not a default rendering and if the Hebrew meaning is clear from the context, it is likely to be a calque.

2. *Some Litmus Tests in Semantics*

The following examples represent attempts at solving typical semantic
problems encountered in Leviticus. I have chosen some stereotypical
renderings and approached them first of all as standard Greek. It soon
became apparent that here and there a case could be made for letting the
semantic range of the Hebrew determine that of the Greek by bringing
into play the above rules for calques and stereotypes.

Example 1: ἁμαρτία as Equivalent to the Hebrew חטאת[28]
Leviticus 4 is the first occurrence in the Bible of this word-pairing and
is a good source for the diverse range of meaning accorded to it. In the
entire chapter ἁμαρτία is the equivalent of the Hebrew חטאת. Other
examples are found in chs. 9 and 10, again as equivalents of the same
Hebrew word ('equals to' here means 'is the equivalent of the Hebrew').

1. τῆς ἁμαρτίας = חטאת as *sin offering*. Occurring in the genitive
with the article, τῆς ἁμαρτίας here refers to 'sin offering', as in the typical expression (e.g. 4.20, 29) τὸν μόσχον τὸν τῆς ἁμαρτίας, 'the sin
offering calf'. More often the genitive τῆς ἁμαρτίας occurs alone, for
example, ἀπὸ τοῦ αἵματος τοῦ τῆς ἁμαρτίας 'of the blood of the sin
offering'. In v. 29 another word, ἁμάρτημα, is the functional equivalent
of τῆς ἁμαρτίας as used in v. 33. In each case, the suppliant is to lay his
hand on its head.

2. ἁμαρτία = חטאת as *sin*. In 4.20b and elsewhere, ἁμαρτία refers to
sin itself. Unlike the following example, this particular case of ἁμαρτία
following περί, for example, in v. 28b, is not a fixed expression and
means 'for sin'.

3. περὶ τῆς ἁμαρτίας = חטאת as *sin offering*. περὶ τῆς ἁμαρτίας is

developed feeling for the language on the borrower's part' (*Lexical Borrowing*,
p. 643).
28. S. Daniel, *Recherches sur le vocabulaire du culte dans la Septante* (Paris:
Klincksieck, 1966), pp. 301-305, discusses in detail the Greek translator's mode of
employing this Greek word for the Hebrew. See also J.W. Wevers, *The Text History
of the Greek Leviticus* (Göttingen: Vandenhoeck & Ruprecht, 1986), p. 117.

used as a substantive in itself, referring to 'sin offering' (in 10.19 περὶ τῆς ἁμαρτίας is something you can eat). In 9.7 τὸ περὶ τῆς ἁμαρτίας is the sin offering to be performed and in 9.8 the phrase is used in apposition to τὸ μοσχαρίον.

4. ἁμαρτία = חטאת as *sin offering*. In 4.32 εἰς ἁμαρτίαν need not necessarily, but should be rendered by 'for a sin offering' instead of 'for sin'. Also, in 4.21b and 4.24b ἁμαρτία clearly means a sin offering. Wevers observes that the Greek translator normally uses τῆς ἁμαρτίας to help the reader distinguish between 'sin' and 'sin offering', something the Hebrew cannot do, and prefers the reading ἁμαρτίας in 4.21b and 4.24b, which would have the semantic range of 1, above.[29]

Harlé and Pralon[30] mention that in 78 cases, when the translator saw חטאת he used ἁμαρτία in Greek. One's first reaction is that, statistically, this is a stereotype, but when one looks at the definition of stereotype, one fails to see from the above examples that in the mind of the translator the word has a normal Greek meaning,[31] except for example 2. In the others, it is obvious that the opposite is happening, that is, that the Hebrew meanings of חטאת dictated the Greek meanings. The only way one is justified in concluding this is when one is sure that one has found a calque. According to the rules for calques, which are Greek words with Hebrew meanings, one needs to show that this usage has become standard fare in non-translation literature of the same tradition. This is indeed true for ἁμαρτία as 'sin offering'. The translator has created a stereotype, but through continued use in the Greek-reading/-speaking community, it has turned into a calque.[32] In 2 Maccabees, the sin offering is referred to in the following way: διὰ τὸ μὴ βεβρῶσθαι τὸ περὶ τῆς ἁμαρτίας ἀνηλώθη (2.11) 'because the sin offering was not eaten, it was burnt up'. Perhaps slightly less convincing, because of the presence of θυσίαν, is 2 Macc. 12.43 ἀπέστειλεν εἰς ιεροσολυμα προσαγαγεῖν περὶ ἁμαρτίας θυσίαν 'he sent…to Jerusalem to bring a sin-offering'. As a matter of interest, in Bar. 1.10 we also find it as follows: καὶ ἀγοράσατε τοῦ ἀργυρίου ὁλοκαυτώματα καὶ περὶ ἁμαρτίας 'so buy with the money burnt offerings and sin offerings'.

---

29. J.W. Wevers, *Notes on the Greek Text of Leviticus* (Atlanta: Scholars Press, 1997), p. 38.

30. P. Harlé and D. Pralon, *Le levitique* (La Bible d'Alexandrie, 3; Paris: Cerf, 1996), p. 35.

31. Pietersma, *Manual*, p. 39.

32. Pietersma, *Manual*, p. 39.

A similar phenomenon is περὶ τῆς πλημμελείας for הֹאשם which means 'guilt offering' in the Hebrew. This word is not attested in the LXX before Lev. 5.18, and also occurs in the same way in Num. 6.12, 18.9 and Sir. 7.31. It has not been possible to find this Greek word in non-translation Greek, so, strictly speaking, LSJ's entry 'sin offering' with reference to LXX Leviticus[33] is unjustifiable. Nevertheless, I wish to argue that it be accorded calque status by analogy to ἁμαρτία and be translated by 'guilt offering', otherwise it would have to be rendered 'for a mistake' every time it occurs, which would be unfair to the translator and simply incorrect.

Example 2: λαμβανεῖν ἁμαρτίαν as Equivalent to the Hebrew נשא עון *'to Incur Guilt'*
With few exceptions, the Greek translator of Leviticus renders עון with ἁμαρτία, and usually with some form of λαμβάνω, for example, in 5.1. This is not a calque, since 'guilt' is part of the regular semantic range of ἁμαρτία. To my mind, this is a stereotype, since it is a good illustration of the fact that the Greek translator is more interested in the formal detail of the Hebrew 'at the expense of communicating its meaning'.[34] Furthermore, stereotypes have to stand in tension with their context. To my mind, this expression is in tension with its context and should be translated as 'to accept the guilt' rather than 'to incur guilt', which is what the Hebrew means. This is identical to Silva's example λαμβάνειν πρόσωπον for נשא פנים, which is also in tension with its context. It may not be translated as 'show favouritism' (which is what the Hebrew means), but rather as 'lift up the face'. This Silva calls a 'loan translation', in the same way that the Spanish *rascacielo* for *skyscraper* is importing not a foreign word, but a particular word-combination.[35]

Example 3: ἀφαίρεμα 'Something Removed' as Equivalent to תרומה *'Contribution'*
Again, this is the default Greek rendering for the Hebrew expression. However, there is some difference in meaning between ἀφαίρεμα in Greek and the Hebrew תרומה. The entry in LSJ for ἀφαίρεμα, 'that which is taken away as the choice part', is close to the truth, but not quite, because it assumes that the standard meaning of the Greek ought

33. LSJ, p. 1418b.
34. Pietersma, *Manual*, p. 35.
35. Silva, *Biblical Words*, p. 87.

to be maintained. I shall argue that this is a calque and should be rendered by 'contribution'. My reasoning is that since ἀφαίρεμα occurs in the following way as 'contribution' in Josephus, *Ant*. 14.10.12: καὶ τῶν πρὸς τὰς θυσίας ἀφαιρεμάτων 'and for contributions toward their sacrifices', one is justified in assuming that this is a word whose Hebrew meaning has become, in Pietersma's parlance, 'a naturalised Greek citizen'.

Example 4: ἀφαίρεμα as Equivalent to תנופה *(Lev. 8.27) 'Swinging, Waving, Wave Offering'*
The Greek word ἀφαίρεμα has no connotation of swinging or waving, and yet it is used three times as equivalent for this Hebrew word. It is very difficult to prove that this is a calque, since it is not attested in non-translation literature. Hence it would simply have to be translated as 'a taking away'. I agree with Wevers that (unlike the case of πλημμέλεια) the translator of Leviticus was unsure of what תנופה meant, and hence renders it by a number of Greek words.[36] The translator of NETS would have to signal in each of these cases the exact dilemma of the Greek translator.

Example 5: ψυχή as Equivalent to נפש
Wevers has argued that ψυχή is a calque, giving statistical reasons—'of the 735 cases where נפש is translated into Greek, 695 are rendered by ψυχή'.[37] Tov lists it as one of many stereotypical renderings, about which he feels that 'if a certain Greek word represents a given Hebrew word in most of its occurrences, almost by implication it has become a mere symbol for that Hebrew word in translation'.[38] However, Pietersma's dictum,[39] that one should work semantically rather than statistically to determine stereotypes, takes precedence here. Thus, I cannot agree with Wevers or Tov, since ψυχή does not seem to me to be a Greek word with a Hebrew meaning. In fact, most of the Hebrew word's wide semantic range overlaps with that of the Greek word's equally wide semantic range. Therefore, this equivalent ψυχή is in my opinion a contextual rendering for נפש, and in Leviticus it occurs mostly with the meanings 'person' or 'creature'.

---

36. Wevers, *Notes*, p. 96.
37. Wevers, *Notes*, p. 34.
38. 'Three Dimensions', p. 538.
39. Communicated to me via e-mail.

I have tried to show by these five cases how carefully one has to investigate the semantic possibilities of Greek words in translationese before one can use the meanings assigned to them by the lexica. The conclusion that some of the terms may be calques is an applecart that comes precariously close to being overturned by the fact that the terms may have been coined by the translator of Leviticus. A calque is, after all, 'an item moulded by prior linguistic usage rather than one shaped on an *ad hoc* basis by the individual translator'.[40] The chance may just exist though that, as Pietersma himself concedes, the early stage of development from stereotype to calque may predate our corpus of literature.[41]

3. *Sifra and Septuagint Leviticus*

The following examples give some indication of the usefulness of reading the Midrash *Sifra*[42] to Leviticus as a companion to the Greek text. This comparison has a two-way benefit. First, when one reads *Sifra*, having studied the Septuagint and the similarities found between its readings and the other Versions and Qumran, one can only conclude that the Rabbis take up issues that other Jewish communities have already grappled with. To my mind, this is a *sine qua non* for midrashic studies. Secondly, when one reads the Septuagint, while taking note of *Sifra*'s discussions, it is not difficult to understand why certain harmonizations, easy escape routes from difficulties and interpretations, are found in the Septuagint—it has a Jewish legal bent.[43] It may even happen that Greek renderings of biblical Hebrew words shed light on unknown semantic possibilities of those Hebrew words which are then

---

40. Pietersma, *Manual*, p. 40.

41. Pietersma, *Manual*, p. 40.

42. L. Finkelstein, *Sifra on Leviticus* (New York: The Jewish Theological Seminary of America, 1983). The text itself is found in Vol. IIff. The English translation I have used, though it is full of errors, is J. Neusner, *Sifra: An Analytical Translation* (Atlanta: Scholars Press, 1988).

43. Z. Frankel (*Über den Einfluss der palästinischen Exegese auf die alexandrinische Hermeneutik* [Leipzig: J.A. Barth, 1851], p. 133) wrote: 'Dass manche dieser alten Halachas auch dem Vertenten des Levit. bekannt gewesen und er auf sie hindeutet, zeigt manche Stelle deutlich und es tritt hier wesentlich der gedachte Einfluss Palästinas auf Alexandrien hervor'. He hastens to add that there is also Alexandrian halakah to be found in LXX Leviticus.

reflected later in rabbinic writings.[44] Of course, one cannot expect *Sifra* consistently to provide parallels where one might wish it to—it is silent, for example, where the LXX sidesteps the academic debate about Molech, and turns מלד into ἄρχων (Lev. 18.21). Also the interpretation of 19.26, where the prohibition of eating blood על הדם is changed by the Greek to eating ἐπὶ τῶν ὀρέων, a harmonization from Ezekiel,[45] finds no counterpart in *Sifra*.

a. *The Liability of the High Priest: 4.5*

Here one finds an addition in the Septuagint about the credentials of the anointed priest: he has been ordained: ὁ τετελειωμένος τὰς χεῖρας (a Hebrew expression מלא ידים borrowed from 16.32—'he who has had his hands filled'). In *Sifra*'s discussion,[46] it is debated whether the sin he has committed occurs after he was anointed, or while he was still a commoner הדיוט (derived from ἰδιώτης). A Mishnah is then quoted which deals with the liability of the priest. A high priest has to be ordained (התמנה). Now if the sin becomes known to him before he was ordained, and after that he is ordained, he is liable. But if the sin was made known to him after he was ordained, he is exempt. The Septuagint for some reason finds it necessary to stress that the man was ordained.

b. *Strange Fire—The Sin of Nadav and Avihu: 16.1*

MT: בקרבתם לפני ה 'when they came near before the Lord'

LXX: ἐν τῷ προσάγειν αὐτοὺς πῦρ ἀλλότριον ἔναντι κυρίου 'when they brought near strange fire before the Lord'

The Greek is harmonized to the Hebrew of Num. 3.4 and Lev. 10.1, where the Hebrew verb is causative/transitive and the direct object is 'strange fire' (בהקרבם אש זרה). One ought either to suppose the existence of a harmonized *Vorlage*, or reason that the translator must have had strong support for changing an intransitive verb into a transitive one to make a point. The translator probably reasoned that since it was usual for the Aaronids to come near to the altar anyway, the real cause of death had to be included, and therefore the transitive verb had to be

---

44. See for example my 'חסם: Pass Over or Protect?', *BN* 86 (1997), pp. 14-17.
45. See the critical note in *BHS*.
46. *Diburah Dehobah, Parashah* 2 par 36ff. Cf. Finkelstein, *Sifra*, p. 129.

read. In *Sifra*,[47] Akiba weighs up the possibilities: either they died merely by reason of the drawing near, as it says in Leviticus, or by reason of the type of sacrifice mentioned in the alternative passages. He concludes that it was not the drawing near that caused their death, but the אֵשׁ זרה. This is against the view of R. Yose, and Eleazar b. Azariah reckons that it could be either action that was sufficient to cause death. Neusner misreads Akiba here.[48] *Targum Onqelos* and the LXX opt for the type of sacrifice. *Neofiti* makes its own suggestion—the problem was that they brought their sacrifice at an inappropriate time. One may safely say that it was important to the Greek translator to include the harmonized reading because it had halakic implications.

c. *Washing by Immersion: 16.4*

MT: ורחע במים את־בשׂרו 'he shall bathe his body in water'
LXX: καὶ λούσεται ὕδατι πᾶν τὸ σῶμα αὐτοῦ 'he shall bathe his whole body in water'

This is supported by the Samaritan Pentateuch את־כל־בשׂרו. *Sifra* asks[49] why the halakah states that immersion is obligatory (טעון טבילה). The connection between 'the whole body' and 'immersion' is perhaps tenuous, but it may be fair to say that the halakah illuminates the reading of LXX and the Samaritan Pentateuch: he must wash himself from top to bottom.

d. *Azazel: 16.8*

In the Septuagint the לעזאזל is rendered by τῷ ἀποπομπαίῳ 'to the one to be cast off'.

In Mishnah and in Sifra[50] the שׂעיר לעזאזל is known as השׂעיר המשׁתלח 'the goat to be sent away'.[51] Both traditions find a way out of

---

47. *Ahare Mot, Parashah* 1.

48. Neusner, *Sifra*, III, p. 3, says: 'The main point of both Yose and Aqiba is that the two sons died simply because they came in when not wanted, and that of course draws to the surface the implicit sense of Lev. 16.1: not to come at all times, but only at the right time'. However, Aqiba actually goes to great length to refer to the strange fire. Cf. I. Drazin, *Targum Onkelos to Leviticus: An English Translation of the Text with Analysis and Commentary* (New York: Ktav, 1994), p. 145.

49. *Ahare Mot, Pereq* 1.

50. *Ahare Mot, Pereq* 2.

51. Frankel, *Einfluss*, p. 133.

the difficulty by making an association with the Aramaic verb אזל 'leave' or 'depart'.

e. *Community Funds: 16.11*

MT: והקריב אהרן את־פר החטאת אשר לו

LXX: καὶ προσάξει Ααρων τὸν μόσχον τὸν περὶ τῆς ἁμαρτίας τὸν αὐτοῦ καὶ τοῦ οἴκου αὐτοῦ (μόνον)

Wevers comments that Aaron is directed to slaughter the 'bullock intended for the sin offering, which was his own', thereby reading τὸν ἑαυτοῦ.[52] The halakah says that his offering should not be paid for out of communal funds,[53] that is, שלא יביא משל צבור '...that he should not present it from that which belongs to the community', since he has already taken a ram and the two goats from the congregation. Thus, the Septuagint's addition may be understood as emphasizing Aaron's own contribution.

f. *The Rest of the Priests: 16.20*

After Aaron is to make atonement for the tent and the altar, LXX adds that this is to be done for the priests also: καὶ περὶ τῶν ἱερέων καθαριεῖ. Furthermore, in v. 24 after בעדו 'on his behalf', LXX adds καὶ περὶ τοῦ οἴκου αὐτοῦ and after ובעד העם 'on behalf of the people', LXX adds ὡς περὶ τῶν ἱερέων. This is important because in *Sifra* the question is asked,[54] just as the in LXX, what about the other priests? In v. 17, we have the summary of the preliminary atonement: it is done for the two categories (1) Aaron and his family and (2) the people. Only at the end of the chapter (v. 33) do we find reference to the third category, that is, Aaron's fellow priests, but it does not state at which stage atonement is made specifically for them. They are not included in the main body of the legislation in MT. The addition of G, like the halakic discussion, clarifies what MT neglects to mention. It is by the blood of their brother's bull (which does not come from community funds) that they are atoned for, and not by the two goats אשר לעם and the goat for the burnt offering which atone for the community, as it says in *Sifra*:

---

52. Wevers, *Notes*, p. 288.
53. *Ahare Mot, Pereq* 3.
54. *Ahare Mot, Parashah* 4.

שלא יהיו אחיו הכהנים מתכפרים בו ובמה הם מתכפרים בפרו של אחיהם

'...by which his brothers the priest are not atoned for. And by what are they atoned for? By the bull of their brother.'

g. *The Long Addition in the Greek of 17.3-4*

I have treated the important case of 17.4 in detail in another article.[55] In it I have argued that while it may, at face value, be concluded that the repetition of the Septuagint is due simply to haplography,[56] the total text-critical evidence suggests that the shorter reading is original because of the many witnesses that attest to that reading (M T, 11QpaleoLev, Syr, N, O and J), while the longer reading is a more embellished version attested by LXX, Samaritan Pentateuch and 4QLev[d] (and attested by *Sifra*'s discussion). The Greek may have opted for the longer text because it made good halakic sense.

4. *Conclusion*

I have given in this paper some examples in support of the NETS principle that entries where Hebrew meanings are given in the standard lexica need to be treated with caution until the Greek words or expressions can be shown to be calques. Secondly, I have tried to show that there is an intertextual dimension in the translation technique of the translator of Leviticus, which becomes noticeable when one reads the rabbinic midrash *Sifra* to Leviticus. Dependence of one tradition upon another is hard or impossible to prove, but the relationship undoubtedly exists.

---

55. D.L. Büchner, 'Inside and Outside the Camp: The Halakhic Background to Changes in the Septuagint Leviticus, with Reference to Two Qumran Manuscripts', *JNSL* 23.2 (1997), pp. 151-62. Cf. also E. Eshel, '4QLev[d]: A Possible Source for the Temple Scroll and Miqsat Ma'ase HaTorah', *Dead Sea Discoveries* 2 (1995), pp. 1-13.

56. D.N. Freedman, 'Variant Readings in the Leviticus Scroll from Qumran Cave 11', *CBQ* 36 (1974), pp. 525-34, esp. p. 529.

OF GUTTURALS AND GALILEANS:
THE TWO SLURS OF MATTHEW 26.73

Jonathan M. Watt

Introduction

Dialect is nothing less than a linguistic fingerprint. Objectively considered, it may convey such identifying features of its speaker as ethnicity, provenance and socio-economic status. But when subjectively received, dialect is notorious for instigating value judgments about the speaker. For whereas received pronunciations and status codes are considered 'normal' by their speakers and 'desirable' to eager acquirers, regional variants and non-standards are often regarded as malformed or even ignorant. This paper will show that these well-documented dynamics of modern speech communities are portrayed in some biblical narratives as well. In particular, I shall focus on a situation portrayed in the New Testament that hinges on brief comments made during the arrest narratives of Jesus which appear, in various forms, in each of the Synoptic Gospels:

> And a little later the bystanders came up and said to Peter, 'Surely you too are one of them; for the way you talk gives you away'. (Mt. 26.73)

> And after a little while the bystanders were again saying to Peter, 'Surely you are one of them, for you are a Galilean too'. (Mk 14.70)

> And after about an hour had passed, another man began to insist, saying, 'Certainly this man also was with Him, for he is a Galilean too'. (Lk. 22.59)

The Fourth Gospel (18.25-26) likewise indicates that Peter was repeatedly associated with Jesus, but does so only vaguely and relates the observations to sight, not sound. Each of the Synoptics, on the other hand, reports that Peter was being associated with Jesus because he was a Galilean, and at least implicitly that he was identified as a Galilean on the basis of his speech.

The argument of this paper is that the comments made to Peter that evening in the courtyard of Caiaphas's home involved two *slurs*, so to speak. The substance of the first was a popular assessment of Peter's regional dialect, which according to certain writers involved poorly formed, that is, slurred, speech. The second involved a regionally motivated insult relating to Peter's Galilean provenance; it was an indirect slur upon his home region. In other words, the Synoptics portray Peter being convicted of wrongdoing, in popular court, on the grounds of his linguistic fingerprint.

This sociolinguistic inquiry investigates the problematic question concerning the specifics of Peter's speech, and will attempt to clarify certain issues of regional dialect and diachrony that plague many commentaries as they attempt to explain Peter's conversations on the evening of Jesus' arrest. It will bring modern observations on regional dialect to bear upon intra-Palestinian discourse at that time, and will suggest that this type of biblical narrative offers a useful platform for teaching basic linguistic principles to students of the Bible at the college and seminary levels.

The Way You Talk Gives You Away

One should not tacitly presume that what identified Peter as Galilean was his dialect (or, in the words of some older commentators, his 'brogue'). Of the three Gospels that bring up the matter directly, Matthew is the most specific with regard to Peter's speech, noting that a servant in the courtyard said to him 'the way you talk (ἡ λαλία σου) gives you away'. Mark and Luke, on the other hand, mention only the conclusion that some of the onlookers had derived from his λαλία, namely, that Peter was a Galilean.

The ubiquity of the modern scholarly assumption that Peter's λαλία was his accent renders citation unnecessary. Yet there are a few alternate views that should occasion a brief mention. Edersheim (1883: II: 552), for example, thought that Peter's 'restlessness of attempted indifference' amidst the anxiety of the moment is what had exposed him. Nolland (1993: 1096) leaves open the possibility that 'some detail in the manner of his dress' provided the incriminating evidence. Heil (1991: 65) makes the curious suggestion that

> not only does his [Peter's] Galilean dialect disclose his association with
> Jesus the Galilean...but his 'speech' throughout the narrative, especially
> his confession of Jesus' messianic divine sonship (16.16) and his boast-

> ful promise to die with Jesus (26.35), distinguishes him as a special
> disciple

—though how those previous conversations given in private could possibly be recalled in this courtyard scene is left unexplained. Most writers, however, remain with the obvious hypothesis that Peter's manner
of speech, that is, his regional dialect, had betrayed his Galilean origin.

But of *which* language is the dialect under consideration? This paper
adopts the view that the language in question is Aramaic, for the following reasons. First, it has been established that Aramaic had become
the native language (NL, or L1) of Palestinian Jews by the first century
of the modern era. Among those instrumental in documenting this is
Joseph Fitzmyer, who demonstrates (1979: 6-7) on the basis of textual
and inscriptional evidence that while Aramaic had been a Near Eastern
lingua franca since the eighth century BCE, its use in Palestine can be
documented even a century earlier, and that by the time of Jesus 'one
may cautiously conclude' that it was routinely used as the first language
for Palestinian Jews. Secondly, even in the case of multilingual communities (as first-century Palestine indeed had been), one's native language would be the code of preference for informal, private conversations. Since the Synoptics portray Peter as speaking to Jewish servants
in the vicinity of Jewish leaders while standing in a Jewish high priest's
courtyard, the most reasonable conclusion is that Aramaic was the ideal
code for the moment. Though some Palestinian Jews likely had Koine
Greek as a second language (L2) in their verbal repertoire, it would
have been inappropriate for this type of social interaction.

In support of the idea that Peter's Galilean dialect of Aramaic is what
was at issue are two other occasions described in the New Testament
itself in which the speech of Galileans was recognizable to outsiders.
The first is the growing awareness on the part of the Sanhedrin that
Peter and John had been with Jesus (Acts 4), a strange statement to
make in v. 13 when the apostles had already indicated their belief in
Jesus at v. 10, unless Luke is showing the Sanhedrin's growing awareness of provenance, rather than merely their preaching content. The
other account, also from Luke, in which men are recognized as Galileans comes from the Pentecost narrative of Acts 2: 'Jews living in
Jerusalem' (v. 5), along with outsiders, identify the apostolic speakers
as 'Galileans'. It is curious that the contrast is made, not between foreign languages and the language of Levantine Jews in general, but with
that of Galileans in particular.

Hence, I conclude, with the majority of commentators cited above, that the λαλία ('speech') which identified Peter was his regional dialect of Aramaic. The question then arises: exactly *what* were the features of his dialect that Judaeans could identify as specifically northern, or Galilean? And how have popular commentaries by scholars contributed to, or hindered, inquiry into this matter?

Though many commentators admit differences of dialect under one label or another, only some have attempted to be more precise. Of this minority, many have contributed an element of confusion even as they have attempted to remove it. For example, Plummer (1964: 516) is one of many who repeats something along these lines: 'The Galileans are said to have mixed the gutturals in pronunciation, and to have had in some respects a peculiar vocabulary'—though, like most of the other commentators who reiterate this view, he fails to cite any written sources. A.T. Robertson (1930: 220) alleged that 'Galileans had difficulty with the gutturals', though how an entire population can have difficulty with its own native speech, and engage in 'defective pronunciation' (Hoehner 1972: 64), is indeed a mystery. Lane (1974: 542) also repeats this confusion, though he is thorough enough to leave a paper trail that points to the dialect issue:

> The Galileans are often mentioned in the Talmud because of their dialect... They were unable to distinguish between the several guttural sounds that are so important an element in Semitic languages. Peter's speech showed him to be a Galilean...

Confusion has entered the picture because ancient reports (some details of which are forthcoming) of Galilean speech were *subjective opinions about the speech production*: what was really a negative assessment of the regional variety became transformed into a negative view of local speech production. 'Confused' should describe not the speech production of first-century Galilean dialect, but certain commentators' ideas about language competence and production.

Wisely, Dalman (1971: 24) remained vague, claiming that Peter's language 'may in some details have been really somewhat different', and then adding 'But one can be certain that it was only in a few non-essentials, and that this Jewish Galilean dialect was strongly tinged with the impress of that Galilee which, also linguistically, was the homeland of our Lord'. *The Interpreter's Bible* (Buttrick *et al.* [eds.] 1951: 589) also offers one of the more cautious assessments of the issue when it observes that 'The Aramaic of Galilee, like the Arabic spoken there today, had dialectical [*sic*] peculiarities'. Ridderbos (1987: 508) comments simply that when it came to subjective judgments, 'his [Peter's] Galilean dialect (of the Aramaic language) formed enough evidence in the eyes of those around him' (parentheses his). Davies and Allison (1997: 548) assess the situation appropriately:

> Matthew does not help the reader understand why Peter's accent betrays him. Certainly all Galileans in Jerusalem for the feast are not Jesus' followers. Probably the thought is that Peter is already suspected on other grounds of following Jesus. His accent is simply supporting evidence.

But what are the specifics? Lane offered clues that provide a break in the case, though they entail a caveat. He indicated that the Talmud gave evidence of regional varieties, but the specific sources he listed are from the Babylonian Talmud (*b. 'Erub* 53b; *b. Meg.* 24b), that is, something not native to Palestine, and for that matter, not committed to print until centuries after the fact. (We shall return to this problem momentarily.) The other modern writer who left a paper trail was Hoehner, in his book on Herod Antipas. He first addresses (1972: 61-62) the overall language situation in the Galilee, providing a general survey of what is, in the present day, a thorny issue:

> There is little doubt that Aramaic was the popular speech in Galilee... It is generally believed, though, that Greek was used and this would be more true of the Galilaeans than the Judaeans. How much Greek was used by the Galilaeans is not known... Generally it is felt that Jesus made use of both Hebrew and Aramaic in his formal disputations and would have known Greek due to the fact that Nazareth was close to Sepphoris. It is probably true that on the whole the Galilaeans...were trilingual owing to their contact with the Greek-speaking districts such as the Decapolis cities, and to the fact that Greek was the language of the official administration and of international commerce.

Subsequently, Hoehner turns to the problem of the Galilean dialect of what he had called the 'popular speech' of first-century Palestine, designating what should properly be identified as the (assumed) *native* or *first* language (NL or L1) of first-century Galilean Jews, namely, Aramaic. Thus he continues (1972: 63-64):

> On the other hand there is a general impression that the Jews of Jerusalem regarded the dialect or the pronunciations of the Galilaeans with contempt and were at times provoked to laughter over it. The Talmud states that it was basically because the Galilaeans interchanged the gutturals (/h, ch, ?, ' /). It is true that in one place the Babylonian

> Talmud does give several amusing stories with regard to the Galilaean
> dialect. However, this seems to be the exception rather than the rule.
> Maybe the defective pronunciation of gutturals was prevalent in the third
> and fourth century but it is probable that it was not so markedly devel-
> oped in the earlier period of Galilee...

Whether the evidence can ever be sufficient to show the diachronic
aspect of Hoehner's claim is unlikely. And the concept of 'defective
pronunciation' on the part of a normal population *cannot* be supported.
Yet the essence of Hoehner's conclusion is surely correct (1972: 64):
'No doubt Jesus and his disciples were recognized because of their
accent', even though his subsequent point is uncertain, namely, that
'there is no implication of dishonor or ridicule' on the part of Peter's
hearers.

In order to present some order to the mixed message of these writers,
we shall make a brief diversion into the issue of the specific language
involved, and then return to the matter of dialect features and the
literary evidence for them.

Galilean Aramaic Dialect

Thus far, the very concept of a Galilean dialect of Aramaic, even theoretically conceived, is deceptively simple. Not even the term is a given,
for it has been used in at least two different ways depending upon the
scholar and time period under discussion. 'Galilean Aramaic' is a red
herring of its own, as will be clear momentarily.

Safrai (Safrai and Stern [eds.] 1976: 1-2) identifies three 'sectors' of
Aramaic Jewish literature from antiquity. The first is the traditional
scripture known as the 'Written Law', which appears in both Hebrew
and Aramaic. The second is the body of literature known as the deutero-
canonicals, i.e. the Apocrypha, which occurs only in translation from
Hebrew into a number of target languages, including Aramaic. Safrai
includes under this heading the Qumran documents.

The third sector is the 'various collections known by the comprehensive designation of Talmudic literature and known traditionally as
the Oral Law, in contradistinction to the Written Law of the canonical
scriptures'. This last category, significantly, has its 'compilation as written works...[no] earlier than the third century CE', being transmitted
orally from the end of the Second Temple era until its commitment to
print centuries later. Safrai adds (Safrai and Stern [eds.] 1976: 1):

'Some scholars and disciples kept records; but these were only for private use and not textbooks for study: they had no official standing either in the schools or the law court'.

Corresponding to Safrai's sectors/sources is Fitzmyer's fivefold chronological division of the phases of the Aramaic language, with that of the first century being the 'Middle Era'. Qumran Aramaic falls within this category. It has been shown above that the dialogue portrayed in the Synoptic passages, being personal conversation between Palestinian Jews and taking place in an informal and familiar environment, would call for the use of their native Aramaic rather than potential alternatives, such as Greek, Hebrew or Latin (to whatever degree it may have been an option). The most direct link would then be with the Qumran materials, but even here, says Fitzmyer, there is little if any direct evidence that will shed light on Peter's speech. In short, though we can and should hypothesize a first-century Jewish Galilean dialect of Aramaic, it remains to date as nothing more than hypothetical.

'Galilean Aramaic' has been a customary label for such speech at least since the turn of this century, when Dalman appears to have been first to use it. The current terminology is 'Palestinian Jewish Aramaic' (PJA) in contradistinction to other varieties such as Christian Palestinian Aramaic and Samaritan Aramaic. (For discussion of the features of PJA, under the label 'Galilean Aramic', see Beyer 1986, Kutscher 1976, Sokoloff 1978, Yahalom 1996, and Greenfield and Sokoloff 1989.) Unfortunately, most of the sources for these variant forms of speech are Byzantine and medieval, what Fitzmyer calls 'Late Aramaic' (1974). Thus, while 'Galilean Aramaic' has at times been used as the label for the hypothetical speech of Jews such as Peter and Jesus, in the most recent scholarship it refers to the later—*centuries* later—written productions of Jewish writers based at Tiberias and its surrounding areas.

This means that when rabbinic literature of the Targums or Talmud is related to the New Testament, one is bringing *post*-biblical materials to bear upon events that antedate them and are, essentially, unrelated. Matthew Black's well-known book *An Aramaic Approach to the Gospels and Acts* (1967), some of Rendsburg's earlier work on Hebrew diglossia (he addressed these problems in his later publications), and William Lane's commentary on *The Gospel of Mark* in the widely-used NIC series all faced, in one way or another, the difficulty of bringing texts to bear upon documents that predate them.

The relative paucity of ancient materials (in contrast to the virtually unlimited potential present in living language situations) and the disjunction of non-simultaneity haunt linguistic analyses of ancient sources. Fitzmyer aptly summarizes: 'Such PJA is not the kind of Aramaic that Jesus and the Apostles would have spoken, as we know now' (1974). He is now preparing a grammar on first-century Palestinian Aramaic based on what has already been published of a corpus of about 120 Aramaic texts from the Dead Sea Scrolls; when that project is completed, one might dare to address with more authority the problem of regional varieties in the first centuries BCE/CE.

Consequently, one must ask whether any contemporary Jewish sources comment in any way upon Galilean pronunciations of the *first* century. If they do, we must also allow for the fact that such comments may reflect subjective values held by the ancient listener regarding a non-standard language variety more than they objectively inform us of the actual mode of speech itself.

Tertiary Evidence for the Dialect

Though it is clear that little, if any, direct evidence of the specifics of Peter's Aramaic can be cited with confidence, we may bring together three lines of indirect evidence that at least are suggestive about the distinguishing features of Peter's dialect.

a. *Evidence from the Babylonian Talmud (Lane, etc.)*
Spolsky (1991: 90), Lane (1974: 542), Hoehner (1972: 63) and others cite the Babylonian Talmud on this matter. This is the material that the few commentators who do attempt an explanation ultimately lean on. The three passages most frequently cited appear as follows:

> R. Eleazar also said: Moses spoke insolently towards heaven, as it says, *And Moses prayed unto the Lord*. Read not *el* [unto] the Lord, but *'al* [upon] the Lord, for so in the school of R. Eleazar *alefs* were pronounced like *'ayins* and *'ayins* like *alefs* (b. Ber. 32a).

> R. Assi said: A priest from Haifa or Beth Shean should not lift up his hands. It has been taught to the same effect: 'We do not allow to pass before the ark either men from Beth Shean or from Haifa or from Tib'onim, because they pronounce *alif* as *'ayin* and *'ayin* as *alif* (b. Meg. 24b).

> R. Abba requested: 'Is there anyone who would enquire of the Judeans who are exact in their language whether we learned *me'aberin* or

me'aberin and whether we learned *akuzo* or *'akuzo*, for they would know [the correct spelling]'. When they asked they replied: Some authorities learn *me'aberin* while others learn *me'aberin*, some learn *akuzo* while others learn *'akuzo*. 'The Judeans were exact in their language'. For instance?—A Judean once announced that he had a cloak to sell. 'What', he asked, 'is the colour of your cloak?' 'Like that of beet on the ground', he replied. 'The Galileans who were not exact in their language'. For instance?—A certain Galilean once went about enquiring, 'who has *amar*?' 'Foolish Galilean', they said to him, 'do you mean an "ass" for riding, "wine" to drink, "wool" for clothing or a "lamb" for killing?' A women once wished her friend, 'Come, I would give you some fat to eat', but what she actually said to her was, 'My cast-away, may a lioness devour you'. A certain woman once appeared before a judge and addressed him as follows: 'My master slave, I had a child and they stole you from me, and it is of such a size that if they had hanged you upon it your feet would not have reached to the ground'. When Rabbi's maid indulged in enigmatic speech she used to say this: 'The ladle strikes against the jar, let the eagles fly to their nests', and when she wished them to remain at table she used to tell them, 'The crown of her friend shall be removed and the ladle will float in the jar like a ship that sails in the sea' (*b. 'Erub.* 53a-b).

And thus the ridicule of the 'enigmatic' speech of Galileans continues in this section, giving numerous examples of like-sounding words that were alleged to be confused by the 'ignorant' and 'foolish' residents of the region. Galileans were alleged to be careless about their diction, and thus should be regarded with contempt. Ederscheim (1883: I, 225-26) adds to his discussion of these sections of the Talmud that the phrase 'Galilean—Fool' was so a common an expression, it was used even for Jewish scholars from that area.

Unfortunately, all of this evidence for Galilean dialect presents certain problems. For one, the language is not specified (and furthermore, it was customary for biblical and extra-biblical writers to designate Aramaic as 'Hebrew', on which see Fitzmyer 1979: 45) and, more importantly, the time period is too late—by centuries. Dalman (1909: 80) cautions: 'We must not, through following the Galilean dialect as known to us, explain this incident [of Peter's speech] from the consideration that the Galileans were accustomed at a later period to soften the gutturals'. Being quite disenchanted with this explanation, Dalman (1909: 81) states that 'anecdotes told in Babylon centuries later…about the speech of uneducated Galilean women, must be regarded as a caricature of the truth'. In fact, in a note on p. 81, he suggests that the 'softening' (which would more properly, and most likely, be phonemic merger or allophonic variation) of Aramaic gutturals was more typical of Babylonian than Palestinian persons. His alternative preference, which is morpho-phonemic rather than phonological, appears below.

b. *Evidence from Contemporary Texts (Fitzmyer)*

Fitzmyer acknowledges the likelihood of regional variations in first-century Palestinian Aramaic, and asks: was Qumran Aramaic different from that, say, of Jerusalem or the Galilee? The possibility, at least, is consistent with countless modern language situations, but he is more concerned with the lack of *proof* (1979: 9):

> While every one knows that the distinction [between literary and spoken forms] is valid and that it is precisely the spoken form of a language that eventually invades the literary and brings about the development of one dialect or phase of it from another, it is another thing to document this distinction...

Twenty years later, Fitzmyer's opinion has not changed on the matter. Nevertheless, the opinion of the servants in the high priest's courtyard was that they could identify Peter as a Galilean *on the basis of his speech*—that is, they were hearing some kind of language production atypical of their own dialect, but which was recognizable as originating further to their north. Complications plague an already slim horizon, for as Rendsburg (1990: 3) observes: 'The problem arises because at certain times the written dialect of a language is used for speaking and the spoken dialect is used for writing'. It is not true, however, that the spoken language will always, or even frequently, influence the written.

The Synoptics record few of Peter's words, and besides, they are being relayed to readers via Koine Greek. Though there are indeed references in the Gospels to the Aramaic speech of Jesus (e.g. about a dozen transliterated Semitic loanwords throughout Mark's Gospel, or the code-switching from Greek to transliterated Aramaic speech in the raising of Jairus's daughter, Mk 5.41), there is no trace in the arrest narratives of the dialectal specifics that prompted the comments about Peter's speech.

c. *Evidence from Language Contact in General (Thomason and Kaufman)*

It would be reasonable to surmise that with Galilean speakers in such close proximity to the Greek speakers of the Decapolis, social and linguistic contact had prompted some kind of language variation that was characteristic only of the Galilee (see extensive discussion of contact-induced changes in Thomason and Kaufman 1988). Among the possibilities are: lexical borrowing, syntactic/sentence-structural alterations, morphological or phonological adaptations. Within the latter scenario, we might find either a phonemic merger (if the pronunciation changes hinted at in the traditional literature were indeed consistent across the board), or possibly context-sensitive allophonic variations (i.e. in which certain sound environments within a word prompt a particular sound segment to change, but only in that environment).

In fact, Dalman (1905: 80-81) offers a morpho-syntactic explanation. He proposes that Peter's statement οὐκ οἶδα 'I do not know' could have been translated by the Gospel writers from any of three Aramaic phrases, only two of which were characteristically Galilean in idiom. Rendsburg (personal correspondence), on the other hand, suggests that his work (1990) on Hebrew dialects in the biblical period implies that 'When Aramaic began to replace Hebrew in the Galilee, presumably many of these features entered Galilean Aramaic as well... There were [likely to have been] differences in [Aramaic] vowels, something which would surface in speech as well.'

Synthesis of Indirect Evidence

Sociolinguistic inquiry, by definition, deals with language variants. Differences in language, dialect or register constitute the independent variables of a sociolinguistic analysis. Apart from these postbiblical references and peripheral connections, I was unable to find direct evidence of specifically Galilean speech from the first century that might confirm the specifics of Peter's dialect implied in the Synoptic narratives. Inference alone must suffice for the present.

Three features of language production suggest themselves as candidates for regional differences in the case of Peter's speech: phonological, morpho-syntactic, and lexical. The lexical possibility might involve the use of synonyms (for example, the beverage called 'soda' in Buffalo is identified as 'tonic' in Boston). Morpho-syntactic difference is not as common: 'The car needs cleaned' is grammatically acceptable to native Western Pennsylvanians but not to many others. Perhaps the most likely feature of regional dialect that would offer itself to even casual listeners is phonology, or accent. For example, distinct pronunciations within greater Boston may indicate not only the provenance of the speaker but his or her socio-economic status as well, as even the untrained ear will be able to identify in the popular English language study video entitled 'American Tongues'. The marked second-person plural pronoun of the Western Pennsylvania region is also specifically indicative of provenance: 'you'-pl is monosyllabic *youns* near the Ohio border, bisyllabic *you-uns* down toward West Virginia, and *yins* further east beyond Pittsburgh. A similar instance of regional phonological variation appears in the book of Judges (12.5-6), indicating differences in pronunciation of a voiceless fricative as either /s/ or /sh/ on opposite sides of the Jordan River near the Dead Sea at the time of the Israelite judges.

Significantly, most of the examples cited here from modern times never appear in writing. Not even the ubiquitous non-pre-vocalic *r*-lessness of British and New England dialects today, which is easily identified even by the untrained ear, impacts the written language. Therefore, whether it was phonetic (vocalic or consonantal) or lexical variation—these are most likely to have been the identifying features of Peter's speech—the conclusion remains that something in Peter's dialect indicated his Galilean provenance as he stood there, surrounded by his Judaean contemporaries. And that was sufficient to undergird their informal, yet accurate, conclusion that he must have accompanied Jesus. Fingerprints do not lie, whether they appear on hard surfaces or in living speech.[1]

BIBLIOGRAPHY

Beyer, K.
    1986   'The Pronunciation of Galilean Aramaic According to the Geniza Fragments with Palestinian and Tiberian Pointing', in *Proceedings of the Ninth World Congress of Jewish Studies. Jerusalem, August 4-12, 1985.* Division D, 1 (Jerusalem: World Union of Jewish Studies): 17-22.

Black, Matthew
    1967   *An Aramaic Approach to the Gospels and Acts* (Oxford: Clarendon Press, 3rd edn).

Buttrick, George Arthur, *et al.* (eds.)
    1951   *The Interpreter's Bible*, VII (New York: Abingdon Press).

1.   I wish to thank Joseph A. Fitzmyer, SJ, for assistance in identifying certain key issues addressed in this paper, and for providing some of its bibliographic references (personal correspondence dated 3 January 1998.)

Dalman, Gustaf
  1905   *Grammatik des jüdish-palästinischen Aramäisch* (repr. 1960; Darmstadt: Wissenschaftliche Buchgesellschaft).
  1909   *The Words of Jesus* (Edinburgh: T. & T. Clark).
  1971   *Jesus-Jeshua* (New York: Ktav).
Davies, W.D., and Dale C. Allison, Jr
  1997   *The Gospel According to Saint Matthew* (vol. 3; ICC; Edinburgh: T. & T. Clark).
Ederscheim, Alfred
  1883   *The Life and Times of Jesus the Messiah* (repr. McLean, VA: Mac-Donald).
Epstein, I. (ed. and trans.)
  1938.   *The Babylonian Talmud*, I,V, X (London: Soncino Press).
Fitzmyer, Joseph A.
  1974   'The Contribution of Qumran Aramaic to the Study of the New Testament', *NTS* 20: 382-407.
  1979   *A Wandering Aramean* (Atlanta: Scholars Press).
  1992   'Did Jesus Speak Greek?', *BARev* 18: 58-63, 76-77.
Greenfield, J.C., and M. Sokoloff
  1989   'Astrological and Related Omen Texts in Jewish Palestinian Aramaic', *JNES* 48: 201-14.
Heil, John P.
  1991   *The Death and Resurrection of Jesus* (Minneapolis: Fortress Press).
Hendriksen, William
  1973   *The Gospel of Matthew* (NTCS; Grand Rapids: Baker Book House).
  1978   *The Gospel of Luke* (NTCS; Grand Rapids: Baker Book House).
Hoehner, Harold W.
  1972   *Herod Antipas* (Cambridge: Cambridge University Press).
Kutscher, E.Y.
  1976   *Studies in Galilean Aramaic* (trans. M. Sokoloff; Bar-Ilan Studies in Near Eastern Languages and Culture; Ramat-Gan: Bar-Ilan University).
Lane, Wiliam
  1974   *The Gospel According to Mark* (NICNT; Grand Rapids: Eerdmans).
Mussies, G.
  1976   'Greek in Palestine and the Diaspora', in S. Safrai and M. Stern (eds.), *The Jewish People in the First Century*, II (Philadelphia: Fortress Press): 1007-39.
Nolland, John
  1993   *Luke 18:35–24:53* (2 vols.; WBC, 35C; Dallas: Word Books).
Plummer, Alfred
  1964   *The Gospel According to St Luke* (ICC; Edinburgh: T. & T. Clark).
Rabin, C.
  1976   'Hebrew and Aramaic in the First Century', in S. Safrai and M. Stern (eds.) *The Jewish People in the First Century*, II (Philadelphia: Fortress Press): 1040-64.
Rendsburg, Gary
  1990   *Diglossia in Ancient Hebrew* (New Haven, CT: American Oriental Society).

Ridderbos, N.
1987   *Matthew* (Bible Student's Commentary Series; Grand Rapids: Regency
          Reference Library).
Robertson, A.T.
1930   *Word Pictures in the New Testament* (New York: Harper & Bros.).
Safrai, S., and M. Stern (eds.)
1976   *The Jewish People in the First Century*, I (Philadelphia: Fortress Press).
Sokoloff, M.
1978   'The Current State of Research on Galilean Aramaic', *JNES* 37: 161-67.
Spolsky, Bernard
1991   'Diglossia in Hebrew in the Late Second Temple Period', *SWJL* 10: 85-
          104.
Thomason, Sarah Grey, and Terrence Kaufman
1988   *Language Contact, Creolization, and Genetic Linguistics* (Berkeley: Uni-
          versity of California Press).
Yahalom, Joseph
1996   'Angels Do Not Understand Aramaic: On the Literary Use of Jewish
          Palestinian Aramaic', *JJS* 47: 33-44.

LANGUAGE OF CHANGE AND THE CHANGING OF LANGUAGE: A SOCIOLINGUISTIC APPROACH TO PAULINE DISCOURSE

Jeffrey T. Reed

> Once the familiar and comfortable idea of the homogeneity of linguistic communities is abandoned, the world appears as an ocean of conflicting attractions, convergence here breeding divergence there, with new centres of attraction developing at all times and threatening to disrupt existing ensembles.
>
> André Martinet[1]

While much is being said in New Testament studies about the socio-logical and anthropological dimensions of early Christianity in relation to Paul, relatively little is being said about the sociological roles which *language* played in Paul's theology and ministry. The imbalance in New Testament scholarship can be likened to the two foci of modern sociolinguistics—the term *sociolinguistics* typically refers to studies from the viewpoint of linguistics, whereas the phrase *sociology of language* to those of sociology. Whereas many insightful New Testament studies have investigated the social forces at work in early Christianity (a 'sociology of language' approach), relatively little attention has been directed to the *linguistic* dimensions of, say, social identity (a 'sociolinguistic' approach). What is perhaps needed is more concentrated attention to the relationship between language as a symbolic system and the society (religious or otherwise) in which it functions. In a study which largely investigates the sociological aspects of early Christianity (including theories about the authors and readers behind the New Testament texts), Wayne Meeks poses the task before us:

> Society is viewed as a process, in which personal identity and social forms are mutually and continuously created by interactions that occur

---

1. A. Martinet, *A Functional View of Language* (Oxford: Oxford University Press, 1962), p. 105.

by means of symbols... Moreover, there is some real but complex relation between social structure and symbolic structure, and religion is an integral part of the cultural web.[2]

Though the relationship between social structure and language (symbol) may be complex, New Testament scholars may find hope in the concluding remark of one of today's leading sociolinguists:

> No one ever doubted that language played a crucial role in social situations, but until very recently no one could say exactly how it worked or why. We have begun to understand how—and occasionally why—and we have developed methods and means that help us to isolate its essential components.
>
> That challenge of seeing language clearly in social situations in which it is just one strand of a factal web may never be perfectly met, but we have made a start, and it is an auspicious one.[3]

Taking the above quotations as a challenge for more linguistically orientated sociological studies of the New Testament, the present paper seeks to investigate how one area of sociolinguistics (from a particular linguistic viewpoint)—viz. the study of language change (or variation)—may help illuminate Paul's attempt to change language (symbol) so as to create and change the identity and behaviour of his readers. In the first section, the basic task of sociolinguistics is introduced, with special attention given to the study of linguistic variation (the study of changes in the dialects of speech communities). In the second section, linguistic variation in Paul's letter to the Philippians is investigated so as to highlight its sociological functions.

Sociolinguistics and the Study of Linguistic Variation

'Sociolinguistics' typically highlights the 'linguistic' side of social behaviour. From the broader perspective, *sociolinguists* generally seek to understand the social significance of language *usage* (e.g. *parole* as opposed to *langue*, performance as opposed to competence, and text as opposed to code), including topics of research such as interactional sociolinguistics, language planning, language and minorities, power,

---

2. W.A. Meeks, *The First Urban Christians: The Social World of the Apostle Paul* (New Haven: Yale University Press, 1983), p. 6.

3. J.K. Chambers, *Sociolinguistic Theory* (Oxford: Basil Blackwell, 1995), p. 253.

social structure, and social change, register and style, social dialect, and, the particular focus of this study, linguistic variation.[4]

Dialects and Standard Languages

A central concern for sociolinguistics has been whether and in what way it is possible to identify a language X in relation to other languages within and across particular cultural groups. Spurred by questions about *language variation*, sociolinguists have argued that an isolated, fixed language rarely exists, except under certain specific conditions.[5] Rather, *varieties of language* (dialects) exist within and across cultural groups. These varieties of language are the product of changes in particular languages due to social forces. One of the varieties of language found in a particular society is often treated as the standard language, being taught through educational channels and enforced by those in power. Only in the case of *standard languages*, perhaps such as Hellenistic Greek, should one think of a *language* of the New Testament in contrast to what is often termed a *dialect*. A standard language, or *code*, is shared

---

4.   Including the recent work of Chambers (see above), some other informative works include D.H. Hymes (ed.), *Language in Culture and Society* (New York: Harper & Row, 1964); J.J. Gumperz and D.H. Hymes (eds.), *Directions in Sociolinguistics* (New York: Holt, Rinehart & Winston, 1972); W. Labov, *Sociolinguistic Patterns* (Philadelphia: University of Pennsylvania Press, 1972); D.H. Hymes, *Foundations in Sociolinguistics: An Ethnographic Approach* (Philadelphia: University of Pennsylvania Press, 1974); M. Sanches and B. Blount (eds.), *Sociocultural Dimensions of Language Use* (New York: Academic Press, 1975); M. Gregory and S. Carroll, *Language and Situation: Language Varieties and their Social Contexts* (London: Routledge and Kegan Paul, 1978); P. Brown and S. Levinson, 'Social Structure, Groups and Interaction', in K. Scherer and H. Giles (eds.), *Social Markers in Speech* (Cambridge: Cambridge University Press, 1979), pp. 291-347; R.A. Hudson, *Sociolinguistics* (CTL; Cambridge: Cambridge University Press, 1980); P. Trudgill, *Sociolinguistics: An Introduction to Language and Society* (Harmondsworth: Penguin Books, rev. edn, 1983); J.P. Louw (ed.), *Sociolinguistics and Communication* (UBS Monograph Series, 1; New York: United Bible Societies, 1986); N. Fairclough, *Language and Power* (London: Longman, 1989); *idem, Discourse and Social Change* (Cambridge: Polity Press, 1992). For application of sociolinguistics to the New Testament, see F.P. Cotterell, 'Sociolinguistics', *Vox Evangelica* 16 (1986), pp. 61-76.

5.   One of the most significant studies in this direction came from Labov's research on the social stratification of English in New York (*Sociolinguistic Patterns, passim*).

by a group of people. Such standard languages often become a speaker's second variety, and thus provide a way to communicate despite regional and social *varieties*. In other words, whereas the code is shared by the larger society, varieties are unique to various users of the code.[6] Varieties are commonly thought of in terms of pronunciation and referred to as dialects; however, other factors determine variation such as spelling, vocabulary, gestures, and even syntax and discourse features. Variant spelling practices probably due to pronunciation differences, as found in ancient Greek papyri, reveal such varieties of dialect in Egypt. Such varieties of language should be pictured on a continuum with opposite poles representing the greatest disparity between the varieties. If two varieties of language are closely positioned together on the continuum, they are readily understood by the different speakers. Two varieties of language on opposite ends of the continuum are less intelligible to the different users of the code. Although the similarities among the dialects on the continuum are recognizable, Hudson argues that the individual instances on the continuum should not be referred to as particular languages. In a quite bold statement, he claims: 'The concept "language X" has no part to play in sociolinguistics—nor, for exactly the same reasons, can it have any place in linguistics'.[7] Accordingly, it might be argued that there is no such thing as *the* language of the New Testament, but only varieties of language in the New Testament. At most, there are shared features of language which exist between these varieties, although what is shared between two varieties might not be shared with other varieties.

Two key factors—regional and social—affect changes in varieties of languages. Regional factors refer to the geographical locations of the language users. Geographical isolation often results in unique developments of a language variety (e.g. phonological peculiarities). Social factors, such as gender, age, education, and status, all affect the development of varieties of language. In addition, the particular needs of social groups may result in the modification of the standard language. For example, all legal terms used in the Roman legal system may not have been part of the public's vocabulary, but they were a vital part of the variety of language used by lawyers and orators. Similarly, early Christian groups likely developed their own varieties of language; in

6.   Hudson, *Sociolinguistics*, p. 48.
7.   Hudson, *Sociolinguistics*, p. 37.

addition, the evidence suggests that the native languages of Palestinian and diaspora Jews did influence their use of Greek.[8]

Hudson argues that standard languages are the only examples in which one should speak of 'a language X'.[9] A standard language is a variety of language that has become the assumed, widespread language of choice. It may simply be a variety of language that has been accepted (for various reasons) by a larger group of speakers. With the rise of Alexander's empire, Koine Greek (descended from the Attic dialect) first developed as the standard variety of language of the empire, with the result that communication took place across dialectal and cultural varieties. This linguistic *code* was eventually shared throughout regions of the Roman empire, allowing for cross-cultural communication.

Linguistic Variation
By accounting for linguistic varieties within a society, sociolinguists were simply recognizing that languages *change* both diachronically and synchronically. As E. Sapir bluntly put it: 'Everyone knows that language is a variable'.[10] However, although linguistic variation may be obvious, 'no linguists analyzed it systematically until the inception of sociolinguistics in the 1960s'.[11] Indeed, the generation after Sapir invoked what is called the 'axiom of categoricity', the assumption that the data for doing linguistic analysis must be regularized to eliminate all real-world variability and exceptions; or, in Saussure's celebrated dichotomy, language as 'system' or *langue*, not language as *parole* (the social uses of language), provided the data for these linguists.[12] M. Joos

8.   On the latter point, see M. Silva, 'Bilingualism and the Character of Palestinian Greek', *Bib* 61 (1980), pp. 198-219; he demonstrates that on the level of *langue* (language system) New Testament Greek is part of the Koine Greek used throughout the Roman Empire of the day, but that on the level of *parole* (language use) it shows signs of Semitic influence. On the former point, however, I am unaware of any comprehensive attempt to compare the linguistic varieties of early Christian documents to reveal potential sociological (or regional) differences—a macro- and micro-stylistic evaluation of the New Testament and other Christian documents.

9.   Hudson, *Sociolinguistics*, p. 37.

10.   E. Sapir, *Language: An Introduction to the Study of Speech* (New York: Harcourt, Brace, 1949 [1921]), p. 147.

11.   Chambers, *Theory*, p. 12.

12.   F. de Saussure, *Course in General Linguistics* (ed. C. Bally and A. Seche-

divorces even further actual use of language from the grammarians' agenda: 'We must make our "linguistics" a kind of mathematics within which inconsistency is by definition impossible'.[13] This premise, that language can be analyzed as an autonomous system independent of social contexts or its speakers, has been perpetuated in the theories of Noam Chomsky—perhaps the most influential, but least understood, linguist appealed to by biblical scholars.[14] Chomsky distinguishes between what he refers to as 'competence' (*langue*) and 'performance' (*parole*) as a means for going about the task of linguistics:

> Linguistic theory is concerned primarily with an ideal speaker-listener, in a completely homogeneous speech-community, who knows its language perfectly and is unaffected by such grammatically irrelevant conditions as memory limitations, distractions, shifts of attention and interest, and errors (random or characteristic) in applying his knowledge of the language in actual performance.[15]

Not until the development of several fairly recent sub-fields of linguistics has the axiom of categoricity been challenged in the linguistic world—especially relevant to the New Testament scholar are the fields of psycholinguistics, discourse analysis, and, the focus of this paper, sociolinguistics. These alternative linguistics seek instead, to use the language of Saussure, to develop the science of *parole*, whereas linguistics prior to these sub-fields has concentrated on the science of *langue*.

A serious challenge to the axiom of categoricity came with one of the first systematic studies of linguistic variation by J.L. Fischer,[16] but a

haye; trans. W. Baskin; New York and Toronto: McGraw–Hill, 1966 [1916]), pp. 9-15.

13. M. Joos, 'Description of Language Design', *Journal of the Acoustical Society of America* 22 (1950), pp. 701-702.

14. His two major early works include *Syntactic Structures* (The Hague: Mouton, 1957) and *Aspects of the Theory of Syntax* (Cambridge, MA: MIT Press, 1965). See also his *Rules and Representations* (New York: Columbia University Press, 1980).

15. Chomsky, *Aspects of the Theory of Syntax*, p. 3.

16. J.L. Fischer, 'Social Influences on the Choice of a Linguistic Variant', *Word* 14 (1958), pp. 47-56; before this, L. Gauchat ('L'unité phonétique dans le patois d'une commune', in *Festschrift Heinreich Morf: Aus romanischen Sprachen und Literaturen* [Halle: Niemeyer, 1905], pp. 175-232) foreshadowed modern sociolinguists by correlating linguistic variation in a French dialect of Charmey, Switzerland with the sex and age of speakers.

more forceful blow was delivered by the studies in the 1960s and 1970s of W. Labov—studies which are now considered the fountainhead of modern sociolinguistic research.[17] Labov attempted to understand the social significance of linguistic variation. What social factors cause speakers to pronounce, for example, certain morphemes differently? Chambers states the task in the form of three questions: 'Why...does linguistic variation exist at all? What is its purpose or function? What is its adaptive significance for human beings?'[18] Hence, the emphasis is placed on the variation, not the consistency, of language. And if variation is treated as a central concern of the linguist (in this case, sociolinguist), it follows that less emphasis will be placed on language as an autonomous system and more on language as a social device.

What characterizes the sociolinguistic approach is the notion that linguistic variability is a result of social forces. This might seem self-evident in hindsight, but one dominating theory about linguistic change has pushed this perspective into the background (or, in some cases, entirely out of the picture)—the Babelian hypothesis. For many, the story of Babel in the Old Testament book of Genesis (11.1-9) exemplifies what is considered the 'counteradaptive' or dysfunctional role of linguistic variability. Linguistic diversity creates societal antagonism as one language community finds itself at odds with another or, on a more general level, one language community is simply prevented from communicating with another. Hence, linguistic variability is counteradaptive—it prevents those who do not speak a particular language from assimilating into that language community. This view is supported by general observation, that is, many institutions attempt to curtail linguistic diversity in favor of a standard dialect by employing, for example

> prescriptive dictionaries, school grammars, nationalized authorities such as the Académie française, school bussing, training in the dramatic arts, British 'public' schools... International politico-linguistic movements

17. For early collections of Labov's work, see especially Labov, *Sociolinguistic Patterns* and *Language in the Inner City: Studies in the Black English Vernacular* (Philadelphia: University of Pennsylvania Press, 1972). For other formative works in social dialectology, see W.A. Wolfram, *A Sociolinguistic Description of Detroit Negro Speech* (Washington, DC: Center for Applied Linguistics, 1969); Trudgill, *Sociolinguistics*; R. Macaulay, *Language, Social Class and Education: A Glasgow Study* (Edinburgh: Edinburgh University Press, 1977).

18. Chambers, *Theory*, p. 207.

for auxiliary languages such as Esperanto and Basic English have no other rationale but the curtailing of diversity.[19]

On a more personal level, humans quickly learn that linguistic diversity can result in social ostracism. As an American doctoral student in Yorkshire, England, I soon learned how dialectal differences can become a subject of ridicule and goading. We are, as humans, constantly pressured to adapt as far as possible to local linguistic norms. Although the Babelian hypothesis provides a reasonably plausible understanding of linguistic variability,[20] it is clearly not the whole story.

If linguistic diversity is truly counteradaptive, then why do human beings resist standardization? If we want to 'fit in', so to speak, then why is linguistic variability such a universal phenomenon? If regional dialects and socially based varieties of language cause their speakers discomfort, why do they continue to exist? Furthermore, why do dialects continue to increase in number? Or, to ask the question from a functionalist perspective, for what purpose do humans continue to create linguistic variability, despite what would seem to be a strong urge to standardize? Sociolinguistic studies are suggesting that with respect to language change there are competing forces of global counteradaptivity and local adaptivity. On the one hand, 'if one looks critically at the kinds of situations in which linguistic diversity appears to be counteradaptive, they all turn out to be power relationships'.[21] Covert prestige plays a key role in maintaining linguistic diversity. The individual speaker is encouraged by local community bonds to adapt to a linguistic norm. Beyond that (the global), the individual perceives his or her variety of language in terms of ideological differences from other varieties, even though from the linguist's standpoint no variety of language is inherently better than any other as a medium for communication. One of the strategies of the powerful elite is to establish their dialect as the standard one. As Kroch and Small note, linguistic prescriptivism is 'the ideology by which the guardians of the standard language impose their linguistic norms on people who have perfectly serviceable norms of their own'.[22] However, languages do not easily standardize for the

19. Chambers, *Theory*, p. 209.
20. For sociological evidence in support of the hypothesis, see Chambers, *Theory*, pp. 209-12.
21. Chambers, *Theory*, p. 212 (examples on pp. 212-14).
22. A. Kroch and C. Small, 'Grammatical Ideology and its Effect on Speech', in

precise reason that the non-standard dialects provide competing social identities for their speakers (which must be upheld or rejected). Thus, global counteradaptivity is a result of local adaptivity, explaining the enduring power of linguistic diversity in human cultures—or what may be called the persistence of the non-standard varieties of language.

There are two general tenets which explain the causes of linguistic variation.[23] The first is that dialects resist conforming to other dialects due to various natural (economical) tendencies in the grammar and phonology. We often use the principle of least effort in our speech, and if the standard language or another dialect does not follow the 'naturalness' of our dialect, then it will be rejected. The second tenet, and the one most relevant to the New Testament scholar, is that the root of dialectal differences is ideological, not linguistic. So, at the end of amassing data in support of his case, Chambers claims, 'The underlying cause of sociolinguistic differences, largely beneath consciousness, is the human instinct to establish and maintain social identity'.[24] People need to belong somewhere and to define that somewhere in relation to 'otherwheres'. Sociolinguists are demonstrating that one of the most important means (tools or weapons) of marking our territory is by speaking like the other people who live there.

It now remains to demonstrate that Paul creates and attempts to enforce a 'Christian' social identity in his letters by means of linguistic variability.

Language Change in Philippians

The canonical letter to the Philippians, be it an aggregate of two or more originally separate letters or one (so most scholars; see Phil. 1.1 σὺν ἐπισκόποις καὶ διακόνοις) original whole,[25] provides a number of

D. Sankoff (ed.), *Linguistic Variation: Models and Methods* (New York: Academic Press, 1978), p. 45.

23. A. Kroch, 'Toward a Theory of Social Dialect Variation', *Language in Society* 7 (1978), pp. 17-36.

24. Chambers, *Theory*, p. 250.

25. The issue of literary integrity does not weigh heavily on the point of this paper, since even three originally separate letters would have apparently been written within a short span of time, and betray similar language, if not the same purposes. More importantly, almost no one denies the authenticity of the supposed fragments (except for perhaps 3.1); D.J. Doughty ('Citizens of Heaven: Philippians 3.2-21', *NTS* 41 [1995], pp. 102-22), despite approximately a century of general

examples of epistolary expressions which may be paralleled in contemporary and more temporally distant letters. The benefit of this comparative literature is that it helps us to understand ways in which Paul's epistolary expression converges with but also diverges from conventional practice. Such comparison and contrast leads to a better appreciation of the function of Paul's epistolary practice.

The following analysis seeks to demonstrate how Paul's linguistic practice *converges with* both his Pharisaic and Hellenistic Greek dialects and how it *diverges from* his Hellenistic dialect in terms of his use of epistolary formulas. In terms of the above survey, I am interested in the global counteradaptivity and the local adaptivity of Paul's dialect and the social forces at play behind them. In order to narrow the scope of the investigation, I am particularly concerned with Paul's modification of epistolary formulas.[26] The benefit of approaching the question of linguistic diversity in Paul vis-à-vis epistolary linguistic conventions is twofold. First, we possess an abundance of epistolary literature from various regions (even though they are mostly found in Egypt, many of the letters are written from outside of Egypt), with which we may compare the language of Paul's letters. Secondly, since epistolary conventions were required to carry on communication across Greco-Roman regional boundaries, it seems reasonable to assume that epistolary conventions typically reflect the standard language (Hellenistic Greek). Thus, the recipient of a letter would at the very least expect a letter to be written according to standard conventions, with less concern for conformity to local conventions, especially if the sender were not from that region.

A study of *epistolary* language in Paul is, furthermore, a useful place to begin a sociolinguistic investigation, since genre (or what some lin-

scholarly support of Pauline authorship, argues that Phil. 3.2-21 is a non-Pauline interpolation, on the grounds that it contains 'un-Pauline' elements (e.g. the self-conception of the apostle, his Damascus experience, and his controversy with Judaism). The staying-power of his arguments awaits scholarly reaction, but, in any case, ch. 3 does not significantly factor into the analysis of the present study.

26. As a matter of definition, I use the term 'formula' (convention) simply to mean *the use of similar linguistic forms in similar situational contexts (i.e. registers) with similar functions* (cf. T.Y. Mullins, 'Formulas in New Testament Epistles', *JBL* 91 [1972], pp. 380-90, esp. p. 388). Although most studies of linguistic variation concern phonetic changes (not generic changes, as in this study), there has been and is currently a need for studies beyond the phonetic level of language (see Chambers, *Theory*, pp. 237-41).

guists often refer to as 'register') involves a more specific (less abstract) set of features of linguistic *parole* (usage). Whereas a variety of language refers to *language according to user*,[27] register refers to *language according to use*. Registers correspond to linguistic expressions occasioned by common, social activities (e.g. telephone conversations, teacher–pupil interchange, doctor–patient appointments, or ancient letters). Register has been defined as *a configuration of meanings which is associated with a particular situation*.[28] Communicants are able to identify the situation by means of these configurations of meanings (e.g. 'once upon a time', epistolary formulas, and so on), often by the time the first few words of a discourse are spoken. It usually takes only a few seconds, for example, when turning on the radio to identify whether we are listening to a sermon, sports broadcast, news broadcast, disc jockey, commentary, talk show, quiz program, or interview. M.A.K. Halliday's definition hits at the essence of the concept of register:

> A register can be defined as a particular configuration of meanings that is associated with a particular situation type. In any social context, certain semantic resources are characteristically employed; certain sets of options are as it were 'at risk' in the given semiotic environment. These define the register. Considered in terms of the notion of meaning potential, the register is the range of meaning potential that is activated by the semiotic properties of the situation.[29]

Halliday is suggesting that changes in the context of situation contribute to changes in the *use* of language. Speakers conform their discourse to the context of situation, and consequently draw upon accepted forms of language which others recognize as appropriate for that situation. Just as ethnographers have argued that 'much of language use, like a grammar, is rule governed',[30] registers (genres) may be treated as rule-governed structures of language use. Consequently, these linguistic structures invoke corresponding interpretations by listeners, that is, they provide for predictability. The same communicative principle (which is

27. Hudson, *Sociolinguistics*, pp. 48-49.

28. M.A.K. Halliday and R. Hasan, *Language, Context, and Text: Aspects of Language in a Social-Semiotic Perspective* (Oxford: Oxford University Press, 1989), pp. 38-39.

29. M.A.K. Halliday, *Learning How to Mean—Explorations in the Development of Language* (London: Edward Arnold, 1975), p. 126.

30. J.J. Gumperz, *Discourse Strategies* (Studies in Interactional Sociolinguistics, 1; Cambridge: Cambridge University Press, 1982), p. 155.

likely a universal principle along the lines of Grice's 'cooperative' prin-ciple) *prima facie* governed the production of New Testament dis-courses.[31]

This principle of predictability required by register involves five major aspects of discourse: (1) subject-matter (the semantic content of the discourse); (2) situation-type (or context of situation); (3) partici-pant roles (who is communicating with whom; what are the differences or similarities in age, gender, and other social variables); (4) mode (e.g. persuasive, explanatory, and imperative discourses); and (5) medium (spoken or written).[32] Languages develop standard formulas in order to express these features of the discourse. The following diagram illus-trates the fundamental choices of generic formulas made by an author. Once a particular situation invokes a choice of register, the author may choose to support or reject standard convention (formulas). If it is sup-ported, the author must then choose both between an obligatory or optional formula *and* between a canonical or modified one.

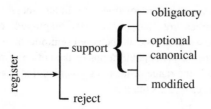

These types of choices involve eight basic questions: (1) what elements must occur (obligatory)?; (2) what elements may occur (optional)?; (3) where must they occur?; (4) where may they occur?; (5) how often must they occur?; (6) how often may they occur?; (7) what function must they have?; and (8) what function may they have?

The above diagram and questions provide a useful heuristic device for analyzing Paul's epistolary formulas for linguistic variation and conformity.

31. H.P. Grice, 'Logic and Conversation', in P. Cole and J. Morgan (eds.), *Syntax and Semantics*. III. *Speech Acts* (New York: Academic Press, 1975), pp. 41-58. 'Appropriateness for the situation', for example, was an important aspect of rhetorical and epistolary theory in Greco-Roman traditions.

32. R. Hasan, 'Code, Register and Social Dialect', in B. Bernstein (ed.), *Class, Codes and Control*. II. *Applied Studies towards a Sociology of Language* (London: Routledge & Kegan Paul, 1973), p. 272.

Epistolary Variation in Philippians

As examples of language change in Paul the following investigation is limited to the epistolary formulas found in Phil. 1.2 (salutation) and 1.12-26 (disclosure and request), since these are not directly affected by the integrity issue and provide clear examples which adequately demonstrate the point.[33]

Salutation (1.2)

Paul's salutations are often treated by commentators in terms of epistolary convention (usually as part of the opening), though they recognize the obvious divergence in Paul's style.

Ancient letter writers commonly follow the superscription and adscription of the letter ('A to B') with some type of salutation (initial greeting): χαίρειν, ἐρρῶσθαι, ὑγιαίνειν, or a combination of the first with one of the other two.[34] These salutations are not obligatory to the epistolary genre, as is evidenced particularly in formal letters (e.g. petitions, complaints, and applications) which often begin with '"To Y [dative] from X", usually omitting the salutation',[35] but they are frequent in personal letters. The salutation plays the same role as the prescript (and other conventions appearing in the opening of the letter), that is, establishing the immediate interpersonal relationship between sender and recipient. Sometimes the salutation appears to be little more than a formal nicety as in the 'appointment' of a village scribe Menches recorded in *Sel.Pap.* II 339 (199 BCE) Ἀσκληπιάδης Μαρρεῖ χαίρειν·

---

33. For my understanding of Phil. 3.1b as an epistolary formula of hesitation, see J.T. Reed, 'Philippians 3:1 and Epistolary Hesitation Formulas: The Literary Integrity of Philippians, Again', *JBL* 115 (1996), pp. 63-90.

34. O. Roller, *Das Formular der paulinischen Briefe: Ein Beitrag zur Lehre vom antiken Briefe* (BWANT, 4.6; Stuttgart: Kohlhammer, 1933), p. 61. Examples abound, but some near the time of Paul include *P.Oxy.* II 297.1 (54 CE) Ἀμμώνιος Ἀμμωνίωι τῶι πατρὶ χαίρειν; BGU VIII 1769.1 (48–47? BCE) Ἑλλάνικος Εὐρυλόχωι τῶι ἀδελφῶι χαίρειν καὶ ἐρρῶσθαι; *P.Oxy.* XXII 2353.1-2 (32 CE) Σινθῶνις Ἀρποχρᾶτι τῷ υἱῶι πλεῖστα χαίρειν καὶ διὰ παντὸς ὑγιαίνειν.

35. D.E. Aune, *The New Testament in its Literary Environment* (Philadelphia: Westminster Press, 1987), p. 163. The expression χαίρειν καὶ ἐρρῶσθαι is typically pre-Pauline (primarily second to first century BCE) and χαίρειν καὶ ὑγιαίνειν is mostly limited to the first century BCE and first century CE; see, however, W. Crönert ('Die beiden ältesten griechischen Briefe', *Rheinisches Museum* 65 [1910], pp. 157-60, esp. p. 157) for this formula in a fourth century BCE Athenian letter inscribed on lead.

Μεγχῆι; in other cases (especially personal letters), its omission might have been taken as an affront by the recipient. Paul's undeniable modification of this optional epistolary formula would have been immediately noticeable to his Philippian readers, who had become accustomed to traditional formulas. It has not been emphasized enough, perhaps because it becomes mundane to the modern reader of the Pauline letters, how ancient readers would have been struck by Paul's modification; his formula was not a ritualistic 'hello' but a means of drawing the reader into a letter with different aims than those to which they were accustomed.

Two reasons suggest that Paul is adapting his salutation from the typical epistolary salutation. First, and most apparent, is his use of the noun χάρις. Although this term is an important part of Paul's religious vocabulary, it also recalls its infinitive cognate χαίρειν ('hello', 'greetings') used as a salutation in letters. The use of the noun χάρις near the salutation is found in *P.Cair.Zen.* III 59526.1 Φιλοκράτης Ζήνωνι χαίρειν, τοῖς θεοῖς πολλὴ χάρις—here it is probably best understood in the sense of thanksgiving ('many thanks to the gods...').[36] Similarly, Gemellos follows his χαίρειν salutation with thanks directed towards the recipient for showing concern for him: *P.Mich.* VIII 498.1-5 (II CE) Γέμελλ[ο]ς Ἀπολιναρίωι τῶι τιμιωτάτωι [ἀ]δελφῶι χαί[ρει]ν, χάρις σοι πλείστη, ἄδελφε, μεριμνήσαντί με. It is unclear, and probably doubtful, that Paul is following this convention. Nonetheless, that Paul had some precedent for changing the infinitive to a nominative is evidenced by this and other adaptations of the χαίρειν formula in epistolary literature. For example, besides the usual χαίρειν, this verb is also found in the optative (χαίροις) and imperative (χαῖρε).[37] These examples demonstrate the possibility of a modification of the conventional form; nevertheless, Paul's switch to the noun form is clearly unconventional. Secondly, Paul's expansion of the salutation is not unparalleled

36. Cf. the same expression in *P.Oslo* III 155.1-2 (II CE).

37. See e.g. *P.Oxy.* III 526.1-3 (II CE) Χαίροις Καλόκαιρε Κύριλλός σε προσαγορεύω and BGU III 821.1 (II CE) χαῖρε κύριέ μου πάτερ Ἡραίσκος σε ἀσπάζομαι. J.L. White ('Epistolary Formulas and Cliches in Greek Papyrus Letters', *SBLSP* 2 [1978], pp. 289-319, esp. p. 295) correctly places such variations of the salutation in the second and third centuries CE—mostly the latter. Later uses do exist (e.g. SB XIV 11588.2 [IV CE]), but BGU VI 1453.2 (323–30 BCE) χαῖρε, if the spelling is correct, may be a pre-Pauline usage. The point stands that authors were not inescapably determined by convention.

in papyrus letters. For example, letter writers frequently employ modifiers to describe χαίρειν (e.g. πᾶσαι [pre-first century CE], πολλά, πλεῖστα).[38] Thus, it would not be unthinkable for Paul to modify his salutation with the prepositional phrase ἀπὸ θεοῦ πατρὸς ἡμῶν καὶ κυρίου Ἰησοῦ Χριστοῦ. Thirdly, salutations not infrequently consist of two or more verbal elements (e.g. χαίρειν καὶ ἐρρῶσθαι and χαίρειν καὶ ὑγιαίνειν).[39] For example, in a letter from Diogenes to his brother Dionysius, the sender not only combines two verbs, but modifies them with πλεῖστα (*P.Oxy.* VII 1061 [22 BCE] Διογένης Διονυσίωι τωι ἀδελφῶι πλεῖστα χα(ίρειν) καὶ ὑγιαίνειν).

Such combinations of verbs in epistolary salutations provide a reasonable parallel for Paul's dual elements χάρις and εἰρήνη. It has become customary for scholars to treat Paul's two-part salutation as a combination of (1) the traditional χαίρειν altered to a more 'Pauline Christian' χάρις and (2) the Jewish salutation שָׁלוֹם translated into the Greek εἰρήνη.[40] The Hebrew and Aramaic epistolary evidence provides a suitable background for Paul's use of εἰρήνη. The author of an embedded letter in 2 Maccabees (1.1-10a), which mostly follows regularities of Hebrew and Aramaic epistolary style, employs the less com-

---

38. See e.g. BGU I 38.1-2 (I CE) Σερῆνος Ἀπολιναρίῳ τῷ πατρεὶ πολλὰ χαίρειν and BGU III 811.1-2 (98–130 CE) Κορνήλιος Ἀπολλῶτι τῶι ἀδελφῶ πλεῖστα χαίρειν.

39. G.F. Hawthorne (*Philippians* [WBC, 43; Waco, TX: Word Books, 1983], p. 11) makes too little of the use of double salutations. I have found at least 35 examples of χαίρειν καὶ ὑγιαίνειν, and at least 27 examples of χαίρειν καὶ ἐρρῶσθαι.

40. See Roller, *Formular*, p. 61; I. Taatz, *Frühjüdische Briefe: Die paulinischen Briefe im Rahmen der offiziellen religiösen Briefe des Frühjudentums* (NTOA, 16; Göttingen: Vandenhoeck & Ruprecht, 1991), p. 112. L.G. Champion (*Benedictions and Doxologies in the Epistles of Paul* [Oxford: Kemp Hall, 1934], pp. 45-75) and T.Y. Mullins ('Benediction as a New Testament Form', *Andrews University Seminary Studies* 15 [1977], pp. 59-64) attribute the 'grace and peace' expressions in Paul's letters to benedictions in the LXX (Deut. 6.24-26) and synagogue worship; contrast R. Jewett, 'The Form and Function of the Homiletic Benediction', *ATR* 51 (1969), pp. 18-34, here p. 31, who is not convinced that these had any formal influence on New Testament expressions. While it is possible that Paul's expressions reflect a functional similarity with these Old Testament benedictions—that is, (1) wish/recipient/divine source or (2) wish/divine source/wish/recipient—the language is very different (e.g. there are no verbs; the source is God and Jesus; dative rather than accusative is used for the recipient).

mon Greek salutation 'To B χαίρειν A',[41] followed immediately (with no conjunction) by a prayer for the welfare of the recipients using εἰρήνη (εἰρήνην ἀγαθὴν καὶ ἀγαθοποιῆσαι ὑμῖν ὁ θεός...).[42] O'Brien notes that in the LXX εἰρήνη can also have the general sense of 'well-being'.[43] This meaning is not far removed from that of another form of the Greek salutation, ὑγιαίνειν, which is used in conjunction with χαίρειν, for example, in 2 Macc. 1.10. In epistolary contexts ὑγιαίνειν and ἐρρῶσθαι often function as the sender's wish for the recipient's health and well-being, and when used with χαίρειν as a double salutation either verb may appear as the *second* element. Rather than alter the verb to a noun form such as ὑγίανσις, Paul may have chosen εἰρήνη in slight contrast to the function of ὑγιαίνειν. In a two-part salutation, the Philippian readers would have expected to find an exhortation to their good health in the second element. Paul, however, wished a type of

41. J.A. Goldstein (*II Maccabees* [AB, 41A; Garden City, NY: Doubleday, 1983], p. 140) maintains that χαίρειν here is a translation (as in 1 Esd. 6.8 and 2 Macc. 12.20) of the Semitic salutation 'peace' (שׁלם). He does not precisely answer how the salutation in the second embedded letter (1.10b–2.18, by a different author)—χαίρειν καὶ ὑγιαίνειν—is a translation of the Semitic formula. In terms of semantics, ὑγιαίνειν better parallels שׁלם than χαίρειν; so P. Dion, 'The Aramaic "Family Letter" and Related Epistolary Forms in Other Oriental Languages and in Hellenistic Greek', *Semeia* 22 (1982), pp. 59-76, esp. p. 68. It may be that there is no one-to-one correspondence in the translation; rather, the author employs a Greek epistolary convention with a similar pragmatic function (viz. to greet the recipient) but not the same semantic one. G. Friedrich ('Lohmeyers These über "Das paulinische Briefpräskript" kritisch beleuchtet', *ZNW* 46 [1955], pp. 272-74, esp. p. 273), in response to Lohmeyer's suggestion that Paul's salutations are liturgical, had already pointed to parallels 'aus neuassyrischer, neubabylonischer Zeit und in den Elephantinepapyri'.

42. The order of the salutation 'To B (greeting) A' is common in Aramaic letters (see J.A. Fitzmyer, 'Some Notes on Aramaic Epistolography', *JBL* 93 [1974], pp. 201-25, esp. p. 211). Concern for the well-being of the recipient is also found in Aramaic prescripts; for examples, see Fitzmyer, 'Epistolography', pp. 214-15. Furthermore, two-part greetings (e.g. 'peace and life'; 'greetings and prosperity') are found in Aramaic prescripts—see examples in Fitzmyer, 'Epistolography', p. 215, and Dion, 'Family Letter', p. 61. Finally, Fitzmyer ('Epistolography', p. 215) notes the difficulty of knowing whether the Jewish salutation formula is just a simple 'greeting' (English 'Hi') or something with a more theological intent ('peace').

43. P.T. O'Brien, *Commentary on Philippians* (NIGTC; Grand Rapids: Eerdmans, 1991), p. 51.

well-being upon them that was not limited to physical health,[44] but one grounded in a 'peace' and 'well-being' from *his* god and lord, not one of the other gods beseeched by letter writers to bestow well-being upon their recipients.

In sum, just as Paul's modification of the obligatory prescript is primarily in terms of his particular theological aims, so also is his modification of the optional salutation. Not only has he departed from the verbal greeting formula in favor of the nouns χάρις and εἰρήνη, which have unambiguous (Jewish-Christian) religious overtones, but he places the source of his greeting in the realm of the supernatural—a quite uncanonical modification of the epistolary salutation. Paul's modification was probably influenced by both Jewish and Greco-Roman traditions (which, of course, were not alienated from one another), as well as his own 'Christian' experience. This is not a naive conflation of different cultures, but a recognition that Paul has consciously drawn from various registers to create his version of the epistolary salutation; it is perhaps the most clear case of his modification of epistolary traditions. Although a linguistically sensitive analysis of Paul's salutation would caution against reading theologically pregnant concepts[45] into what was often less meaningful to the communicative act—both the Greco-Roman and Jewish salutation could be used as a simple 'greeting'—Paul's undeniable modification of convention suggests a calculated effort on his part to communicate something unique at the beginning of his letters. Unless this salutation is part of a pre-Pauline Christian tradition which had become widespread in usage (which must have occurred early, since it occurs in all of Paul's letters), *Paul* created it and, although he probably employed more than one secretary,[46] demanded its use in all

---

44. The common epistolary wish for the physical well-being of the recipient is noticeably absent from Paul's letters. In addition, terms for health such as ὑγιαίνω and ὑγιής, although found throughout the Gospels (esp. John's), are absent from the accepted Pauline letters; only the Pastorals use the word, and there it is not used of physical well-being but of 'healthy, sound' teaching and conduct (1 Tim. 1.10; 6.3; 2 Tim. 1.13; Tit. 1.9, 13; 2.1, 2, 8).

45. It seems unadvisable, for example, to read all of O'Brien's Old Testament and New Testament concepts of 'peace' into Paul's salutation (*Philippians*, p. 51)—perhaps a case of illegitimate totality transfer.

46. Paul at least employed secretaries in Romans (16.22, the only reference to the name of a secretary), 1 Corinthians (16.21), Galatians (6.11), and Philemon (19); cf. Col. 4.18; 2 Thess. 3.17; see E.R. Richards, *The Secretary in the Letters of Paul* (WUNT, 2.42; Tübingen: Mohr–Siebeck, 1991), pp. 169-76. If Tertius was the

his letters (demonstrating, at least in part, his control over the content and style of his letters). It was an essential component of the structure of his letters; and it again demonstrates that Paul chose to modify canonical epistolary conventions to one degree or another. We might, therefore, anticipate similar modifications elsewhere.

Disclosure and Requests/Petitions (1.12-26)

Whereas the salutation of Paul's letters are often treated by commentators in terms of epistolary language, his 'disclosures' (and their concomitant 'requests') typically receive little or no treatment with respect to their similarities to and differences from standard convention. The disclosure and requests found in Phil. 1.12-26 provide several examples of how Paul changes conventional language for his own ideological and rhetorical agenda.

The example of prayer cited in *P.Mich.* VIII 491 (II CE) may serve as an introduction to the next epistolary convention used in Philippians, a disclosure formula with associated requests. After mentioning his prayers to the gods, Apollinarios remarks that he wants his mother to know about his safe arrival in Rome (lines 4-5 γεινώσκειν σε θέλω, μήτηρ, ὅτι...).[47] Similarly, in Phil. 1.12 Paul discloses information to the Philippians about his personal situation and well-being: γινώσκειν δὲ ὑμᾶς βούλομαι, ἀδελφοί, ὅτι τὰ κατ' ἐμὲ μᾶλλον εἰς προκοπὴν τοῦ εὐαγγελίου ἐλήλυθεν 'I want you to know, brothers and sisters, that my situation has come about for the advance of the gospel'.[48] He

secretary of all of Paul's letters—travelling with the Pauline mission—mention of him in one of the other letters might be expected, since Paul is not slow to make note of his co-workers.

47. For other examples near the time of Paul, see e.g. *P.Oxy.* IV 743.27-28 (2 BCE) ἂν τοῦτό σε θέλω γεινώσκειν ὅτι; *P.Oxy.* IV 744.3 (1 BCE) γίνωσκε ὡς...; *P.Koeln.* I 56.3 (I CE) γινώσκιν σε θέλω ὅτι...; *P.Mich.* VIII 464.3-4 (99 CE) γινώσκιν σε θέλω ὅτι...

48. For examples in or near the opening, see Rom. 1.13; 2 Cor. 1.8; Phil. 1.12. J.T. Sanders ('The Transition from Opening Epistolary Thanksgiving to Body in the Letters of the Pauline Corpus', *JBL* 81 [1962], pp. 348-62) and T.Y. Mullins ('Disclosure: A Literary Form in the New Testament', *NovT* 7 [1964], pp. 44-50) conclude that Paul's disclosures signal the end of the thanksgiving section. J.H. Roberts ('Pauline Transitions to the Letter Body', in A. Vanhoye [ed.], *L'Apôtre Paul: Personnalité, style et conception du ministère* [Leuven: Leuven University Press/ Peeters, 1986], pp. 93-99, esp. p. 98) adds to the disclosure other transitional devices: (1) 1.10 eschatological climax and (2) 1.11 doxology. For disclosures in the body of Paul's letters, see Rom. 11.25; 1 Cor. 10.1; 11.3; 12.1; 1 Thess. 4.13.

narrates his situation in vv. 12-26, mostly discussing the preaching of the gospel which resulted from his imprisonment and debating whether he wants to die and be with Christ or to live and further serve the Philippians. The importance of informing friends and family about one's own situation is revealed, for example, in *P.Yale* I 42.5-9 (229 BCE), in which the letter writer complains that he is anxious because up until the present he has heard nothing about the situation of the recipient (τὰ κατά σε).[49] In Phil. 1.27–2.18, Paul then turns to petition the Philippians with respect to their conduct. He uses his own immediate story and a story about Christ as a means to exhort them.

Epistolary formulas disclosing information often take one of the following three forms: γέγραφα οὖν ὅπως... ('I write so that you may know...'), γίνωσκε (ἴσθε, μάθε) ὅτι (ὡς)... ('Know that...') and γινώσκειν σε θέλω ὅτι... ('I want you to know that...').[50] All three formulas primarily serve the task of disclosing information and often, especially in brief letters, supply the 'explanation of the reason for writing'.[51] T.Y. Mullins lists four elements of the third type of disclosure formula: (1) θέλω 'to desire, wish', (2) noetic verb in the infinitive, (3) person addressed, and (4) information.[52] J.L. White lists the lexical choices often found in the formula:

> (i) the verb of disclosure, often a two-membered unit consisting of a verb of desiring (θέλω or βούλομαι) in the first person indicative, and the verb of knowing (γινώσκω) in the infinitive form; (ii) the vocative of address (ἀδελφοί, 'brothers', in the five examples from Paul); and (iii) the subject to be disclosed introduced by ὅτι.[53]

Phil. 1.12 is the only one which has βούλομαι with γινώσκειν. With respect to the other letters, 1 Cor. 11.3 θέλω δὲ ὑμᾶς εἰδέναι ὅτι... is stated in the positive (cf. *P.Hamb.* II 192.17-18 [III BCE] εἰδέναι δέ σε θέλω ὅτι...; PSI XII 1259.4 [II-III CE] εἰδέναι σε θέλω ὅτι...); the remainder in the negative (e.g. Rom. 1.13 οὐ θέλω δὲ ὑμᾶς ἀγνοεῖν, ἀδελφοί, ὅτι...; cf. *P.Cair.Zen.* III 59530.1 [III BCE] οὐκ οἶμαί σε ἀγνοεῖν διότι...; *P.Brem.* I 6.3 [II CE] οὐκ οἶμαι ἀγνοεῖν σε ὅτι...).

49. ἐμοῦ σοι γεγραφότος πλέονας ἐπιστολὰς καὶ οὐθέμ μοι παρὰ σοῦ τί μοι προσπεφώνται, τὸ πλέον ἀγνιῶν ἔνεκα τοῦ μηδ᾽ ἕως τοῦ νῦν ἀκηκοέναι τὰ κατά σε.

50. For further discussion and examples, see J.L.White, *Light from Ancient Letters* (Philadelphia: Fortress Press, 1986), pp. 204-205, 207-208.

51. White, *Light*, p. 207.

52. Mullins, 'Disclosure', p. 46.

53. J.L. White, 'Introductory Formulae in the Body of the Pauline Letter', *JBL* 90 (1971), pp. 91-97, esp. p. 93.

This longer, more polite, form of disclosure is common in private letters, whereas the imperative form (γίνωσκε) is typical of business letters. Phil. 1.12 follows the polite form; only Paul's use of βούλομαι, rather than the more typical θέλω, stands out, but is probably of little functional significance.[54] The actual content of Paul's disclosure is that his circumstances (viz. his imprisonment) have resulted in the advancement of the gospel. His situation has had two consequences (ὥστε): (1) v. 13, the gospel has been brought to those in charge of his imprisonment (and the 'rest'?) and (2) v. 14, others have been emboldened to preach the gospel. Paul then notes that not everyone is proclaiming the gospel out of sincere motives—some (probably Christians) do it apparently to increase Paul's troubles; yet he still rejoices because Christ is being proclaimed. At the end of v. 18, Paul makes a transition (ἀλλὰ καὶ χαρήσομαι...γάρ...) into a discussion about his possible σωτηρία: οἶδα...ὅτι τοῦτό μοι ἀποβήσεται εἰς σωτηρίαν (v. 19). The string of prepositional phrases and a ὅτι clause in vv. 19-20, seemingly cluttered, modifies (directly or indirectly) this main clause.

Despite Paul's difficult clause structure, interpretations of what he means here have focused on the possible semantics of σωτηρία.[55] Two basic interpretations predominate, one emphasizing the theological background of the term (eschatological salvation) and the other pointing to its typical epistolary function (rescue from danger).[56] In support of the former reading, O'Brien points to the exact parallel of the expression ἀποβήσεται εἰς σωτηρίαν in Job 13.16 LXX.[57] Job seeks vindica-

54. For use of βούλομαι rather than θέλω with a noetic verb, see e.g. *P.David* I 14.19-20 (II-III CE); *P.Koeln* V 238.2-3 (IV CE); *P.Oxy.* XLVIII 3399.3 (IV CE); *P.Oxy.* LVI 3862.6-7 (IV-V CE); *P.Stras.* I 35.2-3 (IV-V CE).

55. Unless strong evidence can be proffered, τοῦτο should be taken with its nearest co-textual cohesive tie, viz. the demonstrative pronoun in 1.18 ἐν τούτῳ which itself refers to the ongoing proclamation of Christ (with sincere and insincere motives); *contra* O'Brien (*Philippians*, p. 109) who takes it back to 1.12.

56. O'Brien (*Philippians*, p. 109) lists various options: 'rescue from captivity, preservation of the apostle's life, triumph over his enemies, the salvation (and conversion) of many people, the eternal messianic redemption, or, in general terms, whatever will be salutary for Paul'.

57. This Old Testament parallel is quite clear since (1) Paul only uses the verb ἀποβαίνω here (cf. Lk. 21.13 where it also has the sense of 'result' rather than movement away from) and (2) this verb is rare in the papyri and never used in conjunction with σωτηρία. Yet there is the possibility that this expression represents a Jewish idiom, rather than a conscious use of Scripture (C.D. Stanley, *Paul and the*

tion in the 'heavenly court'; so also, Paul seeks salvation based on God's judgment. However, it is not the function of Job's statements in their context that necessarily determines Paul's usage, but how Paul seeks to incorporate this subtext into his own discourse. And since Paul's usage is what is at issue, the Job parallel proves indeterminate. Indeed, O'Brien can use it to support his eschatological interpretation of σωτηρία and Hawthorne can use it to support his physical interpretation.[58] Paul's use of the noun in his other letters, including Philippians (Rom. 1.16; 10.1, 10; 11.11; 13.11; 2 Cor. 1.6; 6.2; 7.10; Phil. 1.28;[59] 2.12; 1 Thess. 5.8, 9), would suggest that σωτηρία in Phil. 1.19 implies eschatological salvation, that is, deliverance from wrath (Rom. 5.9; 1 Cor. 3.15; 5.5; 1 Thess. 1.10; 5.9) and reception of eternal glory (Rom. 8.18-30; 2 Thess. 2.13, 14).[60] However, in epistolary contexts such as this one, σωτηρία regularly implies the physical welfare (e.g. rescue from the dangers of a sea-voyage) either of the sender or the recipients (cf. 2 Macc. 1.11).[61] R. MacMullen notes that the same is true

---

Language of Scripture: Citation Technique in the Pauline Epistles and Contemporary Literature [SNTSMS, 74; Cambridge: Cambridge University Press, 1992], p. 67 n. 8); thus, appeal to its original context for understanding Paul's use may be misleading.

58. O'Brien, *Philippians*, p. 110, and Hawthorne, *Philippians*, p. 40.

59. Even G.F. Hawthorne ('The Interpretation and Translation of Philippians 1.28b', *ExpTim* 95 [1983], pp. 80-81), who reads σωτηρία in 1.19 as physical deliverance, interprets it as 'salvation of your souls' in 1.28, even though his unique reading of 1.28b would allow for a non-eschatological reading.

60. So O'Brien, *Philippians*, p. 110; D.E. Garland, 'Philippians 1:1-26: The Defense and Confirmation of the Gospel', *RevExp* 77 (1980), pp. 327-36, esp. p. 333; T.F. Dailey, 'To Live or Die: Paul's Eschatological Dilemma in Philippians 1.19-26', *Int* 44 (1990), pp. 18-28, esp. p. 20; M. Silva, *Philippians* (Baker Exegetical Commentary on the New Testament; Grand Rapids: Baker Book House, 1992), pp. 76-78; I.H. Marshall, *The Epistle to the Philippians* (Epworth Commentaries; London: Epworth Press, 1991), p. 24; so also the author of the Latin (translation?) letter to the Laodiceans (late II CE?), who recites Philippians at several points, translates 1.12 with *vita aeterna*.

61. Cf. L. Alexander, 'Hellenistic Letter-Forms and the Structure of Philippians', *JSNT* 37 (1989), pp. 87-101, esp. p. 96. The majority of epistolary uses of σωτηρία are in reference to the welfare (e.g. health, safety) of the recipient (σωτηρία σου) or other family members and friends (e.g. *P.Mich.* VIII 490.12-14 [II CE] καὶ σὺ δὲ μὴ ὄκνει {ωκνι} γράφιν περὶ τῆς σωτηρίας σου καὶ τῆς τῶν ἀδελφῶν μου); however, for an example which concerns the σωτηρία of the letter writer, see the same letter *P.Mich.* VIII 490.6-7 (II CE) ἀνάγκην {ανανκην} ἔσχον σοι

of 'salvific' terms in inscriptions: ' "Savior" in them [inscriptions], or 'salvation', had to do with health or other matters of this earth, not of the soul for life eternal'.[62] Furthermore, the idea that a person's well-being is dependent upon one's own and others' prayers to the gods has been mentioned above with respect to epistolary thanksgivings and prayers; similarly, Paul also attributes his σωτηρία to the δέησις of the Philippians and the provision of the Spirit (1.19).

Consequently, the debate over the meaning of σωτηρία in Phil. 1.19 raises linguistic issues regarding the influence of syntagmatic and para-digmatic choices on word meanings. Scholars have typically focused on paradigmatic choices (i.e. the choices available to him in his mental lexicon) that were at Paul's linguistic disposal (competence) when he used σωτηρία. But if syntagmatic choices (viz. the epistolary context) are taken with equal seriousness, then the interpretation of σωτηρία as 'physical well-being, safety' in Phil. 1.19 is more credible. I find it dif-ficult to believe that Paul, who so far has appeared to be very aware of his epistolary style, would fail to see the connection between his use of σωτηρία and epistolary usage. But as has already been noted, Paul is capable of modifying epistolary convention (especially for ideological reasons), and this is what he has apparently done here. That σωτηρία does not simply mean 'physical rescue' in 1.19 is most evidenced by the final phrase in v. 20: εἴτε διὰ ζωῆς εἴτε διὰ θανάτου—Paul clearly allows for the possibility of his death, regardless of his personal expec-tations.[63] The 'rescue' he envisions is not limited to his mortal life.[64]

δηλῶσαι περὶ τῆς σωτηρίας μου; cf. PSI IV 392.5 τῆς σωτηρίας ἡμῶν (242-41 BCE). Request for information about the recipient's σωτηρία is often combined with a promise to take care of whatever the recipient needs, as in *P.Mich.* III 212.9-11 (II-III CE) γράφε μοι, κύριε, σὺν [τ]οῖς ἑτ[έ]ροις περὶ τῆς σωτηρίας σου καὶ περὶ ὧν χρήζεις ἀπ' ἐμοῦ. Personal correspondence often comprised these two elements: information about well-being (σωτηρία) and request for goods and services (χρεῖαι).

62. R. MacMullen, *Paganism in the Roman Empire* (New Haven, CT: Yale University Press, 1981), p. 57.

63. In a mostly convincing reading of σωτηρία as physical deliverance, H.A.A. Kennedy ('The Historical Background of the Philippians', *ExpTim* 10 [1898–99], pp. 22-24, here pp. 23-24), however, fails to account for the apparent implications of this prepositional phrase. R.R. Reeves ('To Be or Not to Be? That is Not the Question: Paul's Choice in Philippians 1.22', *Perspectives in Religious Studies* 19 [1992], pp. 273-89, esp. p. 286), who also adopts the interpretation of physical deliverance, gets around this problem by interpreting 'whether by life or by death'

Paul makes the qualification in v. 20, that is, that whether he lives or
dies Christ shall be magnified through him, so as to redirect the implied
epistolary reader's mental script (i.e. the way in which they typically
interpret σωτηρία language) in a way that challenges their need for
deliverance from physical sufferings—and what more striking way to
do this than to manipulate conventions of language probably familiar to
the reader. Paul is less ambiguous about the meaning of σωτηρία in
1.28-30: God's salvation (v. 28 σωτηρία) does not preclude suffering
(v. 29 πάσχειν) in the Christian's life. Clearly σωτηρία here does not
imply physical rescue, which would not serve Paul's ensuing argument
that 'suffering' is fundamental to Christian existence. In 1.19, Paul
seeks a σωτηρία that is not solely based on physical deliverance but on
eschatological vindication;[65] the Philippians should adopt the same
attitude toward 'suffering' that he has (1.30).

The remainder of Paul's disclosure develops out of the last phrase of
Phil. 1.20, that is, he desires to die and be with Christ but also to remain
and serve the Philippians (1.21-26). This eventually becomes a travel-

metaphorically, i.e. 'dying' means staying in prison; but the context does not prompt
a metaphorical reading and his appeal to 2 Cor. 1.9-10 could just as well support a
'physical death' interpretation of Phil. 1.20. Furthermore, his claim that Paul's
absence/presence language in 1.27 'is inexplicable if the apostle believed that he
was going to die in prison' (p. 288 n. 96) is unwarranted if Paul is simply referring
to his receipt of news about them *while he is still in prison*. Reeves's larger
argument that Paul here is debating whether or not to use the Philippians' monetary
gift as a bribe to secure his release, while plausible (Acts 24.26), requires reading
much into the text that is not explicitly stated.

    64. τοῦτο in v. 19 probably refers back to the activity of those who preach
Christ so as to afflict Paul. Their activity will result in Paul's ultimate vindication
(salvation) before God, since he, like Job, is innocent.

    65. Cf. Garland, 'Defense', p. 333. 2 Tim. 4.10-18, whether it is Pauline or not,
provides a comparable intertextual reading of how I interpret Paul's statement here.
Paul, in his defence of the gospel in prison, is confronted by two sets of *Christians*—one supporting him and the other not. Thus, he has been deserted in his imprisonment. He expects God to rescue him, in spite of the possibility that ultimately
he may die. His rescue is one that will bring him into the heavenly kingdom. Cf.
C. Clemen, *Die Einheitlichkeit der paulinischen Briefe an der Hand der bisher mit
Bezug auf sie aufgestellten Interpolations- und Compilationshypothesen* (Göttingen:
Vandenhoeck & Ruprecht, 1894), p. 141, who notes a possible historical connection
between 2 Tim. 4.9-15 and Paul's earlier letter (A) to the Philippians.

ogue statement in v. 26 (διὰ τῆς ἐμῆς παρουσίας πάλιν πρὸς ὑμᾶς).[66] The rhetorical importance of such statements in Paul's letters has already been noted in the above treatment of prayer formulas. It remains here to note that letter writers sometimes discuss their travel plans in relation to their circumstances. For example, in *P.Mich.* III 203 (98-117 CE), the author Saturnilus uses a disclosure formula (γεινώσκειν σε θέλω ὅτι...) to reveal that he has not had an opportunity to visit since he was last there (line 8) and then he employs another disclosure formula to reveal that he may not be able to visit again for some time (line 13). On the one hand, letter writers such as Paul seem obliged to make known their future travel plans; on the other hand, the same letter writers often apologize for previous and future failures to visit. Much of Paul's travel language is paralleled in the non-literary papyri;[67] Mullins is not exaggerating when he claims that non-literary papyri 'are full of visit talk'.[68] Paul's use of μένω-terms in 1.24-25, παρουσία in 1.26, and the participles ἐλθών, ἰδών, ἀπών in 1.27 are all common terms of 'visit talk' in personal letters.[69]

Regarding the structure of this section, the use of requests after a disclosure formula may illuminate the function and location of 1.27-30, as well as the additional exhortations in 2.1-18. L. Alexander has rightly pointed out the petitionary beginning at 1.27 and that the clause ἵνα...ἀκούω τὰ περὶ ὑμῶν may be 'an implied request for news'.[70] The exhortations of 2.1-18, signaled by οὖν, would then represent Paul's new petitions to the Philippians. In other words, 1.27-30 (a petition following a disclosure) addresses their immediate situation, and 2.1-18

66. On the concept of παρουσία in letters, see K. Thraede, *Grundzüge griechisch-römischer Brieftopic* (Munich: Beck, 1970), pp. 146-56.

67. For a formal study which gives more attention to epistolary literature than Funk's notion of 'Apostolic Parousia', see T.Y. Mullins, 'Visit Talk in New Testament Letters', *CBQ* 35 (1973), pp. 350-58.

68. Mullins, 'Visit Talk', p. 352.

69. Besides the examples in Mullins, see BGU XIV 2420.2-3 (I BCE) προσμένω τὴν παρουσίαν σοῦ; *P.Oxy.* XLVIII 3357.7-8 (I CE) ἀναμεῖναι τὴν Φανίου παρουσίαν; *P.Oxy.* LVI 3852.17-18 (II CE) ἡ σὴ παρουσία ἔσται ἡμεῖν; *P.Oxy.* IV 744.5. (1 BCE) ἐγὼ ἐν Ἀλεξανδρε<ί>α μένω; CPR VII 55.7-8 (II CE) παραμένω ἐν τῆι οἰκίαι; *P.Leit.* I 5.6 (c. 180 CE) σ[οῦ] ἀπών; SB VI 9228.5 (160 CE) ὁ Πάστωρ ἀπών; PSI XII 1241.19-21 (159 CE) ἐλθὼν ἀνθομολογηθῇ μοι περὶ τῆς εὐστ[α]θείας ὑμῶν; *P.Oxy.* IX 1215.2 (II-III CE) καλῶς {αλως} ποιήσεις {πυησις} ἐλθὼν πρὸς ἐμέ {αιμαι}.

70. Alexander, 'Letter-Forms', pp. 95-96.

brings to bear new exhortations. Throughout this entire section (1.12–2.18) Paul's own situation—the content of the initial disclosure formula—is a recurrent topic (1.13, 17, 20-26, 30; 2.12, 17). His situation is interwoven with exhortations to the Philippians. The combination of a disclosure formula and petitions is a useful epistolary strategy, obviously because letter writers would want to reveal their own situation, reiterate previous commands, address the immediate situation of the recipients, and add any new commands that require their attention.

J.L. White has identified three main parts to epistolary petitions (and requests): (1) *background*, in which the petitioner recites the circumstances which necessitate the request; (2) *request*; and (3) *acknowledgment* that the letter writer will be benefited if the request is fulfilled.[71] These can be discussed briefly. (1) White observes that 'in letters where request is only one of the functions in the body, the "background" is often omitted as a formal element. It is functionally present, however, in ἵνα, ὅπως and γάρ clauses which follow the request and provide explanation of it.'[72] Similarly, Paul's initial πολιτεύεσθε request is explained by the following ἵνα clause, that is, his request is based on his desire to receive future news of their steadfastness (v. 27) and fearlessness (v. 28). More than that, however, the disclosure about Paul's situation in prison serves as a background to his petitions in 1.27-30; he uses his own situation as an example for the conduct of the Philippians. This background–petition structure in Philippians may be explained in terms of epistolary literature; so White notes that 'the initial disclosure may serve…as background information to justify the request'.[73] Lastly, there is no inherent epistolary reason why a letter may only make one request or petition; thus, Paul's multiple exhortations are not entirely unconventional. In *P.Mich.* III 203 (98-117 CE), after using four disclosure formulas, the author makes five different requests—take care of my pigs; send allowance to Julas; send his brother to me; send olives; write to me concerning Julius—before closing the letter with greetings. Obviously, that which makes Paul's petitions stand out is their moral

---

71. White, *Light*, p. 204; see also his more detailed treatment *The Form and Structure of the Official Petition: A Study in Greek Epistolography* (SBLDS, 5; Missoula, MT: Scholars Press, 1972), although this mainly treats official and administrative petitions. Personal letters sometimes employ a simple imperative to make a request.

72. White, *Light*, p. 204.

73. White, *Light*, p. 198.

character. (2) Paul uses two clearly marked linguistic transitions to begin his two sets of requests/petitions: 1.27 μόνον[74] and 2.1 οὖν.[75] Yet the transition to 1.27 is still stated in the context of his travelogue. In other words, Paul's initial set of petitions is occasioned by the travelogue discussion. Paul wants the Philippians to 'conduct themselves' or 'exercise their citizenship' in a manner worthy of the gospel,[76] whether or not he is able to visit them. In *P.Oxy.* III 532.10-18 (II CE), the letter writer warns that if a payment is not made at once then he will have to come in person and dispute over it: ἀναγκαίως οὖν τῷ ἀναδιδόντι {αναδιδουντι} σοι τὸ ἐπιστόλιον τοῦτο εὐθέως ἀπόδος...ὅρα οὖ<ν> μὴ ἄλλως πράξῃς καὶ ποιήσῃς με πρὸς σε ἐλθεῖν συνζητήσοντα σοι.[77] Paul, in contrast, does not want their conduct to be motivated by a potential visit. (3) Lastly, at the end of Paul's second set of petitions, he perhaps states his *acknowledgment* of the benefit he will receive if the Philippians carry out his petitions: specifically, their obedience will result in καύχημα ἐμοὶ εἰς ἡμέραν Χριστοῦ because οὐκ εἰς κενὸν ἔδραμον οὐδὲ εἰς κενὸν ἐκοπίασα (2.16).

In sum, the requests are closely tied in a structural way to Paul's disclosure of his situation—the two work together. It was perfectly natural for Paul to make requests of his recipients in an epistolary context; this is not something that differentiates his letter-writing style. However, Paul, as is typical of his modification of epistolary convention, composes his requests so as to serve his own religious purposes (in contrast to the seemingly mundane 'Send me some olives, mother'). That is, the rhetoric behind his requests seeks moral and ethical change in his readers.

In conclusion, Paul changes the language of epistolary convention to

---

74. On the use of μόνον with an imperative, see LSJ s.v. μόνος B.II.

75. White (*Light*, p. 204) notes that οὖν is one of the conjunctions used to connect a request to a background. Accordingly, the petitions beginning at 2.1 probably follow from the petitions and situations stated in 1.27-30; this understanding is supported by Paul's use of the imperative πληρώσατε. Paul will be pleased if they carry out the petitions of 1.27-30, but his joy will be made complete if they carry out the ensuing petitions.

76. For various interpretations of πολιτεύεσθε, see T.C. Geoffrion, *The Rhetorical Purpose and the Political and Military Character of Philippians: A Call to Stand Firm* (Lewiston, NY: Edwin Mellen Press, 1993), pp. 42-48, who defines it in political terms.

77. For epistolary formulas used to summon responsible action, see White, 'Formulas', pp. 305-307.

serve his own communicative goals. His disclosure is used to narrate his own situation in order later to exhort the Philippians to behave in the same way. In other words, Paul's modification of epistolary convention may be summarized in the statement that *he discloses information about himself and then uses this for paraenetic purposes.*[78] In addition, the mention of his 'safety' (σωτηρία) in the context of his disclosure, as is common in epistolary literature, is not limited to a physical, earthly rescue—the type his audience was seeking—but an eschatological, salvific rescue.

Summary

We have only investigated Paul's changing of language in two epistolary conventions in Philippians—the prescript and the disclosure/ requests. Much more could be said about the letter as a whole in terms of language change, but the following summary of language change in Philippians, which stems from my more detailed discourse analysis of Philippians,[79] must suffice here.

In the prescript, Paul employs 'Christian' religious language (δοῦλοι Χριστοῦ Ἰησοῦ...τοῖς ἁγίοις) to establish the current relationships between the communicants, in contrast to the familial and friendship expansions found in most prescripts of personal letters. In the salutation, he departs from the verbal greeting formula (χαίρειν) in favour of the nouns χάρις and εἰρήνη, which have unambiguous religious overtones (Jewish and Christian); in addition, the source of his greeting involves the supernatural—a quite unconventional modification of the epistolary salutation. In the thanksgiving, (1) Paul gives thanks to only *one* god (a Jewish one at that) who is identified in relation to himself (θεῷ μου) and (2) Paul thanks his god for the 'moral' (or 'spiritual') welfare of his recipients,[80] that is, their participation in the gospel (both

78. So P. Wick (*Der Philipperbrief: Der formale Aufbau des Briefs als Schlüssel zum Verständnis seines Inhalts* [BWANT, 135; Stuttgart: Kohlhammer, 1994], p. 158) rightly claims, 'Paulus seine Selbstdarstellung ebenfalls dazu benutzt, um damit den Philippern ein Beispiel für die Paränese zu geben'; for example, 'Für Seneca ist der Tod die höchst mögliche Form der vorbildlichen Selbstdarstellung. Auch für Paulus ist seine mögliche Hinrichtung ein Weg, ein Vorbild der Gesinnung Christi für die Philipper zu sein.'

79. See J.T. Reed, *A Discourse Analysis of Philippians: Method and Rhetoric in the Debate over Literary Integrity* (JSNTSup, 136; Sheffield: Sheffield Academic Press, 1997), Chapter 4.

80. Cf. White, *Light*, p. 20: 'Though Paul never cites the conventional wish for

experientially and in practice), rather than their physical or material welfare. In the disclosure formula, Paul narrates his own situation in order later to exhort (petition/request) the Philippians to behave in the same way. In the commendations (2.19-30), Paul's use of epistolary forms is both conventional (i.e. he commends Timothy and Epaphroditus into the care of the Philippians) and modified (i.e. he sets up at least one of the commended persons, Epaphroditus, as a model of moral imitation). In the final set of petitions/requests (4.2-9), after his initial petitions to individuals in vv. 2-3, Paul turns to more general, ethical requests, rather than the typical business and personal ones (so most papyri), using mostly 'religious' language to do so (v. 3 ἐν βίβλῳ; v. 4 χαίρετε ἐν κυρίῳ; v. 5 ὁ κύριος ἐγγύς; v. 6 prayer terminology). In the 'joy' expression (4.10-20), Paul's adaptation of convention is not to be found in a 'thankless thanks' but in his method of repaying the Philippians for their gift, that is, God is the one who will take care of their every need (χρεία) and he is the one to whom praise is to be given (4.19-20). Paul found nothing theologically objectionable in the standard convention of closing greetings; hence, we find no divergence from most other letters. In the closing grace wish, Paul almost entirely abandons epistolary convention (i.e. he chooses to 'reject' epistolary convention); his grace wish contrasts with the typical closing 'farewell' in which the author shows concern for the well-being of the recipient, although it still retains the function of concluding the communicative act and maintaining social relationships with the recipients. Paul, like the Gospel writers, is unmistakably engaged in a process of not only reusing traditional generic forms but also rewriting them for his own religio-rhetorical ends.

I would propose that what is happening in much of Paul's use of epistolary convention is linguistic variation, that is, Paul is or has already been changing his Pharisaic[81] Greek dialect as well as his local

health, he does express his concern for his recipients' welfare; his concern is not with ordinary well-being, but with his recipients' spiritual conformity to the standards of a new spiritual age'.

81. Based on Phil. 3.5 and Acts 26.4-5, I conclude that Paul at least received the majority of his Pharisaic upbringing in Jerusalem, wherein he would acquire a variety of language which is referred to here as 'Pharisaic', for the lack of a better word. On a broader level, this dialect might be related to that of Palestinian Greek, but I would still assert that Paul's Pharisaic enculturation would also have had a particular influence on his linguistic capabilities.

Hellenistic dialect (a Tarsian dialect?) and standard Greek dialect (typically referred to as Hellenistic or Koine Greek, though its existence as an autonomous code might be challenged on the grounds mentioned above) so as to communicate his own ideology on certain religious matters.[82] Or, to recall the above analysis, *global counteradaptivity is a result of local adaptivity, explaining the enduring power of linguistic diversity in human cultures.* On the one hand, Paul must diverge from his Pharisaic dialect, including certain words and perhaps 'ways of saying' things for essentially two reasons: (1) he may disagree ideologically with the meaning of some of the language, and (2) the dialect might incorrectly convey the intended meaning to the audience. If (2) is the reason, then Paul is actually converging his Pharisaic dialect towards his Hellenistic dialect. On the other hand, Paul must diverge from his Hellenistic dialect (or that of his audience, which may or may not have been the same), because it may conflict ideologically and ethically with those parts of his Pharisaic dialect that he upholds, or with his own *idiolect* (the unique particularities of his dialect or features found in a 'Christian' dialect). This dialect of divergence and convergence thus creates another dialect which might be called a 'Christian dialect', but at least for our purposes may be referred to as the dialect of the text in this study—'Paul's dialect':

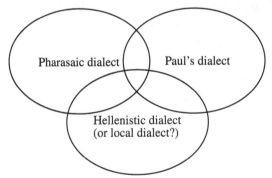

Though this diagram may be overly simplistic, it at least captures two of the dialects which Paul probably learned growing up in Tarsus and

82. White (*Light*, p. 19) has made a similar claim about Pauline epistolary style, but without discussing the sociolinguistic implications: 'The Apostle Paul appears to be the Christian leader who was responsible for first introducing Christian elements into the epistolary genre and for adapting existing epistolary conventions to express the special interests of the Christian community'.

being educated in Jerusalem (if, of course, Luke is historically accurate) and which were at play in the development of his own use of language as a new member of the 'Christian' movement. The overlapping sections represent 'code' or 'language' shared in common (what would typically represent the 'standard language'). The other sections are not shared by the other varieties of language because either (1) the language users have consciously rejected elements of the other variety's lexicogrammar for ideological or phonological (naturalness) reasons, or (2) the language users are unaware of those elements of the other variety's lexico-grammar. In the case of those epistolary elements of Hellenistic Greek studied here, it becomes clear that Paul, although aware of standard convention, elects to depart from convention for various ideological purposes.

From an exclusively epistolary point of view, Paul is expected by the standard language to adopt conventional practice. He is, however, also pressured to conform to other dialects familiar to him (Jewish and Christian), even when these diverge from the standard language (the principle of local adaptivity). He is also faced by the dilemma of global counteradaptivity at the risk of being rejected by his audience (who expect the standard language). From a sociolinguistic perspective, although 'there are social pressures that promote standard dialects, there must also be counter-pressures favoring the local, the informal and the vernacular in speech'.[83] Though Paul is pressured to conform to the standard dialect, sociolinguistic studies have demonstrated that 'all social strata, not just the empowered stratum [the standard dialect creators and users], feel the need to assert their linguistic identity'.[84] By altering the standard convention to conform to the ideology underlying his local dialect, Paul is placing pressure on his readers to conform to his dialect, and hence the ideology that comes with speaking in a certain way. That is, linguistic variation for Paul is a powerful tool for 'evangelism'. Paul's language (discourse) of ideological and behavioural change is in part accomplished by changing language.[85]

---

83. Chambers, *Theory*, p. 221.

84. Chambers, *Theory*, p. 252.

85. An interesting corrolary of this is that whereas subjects of sociolinguistic studies repeatedly assign status qualities of intelligence, education, wealth, success and achievement to speakers of a standard language (E.B. Ryan, 'Why Do Low-Prestige Language Varieties Persist?', in H. Giles and R. St Clair [eds.], *Language and Social Psychology* [Oxford: Basil Blackwell, 1979], p. 151), Paul, the standard-

Therefore, I wish to argue here that Paul is attempting to create a standard 'Christian' (albeit his version of 'Christianity') dialect. A dialect becomes the standard one because its speakers possess various powers—economic, military, political, spiritual.[86] If Paul's dialect becomes the norm, then all of the cultural baggage that is inseparably linked with it also becomes the norm. Perhaps herein lies the key motivation behind the gradual canonization of Paul's letters and, indeed, Paul's original motivation for 'writing' to his churches rather than simply sending oral messengers—the perpetuation of a linguistic standard requires codification. In modern society,

> the accumulation of dictionaries, grammars, usage guides, spellers...and readers forms an educational base for preparing future generations of standard bearers. It also forms a bedrock of authorized language in the event of linguistic challenges. Enshrining the standard dialect in print inhibits change as far as possible, although that is never very far.[87]

This may provide a partial explanation for Paul's letters being canonized in linguistic form, and yet can never prevent ecclesiastical diversity. While New Testament scholars typically recognize the need to investigate various social forces at play in the formation of Pauline churches, it is less obvious from the secondary literature that they have investigated how language per se may have been used as a tool for creating social identity in early Christianity. Along these lines, sociolinguistics has much to contribute to the New Testament scholar's study of the sociology of early Christianity.

Conclusion

This study has drawn from sociolinguistic studies of language variation, which maintain that *linguistic variation* in speech communities (both regional and standard dialects) is the direct result of sociological forces. The goal has been to demonstrate this axiom at work in one of Paul's letters at one level of language (conventions of the epistolary genre),

---

language deviant, frequently downplays such qualities in his letters. This is especially true in Philippians. Although impossible to prove causally, it is an interesting coincidence that Paul's ideology at least reflects his non-standard use of the epistolary genre.

86. Chambers, *Theory*, p. 251.
87. Chambers, *Theory*, p. 251.

suggesting that Paul changed the standard language so as to seek ideological and behavioural changes in his readers.

One overriding sociologically based cause for linguistic variation in Pauline discourse is to be found in Paul's missiology. Though always a Jew, Paul clearly moved beyond the Judaism he knew before his 'conversion' and 'calling'. He had to negotiate this Jewish Christianity with his conviction that he was called to the Gentiles, and his subsequent stance that Gentiles did not have to participate in the 'works of the law'[88] in order to remain in the community of God's people. In a sentence: the Gentiles could become (messianic) Jews without becoming entirely Jewish. Consequently, as a missionary seeking social change amongst Gentiles, Paul was faced with the problem of discoursing in a Jewish dialect (i.e. a language determined and created by various Jewish cultural norms) with non-Jewish peoples. To accomplish social change in his readership without losing them, so to speak, in the language, he had to change not only the language of Judaism but also the language of his readers. In other words, in grappling with the 'newness' of the Christ event for the people of God, Paul sought a new citizenship (Phil. 3.20)—a new society with its own dialect. Or, to recall Martinet's quotation at the beginning of this study, Paul was fighting for a 'Christian' identity for himself and his readers in an 'ocean of conflicting attractions'. But just as all dialects diverge from and converge with other dialects, Paul's new dialect was pulled in conflicting directions. If Paul does not at least speak on the fringes of his readers' dialect by using similar words and grammar, he risks being rejected as a complete outsider—'he doesn't speak like us!' Such a strategy would go against his missiological universalism (1 Cor. 9.19-23). To speak solely within his readers' dialect—complete convergence—would run the risk of not changing his readers' identity. Such a strategy would counter the theological motivation for Paul's missiology (Rom. 15.15-16; 1 Thess. 2.16). These conflicting forces underlie Paul's changing of epistolary convention in Philippians.

While not denying outright the existence of a Greek code (or standard dialect), this study has emphasized how a dialect (or variety of the stan-

---

88. While agreeing with Dunn that 'works of the law' primarily functions in Pauline rhetoric as designating legal ethnocentricity (see esp. the essays in his *Jesus, Paul and the Law: Studies in Mark and Galatians* [London: SPCK, 1990]), I do not doubt that Paul saw behind this some Jewish emphasis on personal attainment of righteousness.

dard dialect) diverges from and converges with the standard dialect, as well as other dialects. This *dialectic* of change and uniformity, it was argued above from sociolinguistic studies, is typically the result of sociological forces (e.g. gender, age, religion, occupation, status, and so on). Thus, when we discover linguistic variation from the norm (either the standard dialect or the localized dialect of the audience), we should seek to understand the sociological function behind Paul's (or any New Testament author's) changing of 'language'. Many more texts need to be analyzed to see if, and in what way, this thesis is true for other New Testament texts, as well as for other linguistic formulations (e.g. word meanings, grammatical choices, genre formation); indeed, I have only investigated one area of linguistic variation (changes in generic formulas). Beyond these limitations, it is worthwhile concluding with a question that challenges especially how studies of New Testament Greek grammar and linguistics (and, *a fortiori*, New Testament exegesis) should be carried out. In the light of the growing emphasis in sociolinguistics (as well as in psycholinguistics and discourse analysis) on the functional *use* of language, is it even possible to speak of the language of the New Testament—*langue*, to invoke Saussure, or competence, to beckon Chomsky—or is it only possible to investigate the dialectal varieties of Greek—*parole* or performance—found in the New Testament? Do we need grammars of New Testament Greek, rather than a single grammar? Or, to speak in more consequential terms, must we abandon the view of the homogeneity of New Testament linguistic communities and the exegetical conclusions based upon simplistic cross-referencing of New Testament passages? These questions are obviously stated in extreme terms, but they nonetheless raise sociolinguistic questions of the New Testament which have been typically ignored by New Testament exegetes, who all too often assume that all we need to know about Greek grammar and lexicography may be found in a handful of standard reference works.

SEMANTICS AND PATTERNS OF ARGUMENTATION IN THE BOOK OF ROMANS: DEFINITIONS, PROPOSALS, DATA AND EXPERIMENTS

Stanley E. Porter and Matthew Brook O'Donnell

1. *Introduction*

The semantics and patterns of argumentation in Romans raise a number of provocative questions, not least how it is that the semantic structure of this book forms the basis for its argumentative structure. We do not propose to ask, and much less to answer, all of these questions. Nevertheless, it seems that many of them are related to important broader questions regarding a linguistic interpretation of the New Testament. Several of these issues are here brought into the discussion, and a number of proposals and data-driven experiments are presented as ways forward for future research.

2. *Semantics*

a. *Historical Overview*
The initial question that must be asked regarding semantics in Romans is 'what is semantics?' Semantics is now a word that is quite frequently found and used in biblical studies. This came about probably first because of the widely invoked, yet still greatly under-used, work by James Barr, *The Semantics of Biblical Language.*[1] This was not only a clarion call to those in biblical studies that much of their linguistic method (if it could be called method) was flawed, but probably introduced the word 'semantics' as a technical concept that biblical scholars needed to be aware of. The path of Barr was followed and extended by the still important, yet rarely cited, work of Arthur Gibson, *Biblical*

---

1.   Oxford: Oxford University Press, 1961.

Semantic Logic.[2] For most New Testament scholars, however, the widespread use of the concept of semantics is probably attributable to a number of works that appeared in the 1980s, such as Moisés Silva's *Biblical Words and their Meaning*,[3] and the several works of Eugene Nida and Johannes Louw, including especially their *Greek–English Lexicon, Based on Semantic Domains.*[4]

Such widespread use of the word has not always been the case. This is certainly true of biblical studies, and, arguably more importantly, of modern linguistics. Semantics as a concept was first introduced into the discussion in 1897 by M. Breál in his work entitled (in English) *Semantics: Studies in the Science of Meaning*,[5] an exploration from a historical linguistic perspective. Nevertheless, semantics—concerned with a synchronic discussion of the meaningful structures in language—did not become a subject of significance in modern linguistics until the constituent analysis of the Bloomfield school had begun to fade and the issue of meaning in language was finally allowed to come to the fore. Since then, of course, the issue of meaning has become one of the major preoccupations of modern linguistics.[6]

Until a few years ago, however, the question of meaning in linguistics and biblical studies was answered in a fairly simple way. For linguists, as a heritage of logical positivism, meaning was often equated with a truth-conditional semantics.[7] A truth-conditional semantics is

2. Oxford: Basil Blackwell, 1981, soon to be reprinted by Sheffield Academic Press.

3. Grand Rapids: Zondervan, 1983, with a revised edition including one more essay, by a former student (Grand Rapids: Zondervan, 1994).

4. New York: United Bible Societies, 1988. A book that deserves to be better known is E.A. Nida and J.P. Louw, *Lexical Semantics of the Greek New Testament* (SBLRBS, 25; Atlanta: Scholars Press, 1992).

5. New York: Henry Holt, 1900, a translation of *Essai de sémantique*.

6. For a brief overview of the history and development of this issue in linguistics, see R.H. Robins, *A Short History of Linguistics* (London: Longmans, 2nd edn, 1979), pp. 203-12, 220-32; cf. G. Sampson, *Schools of Linguistics* (Stanford, CA: Stanford University Press, 1980), pp. 57-80; P.H. Matthews, *Grammatical Theory in the United States from Bloomfield to Chomsky* (Cambridge Studies in Linguistics, 67; Cambridge: Cambridge University Press, 1993), esp. pp. 5-48.

7. See R. Kempson, *Semantic Theory* (CTL; Cambridge: Cambridge University Press, 1977), pp. 23-25; J. Lyons, *Semantics* (Cambridge: Cambridge University Press, 1977), pp. 167-73; cf. *idem, Language, Meaning and Context* (London: Collins, 1981), pp. 30-31 and passim.

based upon whether the proposition expressed by a given statement satisfies certain truth conditions. These truth conditions are often defined in terms of reference, that is, having knowledge of what it is that the sentence refers to. The result is that if two sentences satisfy the same truth conditions (in this instance, refer to the same thing) then they are synonymous; if they do not satisfy the same truth conditions, then they are not synonymous. This is essentially a word-based analysis, despite its rather lofty-sounding hypothetical configuration. At best it extends the analysable structure to the length of a sentence, the largest unit of assessment in most formalist linguistic models.

A similar kind of analysis has been practiced in New Testament studies. There are a number of works that will not be dealt with here, because they are probably not suitably or constructively discussed in this context.[8] Suffice it to say that the patterns described above are fairly typical for the ways that such topics are treated in New Testament studies. Most studies of semantics—until very recently—have been confined to the study of the meanings of individual words, or lexical semantics.[9] This is the case, for example, in Silva's important work, sub-titled *An Introduction to Lexical Semantics*. In this book, as one might expect, he deals with the various ways in which words are said or thought to mean. In a work on *biblical* semantics it is perhaps excusable that so much of the work (almost the first two thirds) is taken up with historical semantics, including discussion of the role and relationship of the Septuagint. The latter part covers what one might reasonably expect to find in a book on lexical semantics, what he calls descriptive semantics.

There are three comments worth making. The first is that, if anything, there is simply too little space devoted to the different topics, including consideration of what Silva terms 'style'. to address questions where units larger than the word enter into consideration. The second is that Silva presents what must be seen as a confusing notion of reference. His perspective comes closer to a 'naming' theory (which gives empha-

---

8.   See, for example, G.B. Caird, *The Language and Imagery of the Bible* (Philadelphia: Westminster Press, 1980); W. Egger, *How to Read the New Testament: An Introduction to Linguistic and Historical-Critical Methodology* (Peabody, MA: Hendrickson, 1996). Egger, however, confuses structuralism with text-linguistics.

9.   This is not to say that more should not be done in this area, and has been by, for example, D.A. Cruse, *Lexical Semantics* (CTL; Cambridge: Cambridge University Press, 1986). Others continue to develop grammars based around the word. See, for example, R. Hudson, *Word Grammar* (Oxford: Basil Blackwell, 1984).

sis to referentiality over sense relations) than he probably wishes it to, but he is apparently concerned to protect what he thinks is the objective nature of theological concepts. They become 'things' that can be referred to in the same way as 'this lectern' or 'that screen'. There is further confusion over the referring process, as if referentiality were a thing in itself rather than a function of users of language, with the further consequence that he invokes a rather opaque concept of levels of referentiality (fully, mostly and partly).[10] The third observation is that semantics only seems to extend beyond the word (at least formally, in Silva's analysis) in his discussion of style, where he treats clauses with verbs of knowing.[11] Silva's work has been highly influential, however, so that for many who discuss semantics his categories are determinative.[12]

An earlier and in some ways more promising, though largely ignored, book is that by Johannes Louw, *Semantics of New Testament Greek*.[13] Louw clearly takes a position influenced by the psycholinguistic theories of Chomsky, as can be seen in his definition of semantics in connection with other areas of study, such as anthropology, psychology and philosophy. He then devotes several chapters to talking about issues related to words, before finally asking the question, 'What is Meaning?' In the final two chapters he introduces the notion that semantics is more than the meanings of words and sentences. The first chapter is an exposition of Chomskyan phrase-structure grammar, which does not move much beyond the meanings of words, since the largest unit is the sentence, but often in a greatly simplified form. The second chapter is an exposition of what has come to be known as the South African school of discourse analysis (discussed further below). There is little doubt that this is a movement in the right direction—that is, being concerned with semantic structures that are larger than the word, seen in terms of entire discourses—but the foundation here is subject to criticism. It is not

---

10. Silva, *Biblical Words*, pp. 105-107.

11. See M. Silva, 'The Pauline Style as Lexical Choice: ΓΙΝΩΣΚΕΙΝ and Related Verbs', in D.A. Hagner and M.J. Harris (eds.), *Pauline Studies* (Festschrift F.F. Bruce; Exeter: Paternoster; Grand Rapids: Eerdmans, 1980), pp. 184-207, which presents a fuller form of this argument.

12. See, for example, G.R. Osborne, *The Hermeneutical Spiral: A Comprehensive Introduction to Biblical Interpretation* (Downers Grove, IL: InterVarsity Press, 1991), esp. pp. 64-92.

13. Philadelphia: Fortress Press; Atlanta: Scholars Press, 1982.

clear how one creates criteria to advance beyond the sentence if one starts from a Chomskyan framework.[14]

b. *Redefining Semantics*
From the brief survey above, we can see that work in New Testament semantics could benefit from a reappraisal of the concept of meaning. It seems that appropriately defining and understanding the concept of meaning is foundational for further work regarding the meaning and argumentative force of any text, including one in the New Testament such as Romans. To help provide the basis for such understanding, we offer three examples, before turning to the concept of argumentation, all with implications for study of Romans.

1. *Semantic Domains*. In the area of lexical study, much more could be done that relies upon the concept of semantic fields or domains. Many scholars invoke the concept of semantic domains, rightly we believe, but the concept has not been used as fully as it might be. Most use of the concept is in ways similar to those of the Louw–Nida lexicon. That is, the individual word, and the sentence in which it is found, are still at the centre of attention. One studies this word in relation to other meanings it may have (polysemy), as well as in its various sense relations with other words (e.g. synonymy, antonymy, hyponymy, and so on). The significance of this individual word is then, perhaps, incorporated into the meaning of a sentence, and only rarely into that of a larger unit. How does one determine the significance of this particular word? There is, of course, a certain amount of significance that may attach to its morphology (for instance, if it is a verb used in a particular tense-form or mood, or if it is a noun in a particular case), or that may be indicated by its syntax within a group of words or a clause. But one of the things that Barr emphasized, even though many have ignored him, is that one cannot equate words (or lexical items) and concepts, so that one cannot necessarily invoke a particular concept simply because of the appearance of a given word, and certainly cannot count on this same concept being invoked if this word is used again.

Jeffrey Reed has pioneered use of semantic domain theory in the study of New Testament vocabulary by finding what he calls 'semantic

14. The same kind of unsatisfactory progression is found in D.A. Black, *Linguistics for Students of New Testament Greek: A Survey of Basic Concepts and Applications* (Grand Rapids: Baker Book House, 1988), pp. 120-42.

chains'.[15] These chains are vocabulary that come from the same semantic domain. By studying their appearance over the extent of a discourse unit, in his case the book of Philippians, he contends that one has a better method of determining the ideational structure of the discourse, that is, the way language is used to speak of the world of events and experience. Words that recur in common semantic domains, and subdomains, point the focus of the subject matter in a particular direction. Of course, one may have some quibbles and complaints about the Louw–Nida lexicon forming the basis of such study.[16] Apart from the fact that this lexicon stands as one of the major accomplishments in lexicography, both ancient and modern (compare the revision of Liddell–Scott according to the traditional principles of lexicography),[17] exegetes must come to terms with the importance of the categories of field semantics extended over an entire corpus.[18] This is the only means by

15. J.T. Reed, *A Discourse Analysis of Philippians: Method and Rhetoric in the Debate over Literary Integrity* (JSNTSup, 136; SNTG, 3; Sheffield: Sheffield Academic Press, 1997), pp. 296-331.

16. See S.E. Porter, *Studies in the Greek New Testament: Theory and Practice* (SBG, 6; New York: Peter Lang, 1996), pp. 69-73; D.A. Black, Review of Louw and Nida (eds.), *Greek–English Lexicon, FN* 1 (1988), pp. 217-18; J.P. Louw, 'How Do Words Mean—If They Do?', *FN* 4 (1991), pp. 125-42 (for a presentation of the theory for the Louw–Nida lexicon). For a critical analysis of the lexicon, see J. Lee, 'The United Bible Societies' Lexicon and its Analysis of Meaning', *FN* 5 (1992), pp. 167-89 with a response, J.P. Louw, 'The Analysis of Meaning in Lexicography', *FN* 6 (1993), pp. 139-48. See also S. Wong, 'Leftovers of Louw-Nida's Lexicon: Some Considerations Towards "A Greek–Chinese Lexicon"', *FN* 7 (1994), pp. 137-74; G.H.R. Horsley and J.A.L. Lee, 'A Lexicon of the New Testament with Documentary Parallels: Some Interim Entries, 1', *FN* 10 (1997), pp. 55-84.

17. P.G.W. Glare (ed.), *Greek–English Lexicon Revised Supplement* (Oxford: Clarendon Press, 1996), pp. v-ix.

18. On corpus linguistics, and its relation to a functional grammar (see below), see M. Stubbs, *Text and Corpus Analysis* (Oxford: Basil Blackwell, 1996). On the use of corpus-based techniques in lexicography, see J. Sinclair (ed.), *Looking Up: An Account of the Cobuild Project in Lexical Computing* (London: Collins, 1987); *idem, Corpus, Concordance, Collocation* (Oxford: Oxford University Press, 1991); V.B.Y. Ooi, *Computer Corpus Lexicography* (Edinburgh: Edinburgh University Press, 1998). For an initial investigation into the potential of corpus-based lexicography and Hellenistic Greek, see M.B. O'Donnell, 'Some New Testament Words for Resurrection and the Company They Keep', in S.E. Porter, M.A. Hayes and D. Tombs (eds.), *Resurrection* (RILP, 5; JSNTSup, 186; Sheffield: Sheffield Academic Press, 1999), pp. 136-63.

which lexical study can occur, and should help to remake word studies. Rather than simply studying an individual word in all of its occurrences, or a single word in relation to its semantic field—as necessary as these preliminary stages are—analysing entire semantic domains as they are lexicalized across a corpus, or even corpora, seems to be the way forward in lexical study.[19]

Semantic field study involves an interplay between the conceptual domains and the individual lexical items that fall within those domains. Although there is a long history in linguistics of the use of lexical statistics, we wish to improve upon the simple counting of words that this method sometimes implies. We believe that one can discover something important about the meaning of a text or a group of texts (corpus) by examining the frequency and distribution of specific lexical items in the corpus. On the most basic level, often as a basis for some, if not most, of the worthwhile work mentioned above, this involves first counting the number of times a particular word or group of words occurs in a text. Once repeated for a large enough number of words, it is possible to make statements as to the characteristic words in the text.[20] For example, the 20 most frequent words (considering only verbs, nouns and

---

19. One could well argue that all levels of language, including syntax and discourse features, should be studied across a corpus. A prerequisite for such study is machine readable texts annotated with linguistic information (the most familiar form of linguistic annotation of the Greek New Testament is grammatical annotation available in the texts utilized by search software programs such as GRAMCORD and BibleWorks). This annotation should take place at all levels of discourse from the morpheme up to the paragraph and discourse. For a collection of state-of-the-art essays on corpus annotation, see R. Garside, G. Leech and A. McEnery (eds.), *Corpus Annotation: Linguistic Information from Computer Text Corpora* (London: Longman, 1997).

20. This type of methodology has been particularly popular in the field of authorship attribution, where some have asserted that particular words can be identified as characteristic of a given author (Paul, for instance), and that a high frequency of these words in a text of uncertain origin would suggest authenticity, while a lack of these 'key' words points away from this conclusion. For a survey and evaluation of attribution studies, particularly where they have focused on the authorship of New Testament documents, see M.B. O'Donnell, 'Linguistic Fingerprints or Style by Numbers: The Use of Statistics in the Discussion of Authorship of New Testament Documents', in S.E. Porter and D.A. Carson (eds.), *Linguistics and the New Testament: Critical Junctures* (JSNTSup, 168; SNTG, 5; Sheffield: Sheffield Academic Press, 1999), pp. 206-62.

adjectives) in Romans, and their frequency of occurrence in the book, are as follows:

Table 1

Word	Freq.	Word	Freq.	Word	Freq.
θεός	153	πίστις	40	ἄνθρωπος	27
εἰμί	113	Ἰησοῦς	36	σάρξ	26
νόμος	74	γίνομαι	35	ἔχω	25
πᾶς	70	δικαιοσύνη	34	χάρις	24
Χριστός	65	πνεῦμα	34	ἀποθνήσκω	23
ἁμαρτία	48	λέγω	34	ποιέω	23
κύριος	43	ἔθνος	29		

This kind of frequency list is, on the one hand, a very primitive and blunt device for exploring the meaning of Romans, but, on the other hand, still quite revealing. The most frequent word, perhaps not surprisingly for a Christian religious text, is θεός. More telling for Romans is the rank of the words νόμος, ἁμαρτία and πίστις. At this stage we have learnt little that would not be discovered from asking the question 'What is Romans about?' or 'What are the main themes of Romans?' or even by consulting the introductory section of any commentary on the book.

As mentioned above, the concept of semantic fields or domains has become increasingly popular in New Testament interpretation, and provides a means of moving beyond analysis of individual lexical items. However, few have progressed beyond the use of the concept in an atomistic, word-by-word manner. Even at the word level, it is possible to encode much semantic information, such as the semantic domain a word belongs to, following each word in the corpus.[21] For example, Rom. 5.1 could be annotated as follows:

Rom 5.1 δικαιωθέντες <34> οὖν <89> ἐκ <84> πίστεως <31> εἰρήνην <22> ἔχωμεν <57> πρὸς <84> τὸν <92> θεὸν <12> διὰ <90> τοῦ <92> κυρίου <12> ἡμῶν <92> Ἰησοῦ <93> Χριστοῦ <93>

Here we have used only the major domain for each word from the

---

21. See M.B. O'Donnell, 'The Use of Annotated Corpora for New Testament Discourse Analysis: A Survey of Current Practice and Future Prospects', in S.E. Porter and J.T. Reed (eds.), *Discourse Analysis and the New Testament: Approaches and Results* (JSNTSup, 170; SNTG, 4; Sheffield: Sheffield Academic Press, 1999), pp. 71-117.

Louw–Nida lexicon, and selected the first domain listed for a word in those cases where a word belongs to more than one domain. Such a procedure is not without problems, but will suffice for the present study.[22] Elsewhere, we have demonstrated how a segment of text annotated in this manner can be displayed on a two-dimensional plot, providing a *semantic map* of the text, and revealing specific verses and groups of verses containing a significant number of words from a particular domain or combination of domains.[23]

This method can be extended over the whole book; however, with 433 verses in Romans and 93 domains from the Louw–Nida lexicon, it becomes difficult to isolate key clusters of domains. Initially it is sufficient to list the number of occurrences of each domain per chapter, instead of per verse. The table in Appendix A presents the number of occurrences of each word from each domain of the lexicon[24] in each chapter of Romans, ordered by the total frequency. It should be recognized that, at this point, apart from the decision to ignore alternative domain classifications for words classified in more than one domain, the data in this table are simply a *descriptive abstraction* of the lexicon of Romans. The use of such devices provides a method of handling the vast amount of information that must be taken into account. The table in Appendix A can be used as a means of identifying semantic patterns (at the word level) in Romans. Questions must be asked about what

---

22. For a discussion of semantic disambiguation, see O'Donnell, 'Annotated Corpora', pp. 86-88. Closer examination of the words that are classified in multiple domains in the Louw–Nida lexicon reveals that words such as prepositions are the least clearly defined (reflecting the multiple classification schemes of traditional grammars). The following text shows all the possible major domains for each word in Rom 5.1: δικαιωθέντες <34, 88, 56, 37, 36> οὖν <89, 91> ἐκ <84, 89, 90, 63, 68, 67, 57> πίστεως <31, 33> εἰρήνην <22, 25> ἔχωμεν <57, 18, 31, 49, 74, 90, 13, 90> πρὸς <84, 83, 90, 89, 67, 78, 90, 64> τὸν <92> θεὸν <12> διὰ <90, 89, 84, 67> τοῦ <92> κυρίου <12, 57, 37, 87> ἡμῶν <92> Ἰησοῦ <93> Χριστοῦ <93, 53>. This reveals the limitation of the method we have demonstrated in this study. However, we are not seeking so much to present interpretative conclusions as to demonstrate new methods of investigating semantic patterns in the book of Romans.

23. See O'Donnell, 'Annotated Corpora', pp. 104-107, 112-13 (for plot).

24. We have not included domains that do not occur in the book at all. Linguistically it is often useful to consider not only what is there, but what is not there but potentially could have been. The missing domains from the book of Romans are 48 (*Activities Involving Liquids or Masses*), 50 (*Contests and Play*), 51 (*Festivals*), 54 (*Maritime Activities*), 62 (*Arrange, Organize*), 70 (*Real, Unreal*) and 86 (*Weight*).

exactly constitutes a significant pattern. Are the domains with the highest frequency more or less interesting for establishing the meaning of the letter? What is the minimum total number of occurrences of a particular domain at which one can examine the distribution of words from that domain across the book? These issues will not be addressed here.[25]

For determining the semantic structure of the book, it is perhaps enlightening to examine the pattern of particular domains on a chapter-by-chapter basis and how these interact with other related domains. For instance, consider the distribution of words from domains 23 (*Physiological Processes and States*), 31 (*Hold a View, Believe, Trust*) and 42 (*Perform, Do*) across the book of Romans.

Table 2

	Romans Chapter															
Domain	1	2	3	4	5	6	7	8	9	10	11	12	13	14	15	16
23: Physiological Processes and States	8	2	0	4	15	28	19	18	3	3	2	5	1	29	2	0
31: Hold a View, Believe, Trust	9	0	13	17	2	1	4	0	3	10	4	2	1	5	2	3
42: Perform, Do	6	9	3	4	0	0	3	7	4	0	1	1	4	1	1	6

This table reveals that there is a cluster of words from domain 23 in chs. 5–8,[26] and then again in ch. 14.[27] The four-chapter cluster comes after two chapters (3 and 4) with the highest concentration of words from domain 31.[28] So, simply on the basis of these two semantic

25. It should also be noted that the data presented in this and the following tables are the 'raw' frequency counts and have not been normalized according to the number of words in each chapter. For initial investigation it is sufficient to use raw frequencies. Below we examine the data in Appendix A using multivariate statistical techniques, for which the normalization of data is more important.

26. Chapter 5: θάνατος (6 times), ἀποθνήσκω (5 times), ζωή (4 times). Chapter 6: θάνατος (7 times), ἀποθνήσκω (6 times), ζάω (5 times), νεκρός (4 times), ζωή (3 times), θνητός (1 time), ἀνάστασις (1 time), συζάω (1 time). Chapter 7: θάνατος (5 times), ἀποθνήσκω (4 times), ζάω (4 times), καρποφορέω (2 times), νεκρός (2 times), ἀναζάω (1 time), ζωή (1 time). Chapter 8: ζωή (4 times), ζάω (3 times), νεκρός (3 times), θάνατος (3 times), ἀποθνήσκω (2 times), θνητός (1 time), ζωο-ποιέω (1 time).

27. Chapter 14: ἐσθίω (13 times), ζάω (7 times), ἀποθνήσκω (6 times), βρῶσις (1 time), νεκρός (1 time), πίνω (1 time).

28. Chapter 3: πίστις (9 times), πιστεύω (2 times), ἀπιστία (1 time), ἀπιστέω (1 time). Chapter 4: πίστις (10 times), πιστεύω (6 times), ἀπιστία (1 time).

domains, one might suggest that chs. 3–8 of Romans move from a discussion of belief (and unbelief) to a focus on physical (biological) states, that is, life and death. These are semantic fields utilized throughout the letter, but particularly concentrated in a contiguous manner in the first half of the book. Again, this is not information that could not be gleaned from a cursory reading of the first eight chapters. It should be clear, however, that this kind of analysis could be usefully extended to consider the interaction between a much larger number of domains. Once a significant cluster, such as the concentration of words from domain 23 in chs. 5–8, has been identified, other domains should be examined to see if they coincide with this cluster, through either a significant cluster of occurrences or a lack of occurrences. For example, words from domain 42 (*Perform, Do*) spread across the whole of Romans without significant variance or clustering; however, there is a possibly marked absence of domain 42 words in chs. 5 and 6. The interpretative significance of such observations must be carefully investigated through a close reading of the text, but the method at least provides a tool for the identification of some of the semantic patterns in Romans.

2. *Units Smaller and Larger than the Word*. The second issue in semantics is that we must come to terms with an expanded definition of the concept, one that includes not only what we have been saying about the word, but also units both smaller and larger than the word. Recent work in discourse analysis has been heralded by some as pointing to a period in the future when all linguistics will consist of morphology and discourse analysis.[29] The result of such a scenario implies that one must have both micro- and macro-synoptic views of the linguistic data. Morphology remains an important, and still neglected, area of New Testament Greek studies. By morphology is meant not simply the vagaries of word formation, and so on, such as are found in the second volume of Moulton's grammar or the early sections of BDF,[30] but also what these elements of linguistic substance contribute to meaning. Here is where

29. W. Chafe, 'Looking Ahead', *Text* 10 (1990), pp. 19-22, esp. p. 21; cited with approval by Reed, *Discourse Analysis of Philippians*, p. 405.

30. J.H. Moulton and W.F. Howard, *A Grammar of New Testament Greek*. II. *Accidence and Word-Formation* (Edinburgh: T. & T. Clark, 1928); F. Blass and A. Debrunner, *A Greek Grammar of the New Testament and Other Early Christian Literature* (trans. R.W. Funk; Chicago: University of Chicago Press, 1961), pp. 25-69.

discussion of verbal aspect, mood, voice, and case must *begin*—but they certainly cannot end here. The co-text and context must be analysed to establish the significance of the given form within the constraints of its linguistic environment.[31] There is a tendency to overload one's expectations onto morphology. We have all seen this in exploration of the verb tenses, where the supposed meaning of the tense is invoked in order to give a sharp and precise, even heavily theological, meaning to a usage. This certainly happened before more people became aware of verbal aspect theory,[32] but it has continued as well. A similar thing can happen in the study of the cases, where it is thought that a definition of case provides the solution to most complex semantic problems in the New Testament. Recently, an author has suggested the necessity of studying Greek according to semantic case theory.[33] This is not the place to explore what semantic case theory is, and what its strengths and weaknesses may be. The effort is commendable in that it takes a recognizable category and, appreciating its limitations, redefines it in an attempt to expand the category to larger semantic units. Nevertheless, we do not think that case theory is the solution to understanding the semantics of Greek, much less of the cases, and have elsewhere proposed a modified morphologically-based case theory in its place. In this scheme, there is place for recognition of a definable element of meaning contributed by morphology, while appreciating that there are larger semantic considerations as well that must be taken into account.[34]

31. On the difficult concept of context, see A. Duranti and C. Goodwin (eds.), *Rethinking Context: Language as an Interactive Phenomenon* (Cambridge: Cambridge University Press, 1992).

32. See S.E. Porter, *Verbal Aspect in the Greek of the New Testament, with Reference to Tense and Mood* (SBG, 1; New York: Peter Lang, 1989), esp. pp. 17-65.

33. S. Wong, 'What Case is This Case? An Application of Semantic Case in Biblical Exegesis', *Jian Dao* 1 (1994), pp. 49-73; *idem, A Classification of Semantic Case-Relations in the Pauline Epistles* (SBG, 9; New York: Peter Lang, 1997). A similar theory is found in P. Danove, 'The Theory of Construction Grammar and its Application to New Testament Greek', in S.E. Porter and D.A. Carson (eds.), *Biblical Greek Language and Linguistics: Open Questions in Current Research* (JSNTSup, 80; SNTG, 1; Sheffield: JSOT Press, 1993), pp. 119-51; *idem*, 'Verbs of Experience: Toward a Lexicon Detailing the Argument Structures Assigned by Verbs', in Porter and Carson (eds.), *Linguistics and the New Testament*, pp. 144-205.

34. S.E. Porter, 'The Case for Case Revisited', *Jian Dao* 6 (1996), pp. 13-28; *idem*, 'The Greek Language of the New Testament', in *idem* (ed.), *Handbook to*

As with the concept of lexical semantics discussed above, however, there is a need to move beyond an instance-by-instance or even clause-by-clause analysis of morphological features, such as case. One of the difficulties with such a procedure is the large body of data that must be recorded and processed for the full analysis of even a small text. One way to address this problem is by producing a graphic display to show the frequency of occurrence of selected linguistic features across a text.[35] Table 3 below provides a grammatical plot for the morphological feature of case (instances of nouns, pronouns, adjectives and articles) in Romans 9–11. The cases are arranged in order of markedness—the major divisions being between the least heavily marked nominative and the oblique cases, and the accusative as the least heavily marked of the oblique cases.[36] The verse is not an entirely satisfactory unit of division for counting the distribution of case in this manner (ideally, the clause would serve as the basic unit for such analysis and for the examination of semantic domains as above). However, the verse serves as a readily recognizable unit of reference familiar to those commenting on Romans. We do not comment on the specifics of these data here but simply present them as a method of exploring patterns of morphological features across larger units of analysis than the word.

Exegesis of the New Testament (NTTS, 25; Leiden: E.J. Brill, 1997), pp. 99-130, esp. 119-24.

35. D. Biber, S. Conrad and R. Reppen, *Corpus Linguistics: Investigating Language Structure and Use* (Cambridge Approaches to Linguistics; Cambridge: Cambridge University Press, 1998), pp. 122-30. For an application of a similar grammatical plot to the book of Jude, see O'Donnell, 'The Use of Annotated Corpora', pp. 98-104.

36. The vocative case is not included in this display. Formally, the vocative is only distinguished for first declension masculine singular nouns, second declension masculine and feminine singular nouns and a few instances in the third declension. Grammatically annotated texts of the New Testament are inconsistent on this point; both the Friberg text and the GRAMCORD database allow for vocative articles and participles, and tag formally ambiguous nominative/vocative forms as vocatives. This is one of the instances in which there is a confusion of linguistic levels, with discourse features influencing annotation at the word level; see O'Donnell, 'The Use of Corpus Annotation', pp. 93-95. For more on the hierarchical arrangement of the Greek cases, see Porter, 'The Greek Language of the New Testament', pp. 122-24; *idem, Idioms of the Greek New Testament* (BLG, 2; Sheffield: Sheffield Academic Press, 2nd edn, 1994), pp. 82-83.

Table 3

Verse	Chapter 9				Chapter 10				Chapter 11			
	Nom.	Acc.	Gen.	Dat.	Nom.	Acc.	Gen.	Dat.	Nom.	Acc.	Gen.	Dat.
1	-	1	3	4	4	3	4	-	4	2	5	-
2	4	-	1	3	-	2	1	1	4	4	3	3
3	3	1	8	-	-	5	4	2	2	6	3	-
4	14	-	1	-	2	1	1	2	3	4	1	3
5	7	4	3	-	3	4	2	1	1	1	1	2
6	7	-	3	-	4	3	2	2	3	-	1	1
7	4	-	1	2	2	3	1	-	5	3	-	-
8	7	1	6	-	5	2	5	4	2	3	5	1
9	4	3	1	2	2	3	3	4	3	4	1	1
10	1	1	5	-	-	2	-	2	2	2	4	-
11	2	4	2	-	4	-	-	1	2	2	1	4
12	2	-	2	3	4	3	3	-	8	-	5	1
13	-	4	-	-	2	2	1	-	2	3	2	3
14	1	1	-	2	-	1	1	-	-	3	2	-
15	-	2	-	2	3	2	1	-	7	-	3	-
16	-	-	4	-	3	-	1	4	10	-	-	-
17	2	7	2	6	4	-	3	-	4	-	8	1
18	-	2	-	-	4	5	4	-	3	3	2	-
19	1	-	1	3	3	2	-	3	2	-	-	-
20	5	1	-	3	2	2	-	2	1	1	-	4
21	2	6	5	-	-	8	1	-	2	1	3	-
22	2	6	2	2	-	-	-	-	3	4	2	2
23	-	5	4	-	-	-	-	-	4	1	-	2
24	-	2	2	-	-	-	-	-	3	4	2	4
25	-	4	2	2	-	-	-	-	4	4	4	3
26	3	-	2	3	-	-	-	-	3	1	2	-
27	7	-	7	-	-	-	-	-	3	2	2	1
28	1	1	2	-	-	-	-	-	2	7	-	-
29	4	1	1	1	-	-	-	-	5	-	2	-
30	2	5	1	-	-	-	-	-	1	-	1	4
31	1	2	1	-	-	-	-	-	2	-	-	3
32	-	1	4	2	-	-	-	-	2	5	-	-
33	1	2	2	2	-	-	-	-	7	-	6	-
34	-	-	-	-	-	-	-	-	3	1	2	-
35	-	-	-	-	-	-	-	-	1	-	-	2
36	-	-	-	-	-	-	-	-	4	3	2	1

In their study, Biber, Conrad and Reppen examine the use of verb tense-form and voice in scientific texts, and discover significant correlations between switches from non-past to past tense-forms and active to passive voice, and the major structural sections: Introduction, Method, Results and Discussion. The Introduction sections are written mainly using active voice non-past tense verbs, the Method sections switch to past passive verbs, the Results section continues to use past time verbs but in the active voice, and finally the active voice dominates the Discussion section with no marked preference for either past or non-past verbal forms. After gathering frequency statistics for tense-form and voice in each of these sections in a sizeable corpus of scientific texts, they were able to establish a normal or expected pattern for each section of such a text. Graphical discourse maps can then be 'used to identify systematic departures from the expected patterns, leading to the identification of rhetorically salient shifts in the discourse'.[37]

For our study, a program was developed that allows selection of a chapter of Romans to examine it with regard to the distribution of aspect (see Appendix B). One can select whether to focus upon finite forms (in the indicative, subjunctive, imperative and optative moods), participles or infinitives, or combinations of these three. The Greek text of the selected chapter is displayed with word forms in the perfective aspect (aorist) highlighted in red, forms in the imperfective (present and imperfect) in blue and stative forms (perfect and pluperfect) in green.[38] A histogram of the distribution of the aspects by verse is also provided, as is a vertical 'trace-plot'. The plot moves down the page as words in the text progress. If a perfective form occurs, a point is plotted on the left-hand side of the plot. If an imperfective form occurs, then a point is placed in the middle of the plot. Stative occurrences are marked on the right-hand side of the plot. Appendix C contains a full plot of Romans utilizing this method.[39]

By examining this plot, it is possible to identify sections of text dominated by a particular aspect. For example, throughout Romans 1 we observe a regular fluctuation between perfective and imperfective aspect. The aorist forms are more numerous, thus supporting the understanding of the perfective as the background aspect. However, after the begin-

37. Biber, Conrad and Reppen, *Corpus Linguistics*, p. 127.

38. It is not possible to reproduce the colour effects used by the program to distinguish the three aspects in Appendix B. We have attempted to make these distinctions through the use of shading and underlining in the text window. In the vertical line plot, points on the left represent an occurrence of the aorist form (perfective aspect), points in the middle present and imperfect forms (imperfective aspect) and points on the right perfect and pluperfect forms (stative aspect).

39. All forms of εἰμί have been excluded because they are aspectually vague; see Porter, *Verbal Aspect*, pp. 442-47. The plot includes both finite (indicative, subjunctive, imperative, optative) and infinite (participle, infinitive) verbal forms.

ning of ch. 2, there is a noticeable switch to the consistent use of the imperfective aspect, realized by present tense-forms. There are only two instances of perfective aspect in the entire chapter, both occurring in v. 12: ὅσοι γὰρ ἀνόμως ἥμαρτον, ἀνόμως καὶ ἀπολοῦνται, καὶ ὅσοι ἐν νόμῳ ἥμαρτον, διὰ νόμου κριθήσονται. Another interesting example is the contrast between 7.3-13 and 7.14–8.1 (see plot in Appendix C).[40] In the first section there is a predominance of perfective aspect (the background of discourse), interspersed with 5 instances of foregrounded imperfective aspect (ἐνηργεῖτο, κατειχόμεθα, δουλεύειν, ἔλεγεν, ἔζων) and only 1 instance of stative aspect realized by the perfect tense-form (ἥδειν). Then in v. 14 there are two instances of stative aspect (frontground[41]): οἴδαμεν γὰρ ὅτι ὁ νόμος πνευματικός ἐστιν, ἐγὼ δὲ σάρκινός εἰμι πεπραμένος ὑπὸ τὴν ἁμαρτίαν. This is followed by a string of many instances of imperfective aspect, but none of perfective aspect at all, until 8.2. This would seem to indicate a significant semantic pattern. We are not of course discovering a new insight in Romans 7, or solving the familiar problem of the temporal relationship between these portions of the chapter (see also below). But again, we offer this kind of analysis and the use of graphical plots of grammatical features as a means of discovering semantic patterns throughout Romans.

3. *Discourse and Meaning*. The previous examples illustrate the need in studies of semantics for consideration to be given to units larger than the word, and ultimately to what has come to be called discourse. We take it that discourse analysis, rightly defined, subsumes consideration of such things as analysis of the phrase, clause, pericope or paragraph and, ultimately, the discourse unit.[42] Each of these levels of consideration makes a contribution to the concept of meaning, all of which must enter into any final statement regarding the 'meaning' of a passage. For

---

40. Of course, it is typical for commentators on Romans to draw attention to the shift in tense-forms between Rom. 7.13 and 14. For a survey of discussion, see D.J. Moo, *The Epistle to the Romans* (NICNT; Grand Rapids: Eerdmans, 1996), pp. 441-51. Better at appreciating the use of the tense-forms, however, is M. Seifrid, *Justification by Faith: The Origin and Development of a Central Pauline Theme* (NovTSup, 68; Leiden: E.J. Brill, 1992), pp. 228-44.

41. On planes of discourse in relation to the Greek tense-forms, see Porter, *Idioms of the Greek New Testament*, p. 23.

42. See Porter, *Idioms of the Greek New Testament*, pp. 298-307.

example, ordering of elements in a phrase or clause has an effect on meaning, by bringing to prominence a particular linguistic element. The grammaticalization of an explicit subject inevitably affects word order, since this subject must be syntactically ordered in relation to the other elements, such as the elements of the predicate and any complements or adjuncts. Certain modifiers have varying degrees of tendencies to be placed before or after their head terms, thus altering the significance of a phrase.[43] Clauses are connected together by various means. Sometimes phrases are used, such as participle phrases (including the genitive absolute), but most of the time one of a set of connective words is used. Most analyse these connective words as individual lexical items, when their significance actually comes from how they function by joining together two or more clauses; that is, they are inter-sentential in function and, hence, in meaning. Discourse analysis, rightly understood, unites these other elements into a coherent explanatory whole.

3. *Patterns of Argumentation*

a. *Rhetoric, Discourse and Patterns of Argumentation*
We now turn to the second major part of this paper—patterns of argumentation in Romans. Most recent interpreters of Romans who have looked at argumentation have done so in terms of forms of rhetoric.[44] We wish to approach the subject of argumentation from a more linguistic perspective, particularly in terms of the relationship between semantics and 'patterns of argumentation'. When patterns of argumentation,

---

43. See Porter, *Idioms of the Greek New Testament*, pp. 286-297; *idem*, 'Word Order and Clause Structure in New Testament Greek: An Unexplored Area of Greek Linguistics Using Philippians as a Test Case', *FN* 6 (1993), pp. 176-206; Reed, *Discourse Analysis of Philippians*, pp. 45, 116-18.

44. The range of recent discussion can be conveniently found in S.E. Porter and T.H. Olbricht (eds.), *Rhetoric and the New Testament: Essays from the 1992 Heidelberg Conference* (JSNTSup, 90; Sheffield: JSOT Press, 1993); S.E. Porter and T.H. Olbricht (eds.), *Rhetoric, Scripture and Theology: Essays from the 1994 Pretoria Conference* (JSNTSup, 131; Sheffield: Sheffield Academic Press, 1996); S.E. Porter and T.H. Olbricht (eds.), *The Rhetorical Analysis of Scripture: Essays from the 1995 London Conference* (JSNTSup, 146; Sheffield: Sheffield Academic Press, 1997); S.E. Porter and D.L. Stamps (eds.), *The Rhetorical Interpretation of Scripture: Essays from the 1996 Malibu Conference* (JSNTSup, 180; Sheffield: Sheffield Academic Press, 1999); S.E. Porter (ed.), *Handbook of Classical Rhetoric in the Hellenistic Period 330 B.C.–A.D. 400* (Leiden: E.J. Brill, 1997).

or rhetoric, are discussed in Pauline studies, reference is usually being made to one of two major types of rhetorical study. One, and the most prominently used, is that of classical rhetoric, especially as it is found in the ancient rhetorical handbooks. However, the application of the categories of classical rhetoric to analysis of the Pauline letters, as if this were something that the ancients themselves would have performed, or even understood, is misguided. Classical rhetoric can be a tool for analysis of argumentation, but it is not one that can be privileged on the basis of grounding it in the theory or practice of the ancients. There is little to no evidence that the ancients viewed letters in terms of the categories of rhetoric. In fact, the evidence is that when the ancients speak of letters, apart from the area of style and occasionally forms of arguments, letters and oratory are virtually always distinguished.[45] However, that does not mean that other forms of rhetoric, or other forms of argumentation, cannot be applied to the Pauline letters. The New Rhetoric of Chaim Perelman is probably the best known of these models, but there are others as well, such as the rhetoric of Kenneth Burke.

In terms of the topic of this paper, however, one must try to determine how it is that semantic theory has been, and better yet can further be, utilized to understand the argumentative structure of one of Paul's letters.[46] The relationship between them is not at first readily apparent, although the Scandinavian school of discourse analysis or text-linguistics has had reasonable success in integrating a tripartite syntax–semantics–pragmatics framework with ancient rhetorical theory, as well as communication theory.[47] There are several reasons why this framework, though commendable for its far-reaching and integrative method, does not seem to promise as much for the future, however. One reason

45. See S.E. Porter, 'The Theoretical Justification for Application of Rhetorical Categories to Pauline Epistolary Literature', in Porter and Olbricht (eds.), *Rhetoric and the New Testament*, pp. 100-122.

46. For a discussion of some recent attempts to integrate linguistics and rhetoric, see S.E. Porter, 'Linguistics and Rhetorical Criticism', in Porter and Carson (eds.), *Linguistics and the New Testament*, pp. 63-92.

47. Major proponents include B. Olsson, *Structure and Meaning in the Fourth Gospel: A Text-Linguistic Analysis of John 2:1-11 and 4:1-42* (ConBNT, 6; Lund: C.W.K. Gleerup, 1974); D. Hellholm, *Das Visionenbuch des Hermas als Apokalypse: Formgeschichtliche und texttheoretische Studien zu einer literarischen Gattung.* I. *Methodologische Vorüberlegungen und makrostrukturelle Textanalyse* (ConBNT, 13.1; Lund: C.W.K. Gleerup, 1980); and L. Hartman, *Text-Centered New Testament Studies* (WUNT, 102; Tübingen: Mohr–Siebeck, 1997).

is the troublesome differentiation of syntax, semantics and pragmatics, another is the reliance upon ancient rather than modern rhetorical theory, a third is the invocation of Jakobson's communications model, and the last is the failure to provide a coherent integration of these various aspects.[48]

Several linguists, however, have seen a useful line of connection between ancient rhetorical study and discourse analysis.[49] The line of continuity is that both systems, according to this analysis, are concerned to describe the means by which a text, taken as an entire unit, is seen to be effective or persuasive. Those discourse analysts who discuss this connection, however, also wish to note that ancient rhetoric was a means of textual formation that the *ancients* used. Whatever similarities there may be with modern discourse theory, the two are not to be equated. Discourse analysis, so this theory holds, is the model that moderns should use, since, although common concerns are shared, it has developed explicit methodology in the light of advances in linguistics.

In the light of our discussion above, and the suggestion that discourse analysis provides a means of integrating several of these important factors, including semantics and its bearing on argumentative structure, we wish to examine several works on Romans that appear to have similar concerns. The first is Johannes Louw's discourse analysis of the entire book of Romans, entitled *A Semantic Discourse Analysis of Romans*.[50] Louw has written a very important, though not very widely known, book. The reason it is not better known is undoubtedly because it was printed by the Department of Greek at the University of Pretoria, in a textbook form. This neglect of the book is a shame, for Louw is to be commended for having analysed the entire book of Romans, breaking it down into its constituent colons, or smallest units of meaning, much like a Chomskyan phrase-structure or a Nidean kernel, and then brack-

48. See S.E. Porter, 'Discourse Analysis and New Testament Studies: An Introductory Survey', in S.E. Porter and D.A. Carson (eds.), *Discourse Analysis and Other Topics in Biblical Greek* (JSNTSup, 113; SNTG, 2; Sheffield: Sheffield Academic Press, 1995), pp. 14-35, esp. pp. 30-32.

49. See R. De Beaugrande and W. Dressler, *Introduction to Text Linguistics* (London: Longman, 1981), p. 15; cf. S.E. Porter, 'Rhetorical Analysis and Discourse Analysis of the Pauline Corpus', in Porter and Olbricht (eds.), *The Rhetorical Analysis of Scripture*, pp. 249-74.

50. Pretoria: Department of Greek, University of Pretoria, 1987.

eting these into what he sees as meaningful units for brief comment. There is much to be gained from this analysis. As an example, he notes the differences in the content of the colons in Rom. 5.15, and shows how they are to be arranged on the same structural level, one describing Adam and the other Christ.[51]

However, there are also a number of problems with this model. The first is that it is too dependent upon a Chomskyan-based linguistic model. To be fair to Louw, he tries to position his definition of a colon between the ancient concept of a colon (from which he gets the name of the unit) and what he characterizes as a transformational-grammatical model. He essentially defines a colon in terms of one of the basic phrase-structure rules of Chomskyan linguistics, that is, with a noun and verb component, and all that can be clustered around these units. This well illustrates the difficulty, however, since one must make prior decisions regarding clustering, and the units cannot advance beyond the simplest of sentences. Others have tried to extend Chomskyan analysis beyond the basic sentence,[52] but these attempts have, to date, been unsatisfactory in discourse terms, since they tend merely to invoke super-sentential categories, as if discourse consisted merely of extra large sentences, or to lose their theoretical grounding. As a result, there have been some attempts in the South African school of discourse analysis, of which Louw stands as the figurehead, to re-define the colon. The result has been a move away from more or less precise criteria, however, to an impressionistically based semantic analysis. This seems to undermine the foundation of the model.

A second problem with Louw's model becomes very clear when one moves beyond simple sentences and attempts to link them together. Much of this linkage is performed by sentence conjunctions. In difficult instances, however, these conjunctions are said not to function in the way that one might at first think (for example, εἰ in Rom. 5.15 is not an indicator of a condition), raising the question of what has led to this shift. It seems that Louw has encountered the same difficulties as did constituent analysis in the twentieth century, when identifiable units required a further level of analysis—a semantic level of analysis—to provide the necessary ordering of elements. Whereas the Bloomfield-

51. Louw, *Semantic Discourse Analysis*, p. 63.

52. An attempt at a literary and Chomskyan linguistic analysis is found in E. Schauber and E. Spolsky, *The Bounds of Interpretation: Linguistic Theory and Literary Text* (Stanford, CA: Stanford University Press, 1986).

ians resisted this level of analysis, wishing to perform their analysis solely on formal grounds, Louw apparently wishes to have a semantic level. However, a convincing one has not been found, with the result that often his exposition is left unsupported.[53]

The second study is Hendrikus Boers's book on justification in Galatians and Romans.[54] This book, according to the author, is a text-linguistic, structuralist and semiotic exposition of the concept of justification in Galatians and Romans. Boers makes it clear that he does not want his book to be seen as an instructional book in these disciplinary areas, but as an application of them to his theme in Galatians and Romans. His desire to get to grips with the text is much to be appreciated, but his exposition is more than a bit confusing. After the briefest of expositions of his framework, he first wishes to show how the concept of macro-structure, a very important one in discourse analysis, was anticipated in earlier interpreters of these Pauline letters. When he turns to an exposition of the macro-structure of the letters, however, the difficulty becomes clearer. Boers has apparently equated macro-structure with Chomskyan phrase-structure rules. He takes Teun van Dijk's statement that everyone approaches a text with a macro-structure as tantamount to the statement that everyone has a phrase-structure grammar in mind.[55] What is a surprising disappointment is that the actual structure that Boers proposes is a traditional epistolary structure (based on Romans 1–15 being the original letter), noting also the use of rhetorical questions. This analysis of Boers's conception of discourse is confirmed in his appendix on Principles and Procedures in Discourse Analysis.[56] This reads as if it were simply a more detailed discussion of Louw's definition of the colon, with discussion of bracketing, tree diagrams and Chomsky's now well known example, 'Flying planes can be dangerous'.

53. On the South African school of discourse analysis, see Porter, 'Discourse Analysis and New Testament Studies', pp. 107-16.

54. H. Boers, *The Justification of the Gentiles: Paul's Letters to the Galatians and Romans* (Peabody, MA: Hendrickson, 1994).

55. Boers, *Justification of the Gentiles*, p. 1, citing T.A. van Dijk, *Some Aspects of Text Grammars: A Study in Theoretical Linguistics and Poetics* (Janua Linguarum, Series Maior, 63; The Hague: Mouton, 1972), p. 160. Van Dijk's thought on this topic is conveniently found in his *Text and Context: Explorations in the Semantics and Pragmatics of Discourse* (LLL; London: Longman, 1977), pp. 130-63.

56. Boers, *Justification of the Gentiles*, pp. 229-40.

It is perhaps no wonder that in his recent survey of work on Romans, Robert Morgan cites none of the above work in a way that shows its importance for current study of Romans. This is even though he is well aware of modern issues of biblical interpretation, having written an important survey of the subject.[57] He in fact calls Boers's book on Galatians and Romans 'experimental' and 'demanding'.[58] In the light of what we have said above, it can be called experimental only in so far as no one has done quite what he has done in using Chomskyan grammar as a discourse analytic method and applying it to the New Testament. It can be called demanding only in that it probably demands more from the Chomskyan model than it can deliver. Louw is not mentioned at all.

In the light of these few and somewhat disappointing studies, it comes as no surprise that Moo, who said in the first half of his commentary on Romans, when it was first published, that he would publish a syntactical diagram of the Greek text at the conclusion of his commentary,[59] did not do so when the complete commentary appeared in one volume. In the commentary, Louw is only mentioned for a 1959 article he did on prohibitions in Greek.[60] Boers's book is mentioned twice, using it as an example of recent interpreters who think Romans is about the place of the Jews in salvation history and as an advocate of the subjective genitive in 3.22, a view Moo calls 'exegetically indefensible' and 'theologically dangerous'.[61] In other words, Moo does not introduce or deal with either of these exegetical methods in his commentary. His reticence to hastily adopt new methods, simply because they are new, is to be commended. However, why is it that he, and others who have written commentaries on Romans lately, do not address more of the methodological issues? After all, the commentary has become, and is apparently recognized to be, a compendium of recent thought on the given biblical book. We now have several commentaries on Romans, several of them in multiple volumes. Whereas they have numerous citations of various exegetical conclusions, few if any address questions of method, and what counts for evidence in determining the meaning of various passages that make up the whole of Romans.

---

57. R. Morgan with J. Barton, *Biblical Interpretation* (Oxford: Oxford University Press, 1988).

58. R. Morgan, *Romans* (Sheffield: Sheffield Academic Press, 1995), p. 154.

59. D. Moo, *Romans 1–8* (Chicago: Moody, 1991), p. ix.

60. J.P. Louw, 'On Greek Prohibitions', *Acta Classica* 2 (1959), pp. 43-57.

61. Moo, *Epistle to the Romans*, p. 243.

b. *Functional Grammar and Patterns of Argumentation*
We would like to suggest that Halliday's functional grammar, a sociolinguistically based grammar that works on the principle of interconnecting systems, provides the foundation for such integrative analysis. For Halliday, there are three metalinguistic categories of analysis for describing the relation between a text and its situation, and providing a useful vocabulary for discussion. These three metafunctions and their semantic contribution are: mode, or the textual semantic component; tenor, or the interpersonal semantic component; and field, or the ideational semantic component (already mentioned above in relation to Reed's work).

How would such a Hallidayan analysis of Romans begin to look? We offer the following preliminary studies as an indication of how this model could be utilized in studying the meaningful structures in Romans.

1. *Textual Semantic Component (Mode).* Regarding the textual component, one must recognize the contribution of the Pauline epistolographical conventions. Paul's letters reflect the ancient Greco-Roman letter form, with some noteworthy modifications, such as the development of the thanksgiving and parenetic sections.[62] Despite changing situations addressed in his letters, the constant regarding the shape of Paul's letters, including Romans, is the epistolary structure. It may be revealing, therefore, to investigate the effect of the sections of the Greco-Roman letter form upon the occurrence of linguistic features; or, to state the proposal in reverse, to consider the relation of the occurrence of particular linguistic features to the resulting structure of the letter. As noted above, Biber, Conrad and Reppen suggest that the differences in frequency of occurrence of the forms between different sections of a discourse point to 'differences in terms of the primary communicative purposes of each section'.[63] They focused upon science articles because

---

62. On ancient letter forms, see W.G. Doty, *Letters in Primitive Christianity* (GBS; Philadelphia: Fortress Press, 1973); J.L. White, *Light from Ancient Letters* (FFNT; Philadelphia: Fortress Press, 1986); J.T. Reed, 'The Epistle', in Porter (ed.), *Handbook of Classical Rhetoric*, pp. 171-93; B.W.R. Pearson and S.E. Porter, 'The Genres of the New Testament', in Porter (ed.), *Handbook to Exegesis*, pp. 131-66; S.E. Porter, 'Exegesis of the Pauline Letters, Including the Deutero-Pauline Letters', in Porter (ed.), *Handbook to Exegesis*, pp. 503-53, esp. pp. 539-50.

63. Biber, Conrad and Reppen, *Corpus Linguistics*, p. 124.

these have a strong organizing structure followed in the majority of cases. Their study demonstrates that even though these sections are clearly marked in the text with headings, the headings simply serve to re-enforce the underlying patterns of the discourse. Their findings, however, would seem to be applicable to texts that do not possess such strong or clearly marked divisions, such as an ancient letter, or other books of the New Testament. They conclude that 'frequency counts like these provide useful average characterizations of each section, and by considering such patterns across all four sections, it is possible to obtain an overview of the discourse organization of an article as a whole'.[64]

It is worth exploring whether similar claims can be made about Romans. For instance, is the distribution of the aspects, realized by the tense-forms, similar in the Thanksgiving and Body sections of the letter? Adopting the following outline of Romans: Opening (1.1-7), Thanksgiving (1.8-17), Body (1.18–11.36), Parenesis (12.1–15.33) and Closing (16.1-27),[65] we carried out a series of counts of linguistic features in each section. Each count is normalized to occurrences per thousand words in order to allow comparison between sections of vastly differing length (the majority of Romans is the Body).

Table 4

| Section | Aspect | | |
	Aorist Forms	Present Forms[66]	Perfect Forms[67]
Opening	51.95	25.97	12.99
Thanksgiving	63.69	95.54	6.37
Body	59.74	89.51	12.31
Parenesis	42.43	133.87	15.36
Closing	73.30	60.21	5.24

The first set of counts (Table 4) displays the distribution of the three tense-forms across the five sections of the letter of Romans. The aorist tense-forms occur with a relatively steady frequency throughout the book, though the Parenesis has the lowest frequency per thousand words and the Closing the highest. In contrast, the frequency of the pre-

64. Biber, Conrad and Reppen, *Corpus Linguistics*, p. 126.
65. Taken from L.M. McDonald and S.E. Porter, *Early Christianity and its Sacred Literature* (Peabody, MA: Hendrickson, forthcoming), Chapter 10.
66. Includes imperfect indicative forms and present forms in all moods.
67. Includes pluperfect indicative forms and perfect forms in all moods.

sent tense-forms (including the imperfect) shows some correspondence with the sections of the letter—the Thanksgiving and particularly the Parenesis exhibit higher frequencies. The Thanksgiving and the Closing are interesting due to their low frequency of the perfect tense-forms (including the pluperfect). Previous work has stressed the importance of a systemic view of the Greek aspects in the interpretation of the significance of an occurrence of a particular tense-form.[68] From a distributional standpoint the normal distribution of forms that grammaticalize +perfective and -perfective aspectual semantic features is roughly even (a probability of 0.5/0.5), but slightly skewed towards -perfective forms against +perfective forms in the Pauline corpus (0.67/0.33).[69] From this perspective, the Opening and Closing show significant variation with a high frequency of instances of perfective aspect. In contrast, the Parenesis is marked by the high frequency of instances of imperfective aspect. This would seem to be suitable for the more involved, directive nature of the parenetic material it contains.

Table 5

Section	Voice			
	Active	*Middle*	*Passive*	*Midd./Pass.*
Opening	38.96	25.97	25.97	0.00
Thanksgiving	95.54	19.11	44.59	19.11
Body	121.50	11.19	33.12	12.08
Parenesis	149.96	15.36	26.34	16.83
Closing	68.06	47.12	10.47	15.71

The second set of counts (Table 5) examines the voice system, which grammaticalizes the degree of involvement of the grammatical subject in the process described by the verbal form.[70] The active voice is the

68. Porter, *Idioms of the Greek New Testament*, p. 22.

69. In the 13-letter Pauline corpus there are 1651 +perfective (aorist) forms and 2984 -perfective (non-aorist) forms. For the whole of the New Testament the distribution is 11604 (0.48) to 12383 (0.52). For an exploration of the concept of distributional markedness as it applies to the Greek verbal system, and in particular to the aspect system, see S.E. Porter and M.B. O'Donnell, 'The Greek Verbal Network Viewed from a Probabilistic Standpoint: An Exercise in Hallidayan Linguistics', *FN* (forthcoming).

70. See Porter, *Idioms of the Greek New Testament*, pp. 62-63. The Middle/Passive column is included in the table due to the ambiguous nature of certain forms,

least semantically weighted of the Greek voices and this is the case when the distribution of voice in the New Testament is examined.[71] The Body and Parenesis demonstrate a normal Pauline distribution for voice. In combination with the high frequency of the present tense-forms in the Parenesis noted above, it is interesting to note that the highest occurrence per thousand words of the active voice occurs in this section of the letter. This is as might be expected from the rhetorical purpose of this section of Romans. The large number of middle voice forms in the Closing is due to the repeated use of the aorist imperative ἀσπάσασθε.[72] A comparison of figures from other Pauline and non-Pauline letters would help in the interpretation of these figures. For instance, is the highest occurrence of the passive voice to be expected in the Thanksgiving section as is the case in Romans?

Table 6

| *Section* | *Mood* | | | | | |
	Indicative	*Imperative*	*Subjunctive*	*Participle*	*Infinitive*	*Optative*
Opening	38.96	0.00	0.00	51.95	0.00	0.00
Thanksgiving	108.28	0.00	12.74	12.74	44.59	0.00
Body	112.55	2.91	11.41	37.14	11.64	2.24
Parenesis	84.13	23.41	16.83	54.13	28.53	1.46
Closing	57.59	44.50	7.85	23.56	7.85	0.00

The third set of counts (Table 6) relates to the distribution of mood forms across the epistolary structure of Romans. As might be expected, there is little use of the imperative mood until the Parenesis, where there is a marked increase in frequency, combined with an increase of the subjunctive and non-finite verbal forms (participle and infinitive) and a relative decrease of indicatives. The high frequency of impera-

---

where a decision between middle or passive voice cannot be made on the basis of form alone. This is the case for present, imperfect, perfect and pluperfect forms.

71. There are 18332 active forms and 7089 non-active forms (a 0.72/0.28 ratio) in the New Testament. In the 13-letter Pauline corpus the distribution is slightly more even: 3244 active forms to 1685 non-active forms (0.66/0.34). This may be the influence of the epistolary genre in comparison to narrative in the Gospels and Acts (0.73/0.27 ratio).

72. See comments of Silva on this form, in relation to his discussion of verbal aspect (*Explorations in Exegetical Method* [Grand Rapids: Baker Book House, 1996], p. 118).

tives in the closing is due to the repeated use of ἀσπάσασθε mentioned above. There is much more that could be said about the figures presented in these tables; however, it should be clear how they could be utilized in combination with the vertical plots presented earlier to investigate the texture of Romans.

2. *Interpersonal Semantic Component (Tenor)*. Regarding the tenor of the discourse, detailed investigation of the participant structure is likely to lead to some interesting insights into the interpersonal semantic structure of Romans. Appendix D charts the distribution of person and number reference across Romans (counting finite verbs and personal and intensive pronouns). Some interesting patterns emerge from the data. For example, this is a letter that Paul writes as the only 'author' in 1.1, but the first person singular is not used in the Opening (1.1-7). It does not occur until the Thanksgiving (1.8-17), where a group of second person plurals also occurs (1.6-15), the only cluster until 6.11-22. Despite Paul's authorship, the first person singular is only inconsistently used throughout the book, appearing in higher concentration in several select sections (e.g. 7.7-25—see below; ch. 9 throughout; and 15.14–16.25). However, there are a number of places where he uses the first person plural, a change of number. We must develop a more nuanced set of criteria for discussing this kind of semantic shift in number. Some instances may involve what is traditionally called a hortatory function, in some way including the audience for the sake of developing cohesion in the argument. There are other instances, however, where the first person plural is used to indicate a particular function of first person address, for example, in a rhetorical question as in 4.1, 'what shall we say...'

Other forms of personal reference must also be taken into consideration. For example, there is a noteworthy shift in 1.15, at the end of the Thanksgiving and the beginning of the Body, from first person singular to third person, where Paul describes God's wrath being poured out on all humanity (1.16-28). A consistent use of the third person continues throughout the Body, until the Parenesis begins in 12.1. The use of the third person returns in ch. 13, though not as intensively as before, but returns to its above intensity in chs. 14 and 15. Within the Body, there are several noteworthy uses of person that can be correlated with discussion of particular topics. For example, the second person is used at the beginning and the second half of ch. 2, when Paul is addressing various specific groups, such as judgmental people and Jews. The first person plural is used in 5.1-11, the reconciliation section; 6.1-8, the section on identifying with Christ; and 8.15-28, again a passage on Christian identification. There is of course the notorious problem of the 'I' in 7.7-25. Up until 7.7, the only concentrated occurrence of the first person singular is found in the Thanksgiving section (1.8-17). As would be expected, there is an increase and consistent presence of the second person after the beginning of ch. 12, which marks the start of the Parenesis section. The intention is that analysis of the person structure over the whole of the book would offer insights into some of the notoriously problematic passages, as well as offering general insight into the developing argument of Romans. This interpersonal structure is what creates much of the argumentative force of the text, as various relationships are established, and made prominent through various discourse means (such as mood, word order and voice).

3. *Ideational Semantic Component (Field)*. Regarding the ideational structure of Romans, there is a need for a thorough charting of semantic chains throughout the letter. The examples discussed earlier and the data presented in Appendix A begin to address this need. Utilizing semantic domains, such charting could be further refined by noting how these chains relate to the letter structure. For example, words of thankfulness in high concentration in the Thanksgiving Section of the book would need to be seen as defining the section, but to a large extent as semantically redundant, since they are expected words in such a context. Tables 7 and 8 show the number of occurrences per thousand words of verbs, nouns and adjectives from the 20 most frequent semantic domains in the letter, distributed across the five sections of Romans.

Table 7

Section	Semantic Domain									
	33	88	12	93	13	25	23	59	57	30
Opening	90.91	64.94	90.91	142.90	38.96	12.99	25.97	25.97	0.00	12.99
Thanksgiving	57.32	12.74	44.59	25.48	31.85	31.85	6.37	12.74	25.48	12.74
Body	58.63	49.45	34.46	25.73	28.64	15.66	22.15	16.56	14.32	12.98
Parenesis	45.35	38.77	40.97	26.34	19.02	43.16	27.07	24.87	28.53	12.44
Closing	89.01	20.94	34.03	128.30	20.94	13.09	0.00	20.94	2.62	7.85

Domains:

33: Communication	25: Attitudes and Emotions
88: Moral and Ethical Qualities and Related Behaviour	23: Physiological Processes and States
12: Supernatural Beings and Persons	59: Quantity
93: Names of Persons and Places	57: Possess, Transfer, Exchange
13: Be, Become, Exist, Happen	30: Think

Domain 33 (*Communication*) occurs with high density in every section of the New Testament. It is also the largest domain in the Louw–Nida lexicon. These facts make it one of the least interesting domains to examine across a discourse—one would expect words of communication to occur frequently throughout texts of varying registers, and words from this domain are in some ways semantically redundant. The same could be said for words of existence from domain 13. However, the classification procedure used by Louw and Nida[73] means that certain words have been placed in domain 33 when they might be better or additionally classified elsewhere. νόμος for instance, is listed with three uses in the lexicon: (a) law 33.33, (b) the Law 33.55 and (c) the Scriptures 33.56,[74] but all within domain 33. Certainly in Romans there would seem to be justification for an additional classification in the domain for words to do with control and rule (domain 37), which are found in the sections of the book following the Thanksgiving (see Table 8 below).

Nevertheless, a number of initial observations can be made on the basis of these data regarding the structure of Romans. For example, it is surprising to see that words for moral and ethical behaviour (domain 88) are not more frequent in the Parenesis. Instead, words from domain 25 (*Attitudes and Emotions*), such as ἐλπίς, ἀρέσκω, ὑπομονή, χαρά, εὐδοκέω, χαίρω and ἀγαπάω, are prominent in this section. On the other hand, it is not surprising to see the high frequency of words from domain 93 (*Names of Persons and Places*) in the Closing, given both the function of the closing section of the letter-form in general and Romans 16 in particular.

---

73. See Nida and Louw, *Lexical Semantics*, pp. 107-14.
74. Louw and Nida, *Greek–English Lexicon*, II, pp. 388-445.

Table 8

Section	Semantic Domain									
	8	31	28	10	11	15	67	42	53	37
Opening	12.99	12.99	0.00	38.96	12.99	0.00	0.00	0.00	38.96	0.00
Thanksgiving	0.00	38.22	19.11	12.74	25.48	12.74	0.00	0.00	6.37	0.00
Body	14.32	12.53	12.98	8.73	8.06	8.28	7.38	8.28	7.16	6.27
Parenesis	8.05	7.32	3.66	7.32	8.78	14.63	9.51	5.12	4.39	8.05
Closing	7.85	7.85	18.32	23.56	20.94	0.00	13.09	15.71	5.24	2.62

Domains:

8: Body, Body Parts and Body Products   15: Linear Movement
31: Hold a View, Believe, Trust   67: Time
28: Know   42: Perform, Do
10: Kinship Terms   53: Religious Activities
11: Groups and Classes of Persons and   37: Control, Rule
     Members of Such

The highest frequency per thousand of faith words (domain 31) is found in the Thanksgiving (πίστις and πιστεύω), as is the highest frequency of words from domain 28 (*Know*). The short length of the Opening and Thanksgiving sections tends to skew words from domains of lower frequencies. However, the normalization per thousand words allows for a rough comparison of the different sections, which can lead to the identification of a particular semantic focus. It is also interesting to note the lack of words from domain 42 (*Perform, Do*) until the final section of the letter. This is due to the mention of 'co-workers' in the greetings.

The data presented in Appendix A, along with the tables of the most frequent domains according to the letter structure, allow for the investigation of individual semantic domains. However, it seems intuitively the case that most significant semantic patterns will involve a combination of a number of domains and the absence of others. Careful and detailed study of these data would lead to the discovery of such patterns—but is it possible to identify such patterns in a less observationally intensive matter, allowing the exegete to discover the integrative patterns? The kind of data presented in the table can be analysed using multivariate statistical methods.[75] The data for these methods are

75. For an introduction to multivariate statistics, see B.F.J. Manly, *Multivariate Statistical Methods: A Primer* (London: Chapman & Hall, 1986). Common statistical methods (such as the χ^2 and *t*-test) are univariate statistical methods as they

arranged in a table with p columns representing p different variables measured for n subjects. So transposing the table in Appendix A, that is, swapping the rows and the columns, we have a table of $p = 82$ variables (each representing the number of occurrences of words from a semantic domain in a particular chapter) and $n = 16$ subjects (the chapters of Romans).

Table 9

Chap.	1	3	6	8	9	10	11	12	13	15	22	23	24	25	26
						Semantic Domain									
1	3	2	1	2	2	6	5	27	14	3	2	8	3	12	3
2	0	0	1	1	6	0	8	12	9	4	3	2	2	5	4
3	5	0	0	10	3	0	4	17	19	1	2	0	1	2	0
4	1	3	1	3	2	7	8	8	14	1	0	4	0	6	0
5	2	0	0	2	6	1	0	11	6	2	3	15	0	9	1
6	0	2	2	8	1	1	0	8	12	1	0	28	0	2	1
7	0	0	0	8	12	2	0	7	17	1	3	19	2	4	2
8	1	0	2	17	0	12	0	41	12	3	4	18	6	21	6
9	3	4	6	3	1	11	5	13	13	9	0	3	0	8	1
10	4	0	0	5	1	1	4	9	6	6	0	3	7	4	5
11	3	16	5	6	1	3	7	15	14	8	2	2	5	3	3
12	0	2	0	7	2	1	0	7	4	2	1	5	0	17	5
13	0	0	3	1	0	0	0	7	8	2	1	1	0	13	1
14	0	1	2	2	2	5	0	21	6	5	2	29	0	5	3
15	1	2	1	1	0	4	12	21	8	11	2	2	3	24	2
16	1	1	2	3	0	9	8	13	8	0	1	0	2	5	2

There are a number of different statistical methods that could be applied to these data, depending upon the desired end. One possible application is the semantic grouping of sections of text (in this case chapters) according to semantic domain. This would provide a means of demonstrating that chapters X and Y are semantically very similar, but distant from chapter Z. Cluster analysis provides suitable statistical methods for this task. Manly explains: 'The problem that cluster analysis is designed to solve is the following one: given a sample of n objects, each of which has a score on p variables, devise a scheme for grouping the objects into classes so that "similar" ones are in the same

concentrate on analysing the significance of variation in one variable. In contrast, Manly states that 'the whole point of multivariate analysis is to consider several related random variables simultaneously, each one being considered equally important at the start of the analysis' (*Multivariate Statistical Methods*, p. 1).

class'.[76] There are two main types of cluster analysis: hierarchical and partitioning methods. Hierarchical methods aim to show the relationship between objects in terms of similarity—the most closely related are joined together first, then the resulting groups are joined to their next closest object or group. Partitioning methods seek to place all objects into a specified number of groups so that objects in a particular group are closely related to other objects in the same group.[77] The basis of all clustering methods is a measure of the distance between two objects, referred to as the *distance coefficient*. Given a data matrix of the scores on p variables of n objects, it is possible to calculate a distance matrix that contains the distance between the first object and the second object ($dist_{12}$), between the first and third objects ($dist_{13}$), up to the first and n^{th} objects ($dist_{1n}$) and so on.[78] For example, suppose there are four objects, A, B, C, D, with the following distance matrix:

	A	B	C	D
A	-	-	-	-
B	6	-	-	-
C	1	4	-	-
D	7	2	5	-

Given these distances, partitioning objects A, B, C, D into three groups would result in groups: (A, C) (B) (D), given that the distance between A and C is smaller than the distance between the next closest pair. Partitioning into two groups would result in groups (A, C) and (B, D).

A hierarchical method begins at $t = 0$ with all four objects ungrouped. Then the plot progresses, A and C are the first objects to cluster ($t = 1$), then B and D ($t = 2$). These two clusters ([A C] and [B D]) remain ungrouped at $t = 3$, finally joining at $t = 4$.

76. Manly, *Multivariate Statistical Methods*, p. 100.

77. See Manly, *Multivariate Statistical Methods*, pp. 100-101; M. Oakes, *Statistics for Corpus Linguistics* (Edinburgh Textbooks in Empirical Linguistics; Edinburgh: Edinburgh University Press, 1998), pp. 115-20; A. Woods, P. Fletcher and A. Hughes, *Statistics in Language Studies* (CTL; Cambridge: Cambridge University Press, 1986), pp. 249-61.

78. On various distance measures, see Manly, *Multivariate Statistical Methods*, pp. 42-58.

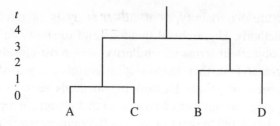

This kind of plot is called a dendrogram. Taking a matrix of $n = 16$ (chapters in Romans) and $p = 38$ (semantic domains that occur more than 20 times in Romans) as the data for a hierarchical clustering algorithm produces the denogram presented in Appendix E. We shall not explore all of the possible implications of this clustering in detail here. However, the groupings produced from the hierarchical clustering of the most frequent semantic domains in Romans are as would be expected in some cases (according to the results of traditional exegesis), but somewhat surprising in others. For example, the close semantic relationship between consecutive chapters is not surprising. Romans 3 and 4 are two of the first to cluster,[79] and later chs. 12 and 13, which mark the beginning of the Parenesis. Somewhat surprising, however, is the first grouping to occur—chs. 9 and 15. A closer look at Appendix A indicates that the high frequency of words from domains 12 (*Supernatural Beings and Powers*), 93 (*Names of Persons and Places*) and 13 (*Be, Become, Exist, Happen*) might be responsible for this grouping. The next group to join with chs. 9 and 15 is the grouping of chs. 2 and 10. This is again an unexpected result, and it is not immediately clear which domains are responsible for this grouping. These four chapters next join with ch. 16, making a group of five chapters that remain distant from the rest of the book until the final grouping. We leave the reader to explore the possible interpretative implications of Appendix E. We offer the method here as a possible tool that, with some careful refinement, might be used to offer insight into semantic and argumentative patterns in Romans.

At this point we must offer the following caveat. Clustering algorithms will find clusters even within randomly generated data and different clustering algorithms may produce variations in the clusters they

---

79. The clustering in the chart moves from the left hand side, where all chapters are ungrouped, to the right hand side, where they have been joined into one group.

find for the same data set.[80] At present there is no agreement as to the best clustering algorithm, as different problems are suited to different methods. As with the use of any statistical methods for the interpretation of both linguistic features and extra-linguistic features (such as authorship) of texts, the interpreter should proceed with caution and seek to support the statistical results with other exegetical tools. In the light of this, we also decided to examine the semantic data using a non-hierarchical (partitioning) clustering algorithm.

Greenwood has carried out a number of studies of the vocabulary of the Pauline corpus and Luke–Acts using a combination of non-hierarchical clustering and non-linear mapping[81] to address questions of authorship.[82] For the Pauline letters he shows how what he labels the Missionary (Romans, 1 and 2 Corinthians and Galatians), Captivity (Philippians, Colossians, Ephesians) and Pastoral (1 and 2 Timothy and Titus) Epistles form three clusters on the basis of the frequency of the ten most common words in the Greek text. Though his concern is with the classification of letters as a whole, he chooses to use the chapter as the basic variable for scoring these ten words. In this study, we have used the same method but are interested in the way in which individual chapters within Romans cluster. Table 10 below shows the results of applying a non-hierarchical clustering (partitioning) algorithm to the data described above, requesting two-, three- and four-cluster solutions.

---

80. See warnings in Manly, *Multivariate Statistical Methods*, pp. 104-105. Oakes states that 'clustering methods will find patterns even in random data, and thus it is important to determine the validity of any categorisation produced by a clustering method' (*Statistics for Corpus Linguistics*, p. 120).

81. There are a number of multivariate statistical techniques, such as Principal Components Analysis, Correspondence Analysis and Multidimensional Scaling, that can be classified as *mapping* techniques in that they aim to reduce the dimensionality of the data so that they can be more easily interpreted and plotted. See Woods, Fletcher and Hughes, *Statistics in Language Studies*, pp. 273-90; Manly, *Multivariate Statistical Methods*, pp. 59-71, 126-40.

82. H.H. Greenwood, 'St Paul Revisited—A Computational Result', *Literary and Linguistic Computing* 7 (1992), pp. 43-47; *idem*, 'St Paul Revisited—Word Clusters in Multidimensional Space', *Literary and Linguistic Computing* 8 (1993), pp. 221-29; *idem*, 'Common Word Frequencies and Authorship in Luke's Gospel and Acts', *Literary and Linguistic Computing* 10 (1995), pp. 183-87.

Table 10

Non-Hierarchical Clustering	Chapters of Romans
2-Cluster Solution	1 2 3 4 9 10 11 15 16
	5 6 7 8 12 13 14
3-Cluster Solution	1 2 3 4 9 10 11
	5 6 7 8 12 13 14
	15 16
4-Cluster Solution	1 3 4 7 12
	2 9 10 15 16
	5 6 13
	8 11 14

Here we will comment only on the three-cluster solution. The first and most obvious result is the grouping of Romans 15 and 16 as a separate cluster. Some might not find this surprising in the light of the discussion of the originality of ch. 16 and parts of ch. 15.[83] The other two clusters contain equal numbers of chapters. The first cluster contains chs. 1–4 and then 9–11. It is fascinating to see that commentators have also identified these units, particularly 9–11, for a considerable amount of time. In the second cluster, chs. 5–8 makes a unit, along with the bulk of the parenetic material. Greenwood uses a non-linear mapping algorithm[84] to represent all the information found in a multidimensional space in two or three dimensions. The plot in Appendix F shows the result of the application of Sammons's algorithm with the clusters from the three-group partitioning superimposed on the plot.[85]

A comparison of Appendix E and Appendix F illustrates the variation that can occur when utilizing different multivariate techniques. But the same points noted from the hierarchical plot, such as the unexpected grouping of chs. 9 and 15, and chs. 1 and 11, can be seen in the close proximity of these chapters in the two-dimensional mapping in Appendix F. In the future, more detailed studies are required to improve and

83. See H. Gamble, Jr, *The Textual History of the Letter to the Romans: A Study in Textual and Literary Criticism* (SD, 42; Grand Rapids: Eerdmans, 1977).

84. J.E. Sammons, 'A Nonlinear Mapping for Data Analysis', *IEE Translations on Computers* 18.5 (1969), pp. 401-409.

85. Greenwood plots an ellipsis with its centre calculated from the clustering data. We have not attempted to carry out such a precise procedure. The purpose of the groupings on the plot in Appendix F is simply to illustrate the results of both procedures (non-linear mapping and non-hierarchical clustering) together.

refine these methods for application to the study of the New Testament. However, in our opinion these initial explorations offer considerable potential for understanding the meaningful structures not only of Romans, but of other books of the New Testament as well.

4. *Conclusion*

This paper has attempted to present in a brief summary some of the past and present work being done in New Testament studies, and in particular on the book of Romans, from a linguistic standpoint. We have concentrated on two interrelated dimensions—semantics and patterns of argumentation. We have tried to show that these two areas are closely related. The basic semantic information gathered through a study of a variety of analytical means—including semantic domains, morphology, and discourse features—can be utilized in an effort to understand the larger structure of the book of Romans. When the two are integrated, patterns of meaning that apply to the overall strategy of the book can be assessed in terms of the particular linguistic features of which these patterns are composed. In order to perform the kind of analysis that we are suggesting here, we believe that more advanced semantic tools must be developed for New Testament studies. These involve extension and development of many recent developments in New Testament linguistic study. Although some of these include application of a variety of statistical and corpus-based techniques, these tools are seen to be applied in the service of greater understanding of the text itself. That is why we have also maintained and attempted to develop further the importance of the Pauline letter form as an important interpretative guide. We have set this within a Hallidayan functional grammatical model as what we consider the most productive linguistic framework for analysis of texts in terms of both micro- and macro-structural patterns of meaning. In a paper of this sort, we have only been able to be brief and suggestive, beginning with the current state of play and attempting to build upon this. We recognize that much more needs to be done in refining and applying the concepts introduced here. Our hope is that such work will have application in more traditional exegesis, including the writing of commentaries, where such information can be more easily integrated and disseminated for the benefit of exegetes.

APPENDIX A

Distribution of Semantic Domains in Romans

Semantic Domain	(Occurrences per Chapter)															
	1	2	3	4	5	6	7	8	9	10	11	12	13	14	15	16
33 Communication	25	44	28	21	11	5	33	22	38	34	17	12	6	8	36	34
88 Moral and Ethical Qualities and Related Behaviour	26	18	21	16	31	30	31	8	19	10	18	22	13	8	10	8
12 Supernatural Beings and Powers	27	12	17	8	11	8	7	41	13	9	15	7	7	21	21	13
93 Names of Persons and Places	15	7	8	10	15	9	3	14	25	12	12	1	2	4	29	49
13 Be, Become, Exist, Happen	14	9	19	14	6	12	17	12	13	6	14	4	8	6	8	8
25 Attitudes and Emotions	12	5	2	6	9	2	4	21	8	4	3	17	13	5	24	5
23 Physiological Processes and States	8	2	-	4	15	28	19	18	3	3	2	5	1	29	2	-
59 Quantity	8	4	12	5	18	1	1	7	8	7	7	7	4	9	14	8
57 Possess, Transfer, Exchange	11	8	1	7	8	5	1	9	4	3	11	12	8	8	11	1
30 Think	5	10	7	13	-	1	7	6	7	-	5	2	2	13	-	3
8 Body, Body Parts and Body Products	2	1	10	3	2	8	8	17	3	5	6	7	1	2	1	3
31 Hold a View, Believe, Trust	9	-	13	17	2	1	4	-	3	10	4	2	1	5	2	3
28 Know	10	11	5	-	1	4	8	7	5	3	7	-	2	1	2	7
10 Kinship Terms	6	-	-	7	1	1	2	12	11	1	3	1	-	5	4	9
11 Groups and Classes of Persons and Members of Such Groups and Classes	5	8	4	8	-	1	-	-	5	4	7	-	-	-	12	8
15 Linear Movement	3	4	1	1	2	1	1	3	9	6	8	2	2	5	11	-
67 Time	2	3	1	2	3	6	3	5	3	2	3	1	7	4	1	5
42 Perform, Do	6	9	3	4	-	-	3	7	4	-	1	1	4	1	1	6

Semantic Domain	Occurrences per Chapter															
	1	2	3	4	5	6	7	8	9	10	11	12	13	14	15	16
53 Religious Activities	7	6	3	7	1	5	-	1	1	-	5	2	-	1	3	2
37 Control, Rule	-	1	1	-	7	6	2	9	1	1	-	-	8	2	1	1
9 People	2	6	3	2	6	1	12	-	1	1	1	2	-	2	-	-
26 Psychological Faculties	3	4	-	-	1	1	2	6	1	5	3	5	1	3	2	2
3 Plants	2	-	-	3	-	2	-	-	4	-	16	2	-	1	2	1
92 Discourse Referentials	2	-	2	1	1	1	2	2	3	1	2	2	5	4	5	-
85 Existence in Space	-	-	1	1	1	6	5	3	2	'	5	1	1	4	-	1
24 Sensory Events and States	3	2	1	-	-	-	2	6	-	7	5	-	-	-	3	2
34 Association	2	1	7	2	3	1	1	3	1	-	4	2	-	-	2	2
58 Nature, Example, Class	4	5	1	1	-	-	4	2	1	1	5	2	2	-	-	2
79 Features of Objects	6	2	5	1	1	1	-	2	4	1	2	-	-	1	1	-
74 Able, Capable	4	-	-	2	1	1	-	7	1	-	-	-	-	3	6	2
6 Artifacts	1	1	-	1	-	2	-	2	6	-	5	-	3	2	1	2
22 Trouble, Hardship, Relief, Favorable Circumstances	2	3	2	-	3	-	3	4	-	-	2	1	1	2	2	1
36 Guide, Discipline, Follow	2	4	-	1	3	5	-	-	-	2	4	-	-	2	2	2
87 Status	2	2	-	-	-	9	2	1	3	-	-	2	2	-	-	1
1 Geographical Objects and Features	3	-	5	1	2	-	-	1	3	4	3	-	-	1	-	1
90 Case	3	2	3	1	-	-	5	-	3	1	-	1	3	-	1	1
60 Number	-	-	3	-	12	-	-	-	2	-	1	3	-	-	1	-
27 Learn	2	2	1	-	2	-	2	1	-	3	4	1	1	1	-	1
21 Danger, Risk, Safe, Save	1	-	-	-	2	-	1	2	1	4	4	-	1	-	1	1
35 Help, Care for	-	1	-	-	-	-	-	3	1	-	1	2	3	-	5	2

Semantic Domain	1	2	3	4	5	6	7	8	9	10	11	12	13	14	15	16
39 Hostility, Strife	1	-	1	-	1	-	1	3	1	-	1	4	4	1	-	1
56 Courts and Legal Procedures	-	4	2	-	3	-	-	3	-	-	1	2	1	1	-	-
20 Violence, Harm, Destroy, Kill	1	1	1	-	-	1	2	4	1	-	2	-	1	2	-	-
41 Behaviour and Related States	1	3	-	3	1	-	6	-	-	-	-	1	-	-	1	-
63 Whole, Unite, Part, Divide	2	-	-	-	-	-	-	3	1	1	3	1	1	-	2	1
65 Value	2	3	4	-	-	-	-	2	-	-	3	-	1	-	-	-
18 Attachment	1	-	-	1	2	-	3	2	-	-	4	-	1	2	2	-
32 Understand	5	1	1	-	-	-	-	-	1	1	4	1	-	-	1	-
68 Aspect	-	1	1	1	-	-	-	1	2	-	-	5	2	1	1	-
17 Stances and Events Related to Stances	-	-	-	2	-	2	1	3	-	1	-	-	1	1	1	-
19 Physical Impact	-	-	-	-	-	-	-	-	1	-	5	-	-	1	1	1
71 Mode	1	-	-	2	-	-	-	1	1	-	1	2	-	-	1	-
72 True, False	2	3	2	-	-	-	-	-	1	-	-	-	-	-	1	-
4 Animals	3	-	1	-	-	-	-	1	1	-	-	-	-	-	-	-
7 Constructions	-	-	1	-	-	-	-	-	-	-	-	-	-	2	2	1
14 Physical Events and States	1	1	-	-	-	-	1	-	-	1	1	-	1	-	-	-
40 Reconciliation, Forgiveness	-	-	1	1	3	-	-	-	-	-	1	-	-	-	-	-
43 Agriculture	-	-	-	-	-	-	-	-	-	-	6	-	-	-	-	-
2 Natural Substances	-	-	-	-	-	-	-	-	4	-	-	1	-	-	-	-
5 Foods and Condiments	-	-	-	-	-	-	-	-	-	-	-	-	-	5	-	-
64 Comparison	1	-	-	-	1	1	-	1	1	-	-	-	-	-	-	-
81 Spatial Dimensions	-	-	-	-	-	-	-	1	-	-	2	2	-	-	-	-
49 Activities Involving Clothing and Adorning	-	-	-	-	-	-	-	1	-	-	-	-	3	-	-	-

Occurrences per Chapter

Semantic Domain	Occurrences per Chapter															
	1	2	3	4	5	6	7	8	9	10	11	12	13	14	15	16
80 Space	-	-	-	-	-	-	-	-	1	1	-	1	-	-	1	-
16 Non-Linear Movement	-	-	1	-	-	-	-	-	-	1	-	-	-	-	1	-
29 Memory and Recall	1	-	-	-	-	-	-	-	-	1	-	-	1	-	1	-
38 Punish, Reward	1	-	-	-	-	-	-	-	-	-	-	-	1	-	-	1
46 Household Activities	-	-	-	-	-	-	-	-	-	-	-	-	-	1	-	1
47 Activities Involving Liquids or Masses	-	-	1	-	1	-	-	-	-	-	-	-	-	1	-	-
73 Genuine, Phony	-	-	-	-	-	-	-	-	-	-	-	2	-	-	-	-
84 Spatial Extensions	-	1	-	-	-	-	-	-	-	-	-	-	1	-	-	-
89 Relations	-	-	-	-	-	1	-	-	-	-	-	1	-	-	-	-
44 Animal Husbandry, Fishing	-	-	-	-	-	-	-	-	-	-	1	-	-	-	-	-
45 Building, Constructing	-	-	-	-	-	-	-	-	-	-	-	-	-	-	1	-
52 Funerals and Burial	-	-	-	-	-	1	-	-	-	-	-	-	-	-	-	-
55 Military Activities	-	-	-	-	-	-	1	-	-	-	-	-	-	-	-	-
66 Proper, Improper	1	-	-	-	-	-	-	-	-	-	-	-	-	-	-	-
75 Adequate, Qualified	-	-	-	-	-	-	-	-	1	-	-	-	-	-	-	-
76 Power, Force	-	-	-	1	-	-	-	-	-	-	-	-	-	-	-	-
77 Ready, Prepared	-	-	-	-	-	-	1	-	1	-	-	-	-	-	-	-
78 Degree	-	-	-	-	-	-	-	1	-	-	-	-	-	-	-	-
82 Spatial Orientations	-	-	-	-	-	-	-	-	-	-	-	-	-	-	-	-

APPENDIX B

Aspect Domain Browser

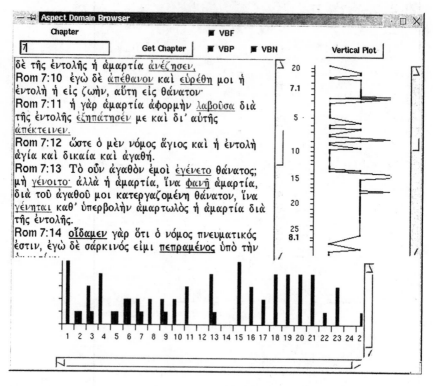

Aspect Domain Browser

Text Window: underline = aorist (perfective aspect)
shaded = present and imperfect (imperfective aspect)
shaded and underline = perfect and pluperfect (stative aspect)

Vertical Plot: left points = aorist
middle points = present and imperfect
right points = perfect and pluperfect

Histogram: For each verse (x-axis) there are three potential bars (height on y-axis represents number of occurrences per verse)
First bar (medium shading) = aorist
Second bar (dark shading) = present and imperfect
Third bar (light shading) = perfect and pluperfect

This Aspect Domain Browser is available at http://www.OpenText.org/romans

APPENDIX C

Vertical Plot of Aspect across Romans

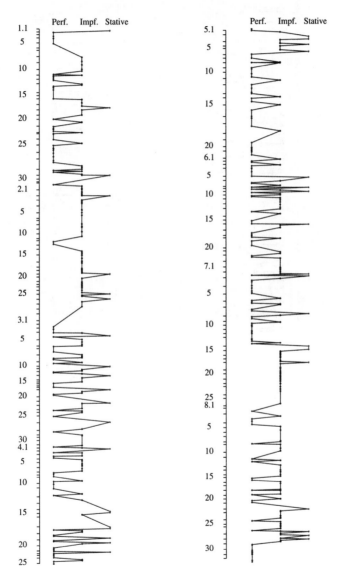

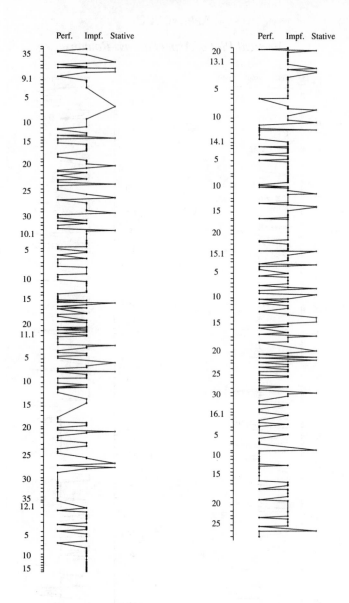

APPENDIX D

Distribution of Person and Number in Romans
(Occurrences per Verse)

Chapter 1

	1	2	3	4	5	6	7	8	9	10	11	12	13	14	15	16	17	18	19	20	21	22	23	24	25	26	27	28	29	30
1s	-	-	-	-	-	-	-	-	-	-	-	-	-	1	1	1	-	-	-	-	-	-	-	-	-	-	-	-	-	-
1p	-	-	-	1	1	-	-	-	4	2	2	1	4	1	-	-	-	-	-	-	-	-	-	-	-	-	-	-	-	-
2s	-	-	-	-	-	-	1	-	-	-	-	-	-	-	-	-	-	-	-	-	-	-	-	-	-	-	-	-	-	-
2p	-	-	-	-	-	2	-	2	1	1	3	2	3	-	1	-	4	1	2	3	-	-	-	-	-	-	-	-	-	-
3s	-	2	1	-	1	-	-	1	2	-	-	1	-	-	-	1	-	-	3	1	5	1	1	1	1	1	1	1	-	-
3p	-	-	-	-	-	-	-	-	-	-	-	-	-	-	-	-	-	-	-	1	1	1	1	4	3	3	3	2	-	-

Chapter 1

	31	32
1s	-	-
1p	-	-
2s	-	-
2p	-	-
3s	-	-
3p	-	-

Chapter 2

	1	2	3	4	5	6	7	8	9	10	11	12	13	14	15	16	17	18	19	20	21	22	23	24
1s	-	-	-	-	-	-	-	-	-	-	-	-	-	-	-	1	-	-	-	-	-	-	-	-
1p	-	1	-	-	-	-	-	-	-	-	-	-	-	-	-	-	-	-	-	-	-	-	-	-
2s	4	-	3	2	2	-	-	-	-	-	-	-	-	-	-	-	4	2	1	-	2	2	2	1
2p	-	-	-	-	-	-	-	-	-	-	-	-	-	-	-	-	-	-	-	-	-	-	-	2
3s	-	1	-	2	-	2	-	-	-	-	1	-	-	-	-	1	-	-	-	-	-	-	-	-
3p	-	-	1	-	-	-	-	-	-	-	-	4	1	2	3	-	-	-	-	-	-	-	-	-

Chapter 2   **Chapter 3**

	25	26	27	28	29	1	2	3	4	5	6	7	8	9	10	11	12	13	14	15	16	17	18	19	20	21	22	23	24
1s	-	-	-	-	-	-	-	-	-	1	-	2	-	-	-	-	-	-	-	-	-	-	-	-	-	-	-	-	-
1p	-	1	-	-	-	-	-	-	4	2	-	-	3	2	-	-	-	-	-	-	-	1	-	1	-	-	-	-	-
2s	3	-	1	-	-	4	-	-	-	-	-	-	-	-	-	-	-	-	-	-	-	-	-	-	-	-	-	-	-
2p	-	-	-	-	-	-	-	-	-	-	-	-	-	-	-	-	-	-	-	-	-	-	-	-	-	-	-	-	-
3s	2	3	1	1-	-	-	1	-	3	1	2	2	2	-	2	2	2	-	1	1	1	1	1	4	2	1	1	1	1
3p	-	-	-	-	-	-	1	2	-	-	-	-	1	-	-	-	2	4	-	-	1	-	-	-	-	-	-	2	-

Chapter 3   **Chapter 4**

	25	26	27	28	29	30	31	1	2	3	4	5	6	7	8	9	10	11	12	13	14	15	16	17	18	19	20
1s	-	-	-	-	-	-	-	-	-	-	-	-	-	-	-	-	-	-	-	-	-	-	-	1	-	-	-
1p	-	-	1	-	-	-	-	-	2	-	-	-	-	-	-	1	-	1	-	-	-	-	1	-	1	1	-
2s	-	-	-	-	-	-	-	-	-	-	-	-	-	-	-	-	-	-	-	-	-	-	-	-	-	-	-
2p	-	-	-	-	-	-	-	-	-	-	-	-	-	-	-	-	-	-	-	-	-	-	-	-	-	-	-
3s	3	2	1	-	-	-	1	-	-	4	1	2	2	-	1	1	1	2	-	2	2	2	2	2	3	1	2
3p	-	-	-	-	-	-	-	-	-	-	-	-	-	2	-	-	-	-	1	-	-	-	-	-	-	-	-

Chapter 4   **Chapter 5**

	21	22	23	24	25	1	2	3	4	5	6	7	8	9	10	11	12	13	14	15	16	17	18	19	20	21
1s	-	-	-	-	-	-	-	-	-	-	-	-	-	-	-	-	-	-	-	-	-	-	-	-	-	-
1p	-	-	-	2	2	2	3	1	-	2	1	-	3	1	2	2	-	-	-	-	-	-	-	-	1	-
2s	-	-	-	-	-	-	-	-	-	-	-	-	-	-	-	-	-	-	-	-	-	-	-	-	-	-
2p	-	-	-	-	-	-	-	-	-	-	-	-	-	-	-	-	-	-	-	-	-	-	-	-	-	-
3s	2	2	4	1	2	-	-	1	-	2	1	2	2	2	2	-	2	2	2	1	-	1	-	4	2	-
3p	-	-	-	-	-	-	-	-	-	-	-	-	-	-	-	1	-	-	-	1	-	-	2	-	-	-

Chapter 6

	1	2	3	4	5	6	7	8	9	10	11	12	13	14	15	16	17	18	19	20	21	22	23
1s	-	-	-	-	2	-	-	3	-	-	-	-	-	-	2	-	-	-	1	-	-	-	-
1p	2	2	2	3	2	2	-	-	-	-	-	-	-	-	-	-	-	-	-	-	-	-	1
2s	-	-	-	-	-	-	-	-	-	-	-	-	-	-	-	-	-	-	-	-	-	-	-
2p	-	-	1	-	-	-	-	1	-	2	2	1	4	2	-	4	3	1	5	2	2	2	-
3s	1	2	1	2	1	2	1	1	3	4	-	2	-	1	1	-	-	-	-	-	2	-	-
3p	-	-	-	-	-	-	-	-	-	-	-	-	-	-	-	-	-	-	-	-	-	-	-

Chapter 7

	1	2	3	4
1s	1	-	-	1
1p	-	-	-	1
2s	-	-	-	-
2p	1	-	-	3
3s	2	3	5	-
3p	-	-	-	-

Chapter 7

	5	6	7	8	9	10	11	12	13	14	15	16	17	18	19	20	21	22	23	24	25
1s	-	-	2	1	2	3	1	-	2	2	6	3	3	4	4	6	3	1	5	2	2
1p	2	3	1	-	-	-	1	-	-	1	-	-	-	-	4	-	-	-	-	-	1
2s	-	-	1	-	-	-	-	-	-	-	-	-	-	-	-	-	-	-	-	-	-
2p	-	-	-	-	-	-	-	-	-	-	-	-	-	-	-	-	-	-	-	-	-
3s	1	-	2	1	1	1	3	-	4	1	-	-	1	3	-	1	1	-	5	1	-
3p	-	-	-	-	-	-	-	-	-	-	-	-	-	-	-	-	-	-	-	1	-

Chapter 8

	1	2	3	4	5	6
1s	-	-	-	-	-	-
1p	-	-	-	1	-	-
2s	-	-	1	-	-	-
2p	-	-	-	-	-	-
3s	1	2	2	1	-	1
3p	-	-	-	-	1	-

Chapter 8

	7	8	9	10	11	12	13	14	15	16	17	18	19	20	21	22	23	24	25	26	27	28	29	30	31	32	33	34
1s	-	-	-	-	-	-	-	-	-	-	-	1	-	-	-	-	-	-	-	-	-	-	-	-	-	-	-	-
1p	-	-	-	-	1	-	-	-	1	2	2	1	-	-	-	1	3	1	3	3	-	1	-	-	-	-	-	-
2s	-	-	-	-	-	4	-	-	2	-	-	-	-	-	-	-	-	-	-	-	-	-	-	-	-	-	-	-
2p	-	3	3	1	3	4	-	-	-	-	-	-	1	2	2	2	-	3	4	-	2	1	4	6	-	-	-	-
3s	2	-	4	-	2	2	-	-	2	2	-	-	1	1	2	2	-	-	4	4	2	-	-	-	-	-	-	-
3p	-	1	-	-	-	-	2	-	-	-	-	-	-	-	-	-	-	-	-	-	-	-	-	-	-	-	-	-

Chapter 8 | Chapter 9

	35	36	37	38	39	1	2	3	4	5	6	7	8	9	10	11	12	13	14	15	16	17	18	19	20	21	22	23
1s	-	-	-	-	-	4	2	4	-	-	-	-	-	1	-	-	-	2	1	4	-	4	-	-	1	-	-	-
1p	-	-	-	-	-	-	-	-	-	-	-	-	-	-	-	-	-	-	1	-	-	-	-	-	-	-	-	-
2s	-	-	-	-	-	-	-	-	-	-	-	1	-	-	-	-	-	-	-	-	-	2	-	1	-	-	-	-
2p	-	-	-	-	-	-	-	-	-	-	1	-	2	-	-	1	-	-	-	-	-	-	-	-	-	-	2	3
3s	-	-	-	-	-	-	1	-	-	-	1	1	2	1	-	1	3	1	1	2	-	2	4	3	1	1	2	-
3p	-	-	-	-	-	-	-	1	-	-	1	-	-	-	-	-	-	-	-	-	-	-	-	-	-	-	-	-

Chapter 9 | Chapter 10

	24	25	26	27	28	29	30	31	32	33	1	2	3	4	5	6	7	8	9	10	11	12	13	14	15	16	17	18
1s	3	1	-	-	-	-	-	-	-	-	-	1	-	-	-	-	-	1	-	-	-	-	-	-	-	-	-	1
1p	1	-	-	-	-	3	1	-	-	-	-	-	-	-	-	2	-	3	5	-	-	-	-	-	-	-	-	-
2s	-	-	-	-	-	-	-	-	-	-	-	-	-	-	-	-	-	1	-	-	-	-	-	-	-	-	-	-
2p	-	1	-	-	-	-	-	-	-	-	-	-	-	-	-	-	-	-	-	-	-	-	-	1	-	-	-	-
3s	1	1	2	3	3	2	1	-	-	-	2	-	-	-	2	3	2	3	2	3	-	2	2	2	-	1	1	-
3p	-	2	2	-	-	-	1	-	-	1	2	2	-	4	2	-	-	1	-	-	2	-	-	-	-	-	-	3

Chapter 10 | Chapter 11

	19	20	21	1	2	3	4	5	6	7	8	9	10	11	12	13	14	15	16	17	18	19	20	21	22	23	24	25
1s	4	4	2	3	-	3	-	-	-	-	-	-	-	1	-	5	3	-	-	2	5	1	4	1	-	5	-	3	1
1p	-	-	-	-	-	-	-	2	-	-	-	-	-	-	-	-	-	-	-	-	-	-	-	-	-	-	-	-
2s	-	-	-	-	-	2	-	-	-	-	-	-	-	-	-	-	-	-	-	2	1	-	4	1	-	-	3	-
2p	2	-	-	-	1	-	-	-	1	-	-	2	-	1	-	-	1	-	-	-	-	1	-	-	2	-	-	2
3s	2	2	1	3	-	3	2	-	2	3	2	2	-	1	-	1	1	-	-	2	-	2	1	2	-	1	1	2
3p	-	-	-	3	-	1	-	3	2	1	1	4	3	-	2	-	1	1	-	2	-	1	2	-	3	1	2	-

Chapter 15

	16	17	18	19	20	21	22	23	24	25	26	27	28	29	30	31	32	33
1s	1	1	2	1	1	-	1	-	3	1	-	-	1	2	3	-	-	-
1p	1	-	-	-	-	-	-	-	-	-	-	-	-	-	1	-	-	-
2s	-	-	-	-	-	-	-	-	-	-	-	-	-	-	-	-	-	-
2p	1	-	-	-	1	3	1	1	3	-	-	-	1	1	1	-	-	-
3s	1	-	1	-	1	3	-	-	-	-	-	-	-	-	-	-	-	-
3p	-	-	-	-	-	3	-	-	-	-	1	7	1	-	-	-	-	-

Chapter 16

	1	2	3	4	5	6	7	8	9	10
1s	1	1	1	3	1	-	3	1	1	-
1p	1	-	-	-	-	-	-	-	1	-
2s	-	-	-	-	-	-	-	-	-	-
2p	1	3	1	-	1	2	1	1	1	2
3s	-	5	-	-	1	1	-	-	-	-
3p	-	-	-	1	1	-	2	-	-	-

Chapter 16

	11	12	13	14	15	16	17	18	19	20	21	22	23	24	25	26	27
1s	1	-	1	-	-	-	1	-	2	-	2	2	1	-	1	-	-
1p	-	-	1	-	-	-	1	1	-	1	2	-	-	-	-	-	-
2s	-	-	-	-	-	-	-	-	-	-	-	-	-	-	-	-	-
2p	2	2	1	1	1	2	4	-	3	2	1	1	2	-	1	-	-
3s	-	1	1	-	1	-	-	-	1	1	1	-	2	-	-	-	-
3p	-	-	-	1	1	1	1	2	-	-	-	-	-	-	-	-	-

APPENDIX E

Dendrogram Illustrating Semantic Clustering of
Individual Chapters of the Book of Romans

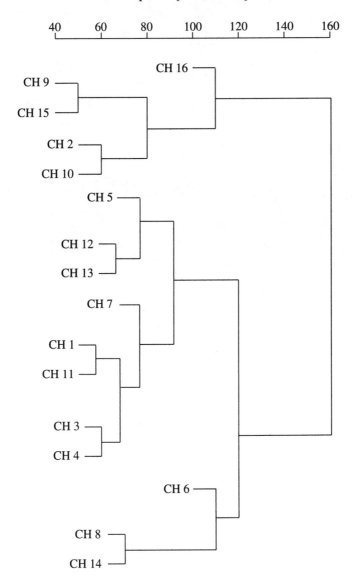

APPENDIX F

Sammon Non-Linear Mapping of Semantic Domains in Romans

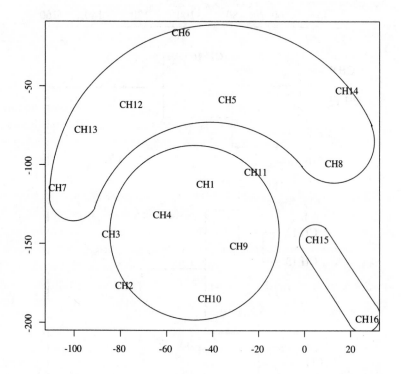

IDEOLOGY AND POINT OF VIEW IN GALATIANS 1–2:
A CRITICAL LINGUISTIC ANALYSIS

Edward Adams

This essay experiments with a style of textual analysis known as 'critical linguistics', a mode of investigating texts now well established in literary and media studies but yet to make an impact in New Testament scholarship.[1] The approach was developed by Roger Fowler and his colleagues at the University of East Anglia during the 1970s. It draws on literary criticism, especially Russian literary theory, and Michael Halliday's model of functional linguistics. It seeks, by scrutinizing the linguistic structures of a text, to bring to the surface 'ideological patterns' encoded in the language.[2]

In their analyses, the practitioners of critical linguistics explore the ways in which language-uses in texts reflect and serve dominant ideologies and reinforce asymmetrical power-relations in societies and

---

1. S.E. Porter considers the potential of this and similar types of analysis for New Testament interpretation in 'Is Critical Discourse Analysis Critical? An Evaluation Using Philemon as a Test Case', in S.E. Porter and J.T. Reed (eds.), *Discourse Analysis and the New Testament: Approaches and Results* (JSNTSup, 170; SNTG, 4; Sheffield: Sheffield Academic Press, 1999), pp. 47-70. T. Klutz takes up critical linguistic methodology in 'Naked and Wounded: Foregrounding, Relevance and Situation in Acts 19:13-20', pp. 258-79 of the same volume. These studies were unavailable to me at the time of writing. In my book *Constructing the World: A Study in Paul's Cosmological Language* (SNTW; Edinburgh: T. & T. Clark, 2000), I apply critical linguistic analysis to Paul's usage of the terms κόσμος (world) and κτίσις (creation).

2. R. Fowler, 'Critical Linguistics', in K. Malmkjaer and J.M. Anderson (eds.), *The Linguistics Encyclopaedia* (London and New York: Routledge, 1991), pp. 89-93, esp. p. 89. For a fuller statement of the critical linguistic perspective, see R. Fowler and G. Kress, 'Critical Linguistics', in R. Fowler, B. Hodge, G. Kress and T. Trew (eds.), *Language and Control* (London: Routledge & Kegan Paul, 1979), pp. 185-213.

groups. From a critical linguistic perspective, 'ideology' is the 'system of beliefs, values, and categories by reference to which a person or a society comprehends the world'.[3] A 'dominant' ideology is the ideology of a large and powerful group.[4] Fowler, in his work, is especially interested in linguistic usages which question, resist and challenge dominant ideologies.[5]

A key analytical category in critical linguistics is 'point of view', a concept derived from narrative criticism. Narrative discourse, whether novels, short stories or newspaper reports, is the principal interest of Fowler and his associates. 'Point of view' is the angle from which a story is told. Literary critics distinguish between the basic content of a story (what the Russian Formalists called *fabula*) and its treatment in the narrative (what the Formalists called *sjuzhet*).[6] The same story may be told from different perspectives, reflecting different attitudes and assumptions. Fowler (adapting the scheme of Boris Uspensky) identifies four categories of point of view: *temporal, spatial, psychological* and *ideological*.[7] These are not independent viewing points but intersecting ones. Each 'plane' of point of view calls on specific features of language for its construction.

The present study is an attempt to apply this framework for analysing narrative discourse to a New Testament narrative text, Gal. 1.13–2.14. As well as Fowler's work, use will be made of the work of Paul Simpson.

In recent treatments of Paul's letter to the Galatians in terms of Graeco-Roman rhetoric, the passage has been classified as a *narratio*.[8] Paul writes in autobiographical mode, reviewing his pre-Christian career in Judaism, his conversion/call, his movements immediately thereafter, his first post-conversion trip to Jerusalem, his departure into Syria and

---

3.   R. Fowler, *Linguistic Criticism* (Oxford: Oxford University Press, 2nd edn, 1996 [1986]), p. 165.

4.   P. Simpson, *Language, Ideology and Point of View* (Interface; London and New York: Routledge, 1993), p. 5.

5.   See especially Fowler, *Linguistic Criticism*, pp. 54-71.

6.   Fowler, *Linguistic Criticism*, p. 161.

7.   Fowler, *Linguistic Criticism*, p. 162.

8.   H.D. Betz, *Galatians* (Hermeneia; Philadelphia: Fortress Press, 1979), pp. 16-18; R.N. Longenecker , *Galatians* (WBC, 41; Dallas: Word Books, 1990), pp. 20-22; B. Witherington III, *Grace in Galatia: A Commentary on St Paul's Letter to the Galatians* (Edinburgh: T. & T. Clark, 1998), pp. 95-97.

Cilicia and ministry in these territories, his second visit to Jerusalem and, finally, his confrontation with Peter in Antioch. Paul composes the narrative, in large part, as a self-defence.[9] A different account of (at least some of) these events, it appears, had come to the ears of the Galatians. Paul writes to give *his* version. He seems to be countering suggestions, most likely propounded by the agitators in Galatia, that his commission and message *derived* from the apostles in Jerusalem, that his apostleship is secondary to and *dependent* on that of the Jerusalem authorities, and that the message which he now preaches to the Gentiles *deviates* from the gospel he originally received.

As he recounts past events to his readers, Paul expresses himself with an economy of words. He imparts no more than the amount of information required to establish his argumentative points, leaving out (what he considers to be) extraneous material and superfluous details. He gives a great deal of thought to his *choice* of words and linguistic structures (though he does not consistently observe the 'rules' of grammar) and emphasizes this by taking the solemn oath: 'What things I write to you, before God, I do not lie' (1.20). The level of care and attention given by the author to both the form and content of his narrative entitles us (as if any entitlement were needed!) to subject his linguistic choices to a fair degree of scrutiny.

The question of power-relations is a prominent one in this text. A key point at issue between Paul and his critics is his role and status within the social network and power-structure of the early Christian movement, specifically his status *vis-à-vis* the authorities in Jerusalem. The authority issue here makes this text an especially appropriate object for critical linguistic analysis.

The essay proceeds as follows: I shall consider, in order, the temporal, spatial, psychological and ideological viewpoints of this narrative, giving a definition of each 'plane' of point of view before investigating its particular linguistic manifestation in the text.

---

9. With the majority of scholars, I take the view that the narrative is in large measure apologetic in nature, i.e. written in response to accusations. However, I would not dispute that Paul also 'presents his "autobiography" as a paradigm of the gospel of Christian freedom': so G. Lyons, *Pauline Autobiography: Towards a New Understanding* (SBLDS, 73; Atlanta: Scholars Press, 1985), p. 171.

1. *Temporal Point of View*

The temporal point of view relates to 'the impression which a reader gains of events moving rapidly or slowly, in a continuous chain or isolated segments'.[10] It encompasses the *order* of the events narrated—including flashbacks, flashforwards and disruptions of the 'natural' sequence—and the *duration* of events, i.e. the temporal span of the narrative and the ways in which certain episodes within it are 'accelerated or decelerated relative to the story as a whole'.[11] We will deal first with the order of events.

a. *The Order of Events*
In the narrative of Gal. 1.13–2.14, Paul sets outs the events he describes in consecutive order. Betz points out that this was the standard procedure in a *narratio*.[12] A series of temporal markers in Gal. 1.13–2.14 helps to establish the linear progression.

1.13   ποτε, 'former'
1.15   ὅτε δέ, 'but when'
1.16   εὐθέως, 'immediately'
1.18   ἔπειτα, 'then'
1.18   μετὰ ἔτη τρία, 'after three (full) years' or 'in the third year'
1.18   ἡμέρας δεκαπέντε, 'fifteen days'
1.21   ἔπειτα, 'then'
2.1   ἔπειτα, 'then'
2.1   διὰ δεκατεσσάρων ἐτῶν, 'after fourteen (full) years' or 'in the fourteenth year'
2.11   ὅτε δέ, 'but when'
2.12   πρό, 'before'
2.12   ὅτε δέ, 'but when'
2.14   ἀλλ᾽ ὅτε, 'but when'

Rarely does time move in a consistently forward-moving direction in narratives, with each successive statement relating an event subsequent to the one before it. There are usually 'flashbacks' and 'flashforwards' within the line of time, if not in the broad sweep of a narrative, then at

10. R. Fowler, *Linguistic Criticism* (Opus; Oxford: Oxford University Press, 1986), p. 127 (this sentence is not in the second edition, used elsewhere in this article).
11. Simpson, *Language*, p. 20.
12. Betz, *Galatians*, p. 61.

the micro-level of the textual development. Backward references to earlier events in the narrative and forward references to later ones (within certain limits), far from breaking up the narrative, enhance its cohesion. Within the temporal progression and linear sequence of Galatian 1–2, there are instances of both flashback and flashforward, as listed below.

1.15 ἐκ κοιλίας μητρός μου, 'from my mother's womb': flashback to the time of Paul's birth

1.17 τοὺς πρὸ ἐμοῦ ἀποστόλους, 'those who were apostles before me': flashback to the time when the Jerusalem apostles received their commissioning, a time anterior to Paul's own apostolic call

1.20 ἃ δὲ γράφω ὑμῖν, ἰδοὺ ἐνώπιον τοῦ θεοῦ ὅτι οὐ ψεύδομαι, 'what things I write to you, before God, I do not lie': flashforward to the present time of writing

1.23 ὁ διώκων ἡμᾶς ποτε, 'the one who formerly persecuted us': flashback to the time of Paul's former life in Judaism (1.13)

1.23 ἥν ποτε ἐπόρθει, 'he once tried to destroy': flashback to the time of Paul's former life in Judaism (1.13)

2.5 ἵνα ἡ ἀλήθεια τοῦ εὐαγγελίου διαμείνῃ πρὸς ὑμᾶς, 'so that the truth of the gospel might remain [intact] for you': flashforward to the time of the founding of the Galatian churches

2.6 ὁποῖοί ποτε ἦσαν, 'what they once were': flashback to the time of the ministry of the historical Jesus

2.7 πεπίστευμαι, 'I had been entrusted': flashback to the time of Paul's commissioning (1.15-16a)

2.7 καθὼς Πέτρος, 'as Peter [had been entrusted]': flashback to the time of Peter's commissioning

2.9 γνόντες τὴν χάριν τὴν δοθεῖσάν μοι, 'recognizing the grace given to me': flashback to the time of Paul's commissioning (1.15-16)

2.11 κατὰ πρόσωπον αὐτῷ ἀντέστην, 'I opposed him to the face': flashforward to the last event in the sequence (2.14)

The flashbacks and flashforwards are both to events *between* the narrative poles (the starting-point and end-point of the narrative)—these poles being Paul's adult life in Judaism and his rebuke of Peter—and to events *before* and *after* these poles, such as Paul's birth and the time of writing the epistle.

These shifts back and forth in time are never allowed to fragment the chronological progression. For the most part, they are linguistically subordinate to the continuative sequences, being related within noun-phrases (e.g. ὁ ἀφορίσας με ἐκ κοιλίας μητρός μου, 1.15; τοὺς πρὸ ἐμοῦ ἀποστόλους, 1.17a) or in dependent clauses (e.g. ἥν ποτε ἐπόρθει, 1.23; ἵνα ἡ ἀλήθεια τοῦ εὐαγγελίου διαμείνῃ πρὸς ὑμᾶς, 2.5).

The time markers indicating temporal progression, on the other hand, are all prominently positioned, occurring mainly at the beginning of sentences. These markers serve to structure and direct the flow of the whole narrative.

The temporal order of events, however, is unclear in 2.4-5, a parenthesis within Paul's description of his meeting with the 'pillar' apostles at Jerusalem. Having stated in 2.3b that at Jerusalem 'not even Titus...was compelled to be circumcised', he goes on in 2.4-5 to talk about false brothers who 'intruded' and to whom he did not 'yield in submission'. Martyn describes the sentence of 2.4-5 as a 'grammatical shipwreck'.[13] It is an anacoluthon, without main subject or verb. The clause διὰ δὲ τοὺς παρεισάκτους ψευδαδέλφους is not completed.[14] The events described in 2.3b-5 are obviously interconnected, but Paul's inattention to grammar makes their temporal relation difficult to discern. It is best supposed that the non-circumcision of Titus related in 2.3b is the climax of a short chain of events.[15] Having stated first the outcome, Paul moves back in time to relate the events that led to it, leaving some gaps in the sequence. The logical chronological order of 2.3b-5 would seem to be as follows.

1.   The false brothers were 'smuggled' into and 'intruded' some setting (2.4b)
2.   At the Jerusalem meeting, they demanded that Titus be circumcised (2.3b-4a)[16]

---

13.   J.L. Martyn, *Galatians: A New Translation with Introduction and Commentary* (AB, 33A; New York: Doubleday, 1997), p. 195.

14.   Martyn (*Galatians*, p. 195) suggests that the breakdown in Paul's grammar relates to 'an increase in his pulse rate', as he considers the enormous damage which could have been done by these individuals had they succeeded in their aims.

15.   A different order of events is suggested by F.F. Bruce, *The Epistle to the Galatians: A Commentary on the Greek Text* (NIGTC; Exeter: Paternoster, 1982), pp. 116-17. He argues that the infiltration and the demand for circumcision happened *after* the Jerusalem meeting described in 2.1-10. The point of 2.3b-5, according to Bruce, is that not even Titus was compelled to be circumcised because the question of the circumcision of Gentile converts was not raised until later, when certain false brothers infiltrated the church at Antioch. But this interpretation of the course of events is forced. It does not arise from Galatians 2 itself but is an attempt to make the narrative cohere with Acts 11 and 15.

16.   The words ἠναγκάσθη περιτμηθῆναι in 2.3b point to an unsuccessful attempt to have Titus circumcised, while the words διὰ...ψευδαδέλφους in 2.4a indicate that the demand for his circumcision came from the false brothers.

3. Paul steadfastly resisted this demand (2.5a)
4. Titus was not circumcised (2.3b)

But this is the only point in the narrative where it is difficult to get a clear idea of the chronological flow of events. The overwhelming impression conveyed by the narrative is of a series of events in linear continuity.

Paul is not only concerned to communicate the chronological order of events, between 1.16b and 2.1, where he outlines his movements between his call and his second post-conversion visit to Jerusalem, he is keen to convey a sense of the *time relationship* between events. With the temporal indicator εὐθέως in 1.16b, he indicates what he did and did not do 'immediately' after his conversion.[17] He did not go to Jerusalem but went away to Arabia, then returned to Damascus. The adverb ἔπειτα in 1.18 introduces what he did next: he went up to Jerusalem. The time marker is backed up with the mention of a specific number of years, μετὰ ἔτη τρία, which could mean either 'after three (full) years' or 'in the third year'.[18] The point from which Paul takes this chronological measurement is not specified. It could be either his conversion or the return to Damascus mentioned in the preceding clause.[19] Despite the relative imprecision, the main point Paul wishes to establish is clear: there was a considerable lapse in time before he made his first post-conversion visit to Jerusalem. The time reference in 1.18, ἡμέρας δεκαπέντε, 'fifteen days', indicates the duration of this visit. The temporal adverb ἔπειτα in 1.21 specifies what Paul did next: he went to Syria and Cilicia. The third narrative occurrence of ἔπειτα, in 2.1, signals Paul's second (πάλιν) post-conversion visit to Jerusalem. The adverb is combined with the expression διὰ δεκατεσσάρων ἐτῶν, meaning either 'after fourteen years' or 'in the fourteenth year'. As with μετὰ ἔτη τρία in 1.18, the point from which Paul reckons this period of time is unclear. He could be measuring the time either from his conver-

---

17. Commentators debate whether εὐθέως regulates the two negative clauses οὐ προσανεθέμην σαρκὶ καὶ αἵματι and οὐδὲ ἀνῆλθον εἰς Ἱεροσόλυμα πρὸς τοὺς πρὸ ἐμοῦ ἀποστόλους or the affirmation ἀπῆλθον εἰς Ἀραβίαν. Most probably, it governs all three clauses. So J.D.G. Dunn, *The Epistle to the Galatians* (BNTC; Peabody, MA: Hendrickson, 1993), p. 68.

18. Witherington, *Grace in Galatia*, p. 118.

19. Most commentators take Paul's conversion as the chronological anchor since that event serves as the reference point for the temporal marker εὐθέως in 1.16b-17.

sion or from his first visit to Jerusalem.[20] But again, the argumentative point is plain: there was a very lengthy temporal gap between Paul's first and second visits to Jerusalem.

Paul's time-measurements, therefore, in this stretch of the narrative have a clear argumentative function: to demonstrate the independence of his message and ministry from Jerusalem. He stresses the length of time he spent away from Jerusalem and the brevity of his only visit to Jerusalem prior to his crucial meeting with the so-called 'pillars'.

The concern to measure the passing of time is not apparent after 2.1. The length in time of the second visit to Jerusalem is not specified. No mention is made of the time gap between this episode and the next one, the Antioch incident.[21] No indication is given as to the duration of the Antioch episode or the time relationships between the events within it, though the precise sequence of occurrences is abundantly clear. It becomes clear that after 2.1, the quantifying of time is no longer required by Paul to make his case. Having firmly established the long time-span between his call and his critical meeting with the Jerusalem leaders, he dispenses with the chronological specificity.

b. *The Duration of Events*

The other aspect of the temporal point of view is the *duration* of time. Key concepts here are 'acceleration' and 'deceleration', the speeding up and slowing down of narrative time. Simpson points out that whereas the temporal span of James Joyce's *Ulysses* covers only a single day, one short paragraph in John Fowles's *The Magus* compresses a sweep of nearly twenty years.[22]

In the first section of the narrative, 1.13-24, events proceed at a rapid

20. As Longenecker (*Galatians*, p. 45) states, determination of the matter 'can only be made in connection with a number of other issues having to do with the addressees and date of the letter'.

21. The suggestion that this event is presented out of sequence, occurring logically before the Jerusalem visit narrated in 2.1-10 (e.g. G. Luedemann, *Paul, Apostle to the Gentiles: Studies in Chronology* [Philadelphia: Fortress Press, 1984], pp. 75-77) cannot be supported grammatically. Paul uses the words ὅτε δέ in 1.15 and 2.14 to refer to an event which occurs *after* the immediately preceding one, so the likelihood is that he does so at 2.11 when introducing the Antioch episode. Moreover, as Martyn (*Galatians*, p. 231 n. 87) points out, there is no reference to food laws in the account of the Jerusalem meeting in Gal. 2.1-10 which is odd if the Antioch incident preceded it.

22. Simpson, *Language*, p. 20.

pace. The temporal span of this segment exceeds the 'fourteen years' (whatever precisely this means) mentioned in 2.1. Paul compresses into a couple of short paragraphs a long period of time. This section of the narrative comprises four distinct episodes: Paul's pre-conversion career in Judaism (1.13-14); his call and subsequent movements (1.15-17); his first post-conversion visit to Jerusalem (1.18-20); his activity between his first and second visits to Jerusalem (1.21-24). The speed slows down dramatically at 2.1. The second section of the narrative, 2.1-10, is the longest and is given over to a single episode: the meeting with the Jerusalem church leaders. The third section, 2.11-14,[23] also narrates one episode: the Antioch incident. We shall look briefly at the 'durative' element in each episode.

Episode One (1.13-14). Paul's career in Judaism is presented summarily. Its actual temporal duration is unspecified. The main verbs in 1.13-14 (ἐδίωκον, ἐπόρθουν, προέκοπτον) are all in the imperfect tense, indicating continuing or progressive actions. The present participle ὑπάρχων refers to a state of being. Paul thus relates this period of his life in terms of the general activities and disposition which characterized it: persecuting and trying to destroy the church, advancing in Judaism, being zealous for his ancestral traditions.

Episode Two (1.15-17). Paul's conversion (1.15-16a) is narrated within a subordinate clause. It does not receive narrative emphasis. Attention

23. Whether Paul's speech to Peter at Antioch ends at 2.14 or continues into 2.15-21 has long been debated. Betz (*Galatians*, p. 114), in his rhetorical analysis of Galatians, takes 2.15-21 not as part of the *narratio* but as the *propositio* of the letter: it 'sums up the *narratio's* content' and 'sets up the arguments to be discussed in the *probatio*'. In this he is followed by Longenecker (*Galatians*, pp. 80-81) and Witherington (*Grace in Galatia*, pp. 169-72). The view taken here is that in 2.15-21, there is a gliding transition from the Antioch incident to the Galatian situation, Paul continuing his attack on Peter, while moving beyond it to deal with specifically Galatian issues. I see this as a deliberate textual tactic on Paul's part, luring his readers into a rhetorical trap and springing it in 3.1 with the words, 'You foolish Galatians!' (in the manner of Nathan's charge against David in 2 Sam. 12.7, 'You are the man!'). Here he reveals that in addressing Peter, he was also speaking to them. Cf. J.K. Riches, 'Defamiliarisation and Conceptual Change', unpublished paper, 1995. It is recognized, then, that the narrative does not come to a clear 'closure'. However, a line has to be drawn somewhere, and for the purpose of this exercise, the textual boundary will be marked at 2.14.

focuses on what happened and what did not happen immediately *after* that event (1.16b-17). The four verbs used in this subsection (προσα-νεθέμην, ἀνῆλθον, ἀπῆλθον, ὑπέστρεψα) are aorist indicative, relating definite, completed actions.

Episode Three (1.18-19). The actual duration of Paul's first post-conversion Jerusalem visit (1.18-19) is very precisely delimited: fifteen days. Again, the main verbs in this subsection are aorist indicative (ἀνῆλθον, ἐπέμεινα, εἶδον). Paul narrates the visit very briefly, no doubt to minimize its importance, giving only those details germane to his argument: why he went (to get to know Peter), with whom he stayed (Peter), whom he saw (James) and whom he did not see (any other apostle).

Episode Four (1.21-24). Paul's movements and activities between the first and second visits to Jerusalem constitute the longest period (in actual time) of the narrative, on any estimate covering over a decade. Time here is massively accelerated. The aorist indicative is used to relate Paul's departure from Jerusalem into the regions of Syria and Cilicia (ἦλθον). The periphrastic imperfect (ἤμην ἀγνοούμενος, ἀκού-οντες ἦσαν), the present (εὐαγγελίζεται) and the imperfect (ἐδόξα-ζον) are then used to convey the main characteristics of this period: Paul was personally unknown to the Judean Christians all this time; they were hearing good things about Paul; Paul was engaged in preaching the gospel; the Judean Christians were glorifying God on account of Paul.

Episode Five (2.1-10). Deceleration takes place at 2.1. Paul zooms in on the meeting with the Jerusalem authorities. This incident clearly constitutes the 'peak' episode of the narrative. The three key features of peaking are evident here: the sudden change of pace; the gathering together of the key characters involved in the narrative; the change of locus.[24] The chronological markers from 1.16c onward build up to this episode. Its narrative importance is also made clear by the signal of apprehension at 2.2d. Paul indicates that he embarked on the journey to Jerusalem with some unease, knowing that a negative outcome at the meeting could render his past and future ministry ineffective ('lest

24. P. Cotterell and M. Turner, *Linguistics and Biblical Interpretation* (London: SPCK, 1989), pp. 246-47.

somehow I should run or had run in vain'). But having introduced an element of suspense into the narrative, he immediately kills it by stressing that 'not even...Titus was compelled to be circumcised'. The potential danger was not realized. It is overwhelmingly more important to Paul to allay suspicions among his readers that there was any disagreement between the Jerusalem leaders and himself as to the substance of the gospel (specifically on the issue of whether Gentile Christians should be circumcised), than to spin out the suspense he has just generated. Having emphatically stated what *did not* happen at the meeting, Paul goes on to narrate what *did* happen: he stood firm against the false brothers; the Jerusalem apostles recognized his apostleship to the Gentiles; they gave to Paul and Barnabas right hands of fellowship; they asked Paul to remember the poor. This section is the most grammatically complex of the narrative, with two long anacolutha (2.3-5, 6-9). The main verbs here are largely in the aorist indicative.

Episode Six (2.11-14). The climax seemingly having been reached, the next and last episode in the sequence, the Antioch incident, comes as something of a surprise. The episode is presented as a sequel to the Jerusalem conference, and a highly important one at that. This is the most dramatic episode of the whole narrative, focusing on the confrontation between Paul and Peter (this is made clear by the immediate flashforward to this event in 2.11b). The Antioch incident serves as a sharp rebuttal of the claim that he departed from the gospel he received from the Jerusalem apostles: *he* did not deviate from the truth of the gospel; *Peter and James did*. No indication is given of the actual temporal duration of this episode. Peter's eating with the Gentiles is related in the imperfect (συνήσθιεν), indicating that this was his normal and sustained practice. The temporal note (ὅτε δὲ ἦλθον) signalling the arrival of certain men from James in 2.12b begins a short series of sequences narrated mainly with verbs in the aorist indicative (ὑπέστελλεν, ἀφώριζεν, συνυπεκρίθησαν, συναπήχθη, εἶδον, εἶπον), climaxing with Paul's public rebuke of Peter.

2. *Spatial Point of View*

We turn now to the spatial point of view. The spatial dimension concerns the representation of place, direction and spatial relationships in a narrative, i.e. locations, movements and the spatial positioning of people and objects in the story. It also has to do with 'the viewing position assumed by the narrator of a story',[25] whether a bird's-eye view of events or the more restricted viewpoint of a single observer. In describing the notion of narrative viewing position, both Fowler and Simpson draw comparison with the visual arts, especially cinema. They point out that close-ups, long shots and tracking shots all have their parallels in narratives.[26] We will look first at Paul's use of spatial language in the narrative, then briefly consider the viewing position adopted.

a. *Paul's Spatial Language*

The narrative of Gal. 1.13–2.14 is replete with spatial indicators: prepositional phrases relating to location and direction, references to spatial positioning and verbs of movement.

1.13 ἐν τῷ Ἰουδαϊσμῷ, 'in Judaism'
1.14 προέκοπτον ἐν τῷ Ἰουδαϊσμῷ, 'I was advancing in Judaism'
1.16 ἐν ἐμοί, 'in/to me'
  ἐν τοῖς ἔθνεσιν, 'among the Gentiles'
1.17 οὐδὲ ἀνῆλθον εἰς Ἱεροσόλυμα, 'nor did I go up to Jerusalem'
  πρὸς τοὺς πρὸ ἐμοῦ ἀποστόλους, 'to those who were apostles before me'
  ἀπῆλθον εἰς Ἀραβίαν, 'I went away into Arabia'
  ὑπέστρεψα εἰς Δαμασκόν, 'I returned to Damascus'
1.18 ἀνῆλθον εἰς Ἱεροσόλυμα, 'I went up to Jerusalem'
  ἐπέμεινα πρὸς αὐτόν, 'I stayed with him'
1.19 ...οὐκ εἶδον εἰ μὴ Ἰάκωβον, 'I did not see...except James'
1.21 ἦλθον εἰς τὰ κλίματα τῆς Συρίας καὶ τῆς Κιλικίας, 'I went into the regions of Syria and Cilicia'
1.22 ἀγνοούμενος τῷ προσώπῳ ταῖς ἐκκλησίαις τῆς Ἰουδαίας ταῖς ἐν Χριστῷ, 'I was not known by face to the churches of Judea in Christ'
2.1 ἀνέβην εἰς Ἱεροσόλυμα, 'I went up to Jerusalem'
  μετὰ Βαρναβᾶ, 'with Barnabas'
  συμπαραλαβὼν καὶ Τίτον, 'taking along also Titus'
2.2 ἀνέβην, 'I went up'
  ἐν τοῖς ἔθνεσιν, 'among the Gentiles'
  κατ᾽ ἰδίαν, 'privately'
  τρέχω ἢ ἔδραμον, 'I should run or had run'
2.3 σὺν ἐμοί, 'with me'
2.4 παρεισάκτους, 'smuggled in'
  παρεισῆλθον, 'intruded'
2.8 εἰς τὰ ἔθνη, 'to the Gentiles'

---

25. Simpson, *Language*, p. 12.
26. Fowler, *Linguistic Criticism*, pp. 162-63; Simpson, *Language*, pp. 12-13.

2.9 Ἰάκωβος καὶ Κηφᾶς καὶ Ἰωάννης...δεξιὰς ἔδωκαν ἐμοὶ καὶ Βαρναβᾷ κοινωνίας, 'James, Cephas and John...gave to me and Barnabas right hands of fellowship'

ἡμεῖς εἰς τὰ ἔθνη, αὐτοὶ δὲ εἰς τὴν περιτομήν, 'we [might go] to the Gentiles, and they to the circumcision'

2.11 ἦλθεν Κηφᾶς εἰς Ἀντιόχειαν, 'Cephas came to Antioch'

κατὰ πρόσωπον αὐτῷ ἀντέστην, 'I opposed him to the face'

2.12 πρὸ τοῦ ἐλθεῖν τινας ἀπὸ Ἰακώβου, 'before certain men from James came'

μετὰ τῶν ἐθνῶν συνήσθιεν, 'was eating with the Gentiles'

ὅτε δὲ ἦλθον, 'but when they came'

ὑπέστελλεν καὶ ἀφώριζεν ἑαυτόν, 'he withdrew and separated himself'

2.13 Βαρναβᾶς συναπήχθη, 'Barnabas was led astray'

2.14 οὐκ ὀρθοποδοῦσιν πρὸς τὴν ἀλήθειαν τοῦ εὐαγγελίου, 'they were not walking straight in accordance with the truth of the gospel'

ἔμπροσθεν πάντων, 'before them all'

There is a particular concentration of spatial terminology in 1.17–2.2a, where Paul documents his movements from his conversion to his second post-conversion Jerusalem visit. Verbs of linear movement (ἀνέρχομαι [1.17, 18], ἀπέρχομαι [1.17], ὑποστρέφω [1.17], ἔρχομαι [1.21], ἀναβαίνω [2.1]) and geographical locations (Ἰεροσόλυμα [1.17, 18; 2.1], Ἀραβία [1.17], Δαμασκός [1.17], Συρία [1.21], Κιλικία [1.21], Ἰουδαία [1.22]) dominate these verses. We will examine the representation of space in each episode of the narrative.

Episode One (1.13-14). There are no indicators of physical space in this episode. The prepositional phrase ἐν τῷ Ἰουδαϊσμῷ in 1.13-14 serves to locate Paul's pre-Christian activities. But the location is socio-religious, 'Judaism', not geographical. Ἰουδαϊσμός is here presented as a sphere of existence, a realm to which one may belong. With the motion verb προέκοπτον, Paul portrays himself as moving forward, forging ahead, in that sphere.

Episode Two (1.15-17). The ἐν ἐμοί in Paul's description of his call in 1.16 may be locative, 'in me', thus indicating an internal revelation. On the other hand, it may be equivalent to a simple dative 'to me', pointing to a revelation directed at Paul. The latter seems more probable.[27] The prepositional phrase ἐν τοῖς ἔθνεσιν in 1.16 indicates the scope and

27. Cf. Martyn, *Galatians*, p. 158.

location of the mission given to Paul: he is to proclaim Christ 'in the regions of the Gentiles'.[28] Jerusalem receives its first narrative mention in 1.17. It is mentioned three times in all. Each time, Paul speaks of going 'up to Jerusalem' (ἀνῆλθον εἰς Ἱεροσόλυμα, 1.17, 18; ἀνέβην εἰς Ἱεροσόλυμα, 2.1). The city is located in the hill country of Judea. The verb thus indicates the ascent involved in the journey. Travel to Jerusalem is regularly spoken of in the New Testament as 'going up' (usually ἀναβαίνω) to the city.[29] Jerusalem is clearly identified in 1.17 as the headquarters of those who were apostles before Paul: the prepositional phrase εἰς Ἱεροσόλυμα correlates with πρὸς τοὺς πρὸ ἐμοῦ ἀποστόλους. He did not go to Jerusalem, but 'went away' into Arabia and then returned 'again' to Damascus. The adverb πάλιν in 1.17c serves retrospectively to identify Damascus (or the vicinity of Damascus) as the location of his conversion and the point of origin of the movement 'went away'.

Episode Three (1.18-19). Paul states that he 'went up' to Jerusalem. The construction ἐπέμεινα πρὸς αὐτόν, 'I stayed with him' (Peter), signals spatial closeness. Paul was the houseguest of Peter.[30] The verb εἶδον in 1.19 ('I did not see any other apostle except James'), indicates at the very least that Paul made visual contact with James, but the contrast with ἐπέμεινα implies that the sustained spatial closeness Paul enjoyed with Peter was distinctly lacking in his dealings with James.

Episode Four (1.21-22). Paul remarks that he 'went' (from Jerusalem) 'into the regions of Syria and Cilicia'. He mentions these territories in the order in which one would reach them travelling from Jerusalem. He states that he was 'not known by face to the Judean churches', emphasizing his spatial distance from these congregations.

Episode Five (2.1-10). The episode opens with the statement that Paul 'went up again to Jerusalem'. The verb of movement is repeated in the next clause: Paul 'went up in response to a revelation'. A verb of movement, τρέχω, is used in 2.2c, where Paul signals his apprehension in going to Jerusalem. The word τρέχω is metaphorical: the motion of 'running' serves as an image of apostolic service. The prepositional

28. Longenecker, *Galatians*, p. 32.
29. E.g. Mk 10.32-33; Lk. 2.42; Jn 2.13; 5.1; Acts 11.2; 15.2.
30. Martyn, *Galatians*, p. 173.

expression, κατ' ἰδίαν,[31] in 2.2b indicates that the Jerusalem meeting under narration took place in a 'private' setting. Conveyed is the idea of enclosed or restricted space. No hint is given of the physical location of this gathering. Six participants at the meeting are clearly identified. These fall into two groups of three. On the one side, there are Paul and his companions, Barnabas and Titus. These two are very clearly 'with' Paul (ἀνέβην...μετὰ Βαρναβᾶ, 2.1; Τίτος ὁ σὺν ἐμοί, 2.3). On the other side there are the three 'pillar' apostles, James, Cephas and John (2.9). In 2.4, Paul refers to another group, the false brothers. These individuals, Paul states, were 'smuggled into' (παρεισάκτους) and 'intruded' (παρεισῆλθον) into some setting. The language clearly has spatial overtones. The precise setting into which they intruded is unspecified. Was it the private meeting under present discussion,[32] or, as has often been suggested, the church at Antioch?[33] Paul's language in 2.4 seems inappropriate for a private, select gathering: '[they] intruded to spy out our freedom which we have in Christ Jesus'. A Gentile church setting such as Antioch fits better. But it could be that Paul is thinking not of a particular location, but of the believing community in general.[34] On this understanding, the setting into which they intruded would be the Christian movement itself. Nevertheless, they do seem to be present at the private Jerusalem meeting (whether they were actually invited to attend or not), demanding that Titus (and Gentile Christians in general) be circumcised (2.3b-4a). The meeting ends with the pillar apostles extending to Paul and Barnabas 'right hands of fellowship' (2.9). The gesture implies spatial closeness and the bridging of (a measure of) spatial distance. They reach agreement on the spatial orientation of their respective missions. Paul and Barnabas would go to the Gentiles (εἰς τὰ ἔθνη, cf. 2.8), and the Jerusalem apostles would go to the circumcised (εἰς τὴν περιτομήν).

31. It is sometimes debated whether Paul in 2.2 is referring to two meetings in Jerusalem, one public before the whole Jerusalem church, signalled by αὐτοῖς, and one private, with the leaders, James, Peter and John, indicated by κατ' ἰδίαν. That Paul has two events in mind is maintained, for example, by Betz, *Galatians*, p. 86. But the most natural reading of Paul's words is that the κατ' ἰδίαν is an amplification of the previous αὐτοῖς, indicating the one private meeting.

32. E.g. Witherington, *Grace in Galatia*, pp. 135-36.

33. E.g. Martyn, *Galatians*, p. 196.

34. Cf. E.DeW. Burton, *A Critical and Exegetical Commentary on the Epistle to the Galatians* (ICC; Edinburgh: T. & T. Clark, 1921), p. 78.

Episode Six. Spatial indicators proliferate in this episode. Here, there is particular emphasis on the spatial positioning of the narrative participants. The passage opens with an indication of linear movement: Peter came to Antioch (ἦλθεν Κηφᾶς εἰς Ἀντιόχειαν). During this visit, Paul 'opposed him to the face' (κατὰ πρόσωπον αὐτῷ ἀντέστην). The expression indicates close spatial positioning, but obviously not of a friendly kind. Backtracking, Paul relates the sequence of events that preceded this conflict. The problem is traced to the 'entrance' of certain men into the scene (πρὸ τοῦ γὰρ ἐλθεῖν τινας...ὅτε δὲ ἦλθον). It was their 'coming' that forced a change in Peter's behaviour. The prepositional phrase ἀπὸ Ἰακώβου is a marker of source. The trouble-makers came 'from James'. Prior to their arrival, Peter used to eat with the Gentile believers, μετὰ τῶν ἐθνῶν συνήσθιεν. The construction points to intimate spatial relationship. But when they came, he 'withdrew' and 'separated' himself (ὑπέστελλεν καὶ ἀφώριζεν ἑαυτόν). The rest of the Jewish believers followed suit, creating a spatial division (at least at meal times) between Jews and Gentiles in the church at Antioch. Paul employs a spatial metaphor to describe Barnabas's defection: he was 'led astray' (συναπήχθη). A verb with spatial connotations is also used to characterize the activities of the Jewish group as a whole: 'they were not walking straight' (οὐκ ὀρθοποδοῦσιν) in relation to the truth of the gospel. Paul indicates that his rebuke of Peter took place 'before them all' (ἔμπροσθεν πάντων), that is, in public, before the whole congregation. I noted above that 2.11-14 is the most dramatic and vivid episode in the whole narrative. It is largely by means of his use of spatial language in these verses that Paul achieves this effect.

b. *Viewing Position*
No clear visual perspective is conveyed in the first episode. In episode two, Paul's movements—from Damascus to Arabia back to Damascus—are related in the fashion of a filmic 'tracking-shot'. In episode three, the visual perspective moves to 'close-up', as readers are introduced to individual named characters other than Paul. In 1.18, the scene conveyed is that of Paul 'at home' with Peter, enjoying the latter's hospitality. Episode four again 'tracks' Paul's movements as he leaves Jerusalem and travels to Syria, then Cilicia. Then, there is a momentary switch to a 'bird's-eye' camera angle, as Paul relates what was happening in the churches of Judea during the long time of his absence from this region. Episode five is related in 'hidden camera' fashion, the

readers being granted privileged viewing access to a scene 'behind closed doors'. The participants are scanned individually in close-up shots, Paul, Barnabas and Titus at the beginning of the episode, James, Peter and John near the end. The latter three are present from the beginning, but their faces are visually blurred, as it were, until the appropriate point in the narrative when their identity is revealed. The false brothers remain 'masked men'; their identity is never unveiled. The final shot has the main participants shaking hands. Titus, though prominent in the opening verses, is curiously out of the picture in this shot. The scene changes abruptly at the start of the sixth episode, from Jerusalem to Antioch. Readers are immediately given a close-up shot of Paul's and Peter's 'face-off'.[35] A series of close-ups and wide-angled shots convey the action which led up to this. It is noticeable that Paul is out of the picture for these scenes (2.12-13). Like his readers, he is a spectator of the drama rather than a participant in it.[36] When the narrative returns to Paul's confrontation of Peter, the camera-shot is wide-angled, conveying the public nature of the event.

c. *The Representation of Jerusalem*
The most interesting and significant feature of the spatial viewpoint of Gal. 1.13–2.14 is the representation of Jerusalem. There is no doubt that Jerusalem is foregrounded in the narrative. It is the first actual location mentioned in the narrative (1.17). It is named three times in total. Every other geographical location is mentioned only once. It is the geographical point of reference in the travelogue of 1.17-24. Paul establishes his movements and whereabouts in these verses in relation to Jerusalem. The city is also the location for the key episode in the narrative. Within the spatial point of view of the narrative of Gal. 1.13–2.14, then, Jerusalem is clearly *privileged.*

The narrative privileging of Jerusalem reflects the common belief among the first Christians that the city was the geographical centre of the early church. As Holmberg states,

---

35. The term is Witherington's (*Grace in Galatia*, p. 151).

36. Some commentators suggest that Paul was not present in Antioch when these events took place, arriving only when the process of withdrawal was complete (Burton, *Galatians*, p. 110; Longenecker, *Galatians*, p. 77; Witherington, *Grace in Galatia*, p. 150). The text, however, gives no such indication. The impression conveyed is rather of Paul watching from the sidelines.

> This was owing to its role as the Holy City and theologico-juridical
> centre of Judaism, and to the fact that this was the place where Christ
> had died and risen, where the Spirit had been effused, and where the
> Apostles of Christ resided, they being the guardians of the divine Word,
> that tradition of and from Jesus which had gone out from Jerusalem.[37]

The church at Jerusalem was accordingly viewed as the ecclesiological centre of the emerging Christian movement.[38]

But Paul not only privileges Jerusalem, he also *problematizes* it. He
uses the secular spelling of the word, Ἱεροσόλυμα, rather than the more
sacred form of the word, Ἱερουσαλήμ.[39] By this he seems to be implying that Jerusalem is simply a geographical site. It has no special religious significance. He thus *de-sacralizes* the city. In the travelogue of
1.17-24, Jerusalem serves as a *negative* geographical point of reference.
Paul, to be sure, takes his co-ordinates from Jerusalem, but he is intent
on showing that he was nowhere near Jerusalem for virtually the whole
of the period under discussion. He was not in Jerusalem when he
received his call to be an apostle, but in Damascus (or its vicinity). He
was not in Jerusalem in that crucial period immediately after his call to
be an apostle. When he did go, it was some time later, and he was there
only very briefly. The only reason he went was because Peter was
there.[40] He did not return for a long period of time. He thus demonstrates that the city did not figure highly in his travel plans. Jerusalem
was hardly the centre of his re-constituted world. At 1.22, he speaks in
general terms of 'the churches in Judea', almost certainly counting the
Jerusalem church as one of them. By adding the qualifier 'which are in
Christ' (ταῖς ἐν Χριστῷ), Paul implies that the geographical location of
these churches, though held to be significant by some, is of far less consequence than their socio-religious and theological location in the realm
of Christ.[41]

In the narrative of Gal. 1.13–2.14, then, Paul *works with* a worldview

---

37. B. Holmberg, *Paul and Power: The Structure of Authority in the Primitive
Church as Reflected in the Pauline Epistles* (ConBNT, 11; Lund: C.W.K. Gleerup,
1978), p. 19.

38. This is certainly the impression we get from Acts.

39. Cf. Longenecker, *Galatians*, p. 33. Paul does, however, use Ἱερουσαλήμ in
4.25-26, where he contrasts the present Jerusalem with the Jerusalem which is
above.

40. Lyons, *Pauline Autobiography*, p. 161.

41. Martyn, *Galatians*, p. 176.

which places Jerusalem at the centre (geographically and theologically) but at the same time, and more so, he *works against* that view. He reflects 'the common opinion among the first Christians, that Jerusalem was the centre of the rapidly growing Church'.[42] But he also calls that understanding into question. He indicates that Jerusalem is not theologically and ecclesiologically central to him or his mission.

3. *Psychological Point of View*

The psychological or perceptual point of view 'concerns the question of who is presented as the observer of the events of a narrative'.[43] Fowler distinguishes between internal and narrative points of view. He then splits each of these categories into two sub-types, creating a fourfold classification.[44] Internal narratives divide into what Fowler calls Type A and Type B. Type A narration is narration from the subjective viewpoint of a participating character in the story. It manifests his or her judgments on other characters in the story and his or her evaluations of the events narrated. Type B narration is story-telling from the perspective of an omniscient narrator who has an internal knowledge of the characters of the story, their intentions, thoughts and feelings. External narratives split into Type C and Type D. Type C narratives describe events from a position outside of the consciousness of any participating character. The narrator claims no knowledge of the feelings or thoughts of the characters and offers no judgments on their actions. Type D is again narration from outside the consciousness of the characters of the story. But in contrast to Type C, the author has definite views about the characters and actions in the story.

Galatians 1.13–2.14, as an autobiographical narrative written largely in the first person, is plainly to be classified as an internal narrative of the Type A variety. Paul writes as a participant in the story he narrates, offering his personal judgments on events and on other characters in the narrative. At one stage in the account, 1.23-24, Paul slips into Type B narration, assuming the role of omniscient narrator, reporting what was being heard about him and done because of him where he was not personally present. But this apart, Paul's narrative conforms exactly to Type A.

---

42. Holmberg, *Paul and Power*, p. 19.
43. Fowler, *Linguistic Criticism*, p. 169.
44. Fowler, *Linguistic Criticism*, p. 170.

Type A narratives, according to Fowler, are characterized by *verba sentiendia*—words relating to the feelings, motives and perceptions (these categories obviously overlap) of the narrating character.[45] There are instances of such 'words of feeling' in the narrative of Gal. 1.13–2.14.

1.14b περισσοτέρως ζηλωτὴς ὑπάρχων, 'being extremely *zealous*': feeling and motive

1.18b ἱστορῆσαι Κηφᾶν, 'to get to know Cephas': motive

1.19   εἶδον...Ἰάκωβον, '...[*saw*]...James': perception

2.2   κατὰ ἀποκάλυψιν, 'in response to a revelation': motive

2.2   μή πως εἰς κενὸν τρέχω ἢ ἔδραμον, 'lest somehow I should run or had run in vain': feeling (of apprehension)

2.6b   ὁποῖοί ποτε ἦσαν οὐδέν μοι διαφέρει, 'what they once were *matters* nothing to me': feeling

2.10   ὃ καὶ ἐσπούδασα αὐτὸ τοῦτο ποιῆσαι, 'which very thing I was *eager* to do': feeling

2.14a ὅτε εἶδον ὅτι οὐκ ὀρθοποδοῦσιν πρὸς τὴν ἀλήθειαν τοῦ εὐαγγελίου, 'when I *saw* that they were not walking according to the truth of the gospel': perception

However, there is little here of the introspective element normally expected of Type A narration. It is remarkable that Paul describes his conversion without any emotional involvement. The only glimpses we get into Paul's inner processes are at 1.14b, where he mentions his pre-Christian zeal for his ancestral traditions, and 2.2, where he admits his apprehension in going to meet with the Jerusalem notables.

The perceptual point of view, needless to say, is crucial to Paul's apologetic. The events of which Paul writes are under dispute. A very different account of them had been given to the Galatians by the agitators, and Paul writes to set the record straight. Unlike the agitators, he speaks as an actual participant in these events. He writes to give a first-hand account of what happened. The strong sense of Paul's 'presence' as a character in the narrative thus lends a considerable degree of authority to what he says. A sense of authority is also conveyed by the confidence and astonishing boldness with which Paul expresses his views and judgments. One may be less inclined to challenge someone who is so certain of his claims, and so forthright in his pronouncements.[46]

---

45. Fowler, *Linguistic Criticism*, p. 171.

46. Critical readers, of course, are immediately suspicious of someone who writes like this.

4. *Ideological Point of View*

Of the four planes of point of view discussed by Fowler, the ideological is the most important. As defined by Fowler, the ideological viewpoint of a text is the set of values and beliefs it communicates.[47] Ideological perspective is linguistically manifested in several ways: through the modal structures of a text, through the use of evaluative words, and through the transitivity patterns of a text. We will look at each of these in turn.

a. *Modality*

'Modality', according to Simpson, 'refers broadly to a speaker's attitude towards, or opinion about, the truth of a proposition expressed by a sentence'.[48] Modal operators, such as 'perhaps', 'possibly', 'arguably', 'probably', 'certainly' express the speaker's degree of commitment to the factuality of the propositions he or she utters.

Paul develops his narrative of Gal. 1.13–2.14 largely through *unmodalized*, categorical assertions, that is to say, statements to which no element of doubt or uncertainty is attached. Categorical assertions, Simpson points out, express the strongest possible degree of commitment to the truth of the proposition uttered.[49] It is not insignificant that the issue of 'Who is telling the truth?' is central to the narrative. Paul is clearly concerned to get across the veracity of his version of events. He even pauses the narrative to reassure his readers, under oath, that he is not lying in what he writes (1.20). The non-modal style of narration reinforces this pledge.

Paul's categorical declarations express both positive and negative 'polarity'.[50] That is to say, Paul makes both affirmations and denials. The extent to which we find negative polarity in the narrative is striking. In the course of the argument, he makes the following negative statements:

47. Fowler, *Linguistic Criticism*, p. 165.
48. Simpson, *Language*, p. 47
49. Simpson, *Language*, p. 49.
50. Polarity, according to M.A.K. Halliday (*An Introduction to Functional Grammar* [London: Arnold, 2nd edn, 1994], p. 88), is 'the choice between positive and negative, as in *is / isn't, do / don't*'. Modality is the 'intermediate degrees between the positive and negative poles'.

1.16b οὐ προσανεθέμην σαρκὶ καὶ αἵματι, 'I did *not* consult with flesh and blood'

1.17a οὐδὲ ἀνῆλθον εἰς Ἱεροσόλυμα..., '*nor* did I go up to Jerusalem'

1.19 ἕτερον δὲ τῶν ἀποστόλων οὐκ εἶδον εἰ μὴ Ἰάκωβον..., 'I did *not* see any other apostle except James'

1.20 οὐ ψεύδομαι, 'I do *not* lie'

1.22 ἤμην δὲ ἀγνοούμενος τῷ προσώπῳ, 'I was *not* known by face'

2.3 ἀλλ' οὐδὲ Τίτος...ἠναγκάσθη περιτμηθῆναι, 'But *not* even Titus ...was compelled to be circumcised'

2.5 οἷς οὐδὲ...εἴξαμεν τῇ ὑποταγῇ, 'to whom we did *not* yield in submission'

2.6 ὁποῖοί ποτε ἦσαν οὐδέν μοι διαφέρει, 'what they once were matters *nothing* to me'

2.6 πρόσωπον [ὁ] θεὸς ἀνθρώπου οὐ λαμβάνει, 'God does *not* accept the face of a human being'

2.6 ἐμοὶ γὰρ οἱ δοκοῦντες οὐδὲν προσανέθεντο, 'the men of repute added *nothing* to me'

2.14 οὐκ ὀρθοποδοῦσιν πρὸς τὴν ἀλήθειαν τοῦ εὐαγγελίου, 'they were *not* walking straight in accordance with the gospel'

2.14 εἰ σὺ Ἰουδαῖος ὑπάρχων ἐθνικῶς καὶ οὐχὶ Ἰουδαϊκῶς ζῇς, 'If you being a Jew live like a Gentile and *not* as a Jew...'

The negative line is concentrated in two main stretches of the text: Paul's account of his actions and movements between his conversion and his second post-conversion visit at 1.16b-22, where he is at pains to make clear what he did *not* do as well as what he did; and his discussion of the private meeting in Jerusalem in 2.3-6, where is keen to stress what did *not* happen at this meeting as well as what did. These are the places in the narrative where he is most obviously refuting the false claims (as he regards them) of his opponents in Galatia.

Paul writes with certainty as to his own actions. The only point at which he injects an element of doubt into what he says about his own activity is 2.2, where the proposition that he 'should run or had run in vain' is introduced by the modal expression, μή πως, 'lest somehow'. Paul is here reflecting the concern he had in going to Jerusalem. But while he considered the possibility that this ministry would prove to be for nothing a *real* one, he also considered it an extremely *remote* one. As it turned out, his worst fear was unrealized.

While Paul exhibits a high degree of confidence in the claims he makes for himself, he is less sure about the claims being made for or by other participants in the narrative, in particular the 'false brothers' and the 'men of repute'. The ἀδελφοί in the compound word ψευδάδελφοι in 2.4 indicates that the individuals referred to by this term professed to be genuine members of the believing community, and were accepted as such, no doubt even by the Jerusalem leaders. The prefix ψευδ- is a modal operator. It signifies Paul's estimation of their profession. They say they are true believers but in Paul's opinion they are not. Paul thus passes a negative judgment on these individuals and their claim to be members of the brotherhood of faith. By extension, he also indicts those who accepted their claim but who ought to have known better, that is, the Jerusalem leaders.

The expression οἱ δοκοῦντες, 'those reputed...', is applied to James, Peter and John, the leaders of the Jerusalem church (2.9). This phrase is clearly a modalizing one. It is a well attested formula in Greek. It can be used is a positive way (those *properly* reputed),[51] or in a negative, ironic way.[52] The ironic sense operates here.[53] This is indicated by its repeated use in these verses,[54] and by the obvious ironic intent of simi-lar constructions involving δοκέω elsewhere in Paul.[55] He uses the expression four times between 2.2 and 2.9. Twice οἱ δοκοῦντες stands on its own (2.2 and 2.6c), and twice (2.6a and 2.9) it is amplified, first with εἶναί τι,[56] 'those reputed to be something (of importance)', then, more significantly, with στῦλοι εἶναι, 'those reputed to be "pillars"'.

That Paul gives no further qualification or explanation of the term 'pillars' strongly suggests that this was an established way of referring to James and Peter and John in early Christianity. In other words, it was the common opinion of the early Christians that the Jerusalem leaders were the 'pillars' of the emerging Christian movement. As Longenecker notes, the description very probably connoted 'a theology and ecclesi-ology'.[57] What was presupposed was 'the idea of a heavenly building— the Church as God's temple...which the three who are mentioned bear up as basic pillars'.[58] Aus points out that in Jewish tradition[59] Abraham,

---

51. E.g. Josephus, *War* 3.453; 4.141, 159.

52. E.g. Plato, *Apology* 21B, C, D, E; 22A, B; 36D; 41E.

53. *Contra* Burton, *Galatians*, p. 71; Bruce, *Galatians*, p. 109.

54. So Longenecker, *Galatians*, p. 57.

55. Cf. 1 Cor. 3.18; 8.2; 10.12; 12.22, 23; Gal. 6.3; Phil. 3.4.

56. Cf. Gal. 6.3, εἰ γὰρ δοκεῖ τις εἶναί τι μηδὲν ὤν, φρεναπατᾷ ἑαυτόν. In Gal. 2.6c, Paul does not go as far to say that the Jerusalem leaders are in fact 'nothing'.

57. Longenecker, *Galatians*, p. 58.

58. *TDNT*, VII, p. 735.

59. R.D. Aus, 'Three Pillars and Three Patriarchs: A Proposal Concerning Gal. 2.9', *ZNW* 70 (1979), pp. 252-61, esp. p. 256.

Isaac and Jacob were viewed as the three great pillars of Israel and of the world. He deduces that the early Church's identification of James, Peter and John as 'pillars' reflects this model. He writes,

> As God once 'established the world', the covenant community Israel, on the basis of the three Patriarchs...God was thought of by Jewish Christians as having 'established the world' anew, the new covenant community...on the basis of three new pillars.[60]

The attribution of the term 'pillars' to the three apostles, therefore, represented 'an eschatological evaluation of the place of Peter, James and John' which was tied to 'an institutional view of their position'.[61] The appellation designated them the leadership of the early Christian movement, not just the leaders of the Jerusalem church but the Christian community as a whole.

By using the modal operator οἱ δοκοῦντες...εἶναι, Paul recognizes the claim that the Jerusalem authorities are 'pillars', but does not give his personal assent to it. He resists the ideology and the view of power-relations in the Christian movement which the title 'pillars' encodes, since it accords him a subordinate role and authority in the early Church to James, Peter and John. It is Paul's firm conviction that he has equal status with the Jerusalem leaders in the social network of the growing Christian movement. He believes that his authority as an apostle is as high and as soundly based as theirs.

The grounds on which Paul calls into question the belief that these men are the 'pillars' of God's eschatological community are set out in the parenthesis of 2.6. A three-step argument is here advanced. First, Paul identifies the basis for their claimed rank as pillars: ὁποῖοί ποτε ἦσαν. 'What they once were', as Burton notes,[62] refers to their past associations with the historical Jesus, in James's case his filial relation to Jesus, and in the case of Peter and John, their relationship to Jesus as his closest followers. It is their past standing, says Paul, which is the basis for their current reputation. Secondly, invoking the Stoic notion of *adiaphora*,[63] he identifies this past standing as a 'matter of indifference': οὐδέν μοι διαφέρει. Their previous relationships, Paul insists,

---

60. Aus, 'Three Pillars', pp. 256-57.

61. C.K. Barrett, 'Paul and the "Pillar" Apostles', in J.N. Sevenster and W.C. van Unnik (eds.), *Studia Paulina: in Honorem Johannis de Zwaan* (Haarlem: Bohn, 1953), pp. 1-19 (16).

62. Burton, *Galatians*, p. 87.

63. Longenecker, *Galatians*, p. 54.

'have no argumentative value in the present'.[64] Thirdly, he gives the theological reason for this judgment:[65] πρόσωπον [ὁ] θεὸς ἀνθρώπου οὐ λαμβάνει, 'God does not accept the face of a human being'. This is a generic statement, a universal truth. As Witherington writes, its meaning 'is not so much that God *shows* no partiality...but that he does not evaluate human beings on the basis of their "face", their honor rating or credentials'.[66] Accepting 'face', Witherington points out, is giving regard to the external features of a person's life—wealth, status, power, gender and so on.[67] God does not take account of such distinctions. Paul's point, then, is that the Jerusalem leaders are being venerated as 'pillars' on the basis of a merely human scheme of evaluation, i.e. on worldly criteria. God sets no store by external, human factors such as personal closeness and familial relations, and neither does he.

The modalizers ψευδ- and οἱ δοκοῦντες thus express two quite different judgments on the different groups concerned. The first overtly expresses Paul's complete rejection of the claim of the individuals spoken of to be authentic believers. In Paul's view, they have no place within the community of faith. The second, in a much more subtle and interesting way, contests the exalted claim being made for or by James, Peter and John, that they are the 'pillars' of the developing church. Paul certainly grants Peter and James (and presumably John) the rank and status of apostles (1.19), a rank which Paul of course claims for himself. But he disputes that these three occupy a 'higher' level of authority within the emerging Christian movement, which the attribution 'pillars' presupposes.[68]

b. *Evaluative Words and Expressions*
Another way in which ideological point of view is expressed is through evaluative terminology. Though treated separately here, the use of evaluative terms is an extension of modality.[69] By means of evaluative words and expressions, mainly adverbs and adjectives, the author makes

---

64. Betz, *Galatians*, p. 95.
65. Cf. Betz, *Galatians*, p. 93.
66. Witherington, *Grace in Galatia*, p. 140.
67. Witherington, *Grace in Galatia*, p. 140.
68. The notion of a threefold elite among the circle of apostles/disciples is present in the Gospel tradition: cf. Mk 5.37; 9.2; 14.33.
69. Simpson, *Language*, p. 47.

known his or her judgment on personages and events in the story. In the narrative of Gal. 1.13–2.14, Paul uses a range of evaluative terms—verbs, nouns and noun phrases, adverbs and adjectives—to express his judgments on participants and actions in the narrative. The use of evaluative language is most apparent in 2.4 and 2.11-14, where he expresses particularly strong, negative judgments, but Paul makes value-judgments, however subtle, throughout the narrative: he expresses his opinions of characters and situations in the process of describing them.

Episode One (1.13-14). Paul speaks disapprovingly of his career as a persecutor. The negative judgment is conveyed not so much by the verbs 'persecuted' and 'tried to destroy', as by the object phrase 'the church of God'. The qualifying words τοῦ θεοῦ evaluate his actions as hostility toward God. He identifies the motive for his conduct as 'zeal for my ancestral traditions', ζηλωτὴς ὑπάρχων τῶν πατρικῶν μου παραδόσεων. Again, the negative judgment is encoded in the object phrase (objective genitive) rather than the verb phrase 'being...zealous'.

With the term ζηλωτής,[70] the adverbial expression καθ' ὑπερβολήν (connected to the verb ἐδίωκον) 'excessively', and the comparative adverb περισσοτέρως (connected to ζηλωτής) 'more abundantly',[71] Paul portrays himself as having acted with passion and intensity. He was deeply committed to the cause for which he strove. In the immediate context, Paul's stress on the fervour and vigour with which he operated adds to the loathsomeness of his actions. But it also sets up a contrast with Peter's behaviour later in the narrative. In the overall narrative context, the drive and commitment which Paul displayed 'in Judaism' stand as a counterpoint to the weakness of will and insincerity which marked Peter's conduct in Antioch. Paul acted wrongly, but at least he did so with strength of conviction. Peter, on the other hand, acted *both* wrongly *and* against his own convictions.

---

70. At a later point in this epistle, he will indicate to his readers that 'zealousness' can be directed toward either an improper (ζηλοῦσιν ὑμᾶς οὐ καλῶς..., 'they are zealous for you but not in a good way', 4.17) or a proper goal (καλὸν δὲ ζηλοῦσθαι ἐν καλῷ..., 'it is good to be zealous in a good way', 4.18). The verb ζηλόω is used positively in Rom. 10.2 and 2 Cor. 11.2.

71. The phrase καθ' ὑπερβολήν is used positively in 1 Cor. 12.31 and 2 Cor. 4.17. The adverb περισσοτέρως is used positively in 2 Cor. 1.12; 2.4; 7.13, 15; 11.23; 12.15; Phil. 1.14; 1 Thess 2.17.

Episode Two (1.15-17). Paul's description of his call to be an apostle lays great stress on its divine origin. This is conveyed by the string of verbs 'chose', 'set apart', 'called', 'reveal', with God as (implied) subject. He also emphasizes the sole sufficiency of his call. He states that he did not subsequently consult with 'flesh and blood'. The term σαρκὶ καὶ αἵματι is highly evaluative. It is a euphemism for human beings, in their frailty and weakness, over against God.[72] His point is not simply that he did not confer with anyone, but that having received his message and commission by divine revelation, consultation with a *mere* human being, by definition, *could not* have added anything to it.

Episode Three (1.18-19). With the verb ἱστορέω, 'to make acquaintance of',[73] Paul presents his first visit to Jerusalem after his call as an informal one. His purpose in going was 'to get to know' Peter. The verb excludes any idea that he was subordinating himself to Peter. It also conveys a positive estimate of Peter. He was someone worth going well out of one's way to meet. With the construction ἐπέμεινα πρὸς αὐτόν, Paul implies that he enjoyed good and friendly relations with him during this brief visit. Paul's judgment of Peter in this episode is one of firm approval. As for James, Paul clearly implies that he did not deem this apostle as worthy of 'getting to know' as Peter. Whereas he stayed with Peter, he only 'saw' James. Paul gives no indication that he actively sought him out. He gives James the title 'brother of the Lord', which is obviously evaluative. But it is not clear precisely *what* evaluation is being conveyed. According to Witherington, the title is a 'highly honorific' one, expressing 'the high privilege and status of James'.[74] Plainly, it is not a pejorative label. But it may not be as high an accolade as Witherington thinks. Paul here identifies James on the basis of his filial connections to Jesus. Retrospectively, this has to be viewed in the light of Paul's parenthetical comment in 2.6. James's family ties to the historical Jesus may be a mark of high status to others, but to Paul it means nothing. Paul's attitude toward James here is thus somewhat ambivalent.

Episode Four (1.21-24). Paul passes a highly positive judgment on his activities during this phase of his life. His judgment is conveyed

---

72. E.g. Longenecker, *Galatians*, p. 33.
73. Bruce, *Galatians*, p. 76.
74. Witherington, *Grace in Galatia*, p. 122.

through the report heard by the Judeans and their reaction to it. The report confirms the authenticity of his call by stressing the dramatic change in his life's direction, using the 'formerly'/'now' formula and picking up the language of episodes one (διώκων, ἐπόρθει) and two (εὐαγγελίζεται): the former persecutor is now a proclaimer of the faith. Paul is thus shown to be engaging in that which he was called to do. The report also establishes the authenticity of his gospel: he preaches the *same* faith he previously tried to destroy (τὴν πίστιν ἥν ποτε ἐπόρθει).[75] Paul states that the Judean congregations responded to the report by 'glorifying God' on his account (καὶ ἐδόξαζον ἐν ἐμοὶ τὸν θεόν). 'Glorifying God' is for Paul the loftiest activity in which human beings can engage.[76] To say that the Judeans glorified God for him is not simply to say that they found 'satisfaction'[77] in his missionary work, but that they affirmed its legitimacy in the strongest possible way.

Episode Five (2.1-10). In saying that he went up to Jerusalem 'in response to a revelation' (κατὰ ἀποκάλυψιν, 2.2), Paul indicates that his visit is to be viewed in the same light as his divine commissioning. He wants to make clear that he was not summoned to Jerusalem by the notables there, and that he did not go to them (cap in hand, as it were) seeking their authorization for his mission. Divine leading, he stresses, not human necessity, induced him to make the visit. He states that he 'laid before' them the gospel which he preaches—a gospel which does not require circumcision (2.2). The verb ἀνατίθημι here carries no thought of subordination.[78] There is no suggestion that Paul was submitting his gospel to the Jerusalem authorities for their approval, or that he would have changed it out of deference to them. The assertion, 'lest somehow I should run or had run in vain', as we have noted, signals apprehension. The evaluative adverbial expression 'in vain', 'uselessly' (εἰς κενόν)[79] conveys Paul's judgment that the outcome of the meeting was crucially important for his mission: disagreement between the Jerusalem authorities and his party on the question of whether Gentile believers should be circumcised could have rendered his missionary

75. Cf. Longenecker, *Galatians*, p. 42.
76. Cf. Rom 1.21; 15.6, 9; 1 Cor. 6.20; 2 Cor. 9.13.
77. As Burton (*Galatians*, p. 65) puts it.
78. So Bruce, *Galatians*, p. 109.
79. 1 Cor. 15.10, 14, 58; 2 Cor. 6.1. Cf. Gal. 4.11.

efforts ineffective.[80] But, as he fully expected, there was no such disagreement. The outcome was positive. Titus, whom Paul brought along as a test-case for the circumcision issue, was not forced to be circumcised, proving that the Jerusalem leaders shared Paul's view on this critical point of the gospel.[81]

Paul describes the activities and aims of the false brothers in 2.4 in highly pejorative terms. He states that they 'were smuggled in' (παρεισάκτους). The term connotes military and political conspiracy.[82] It characterizes these men as dangerous and subversive individuals. He identifies them as 'intruders' (παρεισῆλθον) and 'spies' (κατασκοπῆσαι) operating with malicious intent. Their goal, he states, is the 'enslavement' of the Christian community (ἵνα ἡμᾶς καταδουλώσουσιν). With these disparaging words, Paul passes a definite and unmistakable judgment on these men: they are adversaries of Christ who, having somehow been allowed into the camp, are working as enemies within to undermine the gospel and to capture the church for the cause they serve. Paul portrays his refusal to yield in submission to these individuals as a victory for the gospel (2.5).

The words οὐδὲν προσανέθεντο in 2.6 are evaluative. In insisting that the Jerusalem leaders 'added nothing' to him, Paul again stresses the sole sufficiency of his call and message. He is keen to show that the Jerusalem leaders did not confer any status upon him or cause him to make any adjustments to the gospel he received by revelation. He portrays them as recognizing his call to be as legitimate as theirs and his Gentile mission to be as valid as their Jewish mission. He says in 2.9 that they extended to him and Barnabas 'right hands' (δεξιὰς ἔδωκαν). Within Paul's culture, the gesture of giving the right hand would prob-

---

80. That Paul makes such an admission here has baffled interpreters. The concern which he expresses, if he is maintaining a consistent narrative viewpoint, can hardly be theological-vocational: that he had misgivings about the validity of his gospel. He has strongly argued that he had divine assurance of this. Neither can it be ecclesiological: that he needed the recognition of the Jerusalem authorities for his gospel and apostolic service to be considered legitimate. The whole thrust of his argument is against this. The concern must be practical: he recognized, on pragmatic grounds, that the success of his mission among the Gentiles was dependent on apostolic unity on the circumcision issue.

81. As Betz (*Galatians*, p. 88 n. 293) states, the οὐδέ signals 'the evidential value of Titus' case: if it is true for him, it is true in principle'.

82. Betz, *Galatians*, p. 90 n. 305.

ably have implied the social superiority of the giver.[83] It is likely that this is how James, Peter and John, in the historical event, understood the action, that is, they were acting in their assumed role as 'pillars'. Paul's insertion of the word κοινωνίας, however, encodes a different judgment of the action. He views it as a symbol of partnership, mutuality and equality.[84] Paul's qualification in 2.10 that he was 'eager' (ἐσπούδασα) to remember the poor does not lay stress on the spontaneity of his response to the request of the Jerusalem authorities. Rather, it indicates that he would have done this anyway, whether or not they had asked him,[85] thus reinforcing his claim that they 'added nothing' to him.

In this section, the most crucial of the narrative, Paul manifests the following judgments. He did not defer to the leaders of the Jerusalem church, nor did he place himself in their debt. He conceded no ground on the gospel as he interpreted it. He acted throughout in a manner consistent with his divine calling. The Jerusalem leaders, for their part, fully agreed with his understanding of the gospel and acknowledged his divine commissioning to take it to the Gentiles.

Episode Six (2.11-14). Paul's account of the incident in Antioch (2.11-14) is strongly coloured by evaluative terminology, making his judgments of characters and their actions abundantly clear. He states that Peter 'was condemned' (κατεγνωσμένος ἦν). The passive suggests not merely that Peter was in the wrong, but that he stood condemned *before God*.[86] By any standards, this is a damning indictment. He states that Peter's *volte-face* was motivated by 'fear', specifically fear of the circumcision party (φοβούμενος τοὺς ἐκ περιτομῆς). Peter is thus portrayed not only as inconsistent but also as a weak-willed individual. In Paul's judgment, the whole incident was marked by hypocrisy. In withdrawing from table-fellowship with the Gentile believers, Peter was being hypocritical. The Jewish believers, when they followed him, 'joined in the hypocrisy' (καὶ συνυπεκρίθησαν αὐτῷ [καὶ] οἱ λοιποὶ Ἰουδαῖοι). Barnabas was led astray by their hypocrisy (ὥστε καὶ Βαρναβᾶς συναπήχθη αὐτῶν τῇ ὑποκρίσει). Being 'led astray', Barnabas

---

83. So P.F. Esler, *Galatians* (New Testament Readings; London: Routledge, 1997), p. 133.
84. Cf. Longenecker, *Galatians*, p. 58.
85. See the discussion in Longenecker, *Galatians*, pp. 60-61.
86. Longenecker, *Galatians*, p. 72.

incurs a lesser judgment than Peter, but in Paul's view he is still blameworthy because he capitulated when he ought to have held firm (as he did with Paul against the false brothers in Jerusalem). The Blame is not directly attached to James, but he is implicated as the source of the trouble. Paul accuses Peter, Barnabas and the other Jewish Christians in the Antioch congregation of not walking straight in accordance with the truth of the gospel (οὐκ ὀρθοποδοῦσιν πρὸς τὴν ἀλήθειαν τοῦ εὐαγγελίου). The question in 2.14 accuses Peter of inconsistency (εἰ σὺ Ἰουδαῖος ὑπάρχων ἐθνικῶς καὶ οὐχὶ Ἰουδαϊκῶς ζῇς) and worse still, of forcing Gentile Christian converts to become converts to Judaism (πῶς τὰ ἔθνη ἀναγκάζεις ἰουδαΐζειν).

In the Antioch incident, Paul is again shown to be faithful to the gospel he received. The other narrative participants are seen to be disloyal to the gospel.

At this closing stage of the narrative, a sharp contrast between Paul and Peter, the two main characters, becomes detectable. Both individuals undergo a *volte-face*, Paul at the beginning of the narrative, in episodes one and two, Peter at the end, in this last episode. The latter's about-turn is the reverse of the former's.

1. Paul turned from *Judaism* (ἐν τῷ Ἰουδαϊσμῷ, 1.13a, 14a) to proclaim the *gospel* to the *Gentiles* (ἵνα εὐαγγελίζωμαι αὐτὸν ἐν τοῖς ἔθνεσιν, 1.16b). Peter turned from the truth of the *gospel* (οὐκ ὀρθοποδοῦσιν πρὸς τὴν ἀλήθειαν τοῦ εὐαγγελίου, 2.14a) to compel *Gentiles* to *Judaize* (πῶς τὰ ἔθνη ἀναγκάζεις ἰουδαΐζειν; 2.14e).

2. Paul's about-turn was caused by God (ὅτε δὲ εὐδόκησεν..., 1.15-16a), Peter's by acceding to demands of human beings (φοβούμενος τοὺς ἐκ περιτομῆς, 2.12).

3. Paul's activities in Judaism were marked by conviction and commitment (καθ᾽ ὑπερβολὴν...περισσοτέρως ζηλωτής, 1.13b-14); Peter's actions, which were Judaizing in their effect, were marked by hypocrisy and inconsistency (2.13-14).[87]

---

87. As Lyons (*Pauline Autobiography*, p. 163) points out, there is also a contrast between Paul's refusal to yield to the false brothers in order to preserve the truth of the gospel (2.3-5), and Peter's yielding to the men from James and departing from the truth of the gospel (2.12-14).

c. *Transitivity*

A third way in which ideological viewpoint is encoded is through transitivity.[88] Transitivity has to do with the way in which processes and their participants are characterized in sentences. *Processes* relate to the verb element in a clause and may be classified as material processes, verbal processes, mental processes, relational processes and existential processes. *Material* processes are processes of doing. They may be subdivided into *action* processes, if they are performed by an animate actor, and *event* processes, if they are performed by an inanimate actor (e.g. 'the car broke down'). Action processes can be further subdivided into *intention* processes, where an action is performed under the control of an actor (e.g. 'the boy ate the cake') and *supervention* processes, where processes just happen (e.g. 'the girl fell over'). *Verbal* processes have to do with speech. *Mental* processes are sensory processes and include *perceptions* (e.g. seeing, hearing), *affections* (e.g. loving, hating)[89] and *cognitions* (e.g. thinking, understanding). *Relational* processes divide into *intensive* processes (states of being) and *possessive* processes (states of having). *Existential* processes represent something that is.[90]

Participants relate to nouns or noun-phrases in the clause. Participant roles are as follows. In action processes, the main roles are *actor* (the doer of the action) and *goal* (the sufferer or object of the action). In verbal processes, the key roles are *sayer*, *verbiage* (what is said) and *target*. In mental processes, the roles involved are *senser* and *phenomenon*. In relational processes, the role-types are *carrier* and *attribute*. In existential processes, the key role is *existent*. Participant functions common to all process-types are *beneficiary* (indirect object),[91] *range* (cognate object).[92] An important circumstantial element is *place*.[93]

We will first take a detailed look at the clause structure of Gal. 1.13–2.14, then make some broad observations about transitivity patterns in

---

88. The transitivity model is drawn from Halliday, *Functional Grammar*, pp. 106-75. Here I am largely following Simpson's appropriation of it (*Language*, pp. 88-92).

89. I prefer Halliday's term 'affection' (*Functional Linguistics*, p. 118) to Simpson's descriptor 'reaction' (*Language*, p. 91).

90. For existential processes, see Halliday, *Functional Linguistics*, pp. 142-44.

91. Halliday, *Functional Linguistics*, pp. 144-46

92. Halliday, *Functional Linguistics*, pp. 144-49.

93. Halliday, *Functional Linguistics*, pp. 152-53.

the passage, and finally, say something about the portrait of Paul which emerges from this.

1. *Clause-by-Clause Analysis of Transitivity.* The focus of transitivity analysis is the clause (rather than the sentence). All clauses in the text come under inspection, including dependent clauses and embedded clauses. An embedded clause is a clause within a clause, such as a relative clause. In Koine Greek, certain participial constructions count as embedded clauses.

First Episode (1.13-14). The narrative begins with Paul's readers, the Galatians, as logical subject. They are presented as the sensers of the mental process 'heard about'. The phenomenon, the object of the process, is 'Paul's former life in Judaism'. The clauses which follow, 1.13b-14a, describe that earlier life, and the focus quickly shifts from the Galatians to Paul. He is presented as the performer of dramatic actions: 'persecuted', 'trying to destroy', 'was advancing'. He is also the carrier of the motivating attribute 'zealous'.

Episode Two (1.15-17). The long temporal clause, 1.15-16a, describing Paul's conversion has God as subject. He is the senser of the affection process 'chose' ('desired', 'was pleased'). Within the clause (that is to say, in the embedded clauses), Paul is set forth as the goal of actions done by God, 'set apart' and 'called', and as the beneficiary of God's act of 'revealing' his Son. At 1.16b, Paul resumes the role of subject, a role which he retains in the narrative for the next fourteen clauses. The clause 1.16b expresses the purpose of God's decision to reveal his Son to him: Paul is here the sayer of the verbal process 'proclaim', with the 'Gentiles' as the range. In 1.16c, a negative clause, he is again sayer (or non-sayer): he did not 'consult' with flesh and blood. In 1.17, where Paul states his immediate post-conversion movements, he is actor: the verbs here are 'go up'—which he expressly did *not* do—'went away', 'returned', 'went up'.

Episode Three (1.18-19). Galatians 1.18-19, which outlines Paul's first post-conversion visit to Jerusalem, constitutes one sentence in Greek (with five clauses). Paul is actor in 1.18a: he 'went up' to Jerusalem. In 1.18b, which gives the reason for the previously mentioned action, he is senser of the perception process 'get to know', with Peter as phenomenon. In 1.18c, he performs the action 'stayed', with Peter as place. In 1.19, he is ascribed the mental process of perception, 'did not see' (and by implication 'see'). In these verses, Paul is protagonist. He takes the initiative in going to Jerusalem, in seeking out Peter and in staying with him. In 1.20, he is sayer of the verbal processes 'write' and 'do not lie'.

Episode Four (1.21-24). In 1.21, Paul is the doer of the action, 'went'. In 1.22, he is the carrier of the attribute 'unknown by face', with 'the churches of Judea' as the range. Paul could have expressed the same meaning by casting the Judean believers as sensers and by placing himself in the role of phenomenon. But he chooses a pattern of transitivity which enables him to retain his role as subject. Nevertheless, the Judean churches are the subject of the next clause. This is the first point in the narrative since 1.16b at which Paul is not the logical subject of a process. The churches in Judea are ascribed the perception process of 'hearing'. In the projection clause that follows, Paul is again subject, first as actor of the process 'persecuted', next as sayer of the process 'proclaims', then as actor of the process 'tried to destroy'. Paul rounds off this part of the narrative by presenting the Judean churches as actors: they 'glorified God' on his account.

Episode Five (2.1-10). The next and main subsection of the narrative, the account of the meeting in Jerusalem, opens in 2.1 with Paul as actor. Paul 'went up' to Jerusalem with Barnabas, 'taking' with him Titus. The nominative singular participle συμπαραλαβών represents Paul as taking the lead in bringing Titus along. Paul is actor of the process 'went up' in 2.2a. He is actor in 2.2b, the subject of the verb 'laid before' with the 'gospel' as object and 'those of repute' as beneficiaries. The process represented (as distinct from the sense of the verb employed) conveys no thought of Paul subordinating himself to the Jerusalem leaders. The embedded relative clause within 2.2b has Paul as sayer of the verbal process 'proclaim'. In 2.2d, he is the doer of the actions 'run' and 'had run'. In 2.3, there is a shift from Paul to Titus as subject. Titus, however, is here a passive subject. He is the potential goal of the potential action '(not) compelled to be circumcised'. The actor or actors are unspecified. Logically, the actors would be the Jerusalem leaders (not the false brothers, since they are identified in 2.4a as the *causative* agents of the non-action, not the active agents). Paul suppresses their agency perhaps because he does not wish explicitly to ascribe to them the power to control others which the verb 'compel' implies. Titus is also carrier (of the attribute 'Greek') in the embedded clause 2.3(i). The passive adjective παρεισάκτους implies that the false brothers had been brought in by someone or several people.[94] Again, agency is not specified. Could Paul be hinting that one of the pillars was responsible for bringing them into the Christian camp, perhaps James (especially if the false brothers are to be identified with the 'men from James' in the Antioch incident)?

The false brothers are the actors in 2.4b-c: they 'intruded' so that they might 'spy out' the freedom enjoyed in the Christian community. An unspecified 'we' is the carrier of the attribute 'freedom' in the embedded relative clause within 2.4c. The 'we' refers in the first instance to Paul, Barnabas and Titus. But as Longenecker states, 'it also takes in all Jewish and Gentile believers in Christ who hold to "the truth of the gospel"'.[95] The false brothers are the actors of the potential action 'enslave', with 'us' (all genuine believers, especially Gentile converts), as the intended goal of that process. In 2.5a, Paul, Barnabas and (presumably) Titus are the subjects of the non-action 'yield (in subjection)'. The 'truth of the gospel' is the existent in the existential process 'remain' in 2.5b, with the Galatians as beneficiaries.

A new sentence begins at 2.6, and Paul picks up where he left off at 2.3. The clause of 2.6a is incomplete. Had Paul finished the sentence, he would probably have had himself as the subject of the verb 'received'. The noun phrase 'what they once were' in 2.6b is carrier of the (non-)attribute 'nothing' in the intensive process 'matters' (effectively 'is'). Then in 2.6c, God is the actor of the action process 'accept' with 'face' (of a human being) as goal. In 2.6d, Paul completes what he meant to say in 2.6a, and explicates it. He rephrases the sentence, having the men of repute as subject. They are the doers of the action 'added'. But since what they added was 'nothing', this is effectively a non-action. In 2.7a, the men of repute are the perceivers of a phenomenon. In the projection clause (the thing which is perceived), Paul is the goal of the action 'entrusted'. The verb is in the passive voice. The agent, though unspecified, is clearly God. Peter is the goal of the

---

94. Some commentators (e.g. Bruce, *Galatians*, p. 112; Longenecker, *Galatians*, p. 51), however, argue that the passive force of the adjective should not be pressed.

95. Longenecker, *Galatians*, p. 51.

implied action 'entrusted' (the verb is omitted) in the comparative clause which follows. God is the subject of the parenthetical enhancement clause of 2.8. He is the implied actor of the process 'energized', both in its participial form and in its aorist indicative form, with Peter and Paul as goals. The men of repute, named as James, Cephas and John, are sensers in 2.9a. They perceive the phenomenon 'the grace given to me [Paul]'. In 2.9b, they are then the actors of the process 'gave' with 'right hands' as goal and Paul and Barnabas as beneficiaries. In 2.9c, Paul and Barnabas are actors of a probable material process 'go' (the verb is omitted). In 2.9d, James, Peter and John are also actors of this process (again the verb is omitted). In 2.10, Paul and Barnabas are sensers of the process 'remember', and Paul is senser of the affection process 'was eager', with the request made by the men of repute ('this very thing') as the phenomenon.

Episode Six (2.11-14). In this section Peter is the main actor. In 2.11a, he is subject of the action 'came'. The focus immediately shifts to Paul, in 2.11b, the main clause of the sentence, where he is the doer of the action 'opposed', with Peter as goal. Peter is then the carrier of the negative attribute 'condemned'. In the temporal clause of 2.12a, the men from James are the actors, the subjects of the verb 'came'. Peter is the performer of the action 'eat (with)' in 2.12b. The men from James are in view as actors of the clause 2.12c. Then Peter is actor of the processes 'withdrew' and 'separated', with 'himself' as goal (2.12d-e). He is also the senser of the affective process 'fearing' with 'the circumcision (party)' as the phenomenon (2.12-13). The 'rest of the Jews' are then the actors of the action process 'joining [Peter] in the act of hypocrisy' in 2.13a. Barnabas is the goal of the event process 'led astray', with 'their act of hypocrisy' as inanimate actor in 2.13b. Paul is the senser of the phenomenon 'that they were not walking according to the truth of the gospel', with the Jewish believers as actors in the projection clause. He is then the sayer of the question of 2.14, and within the question, Peter is actor, then carrier, then actor.

2. *General Transitivity Patterns.* Of the 77 clauses analysed, 46 represent material action processes (1.13b; 1.13c; 1.14a; 1.15(i); 1.15(ii); 1.16a; 1.17a; 1.17b; 1.17c; 1.18a; 1.18c; 1.21; 1.23b(i); 1.23b(ii); 1.24; 2.1a; 2.1b; 2.2a; 2.2b; 2.2d; 2.3; 2.4a(i); 2.4b; 2.4c; 2.4d; 2.5a; 2.6c; 2.6d; 2.7b; 2.7c; 2.8; 2.8(i); 2.9b; 2.9c (?); 2.9d (?); 2.11a; 2.11b; 2.12a;

2.12b; 2.12c; 2.12d; 2.12e; 2.13a; 2.14b; 2.14d; 2.14e). Action is clearly the dominant type of process in the narrative, vastly outnumbering all the other processes put together. All the actions are intentional. There are no action supervention processes. Nothing in this narrative just 'happens'. Every action takes place at the direction of an actor. The next most common process types are verbal process (1.16b; 1.16c; 1.20a; 1.20b; 1.23b; 2.2b(i); 2.10a (?); 2.14c) and intensive processes (1.14b; 1.22; 2.3(i); 2.6a(i); 2.6b; 2.9b(i); 2.11c; 2.14d(i))). There are several instances each of the mental processes of perception (1.13a; 1.19a; 1.19b; 1.22a; 2.14a), affection (1.15; 2.10c; 2.12-13) and cognition (1.18b; 2.7a; 2.9a; 2.10b). There is one event process (2.13b), one possessive process (2.4d) and one existential process (2.5b).

The principal actor in the narrative is Paul. Many more actions are credited to him (17 in all)[96] than to any other character (1.13b; 1.13c; 1.14a; 1.17a; 1.17b; 1.17c; 1.18a; 1.18c; 1.21; 1.23b(i); 1.23b(ii); 2.1a; 2.1b; 2.2a; 2.2b; 2.2d; 2.11b). His actions are spread over the whole narrative, but are particularly concentrated in the first main section, 1.13-24. He is least 'active' in the Antioch episode. God is credited with six explicit actions (1.15(i); 1.15(ii); 1.16a; 2.6c; 2.8; 2.8(i)). Six actions are also attributed to Peter (2.11a; 2.12b; 2.12d; 2.12e; 2.14d; 2.14e). Peter's six independent actions (as opposed to his actions as a member of the group 'men of repute', 2.6d; 2.9b; 2.9(d?)) are concentrated in 2.11-14. His actions, which are negatively valued, dominate this episode. The actions of the false brothers take centre-stage in 2.4. If we discount the verbless clause of 2.10a, Paul is the only sayer in the narrative (1.16b; 1.16c; 1.20a; 1.20b; 1.22b; 2.2b(i); 2.14c).[97]

3. *The Portrait of Paul.* Paul is presented in this narrative, through its transitivity structures, as an independent agent, performing actions under his voluntary control. When he is acted upon (that is to say, when he is the goal of someone else's action), it is mainly by God (1.15(i); 1.15(ii); 2.7b). The only point in the narrative at which he is the goal of an action (as opposed to non-action) performed by human beings is at 2.8, where he is given the right hands of the Jerusalem leaders, which, as we have seen, Paul interprets as a signal of equality and partnership. James, Peter and John, the men of repute, are mainly sensers, recog-

96. 1.13b; 1.13c; 1.14a; 1.17a; 1.17b; 1.17c; 1.18a; 1.18c; 1.21; 1.23b(i); 1.23b(ii); 2.1a; 2.1b; 2.2a; 2.2b; 2.2d; 2.11b.
97. 1.16b; 1.16c; 1.20a; 1.20b; 1.22b; 2.2b(i); 2.14c.

nizing and perceiving Paul's calling and divine gifting. In the narrative of Gal. 1.13–2.14, Paul is an author and initiator of events rather than a mere participant in them.

In the Antioch incident, it is true, he reacts to what is going on around him, rather than making things happen. But of those present in Antioch (James is not actually there at Antioch, though he is the implied source of the trouble), he is the only one whose behaviour is completely within his control. The others act under duress or under the influence of others. Peter's turn-about is caused by the arrival of certain men. These men were sent by James. Peter acts out of fear of the circumcision party. The rest of the Jews follow Peter. Barnabas is 'led astray' with them. The Gentile believers are 'compelled' to Judaize. Paul is the only personage in Antioch who acts 'freely'.

With the accent firmly on Paul's role as a creative agent, acting either of his own volition or at the behest of God, the transitivity structures of Gal. 1.13–2.14 help to reinforce one of Paul's key argumentative points in the narrative: the independence of his apostolic ministry from all human authorities and influences (cf. Gal. 1.1).

5. Conclusion

The four planes of point of view in the narrative of Gal. 1.13–2.14 converge to serve Paul's rhetorical goals, establishing his 'self-defence' against the accusations of his opponents in Galatia (that his commission and message derived from Jerusalem; that his apostleship is secondary to that of the original apostles; that he has deviated from the message he received). The temporal point of view highlights the long stretch of time between his conversion and his meeting with the leaders in Jerusalem. The spatial point of view places him far away from Jerusalem for virtually the whole of the period under consideration. The psychological point of view helps to create a sense of the 'authoritative' nature of *his* account of events. The ideological viewpoint lays emphasis on the following points: the truthfulness of his version of events (conveyed by the modal structures of the text); the fact that he remained faithful to his call and gospel (expressed through evaluative terminology); his freedom from the control of other human beings, in particular, the Jerusalem leaders (conveyed by the transitivity structures of the text).

The text communicates certain core values: the authenticity, sufficiency and independence of Paul's divine commissioning; the 'truth of the gospel' which is that Gentiles are accepted within God's new community on equal terms with Jews, without undergoing circumcision or submitting to the Jewish law. These are the norms against which characters and actions in the narrative are measured. The narrative establishes that Paul acted consistently with these core values.

In expressing his own ideological perspective, Paul contests a dominant ideology of the emerging Christian movement. He disputes the view that Jerusalem is the power-centre of the developing church and that the Jerusalem leaders are the 'pillars', the dominant authority, of the movement. This view credits him with a subordinate rank and role in the growing church. As Paul sees it, he is equal in rank to all the original apostles, including James, Peter and John.

The foregoing critical linguistic analysis of the narrative of Gal. 1.13–2.14 has not uncovered any 'new' or 'deeper' meaning in the text, nor has it resolved any of the debated exegetical issues relating to the passage. What it has achieved, I believe, is an enhanced understanding of how Paul's language in the narrative works to achieve his rhetorical goals, to communicate the values he wishes to impart, and to call into question a dominant ideology.

APPENDIX

Transitivity Analysis of the Clauses of Gal. 1.13–2.14

In the table which follows, the constituent clauses of Gal. 1.13–2.14 are isolated and classified according to clause type, and their transitivity structures are analysed. The process types and participant roles have been set out and explained in the main essay. The clause types, which are drawn from Halliday's functional grammar,[98] may be summarized as follows:[99]

98. Halliday, *Functional Grammar*, pp. 225-73.

99. For a helpful summary of how New Testament Greek expresses these clause types, see J.T. Reed, *A Discourse Analysis of Philippians: Method and Rhetoric in the Debate over Literary Integrity* (JSNTSup, 136; Sheffield: Sheffield Academic Press, 1997), pp. 91-92.

Primary: the main clause of a sentence
Elaboration: elaborates on the meaning of another clause in one of three
                 ways:
    exposition: restates the thesis of the clause (i.e.)
    exemplification: restates the thesis of the clause by becoming more
                                    specific about it (e.g.)
    clarification: supports the thesis of the clause with an explana-
                                    tory comment (in fact, indeed)
Extension: extends the meaning of another clause by adding something
                 new to it:
    addition: joins one process to another
      positive: expressed by 'and'
      negative: expressed by 'not even', 'nor'
      adversative: expressed by 'but'
    variation: partially or completely replaces another clause
                                    (except for, but instead)
Enhancement: extends the meaning of another clause by qualifying it in
                 one of several ways:
    temporal: enhances by stating time
    spatial: enhances by stating place
    comparison: enhances by making comparison
    causal-conditional: enhances by stating cause, purpose or condition
Projection: projects one clause through another:
    locution: reports what is heard or said
    idea: expresses thought, belief, feeling, assumption,
                                    etc.
Embedded clause: embeds one clause within another

Verse	Clause	Clause Type	Process	Participants
1.13a	ἠκούσατε γὰρ τὴν ἐμὴν ἀναστροφήν ποτε ἐν τῷ Ἰουδαϊσμῷ,	Primary	Mental, perception: 'heard about'	Sensers: the Galatians; Phenomenon: Paul's 'former life in Judaism'
1.13b	ὅτι καθ᾽ ὑπερβολὴν ἐδίωκον τὴν ἐκκλησίαν τοῦ θεοῦ	Elaboration, clarification	Material, action, intention: 'persecuted'	Actor: Paul; Goal: the church of God
1.13c	καὶ ἐπόρθουν αὐτήν,	Extension (of 1.13b), addition, positive	Material, action, intention: 'was trying to destroy'	Actor: Paul; Goal: the church of God ('it')

Verse	Clause	Clause Type	Process	Participants
1.14a	καὶ προέκοπτον ἐν τῷ Ἰουδαϊσμῷ ὑπὲρ πολλοὺς συνηλικιώτας ἐν τῷ γένει μου,	Extension (of 1.13b and c), addition, positive	Material, action, intention: 'was advancing'	Actor: Paul; Range: in Judaism
1.14b	περισσοτέρως ζηλωτὴς ὑπάρχων τῶν πατρικῶν μου παραδόσεων.	Enhancement (qualifying all three clauses of 1.13b-14a), causal-conditional	Relational, intensive: 'being'	Carrier: Paul; Attribute: zealous for my ancestral traditions
1.15	ὅτε δὲ εὐδόκησεν ὁ ἀφορίσας με ἐκ κοιλίας μητρός μου καὶ καλέσας διὰ τῆς χάριτος αὐτοῦ...	Enhancement (of 1.16c), temporal	Mental, affection: 'chose'	Senser: God ('the one who set me apart...'); Phenomenon (from 1.16a): 'to reveal his Son in/to me'
1.15 (i)	ὁ ἀφορίσας με	Embedded clause	Material, action, intention: 'set apart'	Actor: God ('the one...'); Goal: Paul
1.15(ii)	καὶ καλέσας	Embedded clause	Material, action, intention: 'called'	Actor: God; Goal: [Paul]
1.16a	ἀποκαλύψαι τὸν υἱὸν αὐτοῦ ἐν ἐμοί,	Projection, idea	Material, action, intention: 'reveal'	Actor: God; Goal: 'his Son'; Beneficiary: Paul ('in/to me')
1.16b	ἵνα εὐαγγελίζω-μαι αὐτὸν ἐν τοῖς ἔθνεσιν,	Enhancement (of 1.16a), causal-conditional	Verbal: 'proclaim'	Sayer: Paul; Verbiage: God's Son ('him'); Range: 'among the Gentiles'
1.16c	εὐθέως οὐ προσανεθέμην σαρκὶ καὶ αἵματι	Primary	Verbal: 'did not consult with'	Sayer: Paul; Target: 'flesh and blood'

Verse	Clause	Clause Type	Process	Participants
1.17a	οὐδὲ ἀνῆλθον εἰς Ἱεροσόλυμα πρὸς τοὺς πρὸ ἐμοῦ ἀποστόλους,	Extension (of 1.16c), addition, negative	Material, action, intention: 'nor go up'	Actor: Paul; Goal: Jerusalem; 'those who were apostles before me'
1.17b	ἀλλὰ ἀπῆλθον εἰς Ἀραβίαν	Extension (of 1.17a), addition, adversative	Material, action, intention: 'went away'	Actor: Paul; Goal: Arabia
1.17c	καὶ πάλιν ὑπέστρεψα εἰς Δαμασκόν.	Extension (of 1.17b), addition, positive	Material, action, intention: 'returned'	Actor: Paul; Goal: Damascus
1.18a	ἔπειτα μετὰ ἔτη τρία ἀνῆλθον εἰς Ἱεροσόλυμα	Primary	Material, action, intention: 'went up'	Actor: Paul; Goal: Jerusalem
1.18b	ἱστορῆσαι Κηφᾶν	Enhancement, causal-conditional	Mental, cognition: 'get to know'	Senser: Paul; Phenomenon: Peter
1.18c	καὶ ἐπέμεινα πρὸς αὐτὸν ἡμέρας δεκαπέντε,	Extension (of 1.18b), addition, positive	Material, action, intention: 'stayed'	Actor: Paul; Place: Peter
1.19a	ἕτερον δὲ τῶν ἀποστόλων οὐκ εἶδον	Extension, addition, negative	Mental, perception: 'did not see'	Senser: Paul; Phenomenon: 'any other of the apostles'
1.19b	εἰ μὴ Ἰάκωβον τὸν ἀδελφὸν τοῦ κυρίου.	Extension (of 1.19a), variation verbless clause[100]	Mental, perception: ['saw']	Senser: [Paul]; Phenomenon: James

100. The verb εἶδον is here supplied from the previous clause.

Verse	Clause	Clause Type	Process	Participants
1.20a	ἃ δὲ γράφω ὑμῖν,	Enhancement, spatial (of 1.20b)[101]	Verbal: 'write'	Sayer: Paul; Verbiage: 'what things'; Target: the Galatians
1.20b	ἰδοὺ ἐνώπιον τοῦ θεοῦ ὅτι οὐ ψεύδομαι.	Primary	Verbal: 'do not lie'	Sayer: Paul
1.21	ἔπειτα ἦλθον εἰς τὰ κλίματα τῆς Συρίας καὶ τῆς Κιλικίας·	Primary	Material, action, intention: 'went'	Actor: Paul; Goal: 'the regions of Syria and Cilicia'
1.22	ἤμην δὲ ἀγνοούμενος τῷ προσώπῳ ταῖς ἐκκλησίαις τῆς Ἰουδαίας ταῖς ἐν Χριστῷ.	Extension (of 1.21), addition, positive	Relational, intensive: 'was'	Carrier: Paul; Attribute: 'unknown by face'; Range: the churches of Judea in Christ
1.23a	μόνον δὲ ἀκούοντες ἦσαν ὅτι ὁ διώκων....	Extension (of 1.22), addition, positive	Mental, perception: 'were hearing'	Sensers: the churches of Judea; Phenomenon: 'The one...'
1.23b	ὁ διώκων ἡμᾶς ποτε νῦν εὐαγγελίζεται τὴν πίστιν ἥν ποτε ἐπόρθει,	Projection, locution	Verbal: 'is proclaiming'	Sayer: Paul ('The one who formerly persecuted us'); Verbiage: 'the faith...'
1.23b(i)	ὁ διώκων ἡμᾶς ποτε	Embedded clause	Material, action, intention: 'persecuted'	Actor: Paul ('The one'); Goal: the churches of Judea ('us')

101. Taking the accusative here as an accusative of respect, 'in what things I write to you...'

Verse	Clause	Clause Type	Process	Participants
1.23b(ii)	ἥν ποτε ἐπόρθει,	Embedded clause	Material, action, intention: 'tried to destroy'	Actor: Paul; Goal: the faith ('which')
1.24	καὶ ἐδόξαζον ἐν ἐμοὶ τὸν θεόν.	Extension (of 1.23b), addition, positive	Material, action, intention: 'glorified'	Actors: the churches of Judea; Goal: God
2.1a	ἔπειτα διὰ δεκατεσσά-ρων ἐτῶν πάλιν ἀνέβην εἰς Ἱεροσόλυμα μετὰ Βαρναβᾶ	Primary	Material, action, intention: 'went up'	Actor: Paul; Goal: Jerusalem
2.1b	συμπαρα-λαβὼν καὶ Τίτον·	Extension, addition, positive	Material, action, intention: 'taking along'	Actor: Paul; Goal: Titus
2.2a	ἀνέβην δὲ κατὰ ἀποκάλυψιν·	Elaboration (of 2.1a), clarification	Material, action, intention: 'went up'	Actor: Paul
2.2b	καὶ ἀνεθέμην αὐτοῖς τὸ εὐαγγέλιον ὃ κηρύσσω ἐν τοῖς ἔθνεσιν,	Extension (of 2.2a), addition	Material, action, intention: 'laid before'	Actor: Paul; Goal: 'the gospel...'; Beneficiaries: 'them', 'the men of repute'[102]
2.2b(i)	ὃ κηρύσσω ἐν τοῖς ἔθνεσιν,	Embedded clause	Verbal: 'preach'	Sayer: Paul; Verbiage: the gospel ('which'); Range: among the Gentiles
2.2c	κατ᾽ ἰδίαν δὲ τοῖς δοκοῦσιν	Extension (of 2.2b), addition, positive		

102. Taking τοῖς δοκοῦσιν in 2.2c as an elucidation of αὐτοῖς in 2.2b. In 2.2 and 2.6, the participial phase οἱ δοκοῦντες, without amplification, is taken as a noun phrase 'the men of repute'.

Verse	Clause	Clause Type	Process	Participants
2.2d	μή πως εἰς κενὸν τρέχω ἢ ἔδραμον	Enhancement, causal-conditional (of 2.2a and b)	Material, action, intention: 'run or had run'	Actor: Paul; Range: 'in vain'
2.3	ἀλλ᾽ οὐδὲ Τίτος ὁ σὺν ἐμοί,... ἠναγκάσθη περιτμηθῆναι·	Extension, addition, adversative,	Material, action, intention: 'not compelled to be circumcised' [103] passive voice	Goal: Titus; Actor: unspecified
2.3(i)	Ἕλλην ὤν,		Relational, intensive: 'being'	Carrier: Titus; Attribute: a Greek
2.4a	διὰ δὲ τοὺς παρεισάκτους ψευδαδέλφους,	Enhancement (of 2.3) causal-conditional incomplete clause [104]		
2.4a(i)	τοὺς παρεισάκτους ψευδαδέλφους	Embedded clause	Material, action, intention: 'smuggled in' passive voice	Goal: the false brothers; Actor/s: unspecified
2.4b	οἵτινες παρεισῆλθον	Extension (of 2.4a), addition, positive	Material, action, intention: 'intruded'	Actors: the false brothers
2.4c	κατασκοπῆσαι τὴν ἐλευθερίαν ἡμῶν...	Enhancement, causal-conditional	Material, action, intention: 'spy out'	Actors: the false brothers; Goal: 'our freedom...'

103. The auxiliary + infinitive construction ἠναγκάσθη περιτμηθῆναι is here taken as one process 'compelled to be circumcised', rather than as two distinct actions 'compelled' and 'circumcised'.

104. Words such as 'Now this happened' (i.e. pressure for Titus to be circumcised) seem to be assumed. Cf. Longenecker, *Galatians*, p. 50.

Verse	Clause	Clause Type	Process	Participants
2.4c(i)	ἦν ἔχομεν ἐν Χριστῷ Ἰησοῦ	Embedded clause	Relational, possessive: 'have'	Carrier: 'we'; Attribute: freedom ('which')
2.4d	ἵνα ἡμᾶς καταδουλώ- σουσιν,	Enhancement (of 2.4b and c), causal- conditional	Material, action, intention: 'enslave'	Actors: the false brothers; Goal: 'us'
2.5a	οἷς οὐδὲ πρὸς ὥραν εἴξαμεν τῇ ὑποταγῇ,	Enhancement, addition, negative	Material, action, intention: 'did not yield (to)'	Actors: 'we'; Goal: the false brothers ('whom')
2.5b	ἵνα ἡ ἀλήθεια τοῦ εὐαγγελίου διαμείνῃ πρὸς ὑμᾶς.	Enhancement, causal- conditional	Existential: 'remain'	Existent: the truth of the gospel; Beneficiaries: the Galatians ('you')
2.6a	ἀπὸ δὲ τῶν δοκούντων εἶναί τι,	Primary incomplete clause[105]		
2.6a(i)	τῶν δοκούντων εἶναί τι,[106]	Embedded clause	Relational, intensive: 'seem to be'	Carrier: 'those' Attribute: 'something' (of importance)
2.6b	ὁποῖοί ποτε ἦσαν οὐδέν μοι διαφέρει·	Primary	Relational intensive: 'matters to me'	Carrier: 'What they once were'; Attribute: 'nothing'
2.6c	πρόσωπον [ὁ] θεὸς ἀνθρώπου οὐ λαμβάνει	Enhancement (of 2.6b), causal- conditional	Material, action, intention: 'does not accept'	Actor: God; Goal: the face of human being

105. Had Paul completed the clause, after the parenthesis of 2.6, he probably would have said οὐδὲν παρέλαβον: so Bruce, *Galatians*, p. 118.

106. Here and at 2.9, οἱ δοκοῦντες εἶναι is taken as auxiliary + infinitive + attribute: 'those who seem/are reputed to be'.

Verse	Clause	Clause Type	Process	Participants
2.6d	ἐμοὶ γὰρ οἱ δοκοῦντες οὐδὲν προσανέθεντο,	Primary	Material, action, intention: 'contributed'	Actors: 'the men of repute'; Goal: 'nothing'; Beneficiary: Paul ('me')
2.7a	ἀλλὰ τουναντίον ἰδόντες ὅτι...	Extension (of 2.6d), addition, adversative	Mental, perception: 'seeing	Sensers (2:9): 'the men of repute'; Phenomenon: 'that I have been....'
2.7b	πεπίστευμαι τὸ εὐαγγέλιον τῆς ἀκροβυστίας	Projection, idea	Material, action, intention: 'entrusted' passive voice	Goal: Paul; Actor: unspecified; Beneficiaries: 'the uncircumcised'
2.7c	καθὼς Πέτρος τῆς περιτομῆς.	Enhancement (of 2.7a), comparison verbless clause	Material, action, intention: ['entrusted']	Goal: Peter; Actor: unspecified; Beneficiary: 'the circumcised'
2.8	ὁ γὰρ ἐνεργήσας Πέτρῳ εἰς ἀποστολὴν τῆς περιτομῆς ἐνήργησεν καὶ ἐμοὶ εἰς τὰ ἔθνη	Enhancement (of 2.7b and c), causal-conditional	Material, action, intention: 'worked'	Actor: God ('the one who worked through Peter...'); Goal: Paul
2.8(i)	ὁ γὰρ ἐνεργήσας Πέτρῳ	Embedded clause	Material, action, intention	Actor: God ('the one...'); Goal: Peter
2.9a	καὶ γνόντες τὴν χάριν τὴν δοθεῖσάν μοι,	Extension (of 2.7-8), addition, positive	Mental, perception: 'knowing'	Sensers: James, Cephas and John; Phenomenon: 'the grace given to me'

Verse	Clause	Clause Type	Process	Participants
2.9b	Ἰάκωβος καὶ Κηφᾶς καὶ Ἰωάννης, οἱ δοκοῦντες στῦλοι εἶναι, δεξιὰς ἔδωκαν ἐμοὶ καὶ Βαρναβᾷ κοινωνίας,	Extension (of 2.6d), addition, variation (continuing the ἀλλὰ τουναντίον of 2.7a)	Material, action, intention: 'gave'	Actors: James, Cephas and John; Goal: right hands; Beneficiaries: Paul and Barnabas
2.9b(i)	οἱ δοκοῦντες στῦλοι εἶναι,	Embedded clause	Relational, intensive: 'seem to be'	Carrier: those; Attribute: pillars
2.9c	ἵνα ἡμεῖς εἰς τὰ ἔθνη,	Enhancement, causal-conditional verbless clause	Material, action, intention: ['go']	Actors: Paul and Barnabas; Goal: the Gentiles
2.9d	αὐτοὶ δὲ εἰς τὴν περιτομήν·	Extension (to 2.9c), addition, positive verbless clause	Material, action, intention: ['go']	Actors: James, Peter and John; Goal: the circumcised
2.10a	μόνον	Extension (of 2.7a, 2.9), variation Verb missing[107]	Verbal: ['asked']	Sayers: [James, Peter and John]
2.10b	τῶν πτωχῶν ἵνα μνημονεύ-ωμεν,	Elaboration, exemplification	Mental, cognition (with a view to action): 'remember'	Senser: 'we'; Phenomenon: the poor
2.10c	ὃ καὶ ἐσπούδασα αὐτὸ τοῦτο ποιῆσαι.	Elaboration, clarification	Mental, affection: 'was eager to do'[108]	Senser: Paul; Phenomenon: 'this' (remember the poor)

107. A verb such as ᾐτήσατο needs to be supplied here: so Longenecker, *Galatians*, p. 59.

108. Auxiliary + infinitive taken as one process 'eager to do'.

Verse	Clause	Clause Type	Process	Participants
2.11a	ὅτε δὲ ἦλθεν Κηφᾶς εἰς Ἀντιόχειαν,	Enhancement (of 2.11b), temporal	Material, action, intention: 'came'	Actor: Peter; Goal: Antioch
2.11b	κατὰ πρόσωπον αὐτῷ ἀντέστην	Primary	Material, action, intention: 'opposed'	Actor: Paul; Goal: Peter
2.11c	ὅτι κατεγνωσμένος ἦν	Enhancement (of 2.11b), causal-conditional	Relational, intensive: 'was'	Carrier: Peter; Attribute: condemned
2.12a	πρὸ τοῦ γὰρ ἐλθεῖν τινας ἀπὸ Ἰακώβου	Enhancement (of 2.12b), temporal	Material, action, intention: 'came'	Actors: certain men from James
2.12b	μετὰ τῶν ἐθνῶν συνήσθιεν·	Primary	Material, action, intention: 'used to eat (with)'	Actor: Peter; Goal: the Gentiles
2.12c	ὅτε δὲ ἦλθον,	Enhancement (of 2.12c), temporal	Material, action, intention: 'came'	Actors: certain men from James
2.12d	ὑπέστελλεν	Primary	Material, action, intention: 'withdrew'	Actor: Peter
2.12e	καὶ ἀφώριζεν ἑαυτόν	Extension (of 2.12c), addition, positive	Material, action, intention: 'separated'	Actor: Peter; Goal: himself
2.12f	φοβούμενος τοὺς ἐκ περιτομῆς.	Enhancement (of 2.12d and e), causal-conditional	Mental, affection: 'fearing'	Senser: Peter; Phenomenon: the circumcision party
2.13a	καὶ συνυπεκρίθησαν αὐτῷ [καὶ] οἱ λοιποὶ Ἰουδαῖοι,	Extension (of 2.12d and e), addition, positive	Material, action, intention: 'joined in the act of hypocrisy'	Actors: the rest of the Jews

Verse	Clause	Clause Type	Process	Participants
2.13b	ὥστε καὶ Βαρναβᾶς συναπήχθη αὐτῶν τῇ ὑποκρίσει.	Enhancement (of 2.13a), causal-conditional	Event: 'led astray', passive voice	Goal: Barnabas; Inanimate actor: their act of hypocrisy
2.14a	ἀλλ᾽ ὅτε εἶδον ὅτι...	Enhancement, temporal (of 2:14c)	Mental, perception: 'saw'	Senser: Paul; Phenomenon: 'that they were not walking according to the truth of the gospel'
2.14b	οὐκ ὀρθοποδοῦ-σιν πρὸς τὴν ἀλήθειαν τοῦ εὐαγγελίου,	Projection, idea	Material, action, intention: 'were not walking straight'	Actors: the Jewish believers
2.14c	εἶπον τῷ Κηφᾷ ἔμπροσθεν πάντων·	Primary	Verbal: 'said'	Sayer: Paul; Target: Cephas; Verbiage: 'If you...'
2.14d	εἰ σὺ Ἰουδαῖος ὑπάρχων ἐθνικῶς καὶ οὐχὶ Ἰουδαϊκῶς ζῇς,	Projection, locution, Enhancement (of 2:14e), causal-conditional	Material, action, intention: 'live (like a Gentile)'	Actor: Peter ('You')
2.14d(i)	σὺ Ἰουδαῖος ὑπάρχων	Embedded clause	Relational, intensive: 'being'	Carrier: Peter; Attribute: 'a Jew'
2.14e	πῶς τὰ ἔθνη ἀναγκάζεις ἰουδαΐζειν;	Projection, locution, cont. Primary	Material, action, intention: 'compel to live like Jews'[109]	Actor: Peter; Goal: the Gentiles

109. Auxiliary + infinitive taken as one process 'compel to be circumcised'.

DESIGNING AND COMPILING A REGISTER-BALANCED CORPUS OF HELLENISTIC GREEK FOR THE PURPOSE OF LINGUISTIC DESCRIPTION AND INVESTIGATION

Matthew Brook O'Donnell

1. *Introduction*

A distinctive aspect of sociolinguistic approaches to language study, in contrast to those traditionally labeled as 'theoretical',[1] is the acceptance of naturally occurring texts as the appropriate object for analysis. The implication of this orientation is that linguistic analysis becomes a far more involved and complex task than simply discovering a finite number of rules to account for the structure of an invented and highly idealized form of language. The complexity is a result of the fact that language cannot and does not occur in a vacuum—there are always differences between speakers in pronunciation, or variations in the semantic sense associated with particular words and constructions. Numerous factors, such as the age, gender, educational background, and geographical location of speakers, affect their language use. In addition, language serves primarily as a social tool through which individuals can manipulate and communicate with their environment. Thus two significantly different varieties of language may be produced by the same speaker in close temporal succession on account of the differing goals for which language is being utilized.

The linguist who wishes to analyze Hellenistic Greek cannot adopt what Hudson refers to as an 'asocial approach' (1980: 4), focusing on language structure alone, but must instead take into account the geographical, temporal and social background to the texts under investiga-

---

1. It is unfortunate that the label 'Theoretical Linguistics' has become associated primarily with syntactical sentence-based analysis, such as that advocated by Chomsky (see Radford 1980), while approaches dealing with real language data have tended to be seen as 'Applied Linguistics'.

tion. Given that there are no living native speakers of the language, it is not possible for the linguist either to invent his or her own sentences (introspection) or to interrogate another speaker to produce and make judgments concerning sentences (elicitation).[2] Thus the usual sources for studying linguistic competence are inaccessible, and the results of language use (linguistic performance) must be studied instead. In practice, traditional grammarians of Hellenistic Greek have tended to establish a competence/performance dichotomy between Classical Greek and (deviant) Koine.[3] Given that a real-language approach must be taken, the study of Hellenistic Greek is further complicated by the lack of important information concerning the speakers and the social and situational contexts in which the texts were produced.

The functional socio-semantic linguistic model of Michael Halliday has shown itself to be particularly suited to the study of Hellenistic Greek (see Porter 1989, 2000a; Reed 1997a). It posits a predictable relationship between the social situation and the resulting patterns of language (Halliday 1978: 141).[4] Of particular relevance is the centrality of the concept of *register* (language variety according to use) to Halliday's theory (Halliday and Hasan 1985). In differing situations, individuals select particular configurations of the semantic options available to them, which are in turn realized in the lexicogrammatical system. Halliday states that 'since these options are realized in the form of grammar and vocabulary, the register is recognizable as a particular selection of words and structures' (1978: 111). Thus, at least theoretically, it is possible to predict the probable linguistic forms that will be utilized by a speaker on the basis of the situation, and in reverse, to make sugges-

2.   See Williams (1996a) on the different sources of data for linguistic investigation, and particularly the status of corpus data in theoretical linguistics. For an investigation of the notions of *grammaticality* and *linguistic acceptability*, see Quirk and Svartvik (1966). Their study supports the validity of the use of real language, found in a corpus, for linguistic investigation.

3.   See, for instance, Zerwick (1963) who illustrates on many occasions the ways in which the language of the New Testament has simplified and deviated from Classical standards.

4.   Discussing the role of the *situation* as a determinant of a text, Halliday states: 'The [language] system is a meaning potential, which is actualized in the form of text; a text is an instance of social meaning in a particular context of situation. We shall therefore expect to find the situation embodied or enshrined in the text, not piecemeal, but in a way which reflects the systematic relation between the semantic structure and the social environment.'

tions as to the probable situation on the basis of the lexicogrammar of the text (see Porter 2000a).

Unlike modern languages, such as English (the language Halliday has used to develop his theory), for which there is usually both access to the situational information (such as the identity, age, sex and nationality of the speaker) and considerable knowledge of the linguistic system, the study of Hellenistic Greek is restricted by incomplete historical information about the situation giving rise to the texts, and limited understanding of the language system. There is a need for a representative corpus of Hellenistic Greek, organized according to sociolinguistic variables, that will allow the investigation of the relationship between situational and lexicogrammatical features. This paper seeks to lay down some guidelines for the design and compilation of such a corpus, and to present an outline of a small initial corpus (approximately 600,000 words) under construction as part the Hellenistic Greek Text Annotation Project.[5]

2. *Issues in Corpus Design and Compilation*

Though dismissed by Chomsky (1957: 17) as of little value for linguistic science, there has been a steady revival of interest in linguistic circles in the utilization of collections of real language as the data from which theories about language can be developed and tested (Leech 1992; Williams 1996a; McEnery and Wilson 1996: 2-18; Kennedy 1998: 3-5). One of the factors that has made such an approach to linguistic investigation more feasible is the availability of increasingly powerful computers, which facilitate the search and statistical analysis of large amounts of textual data. Before such utilization can take place, however, a suitable collection of texts must be compiled and stored in an electronic form. The purpose of this section is to consider the major issues involved in such an enterprise, and particularly those of relevance to the compilation of a corpus of Hellenistic Greek texts.

a. *An Archive and a Corpus—Is There a Difference?*
The use of the word 'corpus' to describe a collection of texts is certainly not unique to the recent branch of linguistics known as corpus

---

5.   The *Hellenistic Greek Text Annotation Project* is currently being carried out in the Centre for Advanced Theological Research at the University of Surrey Roehampton.

linguistics. Various collections of classical works, ancient papyri and literary texts have been labeled as corpora by scholars from diverse disciplines of study for centuries. Even within linguistics the word is used in a number of different ways. In this paper the term is used in the restrictive sense suggested by Kennedy, where a corpus is defined as 'a collection of texts in an electronic database' (1998: 3); but as Kennedy admits, this definition 'begs many questions'.[6] Leech (1991: 11) makes a distinction between an electronic text archive and a corpus. An archive is a collection of texts with no particular organizational structure or selection criteria for the texts they contain.[7] Texts are included because they are available in an easily accessible form, and questions such as their genre or overall representativeness are not at the forefront. An example of an English archive is the Oxford Text Archive, compiled by the Oxford University Computing Service. A corpus, on the other hand, consists of a group of texts carefully selected in order to *represent* a specific language or sub-language. The notion of representativeness will be discussed in more detail below. However, in statistical terms a representative sample is a sub-population of a larger (perhaps infinite) hypothetical population, from which generalizations can be made about the larger population. Not all corpus compilers place such emphasis on the representative function of a corpus. Atkins, Clear and Ostler suggest that a corpus is a subset of an electronic text library (ETL) 'built according to explicit design criteria for a specific purpose' (1992: 1).[8] The content of the corpus is constrained by the desired use

6.   Definitions of the word 'corpus' even abound within 'corpus' linguistics. Sinclair, widely considered to be a pioneer in the construction of English corpora, offers the following definition: 'A *corpus* is a collection of pieces of language that are selected and ordered according to explicit linguistic criteria in order to be used as a sample of language' (1995: 19 [emphasis orginal]). This offers a good working definition, placing emphasis upon the importance of linguistic criteria in the selection of textual samples and the purpose of compilation: to provide a sample of language.

7.   Atkins, Clear and Ostler define an archive as 'a repository of readable electronic texts not linked in any coordinated way' (1992: 1). Sinclair states that 'words such as *collection* and *archive* refer to sets of texts that do not need to be selected, or do not need to be ordered, or the selection and/or ordering do not need to be on linguistic criteria. They are therefore quite unlike corpora' (1995: 19-20 [emphasis original]).

8.   They divide text collections into four categories: (1) an Archive, (2) an ETL, which is 'a collection of electronic texts in standardized format with certain

of the resulting collection, whether that be lexical (dictionary building), grammatical, didactic (i.e. ESL/EFL) or technical (used to support statistical speech processing or recognition).

In the light of the preceding discussion, how should the most familiar electronic text collection of ancient Greek, the *Thesaurus Linguae Graecae* (TLG), be classified? Is it a corpus or an archive? Project director Theodore Brunner describes the TLG as a 'computer-based data bank of ancient Greek texts' (in Berkowitz and Squiter 1990: vii). Though the term 'thesaurus' seems to imply that the TLG is more of a lexicographical collection—and this was the original intention for the TLG when it was conceived at the end of the nineteenth century—by the time work on the TLG began in the 1970s it was decided that complete texts representing the complete extant evidence for ancient Greek be stored in computer readable format (see Berkowitz and Squiter 1990: vii-viii). When the work first began, it was driven by the general guideline that 'the data bank should reflect all ancient Greek authors and texts extant from the period between Homer and A.D. 600'. However, Brunner points out that the planning conference that produced this guideline did not 'specify precisely which authors and texts would be involved' (Berkowitz and Squiter 1990: viii). At that early point in the history of the TLG it was best classified as a textual archive and not a corpus. The broad goal of complete coverage without specific criteria for representativeness does not meet the definition of a corpus. On the other hand, by 1977 the project team had managed to complete data entry for the majority of texts falling within the time span from Homer to 200 CE. Thus a claim could be made for having achieved representativeness of the (literary) language of this period, simply on the basis of having collected together every extant text.[9] The TLG has continued to expand, incorporating most of the texts from the period 200–600 CE,

---

conventions relating to content', (3) a Corpus and (4) a Subcorpus, which is 'a subset of a corpus, either a static component of a complex corpus or a dynamic selection from a corpus during on-line analysis' (Atkins, Clear and Ostler 1992: 1).

9. The major focus of the TLG project has been upon the literary language of the ancient world, focusing on the canon of texts usually studied by classicists. Brunner states that 'the latter part of the nineteenth century witnessed an ever-growing desire on the part of classicists for two comprehensive thesauri, one of Greek and one of Latin. To nineteenth-century classicists, the term *thesaurus* denoted a comprehensive lexicon citing and defining all (or essentially all) extant words of a language within a specific chronological framework' (Berkowitz and Squiter 1990: vii).

and beginning to collect texts from authors writing between 600 CE and 1453 CE, thus expanding the original time-frame.

As the TLG has grown, it has become necessary to introduce a clas-sification scheme in order to allow for specialist research on particular genres in the data bank.[10] The chosen classification scheme makes a major division between prose and poetry. Within the prose division there is a hierarchy of categories: first, religion or non-religion, within religion, pagan religion or non-pagan religion and so on. Within the poetry group the major division is between hexameter poetry and non-hexameter poetry (see schema in Berkowitz and Squiter 1990: xxxiv). The introduction of these 'generic' categories (see below) has certainly made the TLG more usable for directive research,[11] but there is no attempt to organize the data bank according to these categories or to monitor the number of texts in each category. I do not think these attempts at classification, therefore, are sufficient to class the TLG data bank as a corpus. It is still best described as a comprehensive archive of nearly the entire extant literary evidence of the Greek language from Homer to 600 CE (and eventually 1453 CE).[12] It thus serves as a popu-lation from which representative corpora of a specific time period (such as the Hellenistic period) or specific genres (such as scientific texts) can be sampled.

b. *Defining the Population and Selecting a Suitable Sampling Method*
It has become increasingly important to ground new corpus projects upon a sound statistical basis. Corpus linguistics has lagged somewhat

---

10. Berkowitz and Squitier (1990: xxxi) state that 'as the size of the TLG data bank continues to expand, the need to classify its voluminous contents into a com-prehensible and manageable system grows ever more urgent. Scholars in search of specific philological, stylistic, or linguistic phenomena likely to be encountered only in certain generic categories of literature should not be required to mine the vast resources of the data bank in their entirety.'

11. Berkowitz and Squitier give the following example: 'Anyone looking for instances of ἀγκυλόγλωσσος might reasonably expect to locate this word (along with its inflectional forms) in medical writings, but probably not in hymnal poetry' (1990: xxxi). This kind of search is possible because the relevant texts are marked with the tag 'Med(ica)' in the data bank.

12. In terms of the four categories used by Atkins, Clear and Ostler (1992: 1), the TLG could be classified as an electronic text library (ETL) because it is stored in standardized format. On encoding and storage formats, see O'Donnell 1999a: 92-93 and on the TEI (Text Encoding Initiative), see Burnard 1992 and Johansson 1994.

behind sociolinguistics in this area. The classic studies of Labov in American inner-city speech communities in the 1970s, and his subsequent work on linguistic change and variation (Labov 1976; 1996; Hudson 1980: 138-90), are founded upon rigorous experimental and statistical principles. Sociological studies seek to investigate particular traits or opinions of a chosen group in society. The usual method for these studies is the use of surveys and field research to collect the data. It may be surprising to some observers of such studies after reading the conclusions presented to learn the small number of individuals consulted. There are two factors that make this possible. The first is a clear identification of the population or segment of society about which one wishes to make statements. The other factor is the selection of an appropriate sampling methodology that will provide a high degree of confidence that the results obtained for the small sample of the population will be representative of the population as a whole.

1. *Population*. If one were to study the party political allegiance of British university students, the definition and identification of the population would be relatively simple. The population is every individual currently enrolled to study at higher educational institutions in the United Kingdom.[13] The situation is not so simple in the case of a corpus to represent a given language. Theoretically the population is every utterance and instance (spoken and written) of the given language in a specified time span. However, it is clear that additional boundaries are required. The primary decision facing the corpus compiler is whether to collect the language *produced* by the speakers of the language of interest, or the language that they *receive* (through listening and reading).

It is common in the discussion of the design and compilation of computerized textual corpora to make a distinction between the *production* of texts, on the one hand, and the *reception* of texts, on the other. Atkins, Clear and Ostler suggest that 'for a general-language corpus… there is a primary decision to be made about whether to sample the language that people hear and read (their *reception*) or the language that they speak and write (their *production*)' (1992: 5). If the goal of the corpus compiler is to represent the language use of a given population, then it follows that he or she should seek to collect as many instances as

---

13. Notice the addition of the word 'currently'. As discussed below in the section on sampling methodology, initial statements of desired population frequently need refining to make their investigation feasible.

possible of the speech and writing from a sample of the population, that is, the texts they produce. The obvious difficulty with this approach, even for a modern language, is that the majority of language users in the population do not produce written texts on a regular basis. It is probably not unrealistic to suggest that at least 90 per cent of language production takes place through the spoken medium, and the majority involves only a few participants (private conversation). The task of collecting even a small and partially representative sample of this language is expensive in terms of both resources and time.[14] The notion of demographic sampling is prominent in sociological studies. A claim that a result is representative of the population must be supported by demonstration that the sample characterizes and matches the total population to be described (see Kalton 1983 and Henry 1990; see below).[15] Biber argues that even if the construction of a large demographically representative corpus of a language (such as English) was feasible, it might not be of great interest for linguistic studies. Linguists, he suggests, are interested in describing the complete range of linguistic variation that exists in a language, and not simply the fact that 90 per cent of the language produced is conversation. Of course a demographically representative corpus of Hellenistic Greek is not even theoretically possible for the modern interpreter. Neither is the luxury of rigorously defined sampling procedures. The language population available for sampling is simply all the extant documents written in Greek between the fourth

---

14. Woods, Fletcher and Hughes (1986: 52-54) discuss a study of the language used by children, particularly the increase in the length of utterances in young children over time. They discuss the theoretical possibility of sampling by attaching a microphone 'to the child, which would transmit and record every single utterance he makes over some period of time to a tape-recorder'. If this was carried out for three months it would then be possible to use random sampling techniques to select utterances from this population. Even though they are describing a possible study of just a few children, they conclude that this method 'is clearly neither sensible nor feasible—it would require an unrealistic expenditure of resources'.

15. Biber (1993b: 247) states: 'A simple demographically based sample of language use would be proportional by definition—the resulting corpus would contain registers that people typically use in the actual proportions in which they are used. A corpus with this design might contain roughly 90% conversation and 3% letters and notes, with the remaining 7% divided among registers such as press reportage, popular magazines, academic prose, fiction, lectures, news broadcasts, and unpublished writing.'

centuries of the two eras.[16] The non-literary papyri provide perhaps the sole portal into the language production of a significant proportion of the Greek-speaking community of the Hellenistic period (see below).

The elimination of the demographic sampling of text production necessitates a focus upon language reception: that is, the language produced by a small number of individuals, but received by a significant number of the population. Describing the contemporary situation, Atkins, Clear and Ostler point out that 'defining the population in terms of language reception assigns tremendous weight to a tiny proportion of the writers and speakers whose language output is received by a very wide audience through the media' (1992: 5).[17] The influence of the mass media in the contemporary world means that the language use and style of a handful of script- and copy-writers is received by millions of individuals on a regular basis.

As Biber points out, 'very few people *ever* produce published written texts, or unpublished written and spoken texts for a large audience' (1993b: 237).[18] In the ancient world the situation was probably more extreme, and there is evidence that scribes were often employed for routine written transactions. Many of the non-literary papyri end with lines similar to this one from *P.Ryl.* II 183: ἔγραψεν ὑπὲρ αὐτοῦ Μάρων γρ(αμματυὲς) κτηνοτρόφω(ν) Εὐη(μερίας) διὰ τὸ μὴ ἰδέναι αὐτὸν γράμματα ('Maron, scribe of Euhemeria's herdsmen, wrote for him because he does not know letters'). According to Davis, the phrase 'ἔγραψεν...γράμματα... occurs in hundreds of papyrus documents which were written in whole or in part by a scribe (or other person) for a person who does not know how to write' (1933: 12; see White 1986: 215-16). Estimates vary as to the proportion of the population who were

16. There is a divergence of opinion as to the temporal demarcation of Hellenistic Greek, but 300 BCE is probably a stable initial marker. There is less agreement concerning the cut-off point, some suggesting 400 CE and others 600 CE or later (see Deissmann 1991: 41-42). The population for a corpus of the production of Hellenistic Greek would be all spoken and written instances (utterances) of the language between these two dates.

17. There is a dependent relationship between the texts we produce and those we receive; an individual's language production is shaped by the language to which he or she is exposed on a day to day basis.

18. It would be interesting—but far beyond the scope of this paper—to consider the effect of the internet upon this statement made by Biber. The internet provides a medium for large numbers of people to produce texts potentially accessed by millions of readers (see Murray 1995).

able to read and write in the Hellenistic world, some suggesting only 20 to 30 per cent of males in a given community. Certainly rich urban males would have been the most likely candidates for textual production.[19] To the cost of the basic materials must be added the skill required to physically produce written material.

Rydbeck offers an alternative view to association of the language of the non-literary papyri with the language of the New Testament as examples of the popular language of the day, by positing an intermediate level of Hellenistic Greek between the literary language and the 'vulgar' papyri (Rydbeck 1991). He suggests that the majority of the papyri represent the language of the educated minority. He states that 'a normal papyrus document is a piece of writing which has been composed by a person with a normal language education—hence by somebody who has learned to write Greek, sometimes known to be a professional writer' (Rydbeck 1991: 200). Even though one might question Rydbeck's dismissal of the papyri as evidence for the study of the language of the New Testament (cf. Porter 1989: 151-53; 1996: 93-95), this statement is relevant for the current discussion.[20] The conclusion is that the focus upon textual reception as the population from which the texts that build up a corpus are sampled is both a practical necessity and theoretically and historically justified in the case of Hellenistic Greek.

2. *Sampling Method.* Having identified the population that a corpus seeks to represent, the next step is to utilize a suitable sampling method to achieve the desired representativeness. Engwall (1994: 49-50) sug-

---

19. Porter (2000b: 132) states that: 'According to recent estimates, probably only twenty to thirty per cent of the males in a given Hellenistic community, at the most, would have been able to read *and* write (perhaps a higher percentage could read some), with a much lower percentage among those in the country. Literacy in the ancient world was directly related to levels of education, access to which was primarily focused on the city, and tended to favour males, especially those with economic resources.' He cites Harris (1989: 116-46) in support of this statement.

20. He seems to be reacting to the notion that the 'living language' of the New Testament world can be recovered from the study of the extant written remains. He states: 'the attempt to extract a living language from the written pieces of the past will always be an almost impossible task' (Rydbeck 1991: 200). He suggests that Deissmann 'was always searching for the living language' in his vocabulary studies of the papyri and the New Testament. However, even if Deissmann was over optimistic in his goals, he demonstrated, from numerous examples, the close relationship of the language of the papyri and the language of the New Testament.

gests that there are two approaches available to the linguist seeking to select samples of language to provide a database for investigation. He refers to these methods as *selection by chance* and *selection by choice*. Selection by chance involves bringing together texts and language samples as one comes across them with little regard for their linguistic and sociolinguistic properties, and adding them to the existing corpus. For the linguist seeking to develop a corpus of Hellenistic Greek, with specific interest in the New Testament, this might involve beginning with the texts at hand in the typical library of a New Testament scholar: the Greek New Testament, the LXX, portions of Philo and Josephus, the Church Fathers. The weakness of this approach is that findings from linguistic investigations of the resulting corpus cannot necessarily be generalized to the language as a whole, if the corpus is not agreed upon as representative of this language. The second approach, favoured by Engwall, is to establish selection criteria that will ensure that the resulting corpus reasonably represents the language as a whole. Though there is general agreement among corpus compilers over the basic criteria to be utilized, there is as yet no standardization (see Sinclair 1995). Section c below will discuss a number of the key criteria. Here I will focus upon one issue of relevance to the discussion of sampling method, that of sample size.

The first computer corpora of the English language, compiled in the 1960s and 1970s, such as the Brown corpus and the Survey of English Usage, were around one million words in size, and consisted of 500 textual samples of 2000 words each. The Brown corpus, for example, was compiled from 500 samples of English printed in the United States in 1961, each about 2000 words in length. This policy was adopted for both pragmatic and theoretical reasons. Though small by current standards of corpora, at the time a one million word corpus was at the extremes of technological possibility, and thus to allow it to be representative of a wide range of genres (or registers) 2000 words was settled upon as the sample size. A surprising number of subsequent corpora have followed this decision and still opt for fixed-length samples of one or two thousand words (e.g. the ARCHER diachronic corpus; Biber, Finegan and Atkinson 1994: 4).[21] Debate continues over what

21. The ICE (International Corpus of English) project—a large scale international project aiming to provide representative corpora of English worldwide (see Greenbaum 1992; Greenbaum [ed.] 1993)—follows the Brown and LOB corpora in

sample size is required for the quantitative analysis of linguistic features. As de Haan suggests (1992), the size of sample required varies
according to the linguistic feature under investigation. He shows, for
instance, that certain grammatical features (such as tense-form distribution) can be reliably investigated with samples of 1000-2000 words.
But to investigate word order, the optimum sample size is somewhere
between 15,000 and 20,000 words.[22] In a recent paper on the future of
corpus linguistics, Sinclair lays down some guidelines for what he sees
as the corpora of the future. On the issue of sample size, he is typically
outspoken:

> Personally I would like to see 'whole text' as a default condition, thus
> classifying sample corpora as one of the categories of special corpora,
> but I may not be representing the general opinion at this point and so I
> have kept the matter at discussion stage for the present. To me the use of
> small samples is just a remnant of the early restraints on corpus building,
> and the advantages of whole texts can be set out in powerful argument.
> The use of samples of constant size gains only a spurious air of scientific
> method, since it confers no benefit on the corpus, and is as practical as
> Genghis Khan's fabled policy of having all his soldiers the same height
> (Sinclair 1995: 27-28).

Elsewhere I have pointed out the failure of many authorial attribution
studies of the Pauline epistles to consider the issue of sample size
(O'Donnell 1999b: 245-51). It is simply not possible to draw conclusions concerning the authorship of ancient letters that are only two or
three thousand words in length with the degree of certainty presented in
many of these studies. This does not, however, mean that only the longer texts in the New Testament such as the Gospels, Acts and Revelation can be utilized for quantitative research. Halliday (1978: 141) suggests that:

> A text is...an indeterminate concept. It may be very long, or very short;
> and it may have no very clear boundaries. Many things about language

utilizing text samples of 2000 words, though a small number of larger texts (20,000
words) are also included (see Greenbaum 1991: 87).

22. Similar issues apply to the overall size of the corpus. Kennedy (1998: 68)
suggests that a corpus of just 100,000 words is sufficient to study prosody and morphology and that 'a robustly reliable analysis of the use of verb-form morphology
can be undertaken on a corpus of half a million words'. The study of lexis, on the
other hand, requires a corpus of 20 million words or more (see Sinclair 1991: 18-
20). For a technical consideration of the relationship between text length and
vocabulary in the New Testament documents, see Pruscha 1998.

can be learnt only from the study of very long texts. But there is much to be found out also from little texts; not only texts in the conventional forms of lyric poetry, proverbs and the like, but also brief transactions, casual encounters, and all kinds of verbal micro-operations.

Wherever possible, it seems desirable to incorporate complete texts in any corpus so that full linguistic analysis, such as Halliday mentions, can be carried out. Certain statistical measures of texts, particularly those that rely on the number of distinct words (types), such as a type–token ratio, are sensitive to sample length (see Biber 1992; O'Donnell 1999b: 249-51). Discourse analysis is interested in the development of a text, in particular how topics and participants are introduced (and re-introduced) over the course of the discourse (Reed 1997a: 101-20). Such concepts can only be investigated if the complete text is available for examination.

On the other hand, practical concerns as to the total size of the corpus (for instance a small 500,000 word corpus), and the need to achieve representativeness, mean in practice that certain authors will need to be selectively sampled. For example, the work of Epictetus should certainly be included in a corpus of Hellenistic Greek designed to complement the Greek of the New Testament; yet his *Dissertations* are 78,609 words in length[23]—twice the length of Luke–Acts, the longest text in the New Testament. Should the complete work be included, or a sample of perhaps 20,000 words? Or what about Polybius's *History*? It is more than twice the length of the entire New Testament. Initially it is suggested that 20,000 words be adopted as the sample size for works of considerable length (in light of the findings of de Haan 1992), but that, where possible, complete texts or at least sections of texts be included (i.e. Epictetus, *Dissertations* Book I). In the case of works of less than 100,000 words by authors of considerable importance, the complete text should be included. For example, in his study of the genre of the Gospels, Burridge (1992) used Philo's *Life of Moses*, which has approximately 32,000 words, as a comparison text.

c. *Classification Criteria in Corpus Compilation*
The literature on corpus compilation and well-known corpora projects tends to make a distinction between *internal* and *external* criteria. Internal criteria are linguistically defined in terms of lexicogrammatical

23. Count taken from figures given in the TLG Canon; see Berkowitz and Squitier 1990: 150.

features (lexical and grammatical choices). External criteria are primarily non-linguistic and focus on features similar to those studied by sociolinguists, such as age, nationality and gender of author, geographic region, communicative function and so on (Atkins, Clear and Ostler 1992: 5; Hudson 1980: 143-45).

The majority of corpora have been compiled on the basis of external criteria, that is, in terms of what Halliday (following Firth) would call features of the context of situation (Halliday and Hasan 1985: 5-11; Reed 1997b: 194-95; Porter 2000a). The reason for this practice has partly been to follow the precedent set by sociolinguistic studies (Hudson 1980: 138-57), but is also due to the lack of research into linguistic variation between text types and a satisfactory method for classification by internal criteria. This focus on external criteria has proved to be largely satisfactory for corpora of modern languages[24] where access to these situational variables is relatively easy and can be relied upon. However, this is not always the case for some more recent diachronic corpora of English (Rissanen, Kytö and Heikkonen [eds.] 1997; Biber, Finegan and Atkinson 1994), where exact dates, geographic location and authorship may not be certain. This is even more problematic when dealing with a corpus of ancient texts, such as the proposed corpus of Hellenistic Greek.

1. *Internal Criteria.* Though the emphasis in the compilation of language corpora remains upon external criteria, more recent works (Biber 1988; 1992; Phillips 1989; Nakamura and Sinclair 1995) have developed a typology of English texts and a number of different (yet complementary) methodologies for classification by linguistic criteria. J. Pearson (1998: 53-55) describes what she sees as currently the two main internal criteria for corpus classification: topic and style.

Topic. The concepts of topic and theme are unclearly and variously defined in the field of discourse analysis (see Brown and Yule 1983: 68-

---

24. Commenting on the practice of classifying corpora in terms of external criteria—or, as they refer to it, 'external evidence'—Nakamura and Sinclair state: 'none of these [external criteria] are aspects of the language of the text. They are presumed to correlate with aspects of the language of text, or there would be no motivation to use them' (1995: 99). They complain that in previous projects 'very little use is made of *internal evidence*, the patterns of language of the texts themselves' (emphasis original).

73; van Dijk 1977: 130-31). The identification of the most frequently occurring words in a specific text or discourse does not necessarily reveal what the text is 'about'. What is required is a clause-by-clause analysis, identifying the theme and rheme and the information flow (Brown and Yule 1983: 125-26; Halliday 1994: 37-67; Reed 1997a: 107-109). Discourse possesses a hierarchical nature, reflecting the fact that authors order and group their message in order to make it more understandable to their audience. Brown and Yule suggest that 'thematic organization appears to be exploited by speakers/writers to provide a structural framework for their discourse' (1983: 143).

Phillips (1989: 7-11) presents a discussion of the notion of 'aboutness' in text, and argues that the regularities and patterns of a text at the macro-level are responsible for this ability.[25] He has developed a method, utilizing mutivariate cluster analysis, to discover the macro-structure of scientific texts on the basis of the lexical items (particularly those identified as technical terms) they contain and thus uncover the topic of a text (see also Hoey 1991). Nakamura and Sinclair (1995) build upon the method developed by Phillips and utilize a more powerful statistical procedure to examine the collocates (words that appear within a four-word span either side of the keyword) of the word 'woman' in the Bank of English (a corpus of over 200 million words). They found that this method is able to identify the different uses of the word in four different components (or registers) of the corpus: (1) books, (2) extracts from the *Times* newspaper, (3) spoken language and (4) BBC reporting. They conclude that their methodology could be expanded and used for the classification of corpus texts by internal criteria.

J. Pearson (1998: 53-54) suggests that future corpus-building projects could utilize these kinds of procedure to classify texts according to their topic, though the tools for automatic topic classification are not yet widely available. Initiatives such as the EAGLES project[26] suggest a list

---

25. Phillips states that aboutness 'seems to be a large-scale phenomenon and not a function of particular structures responsible for the local organisation of linguistic expression...it can be argued that aboutness stems from the reader's appreciation of the large-scale organisation of text' (1989: 7).

26. EAGLES (Expert Advisory Groups on Language Engineering Standards) is a European Union project that aims to provide guidelines for the standardization of annotation schemes for language corpora of European languages (see McEnery and Wilson 1996: 29).

of topics to be used for textual classification such as 'the life of the mind, culture, the physical world, living things, society, manufacture, communications' (J. Pearson 1998: 54). J. Pearson thinks that 'the topics proposed appear to be almost too broad to be useful' and suggests that it is best not to attempt topical classification at this time.

Style. Style is a much utilized, yet ill-defined concept within literary and linguistic studies (see Crystal and Davy 1967: 9-10; O'Donnell 1999b: 227-30). In terms of external criteria for the classification of corpora, researchers have tended to make distinctions, such as formal versus informal language, or literary versus colloquial language. As discussed below, perhaps the major division made in modern corpora is between spoken and written texts (Williams 1996b; Knowles, Wichmann and Alderson [eds.] 1996). The variation in style between spoken and written language has received considerable attention (Crystal and Davy 1967: 68-71; Biber 1988: 47-55; Halliday 1994: xxiii-xxv). A groundbreaking study by Biber (1988) set out to provide an empirical investigation of this variation. The result of this work was both a method for studying linguistic variation and a typology of texts (text-types) that could be utilized for textual classification.[27] Biber applied multivariate statistical methods (factor and cluster analysis) to counts of over 60 linguistic features (such as past-tense verbs, noun–verb ratio, analytic negation) for every text in a corpus classified on the basis of external genre (what he refers to as register) categories (e.g. private correspondence, academic texts, private conversation). The factor analysis identified five main dimensions of variation in these data. Each dimension is defined in terms of the high frequency presence of certain linguistic features combined with the absence or low frequency of others. Each of the dimensions is assigned a functional interpretation on the basis of the prominent features. The dimensions are described in terms of oppositions that represent the ends of a continuum upon which individual texts are located: (1) informational vs involved production, (2) narrative vs non-narrative concerns, (3) Explicit (situation-independent) vs situation-dependent reference, (4) overt expression of persuasion and (5) abstract vs non-abstract style. Texts scoring high on the information dimension contain a high number of nouns and prepositions and the words used

27. Biber's method has been applied to a diachronic corpus of Early Modern English by Taavistainen 1997, where external variables regarding the texts (such as authorship and date) are not always known.

tend to be longer than those found in texts of an informational nature in which private verbs, present tense verbs and second person pronouns tend to occur in large numbers (see discussion in Kennedy 1998: 182-90). The potential of Biber's analysis technique is yet to be fully realized by corpus compilers (Biber 1993b), yet its appeal for ancient language corpora—where external criteria are more difficult to quantify—should be clear (see Porter's essay in Part I of this volume).

2. *External Criteria*. External criteria will most likely remain the major measures for classifying texts in a corpus, until further developments are made in the application of the internal measures discussed above. It is unlikely that internal classification will completely replace external criteria, as part of the reason for compiling a corpus in the first place is to carry out analysis of the linguistic features it contains.

External criteria will be familiar to the historical critic of the New Testament, where the critical questions of authorship, date, provenance, audience and purpose are major concerns. Standard New Testament introductions discuss these issues in some detail (see Kümmel 1975; Guthrie 1994; McDonald and Porter forthcoming), and also detail the variety of opinions and disagreements that exist within even mainstream biblical scholarship. Though in some ways scholars of contemporaneous non-biblical ancient material are far less skeptical in their conclusions with regard to the critical questions, there remain large areas of uncertainty over the authorship, dating and provenance of many such texts. Given that the initial design and compilation of a corpus must rely primarily on external criteria, it is inevitable that some will be dissatisfied with the decisions made. For example, in classifying the author of the 13 letters in the Pauline corpus, what should fill the author slot in the classification of the Pastoral Epistles? It is probably best to indicate that a large degree of uncertainty and disagreement exists over their authorship. The purpose of the corpus is primarily to investigate the internal features of the texts it contains and not to solve the critical debates over authorship. On the other hand, there is certainly value in recording as many situational features as is possible—at least with a reasonable degree of certainty, as this will allow for restricted searches and linguistic analysis of a sociolinguistic nature.

General Situational Parameters/Variables. In his discussion of representativeness in corpus design, Biber (1993b) adapts his situational framework for register-based sociolinguistic studies (1993a) based upon the work of Halliday and Crystal and Davy. He states that 'the primary goal of the framework is to specify the situational character-istics of registers in such a way that the similarities and differences between any pair of registers will be explicit' (1993a: 41). The table below from Biber summarizes the major situational parameters or vari-ables he considers essential for corpus compilation projects.

Table 1

		Situational parameters listed as hierarchical sampling strata (Adapted from Biber 1993b: 245)
MODE	1	*Primary Channel.* Written/spoken/scripted speech
	2	*Format.* Published/not published (+ various formats with 'published')
	3	*Setting.* Institutional/other public/private-personal
TENOR	4	*Addressee.*
		(a) Plurality. Unenumerated/plural/individual/self
		(b) Presence (place and time). Present/absent
		(c) Interactiveness. None/little/extensive
		(d) Shared knowledge. General/specialized/personal
	5	*Addressor.*
		(a) *Demographic variation.* Sex, age, occupation, etc.
		(b) *Acknowledgment.* Acknowledged individual/institution
FIELD	6	*Factuality.* Factual-informational/intermediate or indeterminate/imaginative
	7	*Purposes.* Persuade, entertain, edify, inform, instruct, explain, narrate, describe, keep records, reveal self, express attitudes, opinions, or emotions, enhance interpersonal relationship...
	8	*Topics...*

I have grouped Biber's eight parameters according to the three fea-tures of the context of situation, field, tenor and mode, central to Halli-day's theory (Halliday and Hasan 1985: 12-14).[28] A number of these

28. Briefly defined, the field of discourse describes what is happening in the context of situation, the tenor refers to who is taking part in the discourse, and the mode describes the role of discourse in the context (including its form and channel). For a more detailed description of the Hallidayan model and its application to Hellenistic Greek, see Reed 1997a; Martín-Asensio 1999; Porter 2000a. In spite of

parameters are directly transferable to a corpus of Hellenistic Greek. Others, such as whether the text is published or unpublished, are not directly applicable. However, a similar parameter relating to the intended permanency of the original document would be useful. In the case of inscriptions, there was a clear intention to create a text of lasting value. In comparison, a schoolchild's writing exercise on the reverse of a papyrus or ostracon was not intended to be seen by anyone apart from the child and perhaps a mentor or teacher. A continuum of intended permanency could be developed for classifying ancient texts. Josephus's *Jewish War* was written to have lasting value and permanency. What about the letters of Paul to the churches in Galatia or his Corinthian correspondence? There are some indications in the letters themselves that Paul intended them to have at least intermediate permanency and to be circulated and shared with other congregations (Col. 4.16). However, it is unclear whether he intended his letters to be collected together and utilized as a didactic corpus for early Christianity. The purpose of a parameter such as intended permanency is to examine the effect that knowledge and intention of the longevity of the discourse have upon its production. Though it is interesting to consider how the text has subsequently been viewed,[29] the key element—if it is possible to gauge—is the original conception of the permanency of the discourse. In addition, the parameters that include classification of demographic features, such as sex, age and occupation, will prove troublesome for Hellenistic texts, as will the designation of purpose and topic.[30]

the theoretical potential of the concept of *register*, there is still the need for more detailed description and classification of a range of registers. Bateman and Paris describe the use of the concept for developing effective interactive computer systems. They argue that: 'Even though in systemic-functional linguistics register is an important notion which has undergone considerable development and theoretical refinement since its inception, much work on register still does not take us far beyond an intuitive linking of situation and language. Too many attempts at register analysis still fail to set out clearly what the situational features are, beyond statements of very low delicacy which are often insufficient to adequately differentiate the registers of concern from many others' (1991: 84).

29. The fact that a text is under consideration for inclusion in a computerized corpus in the late twentieth century would seem to indicate that it has most likely achieved a permanency beyond its original authorial conception.

30. Under Topic/Subject, Biber (1993a: 41) lists two sub-categories: (A) *Level of Discussion*: specialized/general/popular and (B) *Specific Subject*: finance, science, religion, politics, sports, law, people, daily activities, etc.

Another difficult area is the dating of ancient documents (such as the letters of Paul), because it requires the use of many pieces of historical and textual evidence, as well as a certain degree of ingenuity in placing one particular document into a plausible reconstruction of the author's life (on Paul see Porter 1999; McDonald and Porter forthcoming). Often this information can be deduced relatively easily from the document itself, as is the case with many official documentary papyri, which were usually dated (White 1986: 5-8). In other cases, assumptions as to the supposed situation of a document can lead to the construction of a scenario or *Sitz im Leben* beyond the evidence found in the text itself. For instance, both the popular and critical consensus concerning the book of Philemon is that the character Onesimus is a runaway slave for whom Paul is pleading clemency with Onesimus's master (Philemon). B.W.R. Pearson, in his recent and persuasive article on Philemon, suggests that 'the most interesting aspect of this reconstructed story [of Onesimus as a runaway slave] is that, for the largest part, it does not derive *directly* from the text of Philemon itself' (1999: 254 [emphasis original]). He questions the degree of certainty with which the situation of the letter can be reconstructed, stating that 'the exact situation addressed in the letter is simply too obfuscated to posit a definite solution' (1999: 255), and argues that translators should present an 'open' translation of the letter leaving the reader to make his or her own inferences and observations concerning the background of the text.

The use of external classification criteria for ancient literature is clearly a complex task and in many cases the results are of a largely tentative nature. For the small initial corpus of Hellenistic Greek (described in Section 4, below) designed with specific reference to the Greek of the New Testament, the situational parameters listed above will be assigned to each text where they are available.[31] However, given the initial purpose of this corpus—that is, to provide a collection of additional Hellenistic texts of use for the study of the language of the New Testament—there are two major external criteria that must be considered. These are the language style and the genre of the texts to be included.

Language Style (Types of Hellenistic Greek). Colwell (1962: 480) posits two major divisions within Hellenistic Greek: (1) literary Greek, 'which tended to be artificial in the sense that it was separated from the spoken

31. For an alternative classificatory scheme, see Crystal 1995.

language', and what he refers to as 'Koine' or common Greek, 'which was close to the spoken language'. It is common for compilers of linguistic corpora to posit a division between spoken and written forms of the language under consideration. There are considerable challenges involved in the storage, representation and annotation of spoken material (see Knowles, Wichmann and Alderson [eds.] 1996). For this reason, many existing corpora do not include any spoken texts or have only a small sample of speech (Leech 1996: ix-x). In the case of Hellenistic Greek, all extant evidence is in written form—though there may be certain texts that reflect spoken language quite closely. Arrian, for instance, claims to have produced an almost verbatim record of the discourses of Epictetus (Oldfather 1925; Horrocks 1997: 91). Porter (2000a: 220) suggests that at places 'the Pauline epistles reflect spoken language written down for subsequent reading', thus potentially explaining the complexity of sections such as Eph. 1.3-14. These possibilities should be recorded as features of the text when it is incorporated in the corpus, and are probably best placed within a sociolinguistic framework, such as Halliday's notion of register (as does Porter 2000a). Having said this, many of the texts have been received in written form and gone through an editing process that has most likely included the standardization of spelling and other features.[32]

However, it is not unusual to find reference to spoken varieties of Hellenistic Greek in the secondary literature. Porter (1989: 152) cites Thomson's claim that scholars of Hellenistic Greek have a 'fuller knowledge' of the language, 'spoken and written, than of any other ancient language', in his discussion of the nature of the Greek of the New Testament. Horrocks, in his recent history of the Greek language, devotes considerable space to the analysis of 'spoken Koine' (1997: 60-64, 67-68, 102-27).[33] He posits a diglossic situation in the history of

32. There are at least two possible levels of standardization of the language of material that was originally spoken: (1) the initial transcription of the material by a scribe who may have standardized the spelling and accidence of the language (though the evidence of documentary papyri should be considered here, where variant spellings and abbreviations remain) and (2) the production of a printed edition of the document (either a reading or diplomatic text). If the document has been transmitted and copied, the potential of alteration due to standardization can take effect with each subsequent copying (see O'Donnell 1999: 79-81 on orthographic annotation).

33. In his Introduction, Horrocks notes that 'the historical linguist, working exclusively with written documents, is...faced with severe difficulties in trying to

Greek (following Ferguson's formulation of diglossia [see Ferguson 1959]) where the written language is the high variety shaped primarily by 'the overwhelming prestige of Athens and its literature in the classical period of the fifth and fourth centuries BC', and the low variety consists of 'the spoken language, particularly of the uneducated, evolving in a "natural" way' (Horrocks 1997: 5). As indicated by the essays in the first section of this volume, the debate over diglossia in Hellenistic Greek is complex. I would agree with Porter (see this volume and 2000a) that the Hallidayan concept of register and the use of multivariate analysis (such as Biber 1988) are more useful and potentially productive concepts and methods for the sociolinguistic analysis of Hellenistic Greek than vague and difficult to quantify concepts such as diglossia and dialect (see Hudson 1980: 53-58; also Watt 1997 for an attempt to quantify diglossic features in Luke–Acts).

In other words, the usual division in corpora between spoken and written texts cannot be utilized in the case of Hellenistic Greek. A more nuanced classification is required than the bipolar division offered by Colwell of literary versus Koine. Other possible polar divisions are between private and public language and official and colloquial literature. In the classification of papyri and inscriptions, some have made a distinction between private correspondence and family inscriptions on the one hand and public (official) material such as decrees, treaties and legal documents on the other (see Bubenik 1989: 39-41). Bubenik draws upon the definitions of Woodhead (1959: 36) to classify inscriptions as either private or public.[34] For his sociolinguistic study, Bubenik redefines public inscriptions as 'that variety whose language/dialect choice is determined by an official organ or magistrate' (1989: 39), and private inscriptions as 'that variety whose language/dialect choice is determined by an individual, a private person (as opposed to an official

---

detect and date the changes that took place in spoken Greek. Concrete evidence is often available only in the form of orthographic errors and grammatical or lexical departures from classical usage in texts which, whether by accident or design, exhibit some degree of compromise with the contemporary spoken language' (1997: 5).

34. He suggests that 'a major distinction has to be made between texts inscribed for a *group of individuals* and those inscribed for an *individual* (or family). These two groups have traditionally been called *public* and *private* inscriptions' (Bubenik 1989: 39 [emphasis original]). There is clear overlap between Bubenik's distinction between private and public (in terms of recipients) and Biber's situational parameter of *Addressee* listed above.

organ or magistrate)' (1989: 40). The use of the official versus colloquial distinction is of a similar nature. Though of value for certain types
of texts (Bubenik bases his diachronic study of Hellenistic Greek
entirely on inscriptions), it is not sufficient to cover the complete range
of the language.

In his discussion of the nature of the language of the New Testament,
Porter surveys previous studies and the insistence by some that there is
a certain 'uniqueness' or 'strangeness' to the New Testament language
when compared to other forms of Hellenistic Greek (Porter 1989: 141-
53). He argues that there has been a failure to recognize both the distinction between a language and a dialect (see Hudson 1980: 21-72;
Porter 1989: 149-50) and that between 'code and text or grammar and
style' (Porter 1989: 151).[35] Porter introduces the Hallidayan concept of
register into the discussion of the nature of the Greek of the New Testament and stylistic varieties within Hellenistic Greek in general. He proposes a continuum of varieties that includes these four groups: vulgar,
non-literary, literary and Atticistic (Porter 1989: 152-53; see Table 2).

Table 2

Stylistic Variety	Examples of authors and types of texts
vulgar	papyri concerned with personal matters, monetary accounts, letters etc.
non-literary	official business papyri, inscriptions, scientific texts, and longer texts, e.g., Epictetus, Apollodorus, Pausanias
literary	Philo, Josephus, Polybius, Strabo, Arrian, Appian
Atticistic	Dionysius of Halicarnassus, Plutarch, Lucian

These four groups, coupled with the understanding that they represent
points on a continuum, provide a more satisfactory classificatory scheme
than any of those considered above. On the whole, the New Testament
is closest to the non-literary variety, though parts might be considered
vulgar (e.g. Revelation), while others could be seen as close to literary
(e.g. Hebrews). In compiling a corpus of Hellenistic Greek to represent

---

35. 'The difference between code and text is realized in the difference between
grammar and style. Grammar determines the verbal range of an individual, i.e. the
"range of meaning which that person can express," and the ways that these meanings are realized in the specific formal features of the language, while style describes
the range of possible manifestations of code, i.e. registers' (Porter 1989: 151).

and support the language of the New Testament, it is important to incorporate texts of a matching language variety. It is also important to represent the broader extremes of the continuum, that is, both vulgar and Atticistic language, so that the whole of the language is represented and comparison studies can be undertaken.[36]

Genre. Corpus compilers aim to include in their corpora a representative range of genres, concentrating primarily on external features. Popular text types are newspaper articles, novels, academic papers, private letters, lectures, sermons, and casual conversation. As discussed above, a number of studies seeking to establish a typology of English texts, both modern and early, have chosen to make a distinction between *genre* and *text type*. Biber (1988), followed by Taavistainen (1997), argues that the term *genre* should be used to refer to the classification of texts according to their external characteristics. Thus factors such as authorship, date, purpose and intended audience are used to group texts. In contrast, the term *text type* is used to refer to the classification of texts on the basis of the linguistic features of the text.[37]

The question of the genre of ancient documents is complex. There is continuing debate concerning the genre of the New Testament documents and the use of generic categories for interpretation (Pearson and Porter 1997). There is also a great deal of terminological confusion over what exactly constitutes a genre (Crystal and Davy 1967: 75); for instance, should one refer to a parable within one of the Synoptic Gospels as a genre? Pearson and Porter maintain the distinction between a *literary form* (such as a parable), which characterizes a particular section of a work, and a *literary genre*, which describes a whole work

---

36. The availability of a representative corpus of Hellenistic Greek, with texts ranging from vulgar to Atticistic variety, would allow studies to address questions of the alleged uniqueness or strangeness of the Greek of the New Testament.

37. Taavitsainen argues that 'the distinction between the two types of abstraction [genre and text type] is useful and necessary if we wish to chart the linguistic features that serve as a matrix in distinguishing various text types and pinpoint differences between adjoining groupings' (1997: 187). In their studies, Biber and Taavistainen were seeking to provide a typology of the texts in the corpora under investigation (for Biber a combination of the Brown and LOB corpora, and for Taavistainen the Helsinki Corpus), and they began with the genre classifications already present in their corpora and moved towards a group of types based on internal linguistic features.

(1997: 134).[38] For the purpose of corpus compilation, this distinction is an important one. Each work in its entirety should be classified as to the genre that best describes it. This is obviously a somewhat imprecise and subjective classification, as genre serves merely as a descriptive device.[39] However, it does allow for the initial clustering of texts according to kind, thus providing a measure of the representativeness of the corpus.

As with literary theory, there is considerable variance in the use of the term 'genre' in linguistic theory. Halliday, for instance (followed by Reed 1997b: 194-98 for the New Testament), equates genre with register. Some linguists make reference to spoken and written registers and use the term in a manner equivalent to the literary analyst's use of 'genre'. In their discussion of compiling a representative diachronic corpus, Biber, Conrad and Reppen (1998: 249-53) make reference to 'colloquial registers (such as personal letters and diaries)' as well as 'literary registers, such as fiction, drama and diaries'. However, it is probably more useful to understand genre in a more restricted sense, as an element of the context of culture (Halliday and Hasan 1985), which affects the language user's choice of field, tenor and mode. For example, the Hellenistic letter form (Reed 1997c; Doty 1973: 27-43; White 1986; Porter 1997b: 539-50; McDonald and Porter forthcoming: ch. 9), utilized and expanded by Paul in his letters, should be considered a genre. There are particular formulaic and idiomatic phrases associated with the opening, thanksgiving, body, parenesis and closing sections of the Hellenistic letter form. Virtually all the extant letters from the Hellenistic period follow the opening formula 'from A to B, greetings (χαίρειν)' (see Hunt and Edgar 1932; White 1986: 194). The (Pauline) parenesis section is typically associated with exhortative and prohibitive material, and so often contains a large number of imperative verbal

38. They suggest that 'the distinction between smaller units within complete works and the larger wholes of which they are constituent parts is something important to be aware of at the outset...we do not talk of, for example, the parable as a *genre*, but rather as a literary *form*, which works of many genres may include'.

39. See Pearson and Porter (1997: 134-35) on the difference between the ancient and modern understanding of genre. In general, ancient discussions of genre tend to be more prescriptive and rule based, while modern genre theory is descriptive. Problems can still arise even when the term 'genre' is used to describe whole texts. Crystal and Davy suggest that 'it is undesirable...to use a label like "genre" to refer simultaneously to the kind of difference existing between poetry and prose on the one hand, and essays and letters, both in prose, on the other' (1967: 90).

forms. Such structural features are best classified under genre, while register captures the broader sense of language realizing situational features and meanings (one of which is genre). Paul's writings share the same genre (they are all letters), yet exhibit a certain amount of register variation as a result of their being written at different times in his life, for different purposes and to different audiences (see Porter in this volume).

The three main genres demonstrated in the New Testament are letters, biography (βίος) and history (Pearson and Porter 1997). The Pauline corpus, Johannine letters and the General Epistles (excluding Hebrews) exemplify the letter genre, the Gospels are examples of Greco-Roman biography (Burridge 1992; Hartman 1997: 3-20) and Acts is best classified as history (Pearson and Porter 1997: 147-48; Porter 1999). Hebrews and Revelation are more difficult to classify as to their genre, though the latter is frequently given the label 'apocalypse'. For the purpose of compiling a representative corpus of Hellenistic Greek, with the New Testament as its centre, it is important to make sure that all the genres of the New Testament are represented in the contemporary texts.

3. *Examples of the Application of Compilation Criteria*

This section of the paper presents three examples of the application of compilation criteria discussed in the previous section. The first two examples illustrate the application of the two internal criteria (topic and style) to the whole of the New Testament corpus, and the third example classifies a short papyrus text, a letter from a soldier to his mother, according to the situational parameters discussed in the section on external criteria.

a. *Internal Criteria*
Topic. Porter and O'Donnell (this volume) present a number of experiments utilizing the semantic domains of the Louw–Nida lexicon (Louw and Nida 1988) to provide a simple semantic map of the book of Romans. That study explores the use of statistical clustering techniques that group semantically similar chapters of the letter. It is possible to extend this technique to the entire New Testament corpus, taking entire books as the objects instead of individual chapters. The basis for most multivariate statistical techniques is a data table with n rows of objects (in this case books of the New Testament) and p columns, each column

being a variable such as the number of occurrences of words from a particular semantic domain. The multi-dimensional distances between each book, scored on the semantic variables, can be displayed in two-dimensional form using various multivariate techniques. Appendix B contains a denogram displaying the results of a hierarchical clustering of the books in the New Testament corpus (and the *Didache*) on the basis of the semantic domains of the content words (verbs, noun and adjectives) found in them. The denogram should be read from left to right. The most semantically similar clusters are joined together first. In this instance, Matthew and Luke are the first to group, and then in turn grouping with Mark. This is to be expected, given the similarity and literary relationship between the Synoptic Gospels. The next pair of objects (books) to group is Ephesians and Colossians—again offering semantic confirmation of the generally assumed close relationship between these two books. Other interesting groupings are the joining of 1 and 2 Peter with Jude and the close semantic relationship between 1 and 2 Thessalonians. Worthy of note is the suprising grouping of Romans with Hebrews, followed by 2 Timothy.

Overall, there are three main clusters, two of which contain sub-clusters: (1) the Gospels, Acts and a sub-grouping of Revelation, James and the *Didache*, (2) the Johannine letters that are semantically distinct from the rest of the New Testament and (3) the remaining texts, which include all of the Pauline material and other epistolary texts. Porter and O'Donnell (this volume) discuss the limitations of utilizing clustering methods and the need for careful interpretation of the results. However, this example is presented to demonstrate the potential of internal criteria—specifically that of topic—for the classification of texts where external criteria are unknown or unsure, as is the case with much ancient literature. As new texts are added to a corpus, this process allows for their allocation into a group with similar texts on the basis of topic. For example, when the *Didache* is added to the New Testament, it clusters with the book of James, followed by Revelation; only later does it group with the Gospels and Acts cluster. This is interesting in the light of the debate concerning the relationship between the *Didache* and the Synoptic Gospels.

Text Type/Style. Biber's study of variation in spoken and written language was described above (Biber 1988). One of the findings of this work was that widely utilized dichotomous categories such as spoken and written, and formal and informal, do not correlate with the results of a multi-dimensional analysis of a corpus of texts of these categories. Various written and spoken registers (according to Biber's use of the term) are more closely linguistically related than other registers of the same mode. For example, private letters and private conversation share many common linguistic features and diverge from academic writing and an undergraduate lecture, which in turn exhibit many common features. Other classification schemes have incorporated these kinds of insights (see Crystal 1995); however, the strengths of Biber's study are that: (1) it offers a means of empirically identifying text types on the basis of the texts themselves (internal criteria) and (2) it places texts and registers on a continuum instead of polarizing them (i.e. a text is not *either* informational *or* involved, but may be situated two-thirds of the way from the informational end of the continuum, thus being largely involved).

In his treatment of diglossia in the Greek of the New Testament, Porter (this volume) takes the five dimensions from Biber's study (see above) and presents the results of counting the most significant features of each dimension for each of the letters in the Pauline corpus. As an example of the application of this method to the entire New Testament corpus, I have taken Biber's first dimension (Involved versus Informational production) and counted the number of occurrences per thousand words for each book of the most significant discriminate features for that dimension: (1) private verbs, imperfective aspect, second and first person reference for involved production and (2) nouns, noun–verb ratio, word length and type–token ratio for informational production.

The graph in Appendix C shows the ranking of the books of the New Testament for these informational and involved features. The texts exhibiting the highest frequency of involved features are plotted in the bottom left-hand corner of the chart, while those high in informational features are plotted in the top right.

Tables 3 and 4 illustrate the feature counts for the books at the extremes of the involved–informational continuum (Jude and John) and the one situated in the middle of the cline (Acts). The counts for the involved features are given as occurrences per thousand words, and the rank is the position of the book for that feature for the entire New Testament corpus.[40] John exhibits a much higher frequency of private verbs

---

40. The use of rank serves as a simple means of comparing the scores without utilizing a multivariate statistical method. It slightly exaggerates the differences

(including πιστεύω and γινώσκω), at 36.52 per thousand, compared to the book of Jude (8.68 per thousand). Likewise, John has almost four times as many first person references per thousand than Jude.

Table 3
Features of Involved Production

	Private Verbs		Imperfective Aspect		2nd Person Reference		1st Person Reference	
	freq.	*rank*	*freq.*	*rank*	*freq.*	*rank*	*freq.*	*rank*
John	36.52	5	112.82	8	62.87	10	70.35	8
Acts	24.77	10	84.55	20	31.22	24	34.69	15
Jude	8.68	27	93.28	12	52.06	17	19.52	26

Table 4
Features of Informational Production

	Nouns		Noun–Verb Ratio		Word Length		Type–Token Ratio	
	freq.	*rank*	*ratio*	*rank*	*avg.*	*rank*	*ratio*	*rank*
John	280.84	22	1.23	25	6.02	26	0.06	27
Acts	289.81	18	1.39	20	6.60	8	0.11	23
Jude	340.56	3	1.85	10	7.07	2	0.50	2

Conversely, John scores consistently low on the features associated with informational production. Texts with a large number of nouns and a high noun to verb ratio tend to be of a more informational nature. They are also likely to have a higher average word length and to have dense vocabulary (type–token ratio). The last of these features—type–token ratio—is dependent upon text length (see O'Donnell 1999b: 245-51), and thus one would expect a short book like Jude (with 461 words) to have a high ratio (0.5). Romans (with 7111 words) has a type–token ratio of 0.15; yet after the first 500 words this ratio is 0.41 (see discussion of sample size above).

The implications of the chart in Appendix C cannot be examined in detail here. However, brief note should be made of the similarity between 2 Peter and Jude, supporting theories of literary dependence between the two books. Note also that the Gospel and letters of John all

between the books of the New Testament on the Involved-Informational scale, but it is a satisfactory measure for the purposes of classification.

score high on involved features. The Synoptic Gospels are shown to be more involved than informational, and exhibit very similar scores—as would be expected due to the literary relationships between them. See the comments of Porter in this volume concerning the position of the Pauline epistles on the informational–involved (which he refers to as *interactive*) continuum.

b. *External Criteria*

The following example is an attempt to assign values to the situation parameters adapted from Biber (1993b: 245; see above) for a short papyrus letter (from Hunt and Edgar 1932: 302-304, No. 111) shown below (on classifying papyri letters see White 1986: 5).

Ἀπολινάρις Ταήσι τῇ μητρεὶ καὶ κυρίᾳ πολλὰ χαίρειν.
πρὸ μὲν πάντων εὔχομαί σε ὑγειαίνειν,
κἀγὼ αὐτὸς ὑγειαίνω καὶ τὸ προσκύνημά σου ποιῶ παρὰ τοῖς ἐνθάδε θεοῖς.
γεινώσκειν σε θέλω, μήτηρ, ὅτι ἐρρώμενος ἐγενόμην εἰς Ῥώμην Παχὼν μηνί κε καὶ ἐκληρώθην εἰς Μισηνούς,
οὔπω δὲ τὴν κεντυρίαν μου ἔγνων· οὐ γὰρ ἀπεληλύτειν εἰς Μισηνοὺς ὅτε σοι τὴν ἐπιστολὴν ταύτην ἔγραφον.
ἐρωτῶ σε οὖν, μήτηρ, σεαυτῇ πρόσεχε,
μηδὲν δίσταζε περὶ ἐμοῦ· ἐγὼ γὰρ εἰς καλὸν τόπον ἦλθον.
καλῶς δὲ ποιήσεις γράψασσά μοι ἐπιστολὴν περὶ τῆς σωτηρίας σου καὶ τῶν ἀδελφῶν μου καὶ τῶν σῶν πάντων.
καὶ ἐγὼ εἴ τινα ἐὰν εὕρω γράφω σοι· οὐ μὴ ὀκνήσω σοι γράφιν.
ἀσπάζομαι τοὺς ἀδελφούς μου πολλὰ καὶ Ἀπολινάριν καὶ τὰ τέκνα αὐτοῦ καὶ Καραλᾶν καὶ τὰ τέκνα αὐτοῦ.
ἀσπάζομαι Πτολεμαῖν καὶ Πτολεμαείδα καὶ τὰ τέκνα αὐτῆς καὶ

Apollinarius to Taesis, his mother and lady, many greetings.
Before all I pray for your health.
I myself am well and make supplication for you before the gods of this place.
I wish you to know, mother, that I arrived in Rome in good health on the 25th of the month Pachon and was posted to Misenum, though I have not yet learned of the name of my company; for I had not gone to Misenum at the time of writing this letter.
I beg you then, mother, look after yourself and do not worry about me; for I have come to a fine place.
Please write me a letter about your welfare and that of my brothers and of all your folk.
And whenever I find a messenger I will write to you; never will I be slow to write.
I greet much my brothers and Apollinarius and his children and Karalas and his children.
I greet Ptolemaeus and Ptolemais and her children and Heraclous and her children.

Ἡρακλοῦν καὶ τὰ τέκνα αὐτῆς.
ἀσπάζομαι τοὺς φιλοῦντάς σε πάντας
κατ᾽ ὄνομα.
ἐρρῶσθαί σε εὔχομαι.
ἀπόδος εἰς Καρανίδα Ταήσι ἀπὸ
Ἀπολιναρίου υεἱοῦ Μισηνάτου.

I greet the ones loving you, each by
name.
I pray for your health.
(Addressed) Deliver at Karanis to
Taesis, from her son Apollinarius of
Misenum.

Table 5

Component of Register	Parameter	Values
Mode	*Primary channel*	Written in letter genre utilizing formulaic structure and phrases
	Format and permanency	Papyrus; not intended for 'publication' or for wide consumption; short-term longevity
	Setting	Private-personal
Tenor	*Addressee*	(a) Plurality: individual (b) Presence: absent (c) Interactiveness: indirect (d) Shared knowledge: personal, family (mother) (e) Demographic: female approx. 35-50 (f) Geographic: Karanis, Egypt
	Addressor	(a) Demographic: male, approx. 15-30 (b) Geographic: Misenum, Italy (c) Chronological: second century CE (undated) (d) Occupation: military (recruit)
Field	*Factuality*	Factual communication of personal events experienced by addressor
	Purposes	*Inform* concerning circumstances; *reassure* of well being; *request* for communication and information; exhortation not to worry; *transmission* of greetings to acquaintances
	Topics	Health, location (Rome and Misenum), military (company), family

As these situation parameters are applied to a range of documents in the
corpus, the parameters under each component of register may need to
be refined or new ones added.

4. *Proposal for an Initial Representative Corpus of Hellenistic Greek*

Appendix A contains an outline of the texts that make up a small (596,049 words) corpus of Hellenistic Greek. It is intended initially to be a resource for the study of the Greek of the New Testament and then to serve as the basis for a larger—and more representative—corpus of Hellenistic Greek. The table in Appendix A does not include the detailed application of external criteria with Biber's situation parameters. The two major external criteria discussed above in Section 2c, language style and genre, were assigned to each book of the New Testament. Then contemporaneous documents roughly matching the main genres and language style were selected to add to the corpus. There is not space in this study to justify the inclusion of each text in turn. However, Tables 6 and 7 illustrate the total number of words for each of the four style/formality categories and for the main genres represented.

Table 6

| Style/Formality | Number of Words | | |
	New Testament	*Other*	*Total*
vulgar	39788	30000	69788
non-literary	98624	262243	360867
literary	26829	168295	195124
Atticistic	0	17099	17099

Given that the majority of the New Testament documents are classified as non-literary in style, more than half of the non-New Testament documents (262,243 words) share this category. At this stage we have only included one Atticistic text—Plutarch's *Cato Minor*—but, as the corpus increases in size, this category of writing should be expanded. In terms of genre, the Letter and Bibliography are represented by a selection of texts of similar length to those in the New Testament. History is perhaps over-represented, though the imprecise nature of the classifications should be remembered.

Table 7

Genre	Number of Words		
	New Testament	*Other*	*Total*
Letter	40951	51678	96629
Biography	64967	65394	130161
History	18450	168816	187266
Apocalyptic	10244	42136	52380
Philosophy	0	92182	92182
Geography	0	20000	20000
Speeches	0	20000	20000

Future studies, similar to those presented above in Section 3a, will confirm and correct the representative nature of this corpus. However, both the initial and experimental nature of the corpus must be stressed at this point.

5. *Conclusion*

The linguistic study of the language of the New Testament, and of Hellenistic Greek in general, cannot progress far without reference to the situational and social features of the texts—what Firthian sociolinguists term the *context of situation*. Unfortunately, traditional sociolinguistics, though concerned with such features, has developed utilizing a social-scientific method that requires interaction with native speakers of the language under investigation. The Hellenistic Greek linguist must work primarily with the extant body of documents from the Hellenistic period. In order to make generalizations and test theories concerning the nature of the language, these texts must be classified and grouped in a manner that allows for representative statements to be made. This study has attempted to introduce to the study of Hellenistic Greek the field of corpus compilation and the criteria and methodology utilized by its practitioners. It illustrates the use of both internal (linguistic) and external (situational) criteria for the classification of texts, and presents a tentative corpus of Hellenistic Greek for the sociolinguistic study of the language.

BIBLIOGRAPHY

Aijmer, K., and B. Altenberg (eds.)
    1991   *English Corpus Linguistics: Studies in Honour of Jan Svartvik* (London: Longman).
Atkins, S., J. Clear and N. Ostler
    1992   'Corpus Design Criteria', *Literary and Linguistic Computing* 7.1: 1-16.
Atkins, B.T.S., and A. Zampolli (eds.)
    1994   *Computational Approaches to the Lexicon* (Oxford: Clarendon Press).
Bateman, J.A., and C.L. Paris
    1991   'Constraining the Development of Lexicogrammatical Resources During Text Generation: Towards a Computational Instantiation of Register Theory', in Ventola (ed.) 1991: 81-106.
Berkowitz, L., and K.A. Squiter
    1990   *Thesaurus Linguae Graecae: Canon of Greek Authors and Works* (Oxford: Oxford University Press, 3rd edn).
Biber, D.
    1988   *Variation Across Speech and Writing* (Cambridge: Cambridge University Press).
    1992   'On the Complexity of Discourse Complexity: A Multidimensional Analysis', *Discourse Processes* 15: 133-63.
    1993a   'An Analytical Framework for Register Studies', in Biber and Finegan (eds.) 1993: 31-56.
    1993b   'Representativeness in Corpus Design', *Literary and Linguistic Computing* 8.4: 243-57.
Biber, D., S. Conrad and R. Reppen
    1998   *Corpus Linguistics: Investigating Language Structure and Use* (Cambridge Approaches to Linguistics; Cambridge: Cambridge University Press).
Biber, D., and E. Finegan (eds.)
    1993   *Sociolinguistic Perspectives on Register* (Oxford: Oxford University Press).
Biber, D., E. Finegan and D. Atkinson
    1994   'ARCHER and its Challenges: Compiling and Exploring a Representative Corpus of Historical English Registers', in U. Fries, G. Tottie and P. Schneider (eds.), *Creating and Using English Language Corpora: Papers from the 14th International Conference on English Research on Computerized Corpora, Zürich 1993* (Amsterdam: Rodopi): 1-14.
Brown, G., and G. Yule
    1983   *Discourse Analysis* (CTL; Cambridge: Cambridge University Press).
Bubenik, V.
    1989   *Hellenistic and Roman Greece as a Sociolinguistic Area* (Current Issues in Linguistic Theory, 57; Amsterdam: John Benjamins).
Burnard, L.
    1992   'The Text Encoding Initiative: A Progress Report', in Leitner (ed.) 1992: 97-107.

Burridge, R.A.

1992   *What are the Gospels? A Comparison with Graeco-Roman Biography* (SNTSMS, 70; Cambridge: Cambridge University Press).

Chomsky, N.

1957   *Syntactic Structures* (Janua Linguarum, Series Minor, 4; The Hague: Mouton).

Clear, J.

1992   'Corpus Sampling', in Leitner (ed.) 1992: 21-32.

Colwell, E.C.

1962   'The Greek Language', *IDB*, II: 479-87.

Crystal, D.

1995   'Refining Stylistic Discourse Categories', in Melchers and Warren (eds.) 1995: 35-46.

Crystal, D., and D. Davy

1967   *Investigating English Style* (London: Longman).

Davis, W.H.

1933   *Greek Papyri of the First Century: Introduction, Greek Text, English Translation, Commentary, Notes* (New York: Harper).

Deissmann, A.

1991   'Hellenistic Greek with Special Consideration of the Greek Bible', in Porter (ed.) 1991: 39-59.

Dijk, T.A. van

1977   *Text and Context: Explorations in the Semantics and Pragmatics of Discourse* (London: Longman).

Doty, W.G.

1973   *Letters in Primitive Christianity* (GBS; Philadelphia: Fortress Press).

Engwall, G.

1994   'Not Chance but Choice: Criteria in Corpus Creation', in Atkins and Zampolli (eds.) 1994: 49-82.

Ferguson, C.A.

1959   'Diglossia', *Word* 15: 325-40.

Greenbaum, S.

1991   'The Development of the International Corpus of English', in Aijmer and Altenberg (eds.) 1991: 83-91.

1992   'A New Corpus of English: ICE', in Svartvik (ed.) 1992: 171-79.

Greenbaum, S. (ed.)

1993   *Comparing English Worldwide: The International Corpus of English* (Oxford: Clarendon Press).

Guthrie, D

1994   *New Testament Introduction* (Leicester: IVP, rev. edn).

Haan, P. de

1992   'The Optimum Corpus Sample Size?', in Leitner (ed.) 1992: 3-20.

Halliday, M.A.K.

1978   *Language as Social Semiotic: The Social Interpretation of Language and Meaning* (London: Edward Arnold).

1994   *An Introduction to Functional Grammar* (London: Edward Arnold, 2nd edn).

Halliday, M.A.K., and R. Hasan
    1985   *Language, Context and Text: Aspects of Language in a Social-Semiotic Perspective* (Victoria, Australia: Deakin University).
Harris, W.V.
    1989   *Ancient Literacy* (Cambridge, MA: Harvard University Press).
Hartman, L.
    1997   *Text-Centered New Testament Studies* (WUNT, 102; Tübingen: Mohr Siebeck).
Henry, G.T.
    1990   *Practical Sampling* (Newbury Park, CA: Sage).
Hoey, M.
    1991   *Patterns of Lexis in Text* (Oxford: Oxford University Press).
Horrocks, G.
    1997   *Greek: A History of the Language and its Speakers* (London: Longman).
Hudson, R.A.
    1980   *Sociolinguistics* (CTL; Cambridge: Cambridge University Press).
Hunt, A.S., and C.C. Edgar
    1932   *Select Papyri*. I. *Non-Literary Papyri, Private Affairs* (LCL, 266; Cambridge, MA: Harvard University Press).
Johansson, S.
    1994   'Encoding a Corpus in Machine-Readable Form: The Approach of the Text Encoding Initiative', in Atkins and Zampolli (eds.) 1994: 83-102.
Kalton, G.
    1983   *Introduction to Survey Sampling* (Newbury Park, CA: Sage).
Kennedy, G.
    1998   *An Introduction to Corpus Linguistics* (London: Longman).
Knowles, G., A. Wichmann and P. Alderson (eds.)
    1996   *Working with Speech: Perspectives on Research into the Lancaster/IBM Spoken English Corpus* (London: Longman).
Kümmel, W.G.
    1975   *Introduction to the New Testament* (trans. H.C. Kee; Nashville: Abingdon Press, rev. edn).
Labov, W.
    1976   *Sociolinguistic Patterns* (Conduct and Communication, 4; Philadelphia: University of Pennsylvania Press).
    1996   *Principles of Linguistic Change*. I. *Internal Factors* (Language in Society, 20; Oxford: Basil Blackwell).
Leech, G.
    1991   'The State of the Art in Corpus Linguistics', in Aijmer and Altenberg (eds.) 1991: 8-29.
    1992   'Corpora and Theories of Linguistic Performance', in Svartvik (ed.) 1992: 105-122.
    1996   'The Spoken English Corpus in its Context', Foreword in Knowles, Wichmann and Alderson (eds.) 1996: ix-xii.
Leitner, G.
    1992   *New Directions in English Language Corpora: Methodology, Results, Software Developments* (Berlin: de Gruyter).

Louw, J.P., and E.A. Nida
    1988   *Greek–English Lexicon of the New Testament Based on Semantic Domains* (2 vols.; New York: United Bible Societies).
Martín-Asensio, G.
    1999   'Hallidayan Functional Grammar as Heir to Rhetorical Criticism', in S.E. Porter and D.L. Stamps (eds.), *The Rhetorical Interpretation of Scripture: Essays from the 1996 Malibu Conference* (JSNTSup, 180; Sheffield: Sheffield Academic Press): 84-107.
McDonald, L.M., and S.E. Porter
   forthcoming   *Early Christianity and its Sacred Literature* (Peabody, MA: Hendrickson).
McEnery, T., and A. Wilson
    1996   *Corpus Linguistics* (Edinburgh: Edinburgh University Press).
Melchers, G., and B. Warren (eds.)
    1995   *Studies in Anglistics* (Acta Universitatis Stockholmiensis: Stockholm Studies in English, 85; Stockholm: Almqvist & Wiksell).
Murray, D.E.
    1995   *Knowledge Machines: Language and Information in a Technological Society* (Language in Social Life Series; London: Longman).
Nakamura, J., and J. Sinclair
    1995   'The World of *Woman* in the Bank of English: Internal Criteria for the Classification of Corpora', *Literary and Linguistic Computing* 10.2: 99-110.
O'Donnell, M.B.
    1999a   'The Use of Annotated Corpora for New Testament Discourse Analysis: A Survey of Current Practice and Future Prospects', in S.E. Porter and J.T. Reed (eds.), *Discourse Analysis and the New Testament: Results and Applications* (JSNTSup, 170; SNTG, 4; Sheffield: Sheffield Academic Press): 71-116.
    1999b   'Linguistic Fingerprints or Style by Numbers? The Use of Statistics in the Discussion of Authorship of New Testament Documents', in S.E. Porter and D.A. Carson (eds.), *Linguistics and the New Testament: Critical Junctures* (JSNTSup, 168; SNTG, 5; Sheffield: Sheffield Academic Press): 206-62.
Oldfather, W.A.
    1925   *Epictetus: The Discourses as Reported by Arrian, the Manual, and Fragments* (LCL, 20; Cambridge, MA: Harvard University Press).
Pearson, B.W.R.
    1999   'Assumptions in the Criticism and Translation of Philemon', in S.E. Porter and R.S. Hess (eds.), *Translating the Bible: Problems and Prospects* (JSNTSup, 173; Sheffield: Sheffield Academic Press): 253-80.
Pearson, B.W.R., and S.E. Porter
    1997   'The Genres of the New Testament', in Porter (ed.) 1997: 131-66.
Pearson, J.
    1998   *Terms in Context* (Studies in Corpus Linguistics, 1; Amsterdam: John Benjamins).

Phillips, M.

1989   *Lexical Structure of Text* (Discourse Analysis Monograph, 12; Birming-
        ham: English Language Research, University of Birmingham).

Porter, S.E.

1989   *Verbal Aspect in the Greek of the New Testament, with Reference to
        Tense and Mood* (SBG, 1; New York: Peter Lang).

1996   *Studies in the Greek New Testament: Theory and Practice* (SBG, 6; New
        York: Peter Lang).

1997a   'The Greek Language of the New Testament', in Porter (ed.) 1997: 99-
        130.

1997b   'Exegesis of the Pauline Letters, Including the Deutero-Pauline Letters',
        in Porter (ed.) 1997: 503-53.

1999   *The Paul of Acts* (WUNT, 115; Tübingen: Mohr Siebeck).

2000a   'Dialect and Register in the Greek New Testament: Theory' and 'Register
        in the Greek of the New Testament: Application with Reference to
        Mark's Gospel', in M.D. Carroll R. (ed.), *Rethinking Contexts, Rereading
        Texts: Contributions from the Social Sciences to Biblical Interpretation*
        (JSOTSup, 299; Sheffield: Sheffield Academic Press): 190-208, 209-29.

2000b   *The Criteria for Authenticity in Historical-Jesus Research: Previous Dis-
        cussion and New Proposals* (JSNTSup, 191; Sheffield: Sheffield
        Academic Press).

Porter, S.E. (ed.)

1991   *The Language of the New Testament: Classic Essays* (JSNTSup, 60;
        Sheffield: JSOT Press).

1997   *Handbook to Exegesis of the New Testament* (NTTS, 25; Leiden: E.J.
        Brill).

Pruscha, H.

1998   'Statistical Models for Vocabulary and Text Length, with an Application
        to the New Testament Corpus', *Literary and Linguistic Computing* 13.4:
        195-98.

Quirk, R., and J. Svartvik

1966   *Investigating Linguistic Acceptability* (Janua Linguarum, Series Minor,
        54; The Hague: Mouton).

Radford, A.

1981   *Transformational Syntax: A Student's Guide to Chomsky's Extended
        Standard Theory* (CTL; Cambridge: Cambridge University Press).

Reed, J.T.

1997a   *A Discourse Analysis of Philippians: Method and Rhetoric in the Debate
        over Literary Integrity* (JSNTSup, 136; Sheffield: Sheffield Academic
        Press).

1997b   'Discourse Analysis', in Porter (ed.) 1997: 189-218.

1997c   'The Epistle', in S.E. Porter (ed.), *Handbook of Classical Rhetoric in the
        Hellenistic Period 330 B.C.–A.D. 400* (Leiden: E.J. Brill): 171-93.

Rissanen, M., M. Kytö and K. Heikkonen (eds.)

1997   *English in Transition: Corpus-Based Studies in Linguistic Variation and
        Genre Styles* (Topics in English Linguistics, 23; Berlin: de Gruyter).

Rydbeck, L.
    1991   'On the Question of Linguistic Levels and the Place of the New Testament in the Contemporary Language Milieu', in Porter (ed.) 1991: 191-204.
    1998   'The Language of the New Testament', *TynBul* 49.2: 361-68.

Sinclair, J.
    1991   *Corpus, Concordance, Collocation* (Oxford: Oxford University Press).
    1995   'Corpus Typology—A Framework for Classification', in Melchers and Warren (eds.) 1995: 17-33.

Svartvik, J. (ed.)
    1992   *Directions in Corpus Linguistics: Proceedings of Nobel Symposium 82, Stockholm, 4-8 August 1991* (Berlin: de Gruyter).

Taavistsainen, I.
    1997   'Genre Conventions: Personal Affect in Fiction and Non-Fiction in Early Modern English', in Rissanen, Kytö and Heikkonen (eds.) 1997: 185-266.

Ventola, E. (ed.)
    1991   *Functional and Systemic Linguistics: Approaches and Uses* (Trends in Linguistics: Studies and Monographs, 55; Berlin: de Gruyter).

Watt, J.W.
    1997   *Code-Switching in Luke and Acts* (Berkeley Insights in Linguistics and Semiotics, 31; New York: Peter Lang).

White, J.L.
    1986   *Light from Ancient Letters* (FFNT; Philadelphia: Fortress Press).

Williams, B.
    1996a   'The Status of Corpora as Linguistic Data', in Knowles, Wichmann and Alderson (1996): 5-19.
    1996b   'The Formulation of an Intonation Transcription System for British English', in Knowles, Wichmann and Alderson 1996: 38-57.

Woodhead, A.G.
    1959   *The Study of Greek Inscriptions* (Cambridge: Cambridge University Press).

Woods, A., P. Fletcher and A. Hughes
    1984   *Statistics in Language Studies* (CTL; Cambridge: Cambridge University Press).

Zerwick, M.
    1963   *Biblical Greek: Illustrated by Examples* (Rome: Pontifical Biblical Institute).

Outline of Initial Representative Corpus of Hellenistic Greek

Text	Author	Genre	Style/ Formality	Date	Provenance	Length (words)
Matthew	?Matthew	Biography	non-literary	70–80 CE	Antioch	18346
Mark	?Mark	Biography	vulgar/ non-literary	55–70 CE	?Rome	11304
Luke	?Luke	Biography	non-literary	75–90 CE	?	19482
John	?John	Biography	vulgar/ non-literary	85–100 CE	?Ephesus	15635
Acts	?Luke	History	non-literary/ literary	75–90 CE	?	18450
Romans	Paul	Letter	non-literary	55–60 CE	?Corinth	7111
1 Corinthians	Paul	Letter	non-literary	55–60 CE	?Asia Minor	6829
2 Corinthians	Paul	Letter	non-literary	55–60 CE	Greece	4477
Galatians	Paul	Letter	non-literary	50–55 CE	?Antioch	2230
1 Thess.	Paul	Letter	non-literary	50–55 CE	?Corinth	1481
2 Thess.	Paul	Letter	non-literary	50–55 CE	?Corinth	823
Philemon	Paul	Letter	non-literary	55–65 CE	?Rome	335
Philippians	Paul	Letter	non-literary	55–65 CE	?Rome	1629
Colossians	Paul	Letter	non-literary	55–65 CE	?Rome	1582
Ephesians	Paul	Letter	non-literary	55–65 CE	?Rome	2422
1 Timothy	?Paul	Letter	non-literary	60–100 CE	?	1591
2 Timothy	?Paul	Letter	non-literary	60–100 CE	?	1238
Titus	?Paul	Letter	non-literary	60–100 CE	?	659
1 Peter	?Peter	Letter	non-literary/ literary	75–90 CE	?Rome	1684
2 Peter	?Peter	Letter	non-literary	85–95 CE	?	1099
1 John	?John/ Johannine Community	Letter	vulgar/ non-literary	85–100 CE	?Ephesus	2141
2 John	?John/ Johannine Community	Letter	vulgar/ non-literary	85–100 CE	?Ephesus	245
3 John	?John/ Johannine Community	Letter	vulgar/ non-literary	85–100 CE	?Ephesus	219
Jude	?Jude	Letter	non-literary	70–95 CE	?	461
Hebrews	?	Letter/ Sermon	non-literary/ literary	70–95 CE	?	4953
James	?James	Letter	non-literary/ literary	45–50 or 90–100 CE	?Jerusalem	1742
Revelation	?	Apocalypse	vulgar	50/90 CE	?Patmos	10244
Judges (LXX)	?	History	non-literary/ translation	200–100 BCE	?Egypt	16519

Text	Author	Genre	Style/ Formality	Date	Provenance	Length (words)
Isaiah (LXX)	?	Prophecy	non-literary/ translation	200–100 BCE	?Egypt	28804
1 Maccabees	?	History	non-literary/ translation	200–100 BCE	?	19535
2 Maccabees	?	History	non-literary/ translation	200–100 BCE	?	12762
Didache	?	Manual	non-literary	90–120 CE	?	2200
Shepherd of Hermas	?	Apocalypse	non-literary	130–170 CE	?	27917
Letters of Ignatius	Ignatius	Letter	non-literary	100–120 CE	?Antioch	8105
Geography	Strabo	Geography/ History	literary	44 BCE –21 CE	?Rome/ Egypt	20000
Greece	Pausanias	History	non-literary	100–200 CE	Lydius	20000
Dissertations	Epictetus	Philosophy	non-literary	100–200 CE	?Rome/ Hierapolis	78609
History	Polybius	History	literary	?169 BCE	?Arcadia/ Rome	20000
Cato Minor	Plutarch	Biography	Atticistic	95–120 CE	Chaeronea (Boetia)/ Rome?	17099
Life	Josephus	Biography	literary	40–80 CE	Palestine/ Rome	16293
Moses	Philo	Biography	literary	20–50 CE	Alexandria	32002
Anabasis	Arrian	History	literary	100–200 CE	?Bithynia	20000
Letter of Aristeas	?	Letter/ Philosophy	non-literary	3rd BCE/ 1st CE	?	13573
Book 1	Diodorus Siculus	History	non-literary/ literary	1st BCE	Sicily	20000
2 Edras	?	Apocalypse	non-literary	2nd BCE - 2nd CE	?	14219
Select Speeches	Demosthenes	Speeches	literary	4th BCE	Athens	20000
Roman History Book 1	Cassius Dio	History	literary	200–300 CE	Nicea	20000
Selection of Documentary Papyri	Various	Letter/ Business	vulgar/ non-literary	300 BCE– 300 CE	Egypt (and elsewhere)	30000
					TOTAL	596049

APPENDIX B

A Dendrogram Illustrating the Semantic Clustering of the
New Testament Documents and the Didache

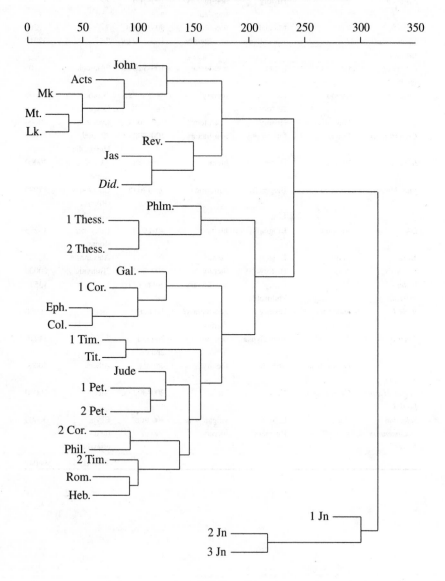

APPENDIX C

Dimension-1: Involved vs Informational Production

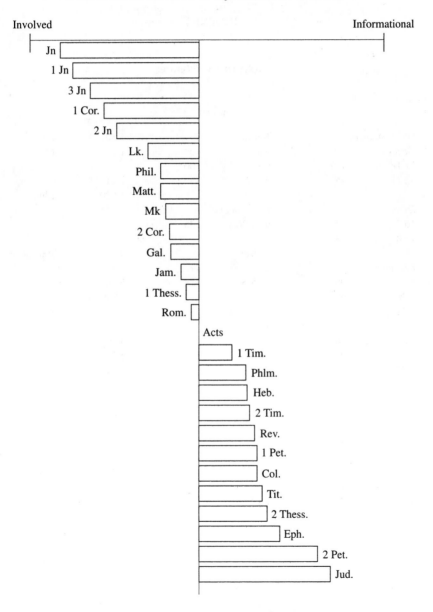

INDEXES

INDEX OF REFERENCES

BIBLE

INDEX OF AUTHORS

JOURNAL FOR THE STUDY OF THE NEW TESTAMENT
SUPPLEMENT SERIES